Aspirational Chinese in Competitive Social Repositionings

Aspirational Chinese in Competitive Social Repositionings

A Re-analysis of Societal Dynamics from 1964 to 2000

Jia Gao

ANTHEM PRESS

Anthem Press
An imprint of Wimbledon Publishing Company
www.anthempress.com

This edition first published in UK and USA 2025
by ANTHEM PRESS
75–76 Blackfriars Road, London SE1 8HA, UK
or PO Box 9779, London SW19 7ZG, UK
and
244 Madison Ave #116, New York, NY 10016, USA

First published in the UK and USA by Anthem Press in 2023

British Library Cataloguing-in-Publication Data
A catalogue record for this book is available from the British Library.

Library of Congress Control Number: 2024951611
A catalog record for this book has been requested.

ISBN-13: 978-1-83999-479-1 (Pbk)
ISBN-10: 1-83999-479-7 (Pbk)

This title is also available as an e-book.

To my grandson, Ethan, wishing he grows up
to achieve his aspirations

CONTENTS

LIST OF ABBREVIATIONS

CASS	Chinese Academy of Social Sciences
CCP	Chinese Communist Party
CCTV	China Central Television
CCYL	Chinese Communist Youth League
CNS	China News Service
COVID-19	Coronavirus 2019
CPC	Communist Party of China, the – see CCP
KMT	Kuomintang, the (Nationalist Party)
MARA	Ministry of Agriculture and Rural Affairs
NBSC	National Bureau of Statistics of China
PLA	People's Liberation Army
PRC	People's Republic of China
SEZS	Special Economic Zones
SOES	State-owned enterprises
TVES	Township and village enterprises

LIST OF FIGURES

LIST OF TABLES

PREFACE AND ACKNOWLEDGEMENTS

In the past four or so decades, a significant amount of research has been undertaken into the rapid and constant social changes happening in China and the dynamics behind this process, resulting in a large body of literature on a wide range of issues and aspects of China's recent transformations. However, most such literature has focused either on political, ideological and policy problems at the macro level or on the different forms of spontaneous resistance and protest at the micro level, providing various perspectives for observing and interpreting what has happened in China. Less studied is the manner in which the majority of everyday Chinese people have reacted to and influenced changes in society over a long period of time. This gap limits our understanding of Chinese society, its societal dynamics and its changing trends to the perspectives of elites and their rivals. Drawing upon a novel perspective of competitive social repositioning, this book seeks to fill this analytical gap by re-analysing the societal dynamics driving social changes in China from 1964, when Mao publicly set out his successor selection criteria, to 2000, when Jiang Zemin promoted his Three-Represents Theory to modify the Chinese Communist Party's (CCP) long-held ideology and practices.

The role of everyday Chinese people in making and influencing social reactions and actions in China is a puzzle that has fascinated me since my youth. I was forced a few years earlier than many teenagers to be a responsible family member and to pay attention to what was taking place in inner Beijing during the early weeks of the Cultural Revolution. A few weeks into the Mao-incited anarchy, a shooting incident that saw bullets fired from a neighbouring school through our house was a sharp awakening, bringing my childhood to an early and abrupt end. In contemporary Chinese political discourse, there is a famous saying that the cannon blast of the October Revolution of Russia delivered Marxism–Leninism to China. In my case, as I have occasionally joked, the shots striking our house shocked me out of my preteen mind. My family was soon relocated to a then-remote, and seemingly safe, university campus in the western outskirts of Beijing.

That was a ridiculous time full of strange things, very different from what I was taught at both home and school. My deepest impression of the Red Guards who repeatedly turned up in our multi-household courtyard to harass my family and a few others was that they appeared to be uncultured and uncouth students by pre-Cultural Revolution standards of social behaviour. The targets of their furious and repeated denunciations seemed to be increasing disciplinary measures at schools and increasing difficulties in coping with school work, which, oddly, they defined as a capitalist reactionary line in education. I was also deeply confused by their anti-common-sense argument that regarded wheat-flour steamed bun as part of what was then called the feudal and capitalist lifestyle. This staple was in short supply in the 1960s, but the Red Guards forgot that wheat-flour food was also deployed as a symbol of a good socialist life in the new China. They were obviously very anti-good-food as they came to our courtyard a few times to check what was cooking on our stoves and to force residents to eat *wotou*, corn-flour steamed bun. This was even more odious and absurd to an always-hungry tween than their anti-school attitudes.

My confusion about what had happened in inner Beijing was not resolved after resettling in a university student dormitory, but exposed to very different socio-political landscapes and climates. The Cultural Revolutionary activities on university campuses were also crazy, but less childish. Unlike the various silly acts of secondary school students in inner Beijing, university campuses were full of daily-refreshed long, big-character posters revealing the alleged historical wrongdoings and political mistakes of those who were active and successful in earlier parts of their life. Residing on campus also exposed me to frequent mass rallies openly denouncing and humiliating many well-known Chinese from a wide range of backgrounds. In those years, I was unable to understand where the anger and hatred of those activists came from, but one thing was clear: these Red Guards, at both high schools and universities, wanted to show their loyalty to Mao, who promised young Chinese that the world and China's future belonged to them. According to what I overheard from other non-activist students, the action of the activist students was their way of striving to be revolutionary 'successors', similar to what we were told in junior primary schools in the early 1960s. The irony was that educated people were one of the major targets of the Cultural Revolution and China's political leading class was then only made up of workers, peasants and soldiers.

Because of the hypothetical importance of workers and peasants – if not soldiers, as their related privileges were not widely shared at the time – our generation was also asked to learn from workers and peasants. One instance of participating in the summer harvest work in a village made me intensely sceptical of the theory of poor peasants being part of the leading class, as well as of their loyalty to the ruling party. At a village meeting to convey the new decision by the ultra-left Maoists to end the entitlement of *ziliudi*, a small piece of land allocated to each rural household, a couple of old and apparently poor peasants stood up and voiced their strong opposition. This silly top-down decision was idealised as a revolutionary measure to 'cut off the tail' of capitalism, implying that those private plots were the final residue of private ownership in China and should not be allowed in the eyes of Maoist radicals. Those peasants were so poor and desperate that they could no longer silently acquiesce in policies to take the land away. They yelled out to the cadres: What shall we eat if not enough food is allocated, like 1961 and 1962, from the brigade? Our panicked teachers quickly asked students to leave the meeting, as such protests were seen to be anti-revolutionary. Thus, many from my generation have long believed that the widely promoted absolute authority of the top leadership was always illusory, and the seeds of rural changes or reforms were planted long ago.

The problems caused by sending millions of urban youth to rural areas led to a brief suspension of the sending-down policy, which altered the fate of my year group. In 1970, school leavers were not sent to villages or agrarian farms in remote regions, except for a handful few who were from deeply troubled families in a political sense. This made us part of China's factory-worker class or the industrial proletariat. My first paid position, assigned by my school, was a sign that all the new workers were from politically problematic families, while earlier groups could be kindly defined as troubled urban residents. This was one of the numerous small- and medium-sized factories that were located in city but under collective ownership, which was at least in name similar to the ownership status of the People's Commune in rural China. This has been a grey area for many students of contemporary China. Some of my old workmates described it as a rural tribe in the city. These factories were originally set up by street-district committees as their voluntary or involuntary response to the Great Leap Forward in 1958. When China run into economic trouble after 1958, these factories were used to absorb urban jobless people, but the workers and factories never gained state-hired and state-owned status.

It must be admitted that what I experienced before the late 1970s was not unique; millions of individuals and families experienced similar or even worse treatment in this era of the Chinese history. As many of my old workmates and friends have often commented, my post-school life in the 1970s was less unfortunate than many others as I was assigned to undergo training first and then work in a factory-run clinic. Besides being free from laborious work as a teenager, my clinic work also provided me with a special chance to learn more about China's urban poor and many other topics that we were unable to learn as a result of the closure of our senior secondary school. I started learning English in the clinic, the exercise of which was protected by the position. During the Cultural Revolution, two special occupations – some scientists and medical doctors or health care workers – were to some extent free from Maoist political correctness, especially from far-leftist class warfare against learned people. My eight-year-long work experience in the clinic serving the urban poor, including one year in Beijing's Capital Iron and Steel Company General Hospital working alongside China's industrial proletariat, helped greatly in readying me for my later unexpected career in the field of applied sociological studies.

As I have noted in the prefaces to my 2015 book, *Chinese Migrants Entrepreneurship in Australia from the 1990s* (Elsevier), the second book of a trilogy on the experiences of new Chinese migrants in Australia and my 2019 co-authored book *Social Mobilisation in Post-Industrial China* (Edward Elgar), I became one of the first group of young Chinese to pass the highly competitive national university entrance examination that was promptly reintroduced in mid-1977, less than one year after Mao's death. Despite competing with the school leavers of preceding 13 years, I passed the selection examination in 1978 and joined the then most prestigious Department of Philosophy at Renmin University of China in Beijing. After four years of study, I was assigned by the university to be a staff member of its administration team as I was found to be more familiar with university operations than other graduates, but I was soon transferred to help establish the new Institute of Sociology at the university. It was there that I became an active researcher in the fields of social psychology and sociology. Before leaving for Australia to conduct my PhD research in mid-1988, I was awarded the first and only national academic prize in the field of sociology by China's National Commission of Education and the Fok Ying Tung Foundation of Hong Kong.

Of course, this book is not about my personal experiences of events in China over the past five or so decades. Instead, this study is based on a systematic and thorough review of the existing scholarship on China's societal dynamics and social change, as well as on data gathered over recent years using multiple research methods. However, the above brief self-introduction offers readers another layer of background information. This is largely because that the topic of this book and the angle to from which I approach that topic are not easy for researchers, even for those young and middle-aged researchers living and working in China.

In fact, the topic of this analysis was often discussed among my colleagues in the mid-1980s when I was working in China. At that time, I developed special research interests in social processes and the dynamics fuelling social reactions and actions. As mentioned several times in my earlier publications, I have long preferred an analytical stance that pays attention to process as opposed to overstressing the role of structure and the impact of shorter time periods. However, the long-term role of everyday people, especially aspirational people, in driving social changes through new social dynamics was not an easy topic to examine in the mid-1980s. It was even more difficult if one wished to foresee what direction Chinese society would take, how far it would move in that way and why it was headed that direction. I can still recollect that general discussions among my old colleagues on this topic often ended with two conclusions. The first was to leave the issue to historians, as researchers were busy in studying many new issues; and the second one was to wait until history reveals more of its details.

Now, more than three decades have passed since the topic was raised and discussed among my Chinese colleagues, and contemporary Chinese history has revealed enough evidence to support a systematic study of what has driven changes in the attitudes and actions of everyday, but aspirational, Chinese in recent decades – what characteristics of their preferences and choices look like at different steps, and how their preferences have given rise to different patterns in China's recent social change. Many readers, including some China observers, are confused by the shifts in China's public sentiment – from the enthusiasm for pragmatic reform under Deng Xiaoping to the resurgence of Mao fever, from post-Mao liberalisation to recent nationalism and from the worship of everything Western to an increasing anti-Western stance. Behind these shifts, China has in fact been pushed along by both the left and the right of the political spectrum, to such a degree that the historic pattern of the 'negation of the negation' has been clearly discernible even within the span of a few decades. This book offers a new way of considering this phenomenon.

As noted at the start of this introduction, this study will adopt a new perspective, competitive social repositioning, the details of which are provided in Chapter one. By applying this new approach, this study offers a new set of evidence and explanations of how China's social dynamics are generated, how ordinary people must keep repositioning themselves within a fast-changing society and how social dynamics work in Chinese society. The novel perspective of competitive social repositioning is carefully tried and tested to enable a focus on ordinary Chinese people's reactions and actions over a long period, thereby overcoming the limitations of previous studies, but with no intention to devalue the latter.

I am deeply indebted to many generous individuals who have either provided me with direct assistance in undertaking of this project or aided me in indirect but valuable ways. Although I started focusing and working on this book during the COVID-19 lockdown, my research preceded the pandemic and has included discussion of crucial events, issues and problems with many people. There are, therefore, too many individuals, both in China and the outside world, to be thanked individually and acknowledged for their assistance and contributions to this project. Since the thank-you list is too long to include here, I would like to collectively thank the WeChat groups established among my old schoolmates and co-workers, as well as my former colleagues. Many of these group members, especially those I interviewed, have been very supportive and helpful to this research project.

I am particularly grateful for the many suggestions and comments from Professor Li Lulu of Renmin University of China, Professor Lin Juren of Shandong University, Professor Fan Ke of Nanjing University and Mr Mi Hedu, one of the prolific researchers among my university mates, and the author of several popular books on China's post-1949 generations. My special gratitude also goes to Dr Zhou Xiang of Renmin University of China for sending me several published memoirs as early as 2015, Dr Rong Liying of Capital Normal University for sharing research materials and Professor Zhou Xiaohong of Nanjing University for offering me access to their oral history database.

In recent years, I have also frequently been supported by a large group of international scholars in the fields of China- and Chinese-related studies. Among them, I would like to thank Professor Chee-Beng Tan of Sun Yat-sen University; Professor Rui Yang of the University of Hong Kong; Professor Min Zhou and Professor Yunxiang Yan of the University of California, Los Angeles; Professor Li Zong of the University of Saskatchewan; Professor Shibao Guo of the University of Calgary; Professor Liu Hong and Dr Zhan Shaohua of Singapore's Nanyang Technological University; Dr Bin Wu of the University of Nottingham; Professor David S. G. Goodman of the University of Sydney; Professor Wanning Sun of the University of Technology Sydney; Professor Bingqin Li of the University of New South Wales; Dr Shenshen Cai of Monash University; Professor Haiqing Yu and Dr Chengju Huang of RMIT University and Professor Manying Ip of the University of Auckland.

Since the mid-2010s, I have benefitted greatly from my conversations and discussions with a group of young Chinese PhD scholars, more than a dozen of them, who have conducted research projects on various applied social science topics at the Asia Institute at the University of Melbourne. I have learned much from them including confirming my own information about events in different Chinese regions. They have all now graduated and worked in different institutions. Among them, special thank go to Dr Pan Qiuping, Dr Yang Yilu, Dr Zhang Qianjin, Dr Song Yao, Dr Guan Tianru, Dr Liu Tianyang, Dr Huang Biao and Dr Jiang Liu.

I am also grateful to the acquisition, editorial and production teams at Anthem Press. I was first contacted by the acquisition team in April 2020, just days after I submitted the manuscript of *Chinese Immigration and Australia Politics* (Palgrave Macmillan, 2020). At the time, Australia was troubled by the COVID-19 pandemic and lockdown restrictions. I thank Lydia Stevens, Molly Grab, Jessica Mack and Megan Greiving for encouraging me to put my ideas in writing. I also appreciate the support and guidance Megan provided during the peer review process. I would also like to thank all the anonymous reviewers for their comments and suggestions on both the proposal and the first manuscript. My thanks also go to Jebaslin Hephzibah and the editorial and production teams at Anthem Press for guiding me through the production process.

The manuscript of this book was edited by Mr Matthew Sidebotham of Canberra-based workwisewords and Dr René Rejón of the Melbourne University Faculty of Arts' Research Assistance team. I am grateful to Matthew and René for their assistance in not only editing the manuscript but also providing me with helpful suggestions. I also thank Ms Wendy Monaghan of Wendy Monaghan Editing Services for helping me connect with highly experienced editors in Australia.

I would also like to thank the Faculty of Arts at Melbourne University for financial support provided under the Faculty Internal Grant Scheme; this funding has partly covered the cost of my fieldwork and editing this manuscript. My special gratitude also goes to Professor Mark Considine, the former dean of the Faculty of Arts and the former provost of the University of Melbourne. Under his deanship, I was provided with chances to travel to China to meet other researchers, and many of the ideas and materials used in this book were collected during those trips.

The unwavering understanding, support and encouragement of my family, which has grown over the past few years, are always important in writing a book like this one, let alone the fact I have been working on several of them in the past 10 or so years. As a result, my wife has taken on almost all household duties. Despite working and living overseas, my son and daughter-in-law have also been very caring and often flown back to Melbourne to help with household duties.

The most significant change to my family life since I finished writing the third book of a trilogy on the experiences of new Chinese migrants in Australia is the arrival of my grandson, Ethan, who was born in the world of social distancing, lockdowns and quarantine in the COVID-19 years. The disruptions of recent years remind me of my own childhood; while very different, both periods remind me that younger generations must be mentally strong and resilient in order to live a happy life in this troubled world. I have therefore decided to dedicate this book to Ethan, wishing him to grow up to be an aspirational person.

Chapter One

THE ABSENCE OF EVERYDAY CHINESE IN THE DICHOTOMOUS PARADIGM

This chapter is the introductory chapter of this book, which starts with an overall historical view of what had happened in China from 1964 to 2000, and why this period is chosen to be re-analysed. The focus of this chapter, however, is on the limitations of the existing scholarship on China's social dynamics and change, which are found to be characterised by the evident absence of ordinary, but aspirational, people in the dichotomous paradigm of examining societal forces at work and possible subsequent changes to socio-economic and socio-political landscape and climate. Since this research aims to fill this knowledge and analytical gap, which has both theoretical and practical implications, the objective of this current chapter is to place the analysis in its historical and theoretical contexts.

As noted in the preface, over the past four or so decades a significant amount of research has studied a fast-changing China. The volume of this body of literature, in both English and Chinese, is such that many new and young researchers, and general readers as well, are often overwhelmed or may even be scared off this overheated research field. Careful review reveals, however, that past research has predominantly centred on either the ruling party or its outspoken opponents, and the so-called silent majority of China's large population is examined only sporadically, if at all. This dichotomous paradigm is reviewed in the second section of this chapter; however, two general epistemological, cognitive and methodological issues seem to be behind the research focus.

The first problem is that of 'herd' or 'flocking' behaviour in the academic research. This is a rather broad issue and beyond the scope of this analysis, but it is worth noting that modern-day academic fields and their practices have certain limits and biases. Flocking behaviour – defined by one French professor, a Nobel Prize winner in economics, as the tendency for a particular subject to 'hog the attention of the scientific community while equally important subjects are neglected' (Tirole 2017, 97) – is one such constraint. In a Chinese phrase, it might be termed *renyun yiyun* (echoing the views of others or repeating what someone has said). In the field of China studies, this herd behaviour refers to at least two types of issues. On the one hand, researchers are often restricted to the search–re-search cycle, limiting many studies not only to established topics but also to existing theories and notions, which has made sections of the field less innovative and led to certain issues never being explored or analysed. On the other hand, despite the claim that academic researchers are intellectually independent, and also despite the fact that many Chinese analysts are often very critical of China's ruling elites, many of them have, in fact, closely followed the topics initiated or advocated by China's ruling party and its establishment. This reality has left much research subject to the direct and indirect influence of China's ruling classes, if not led by them.

The second general issue is the lack of understanding of an important feature of human societies – namely, the role of the likes and dislike of the majority of the population in a society. For more than two thousand years there has been a Chinese saying stressing the role of the masses in defining the fate of the rulers and their followers. This ancient saying is that water can carry a boat, but it can also sink it;[1] it has long been used in Chinese politics to caution that the masses, as the water, can overturn the boat of a ruler or ruling class. The current Chinese socio-political system has thus far survived, but has also been forced to make many changes to it. This well-known ancient political philosophy will be elaborated further in later chapters.

Bearing the above issues in mind, this chapter outlines the context of this study in four sections. The first section provides an overview of the decades from 1964 to 2000, explaining why this research focuses on these decades. The second analyses the existing literature, focusing on what is missing from past research. The third section offers a brief overview of this book's new analytical approach, 'competitive social repositioning'. The fourth and final section outlines the overall structure of this book, which over the course of seven chapters systematically analyses the evidence obtained through the use of multiple methods.

Social Conditions of Post-Famine China

As noted, there are numerous books and other resources available on events in China in the 1950s and 1960s, especially the Anti-Rightist Campaign in 1957, the Great Leap Forward in 1958 and the troubles that triggered open conflict among central and provincial leaders of the ruling CCP in 1959. The internal fight within the CCP in 1959 – which China's top leaders sought to hide from the people – has become known as the Lushan Conference of 1959, a meeting at which the party leadership debated the Great Leap Forward and its socio-economic consequence (MacFarquhar 1974; Teiwes and Sun 1999).[2] The political infighting was a key turning point in the history of the People's Republic of China (PRC) as it entered its second decade. This decade started badly, with severe food shortages and numerous natural disasters. In history, the three years from 1959 to 1961 are known as the Great Chinese Famine among non-Chinese scholars; in China they are called the Three Years of Difficult Period or the Three Years of Natural Disasters.

Table 1.1 lists the main events and changes in China between 1959 and 2000, outlining the overall historical, social and political context of the discussion in this book.

The three years of nationwide famine – which in reality was more than three years in most regions – was a devastating period, but it did trigger changes in the CCP's internal political dynamics and relations. It also saw a period of reflection for the CCP as a new ruling party. The so-called Seven-Thousand Cadres Conference in early 1962 was a symbolic major intra-party event, at which Mao engaged in self-criticism and opted to retreat to what he called the 'second line', withdrawing from daily operational governance (Fu 1993; Baum 1994). As shown in Table 1.1, however, a few

Table 1.1 China's main post-1959 events and changes.

Year	Leadership	Main Events and Changes
1959	Mao Zedong	The Lushan Conference of 1959
1962	Mao Zedong	The Seven-Thousand Cadres Conference in early 1962, at which Mao is sidelined
1962	Mao Zedong	Mao puts forward his 'never forget class struggle' slogan in September 1962
1964	Mao Zedong	Mao openly puts forward his 'five requirements for revolutionary successors'
1966	Mao Zedong	The Cultural Revolution starts in late May
1969	Mao Zedong	Lin Biao is appointed as Mao's successor
1971	Mao Zedong	The September 13 Incident, Lin Biao flees
1976	Mao Zedong	Death of Zhou Enlai, the 1976 Tiananmen Incident and death of Mao
1977	Hua Guofeng	The decision to reintroduce the university entrance examination
1978	Deng Xiaoping	The CCP's Third Plenum of the Eleventh National Congress, focusing on economic construction. Deng assumes his leadership role
1987	Deng Xiaoping	The student protest
1989	Deng Xiaoping	The Tiananmen event of 1989 and Jiang Zemin appointed as the leader
1992	Jiang Zemin	Deng Xiaoping urges further reforms in his inspection tour speeches
1999	Jiang Zemin	The Falun Gong is outlawed
2000	Jiang Zemin	The three-represents theory is put forward

Sources: Complied by the author based on Fu (1993), Baum (1994), Teiwes and Sun (1999), He (2001), Li and Xia (2018).

months after the conference Mao started intervening again, warning the party of the seriousness of class struggle in September 1962. In line with this political tactic, which was partly supported by the first-line leadership, another less well-known campaign, the Four Clean-Ups, was launched (Baum and Teiwes 1968). During this movement, which was originally aimed at rural grassroots cadres who had become corrupt and reckless during the famine, the rift between Mao and his then administrative successor, Liu Shaoqi,[3] who became the second president of the PRC in 1959, not only emerged but rapidly reached an irreversible level, making the Cultural Revolution unavoidable. That is, this tension was an important background to the deterioration of political conditions in China at the time.

Much research has been devoted to the CCP's internal fights, but the new political strategy formed by the first-line leadership – or agreed by Mao and the first-line leaders – has attracted little attention from analysts or researchers. In fact, the four clean-ups campaign exposed a governance dilemma caused by the two-line leadership arrangement and seriously disturbed the CCP. One of the observable results was the difficulty of developing and executing new and unified political narratives suitable to post-famine China. In the post-1959 years, or during and shortly after the famine, there were two new narratives, which provoked very different social reactions.

As first example of the CCP's difficulties in communicating its political message, the four clean-ups campaign was articulated in rather different ways. It was also called the rural socialist education movement when it was first launched in early 1963, and the initial purposes were to audit and monitor daily work points of village-based cadres, the local accounting systems, inventories of storehouses and financial account details. These four original goals gave rise to the name of the four clean-ups. The subsequent changes to its name and scope, however, influenced its socio-political impact. Compared to 'the rural socialist education campaign', the reference to 'clean-ups' sounded combative, resonating with what took place in the political campaigns of the 1950s. Even worse than the name change, however, was the change in objectives, which redirected a rural-focused campaign to broad national action in politics, economics and ideology. The politicisation or escalation of this major post-1959 campaign resulted from the worsening tension between Mao and his frontline leader and successor, Liu Shaoqi. Fortunately, the political thinking in the post-famine period was not one-sided thanks to what Mao defined as the two political lines of command within the CCP, an arrangement also largely influenced by post-famine socio-political and socio-economic climate. At the time, ordinary people were either scared by, or no longer interested in, highly politicised campaigns. Both Mao and his challengers needed a new political narrative to spread encouraging and promising messages to the devastated society and frustrated masses.

The second narrative example, which I call the successor narrative, was the one on which ordinary Chinese pinned their hopes and expectations. Although it was put forward by Mao as part of his attempt to oust his successor, Liu Shaoqi, the successor narrative was re-articulated and utilised by pragmatic frontline leaders. At this juncture, Liu was involved in the formation, or revision precisely, of the successor narrative, which was soon attacked by Maoists as *baizhuan luxian* (the while-expert line) as opposite to Mao's red-revolutionary line (Li and Bachman 1989). Perhaps because there was little else promising in the post-famine years, the plan to train, identify and select successors was seen as a more positive message than the clean-ups campaign, and therefore had a constructive influence on the minds of the general public. This positive narrative was, purposely or accidentally, widely disseminated, playing an important role in offering people opportunities to be hopeful and restoring people's confidence in post-famine China. As will be detailed in Chapter two, several party and state organs and functionaries, such as the Chinese Communist Youth League (CCYL) and the Ministry for Education, involved themselves in actively re-articulating or rebranding the message. Thus, the period of this analysis, from 1964 to 2000, is not arbitrary but, rather, is based on assessments of changing dynamics among both the ruling elites and the governed masses.

As the impact of the successor narrative on post-famine Chinese society will be the key focus of Chapter two, the rest of this section will focus on background information that helps understand why this specific, and almost incidental, narrative was welcomed, if not hailed, by many ordinary Chinese in the 1960s. It is worth noting that the analysis below should be read in conjunction with Chapter two, which will focus on how the narrative was re-articulated and translated into policies and how everyday people responded to this successor narrative. This section, however, focuses on key aspects of underlying social conditions that made the successor narrative popular.

As numerous studies have shown, many social reactions are ultimately related to the size and composition of a country's population. China is not only no exception to this rule, but has also been a case study used to demonstrate the importance of population size, composition and various other aspects in determining and shaping social dynamics and processes. Specifically, in contrast to its recent dwindling birth rate – which fell to just 1.69 births per woman in 2018 and then to 1.3 in 2020, well below the expected population replacement level (2.1 births per woman) – China in the post-famine years was seriously challenged by a different set of demographic issues. Figure 1.1 – based on data from the National Bureau of Statistics of China (NBSC) – reveals that China's population was incredibly young from the early 1950s to almost the early 2000s. In 1964, its median age was as young as 20.2 years, then slowly grew to 22.9 in 1982, 25.3 in 1990 and 30.8 in 2000. This indicates one of the reasons why China in the 1960s could have become an agitated and restless country or a very dynamic society.

What is also surprising is that there 40.7 per cent of the total population in 1964, or more than 281 million people, were aged between 1 and 14. This may sound good to many present-day ageing societies, but China at that time had to cope with difficult food supply issues, in addition to the issues of housing and employment. Importantly, the party-state leadership had also to offer a platform suitable for the young population, something hopeful and positive, and otherwise, they may be as rebellious as youth had been on numerous occasions in China's pre-1949 history. The new successor issue, while not initially intended as such a platform, nonetheless became popular among ordinary families with young children.

China's fertility rate was affected by the famine for several years, with a series of population pyramids covering those born from the 1950s to the 1970s showing an atypical structure with a very lean or narrow layer. This resulted from a sudden and significant drop in the fertility rate over the famine years. Many Chinese have depicted this as a tight belt constricting the body, if not the waist, of the pyramid, while others have described it as a deep wound in the population pyramid. Despite the drastically lower fertility rate during the famine years compared to the rest of the 1950s, China's high

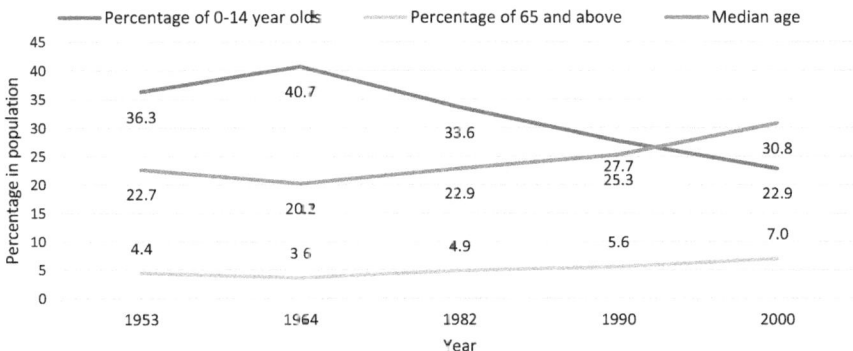

Figure 1.1 China's young population, 1953–2000. *Source*: Created by the author using data from NBSC (2009).

rate of population growth resumed after the famine. In other words, the problem caused by the youth demographic was only one of the various problems faced by China, and the country's massive population base and its rapid growth placed enormous socio-economic pressures upon the party-state system and society.

Figure 1.2 illustrates three sets of statistical data: overall population growth from 1955 to 2000, the rise and recent decline of rural population over the same period of time and the slow and constant growth of the urban population. The trends shown in Figure 1.2 are not just about China's population, but more about its general social conditions, in which people live and work while the state has to govern. Obviously, this was an overpopulated country with an above average birth rate, and the young and inexperienced party-state system was unable to either control it or make perfect use of the birth rate before the end of the 1970s. All these factors made China a rather gloomy and struggling society in the PRC's second and third decades.

In addition, as will be detailed in Chapter two, there was a worsening social structure problem – or 'social contradiction', in the evasive words of Mao – among the many population-related problems in the 1960s. This was the social structural tension or conflict arising from a remarkably young population and the significantly limited opportunities for them to achieve upward social mobility. In fact, following economic downturns and more politicised approaches to new problems, the 1960s saw further policy measures restricting people from moving between social classes or even between rural areas and urban centres. In a popular Chinese saying, there were tens of thousands of people crossing a single-log bridge at the same time (Lin and Sun 2010). For many people, even this narrow bridge did not exist. The narrow channels for social mobility, especially upward social mobility, are discussed in more detail in other chapters, but it was evident in the post-famine years that Chinese society as a whole was suffering from far fewer social mobility opportunities, both horizontal and vertical, even compared to the rest of the 1950s. By the 1960s this reality led to a stronger desire among the public, and the

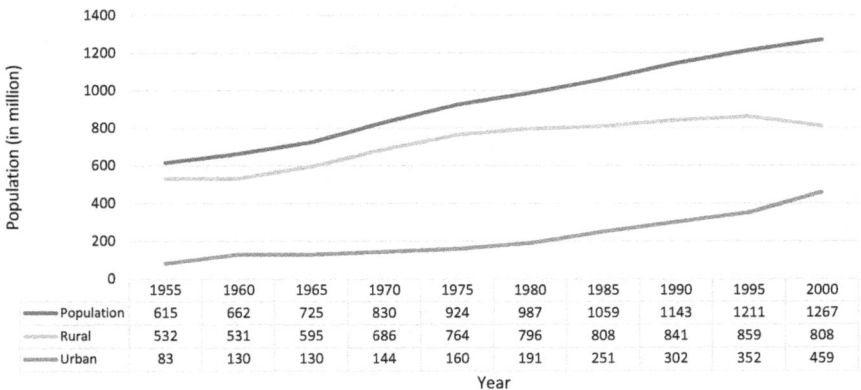

	1955	1960	1965	1970	1975	1980	1985	1990	1995	2000
Population	615	662	725	830	924	987	1059	1143	1211	1267
Rural	532	531	595	686	764	796	808	841	859	808
Urban	83	130	130	144	160	191	251	302	352	459

Figure 1.2 China's population growth and rural–urban distribution, 1955–2000. *Source*: Created by the author using data from NBSC (2020).

use of more sophisticated tactics, to find alternative ways to respond, while the regime's pragmatic leaders were also making efforts to adjust their ways of governing.

After the poor economic conditions during and immediately after the famine years, China enjoyed several years of recovery, including 1964, and there was at least some degree of optimism, despite being still under Mao's leadership. However, from mid-1966 the CCP's actual successor problem, and the tensions created by the two lines of political control, plunged China into what post-Mao reformers have defined as the 10-year chaos of the Cultural Revolution. During this 10-year period of turmoil, China had virtually no horizontal population mobility at all, including in rural–urban migration, let alone vertical mobility allowing citizens to move from one social stratum to another. It was due to the resulting frustration that several generations of Chinese joined forces in the 1970s to resist the country's rigid social control. Of course, China's societal dynamics have significantly altered since the 1980s and 1990s, through a complex and intricate process that is analysed in detailed in Chapters two to eight.

A Scoping Review of the Research Literature

As a result of the shifting social context, the attention of everyday Chinese has long since drifted away from the CCP's political lines, ideology and endorsed narratives. There has always been what may be called public sentiment and opinion, existing in parallel with the narratives endorsed and promoted by the ruling elite, as well as its rivals. From the early to mid-1990s, the attention of China's general public has been increasingly focused on the emerging economic areas and opportunities. This has created cohorts of new business owners and operators, giving rise to a new middle class in China. However, the main drivers of these changes have yet to be explored systematically, especially the role of the needs, desires, pressures and dynamics created by China's huge and young population in creating social change. These hidden forces even triggered a theoretical effort by some open-minded members of the ruling elites and ideologically flexible leaders of the CCP, including Jiang Zemin who put forward his Three-Represents theory in 2000. In Jiang's view, the leading elites must periodically re-evaluate and reset their ideological foundation and goal-setting in order to represent advancing productive forces, culture and the fundamental interests of the majority of the Chinese people.[4] As noted in the preface and the early part of this chapter, however, the ordinary people's side of the story – their influence on social dynamics, changes and processes – is absent from the existing research literature. This section looks at this issue, focusing on what has been studied so far and what areas have not been adequately explored by researchers.

The topic of social change in China has fascinated researchers both within China and in other countries for decades, despite increasingly negative views of a rising China. Such views not entirely displaced memories of China's effective social changes. Few researchers would deny that China has been transformed since Mao's Cultural Revolution. What researchers do not agree on is what has driven these changes and where these driving forces have been generated. The notion of social change was introduced into Chinese scholarship in the late 1970s and early 1980s, and it has soon become a popular analytical idea along with Sinicised Marxism. A few years later, and not long after it emerged as a prevalent framework among Western researchers, the concept of social dynamics also appeared in Chinese sociological literature, reflecting the complexities of the fast-changing socio-political landscape in China.

The notions of social change and dynamics have been used in slightly different ways since they were first introduced in China. Social change has evolved from being an imported descriptive idea to a key analytical notion that is defined from different perspectives. In earlier years, the concept of social change was understood by Chinese specialists as a perceptible transition in society from one state to another in a specific period of time. It has since advanced from focusing on a single aspect – institutional, cultural, socio-structural or behavioural – to a comprehensive one that looks at the various social changes and their effects on society over a long period of time. However, among the three important elements utilised in theorising societal change – process, units of change and human agents (Dwyer and Minnegal 2010) – the main problem in China studies is the lack of proper research efforts probing and theorising human agents of social change. Additionally, the first element, the process in a temporal sense, is often observed based on only a limited time span. The use of the notion of social dynamics in examining Chinese society was initially also more heavily influenced by officially endorsed Marxism than some other newly introduced ideas; however, this problem has been slowly lessening due to the complexities and depth of reform programmes, which has widened the scope of studies. However, as pointed out, there is still no consensus among researchers as to what has been driving change in China. Although analysts have considered this question from different angles, ranging from the group or community level to the national or even international level, the influence of national and international politics has led many analysts to place a somehow excessive emphasis on the ruling party's leadership and the demands for democratisation by opposing forces. As an outcome of these evident deviations, researchers have continued to attempt to identify where dynamics have been produced (Gittings 1990; Bonnin and Chevrier 1991; Hamrin 2003; Zhou 2009; Bian 2015).

The rest of this literature review is organised into three subsections, which discuss, respectively, the research focus on ruling elites and their decisions; the effort to study social reactions and discontents of different social classes towards policy changes; and what has been overlooked by researchers. The review will lead to the proposed framework for this book, which will be detailed in the third section.

The dominance of elitist perspectives on social changes

The excessive research focus on China's party-state system and its role in initiating and implementing – or opposing and impeding, in the eyes of some – various reform programmes and measures arises for two reasons. Politically, China is a one-party state, and historically, its reform was initiated by post-Mao leaders and has since been pushed forward by reformist leaderships. As a result, although the question of how to evaluate China's political system and socio-economic growth was raised soon after its reform (Myers 1987; Liu 1988), the activities of researchers were largely confined to certain directions. These analytical limits were also partly caused by the access problem faced by both foreign and local scholars in China in the early reform years (Thurston 1983; Blecher and Shue 1996). As a result of these constraints, two research focuses initially emerged in the English-language research literature on post-1978 China, focusing on 'an understanding of the dynamics of change and continuity in the Chinese system' (Lieberthal 1995, xvii). Researchers in China had, at the same time, devoted their attention to either assisting policy-making, such as the rural industrialisation strategy of Fei Xiaotong and his team (Zweig 1992; White 1998), or continuing their usual role in praising the leadership. Therefore, both foreign and Chinese researchers focused largely on topics comparable to what Lieberthal defines as the dynamics of change and continuity, but the many obstacles, geographical and political, to research forced them to narrow their focus to politics at the top level. Some crucial questions, such as political bargaining and the reciprocal nature of China's authoritarianism (Lampton 1987), were also raised in earlier years, but research only became possible in later years.

This early focus on the dynamics of change in China, and the narrowed interest in politics at the top as well, produced a huge number of publications. All these were characterised by a temporal variability, highly consistent with what China has reformed and what issues its reform has run into. Other than its temporal characteristics, this research focus also led to a very top-down, institution-oriented or state-centric – if not Beijing-centric – orientation in these early studies and publications. For analytical purposes, this section explores how newly introduced reforms and policies, including their consequences, have been researched and the themes that have evolved along the trajectory of China's reform agendas.

Previous research responses covered almost all main reform areas, including rural reforms, state-enterprise reforms, the depoliticisation of class relations, policies encouraging people to partake in reform and the rise of middle classes in the country.

The early major theme was the rural reforms that began in the late 1970s, a few years earlier than urban reforms. The household production responsibility system was introduced as a result of bottom-up pushes by peasants and village leaders to replace the old collective team system (Lin 1988; Nolan 1988), but the institutional process and its role soon became a key focus, overshadowing other driving forces, including what some analysts called peasant power (Kelliher 1992). In searching for the logic of China's rural reform, an institutional approach has become a favoured analytical tool. Some even believe that economic reforms are based more on political logic than economic logic. This perspective has brought some institutional and political factors, such as party-state relationships, leadership incentives, fiscal decentralisation and even sectoral interests, into consideration as drivers of rural changes (Shirk 1993). These focuses have since turned analytical attention on rural issues away from villagers and village leaders, although many Chinese analysts continue to produce first-hand insights into rural life. This trend became more noticeable when China's agricultural reform entered its rural industrialisation phase (Sigurdson 1977; Zweig 1992). A large number of township and village enterprises (TVEs) formed a powerful engine of rural development after the initial reform and represent a typical case of strong bottom-up pushes for change (Nee and Young 1991; Gilley 2001). However, such dynamic development has only expanded research to a few non-institutional aspects, such as the conduct of local officials and elites (Whiting 2000). Even the latter has then become more concerned with the owner-ship of TVEs and the relations with local governments than rural entrepreneurs (Chen 2000), while the rural–urban divide in income, services and education has remained a theme (Knight and Song 1999). A few decades into China's rural reforms, more studies have been conducted at a meso level than formerly, but the focus remains predomi-nantly on the restructuring of decollectivised rural China (Thøgersen and Bislev 2012). This analytical inertia has in turn limited analysis of China's rural urbanisation, the third phase of the rural reform, to a similar institutional perspective.

The changes in urban China have led to the emergence of another key research theme in studying China's social dynamics and changes. Unlike studies of rural issues, which paid some attention to the roles of peasants and rural leaders, studies of urban reforms were from the very beginning influenced by reformist views on the manage-rial deficiencies in state-owned enterprises (SOEs). The policy attention of early urban reforms was typified by the slogan of 'smashing the iron rice bowl', which sounds puni-tive, if not retaliatory (Gustafsson and Sai 2013, 290). Many urban reform studies also focused on institutional arrangements and policies (Walder 1989; Hughes 2002; Huang 2010b). One outcome of the changes to urban society was issue of laid-off workers, which led to widespread urban protests (Wong 1998; Tang and Parish 2000). The new focus also turned attention to some other aspects of political structure, ideology and related issues (O'Leary 1998; You 1998; Preston and Xing 2003; Huang 2008). Analytically, the focus on the reform's political logic and process has drawn attention to what Chinese elites have advanced in urban areas.

Among many other research topics generated by China's reform, one important and actively studied theme is that of central–local relations as a mechanism to advance structural restructuring (Zhao 1994; Breslin 1996; Goodman 1997; Li 1998). This has been a fertile field of study since the 1980s, and this analytical theme has generated a number of sub-themes, which have turned local governments, leaders and non-official elites at several levels into key actors in the studies. Of course, the depoliticisation of class relations as another Dengist approach has not only been extensively studied, but has also led to a few other sub-themes. China's reform started with a range of Dengist ideas, including the view of science and technology as crucial productive forces. These ideas ended the dominance of Maoist class ideology, liberating many people from dis-crimination (Kraus 1981; Bian 2002; Perry 2007; Andreas 2009; Goodman 2014). This study topic has further entrenched attention to elite ideas and politics.

Even more narrowly focused than the above themes are the studies of China's ruling elites themselves and their thinking, which are partially influenced by academic tradi-tions (Rankin 1986; Chan 1996; Zhang 2000). Various reform policies changed the rule and process of elite politics, and issues were then raised about whether and how the lasting characteristics of the Chinese polity were changing, and so on (Fewsmith 2001; Saich 2001). This focus has since been shifting towards more complex aspects of elite politics. Among them, the analysis of the new leadership has been a fascinating topic, extending consideration to more factors and raising the level of knowledge above that of earlier 'Pekinologists' (Gilley 1998; Lam 1999; Li 2001). While the macro-structure of elites has remained a dominant theme (Zheng 2010; He 2014), the political principles of elite selection and promotion, and the composition of new elites, have all become active topics of research (Walder et al. 2000; Zang 2006; Kou and Zang 2014; Jeffreys 2016; Veg 2019a).

The attention to elites has recently evolved to focus on the emergence of the middle classes in China. Despite warnings that China's middle classes are fragmented and have not yet developed a coherent socio-political consciousness, they are undeniably believed to be a new social class structure driving social-economic and socio-political changes since the late 1990s (Li 2010, 2012). The Chinese state has lately also changed its discourse on the middle classes, accepting them as a socio-political mechanism to deal with risks arising from ongoing changes. As a crucial social structure, these classes are now more than ever considered as legitimate classes and as a norm of citizenship (Ren 2013), and their identity, attitudes and conduct have become active research topics (Chen and Goodman 2013; Miao 2017). However, members of these classes are still largely seen as statistic figures, and their ways of becoming the middle-class members are often abstracted to be a set of external factors and structures without sufficiently considering their motivations and processes.

The second research focus of early studies, on the continuity of China's political system and especially the fate of ideology, also helped strengthen the dominance of elite-oriented research on social change in China. As argued by Fewsmith, China's rise over the past decades 'is largely a political story' (Fewsmith 2013, 1). It is factually correct to see China's reform as both an economic restructuring and a political change, and these areas have been closely examined by Chinese analysts since the early reform years (Wang 1980; Goldman 1981; Pye 1981). These efforts also led to identifying new aspects and emerging themes of China's post-Mao political changes, such as bargaining among players, participation of grassroots people and the changes resulting from reform processes (Lampton 1987; Burns 1988; Stavis 1988). However, these new areas have since the 1980s been overshadowed by the focus on the continuity of China's political system, including the overused continuous revolution theory (Dittmer 1987), democracy (Nathan 1985) and the connection between China's reform and international capitalism (Nee and Stark 1989; Shirk 1993; Sun 1995). These topics have diverted attention from the roles of the masses in driving social changes, including elite politics.

The research interest in the theory and practices of Mao's continuous revolution was a retrograde response to a fast-changing China, which has since the late 1970s hastened the pace of change. Even from the stance of Chinese ruling elites, the Maoist continuous revolution idea had to be abandoned as it was coupled with class struggle actions that were hated, or at least disliked, by a large number of Chinese. Despite the ideological and political disorientation observed in the recent years, the abandonment of the theory was also due to the need for new theories and narratives to back the generational changes of leadership and related changes. Many significant shifts in public sentiment and political climate were also somehow ignored by researchers, who continued to focus on whether China's ruling elites would still follow their revolutionary path. There are two consequences of upholding this study interest. First, the practices developed according to the theory were inaccurately regarded as functional mechanisms in post-Mao China (Dittmer 1987) and were even used to explain why the Gang of Four was removed, an event regarded as an effort to move beyond Maoism (Teiwes 1989). Second, such academic attempts have kept the focus on revolutionary theories and practices in various subsequent studies (Moody 1994; Pei 1994; Gittings 1990). This interest, together with scholarly attention to the next two questions, distracted research from considering emerging issues.

The research interest in democratisation in China arose as a result of China's open-door policies and relaxed controls over people's reading and thinking in post-Mao era. In this political climate, various interest groups emerged to pursue what they believed to be right. This was a decisive step in contemporary Chinese political life, but many studies of these changes have ignored the logic of Chinese societal dynamics (Hsü 1990). Instead, there has been a tendency to fit events in China fit into the researcher's own analytical logic or paradigm. Accordingly, many studies have been done from a democracy perspective (Nathan 1985; Goldman 1994; Mosher 1998; Zhao 2000), which has resulted in the democracy aspect being overemphasised and makes some publications look more like political wishes than academic research. The events of both 1987 and 1989 in China, especially the latter, confused many Chinese analysts (Kelliher 1993; Nathan and Shi 1993; Xu 1999a). They generated a significant outcry and protest, some of which was anti-reform in nature, but were generalised according to the democracy perspective, as a result of which the focus on social changes again turned to two types of elites, ruling and urban-based intellectual.

The above two sub-themes have also been expanded to study the link between China's reform and the global capitalism as part of the effort to evaluate the continuity of China's current system and the fate of Marxist ideology. This focus has arisen despite awareness of the existence of different stances from the Western perspectives, such as the transition to a market economy and the influences of neo-Confucianism, neo-Maoism and neo-conservativism in China (Jeffries 1993; Bell 2010; Misra 2016). Much research has been undertaken in this area, while Dengist pragmatic approaches sought to avoid useless abstract debates and the ideological entanglement with 'isms'. Therefore, there has been a belief that the social changes in post-Mao China are fundamentally a capitalist transformation (Kennedy 2011), with studies then exploring how and when China could become capitalist (Buck 2012; Aglietta and Bai 2013; Keith et al. 2014). This focus disregarded not only Dengist pragmatism, but also new arguments regarding the notional links between capitalism and democracy (Tsai 2007). Also explored were a set of issues of little interest to academics in China, such as links between China's politics, Marxism and capitalism (Chun 2013). In fitting China's reform and social changes into pre-existing paradigms, the overemphasis on these links has assisted in preserving the dominance in the extant research of pre-existing ruling ideology, elites and top-down perspectives, underestimating the impact of strong bottom-up pushes generated by various social changes.

The attention on socio-political reactions to the changes

In addition to the excessive attention on top-level politics and the ideology of China's ruling elites, another enduring focus of research attention has been the increasingly prevalent discontent, anger and protest in China since the late 1970s (Chan 1996; O'Brien 2008; Sun 2008; Wright 2018). Many such studies have in fact been part of research looking at the fate of authoritarianism and democracy in China (Chen 1999a; Chen 2012). However, over the decades these efforts have become a special subfield, producing a large quantity of publications on different forms of social reactions, including protest and resistance, to changing socio-economic and socio-political conditions in China. Despite the expectation that protests would lead to a democratic China, most have been limited in area, spontaneous, narrowly focused and short-lived. Furthermore, they have also been apparently characterised by their own temporal and spatial patterns and trajectories.

The temporal characteristics of the research focus on social responses show a positive correlation with the shifting emphases of China's reform programmes. The latter have sparked a series of protests nationwide in China, starting with students and dissidents, then laid-off workers and a number of semi-religious groups, and continued in many forms of rural protest. These latter protests have lately been joined by urban protests due to rapid urbanisation. On the other hand, the temporal aspect has arisen in part from the spatial characteristics of modern-day popular protests in China. Protests have been slowly spreading from major cities, where youth and intellectuals protested first and urban laid-off workers followed soon after, to medium and small urban centres and then to townships and villages, where the most recent social protests have occurred. Of course, many recent protests have been undertaken in the virtual world. Both the temporal and spatial features confirm that protests in China have been more closely correlated with the country's reform process than the various lofty ideals voiced by protesters. In other words, attention has been given to societal reactions, but some such protests and the intentions of protesters have either been misconstrued by activists or misread by analysts (Yang 2015). The over-theorisation and politicisation of certain protests was a key problem until researchers realised the deficiencies of some pre-existing theories. One result of the early misapprehension of China's protests is the misreading of protesters and their purposes, making these forces subordinate to existing politicised notions.

It seems historically accurate to say that early misunderstandings regarding protests in China were also partly caused by the inadequate articulation of the actual demands of protesters in the late 1970s and 1980s. The Xidan Democratic Wall Movement in Beijing in 1978 and 1979 was a distinctive case of the problem in post-Mao China (Zhao 2003a; Gao 2009). It made strong demands for political liberalisation and democratisation, while the ruling party was forced by the vast majority of the impoverished populace to improve living conditions. The subsequent student protests in many cities throughout the 1980s repeated similar messages, which resonated with many educated urban residents but failed to attract the more economically oriented peasants – who accounted for more than 80 per cent of China's population at the time – as well as other aspirational urban youth who were busy studying at university or elsewhere (Liang and Shapiro 1984; Mason 1994; Cherrington 1997).

This discrepancy between the two sides of post-1978 China was difficult to observe, and the ideological tendency of many researchers in China and abroad made them sympathetic to the arguments of the urban youth and intellectuals. It was at this time that the Western journalistic approach took hold, and since then events in China are often explained according to a set of pre-existing non-Chinese notions or to journalistic needs. In more recent decades there have been fewer student protests, and a better understanding of China's public resentments has also developed. However, there have been few efforts to review why the once highly praised student protests have become less frequent.

Perhaps the most prominent instance of social protest in post-Mao China is the Tiananmen Incident of 1989, which took place before Chinese researchers began to analyse social dynamics independently, and before non-Chinese analysts became familiar with the long-closed China. This episode in fact strengthened the earlier analytical approach to social protest in China and drew attention to the hypothetical possibility of the realisation of democracy in China through urban movements (Barmé and Jaivin 1992; Miles 1997; Barmé 2000). A huge amount of study has been devoted to examining the 1989 incident, including some from different perspectives (Kelliher 1993; Cunningham 2009; Gao 2013a). However, many analyses seem to be based one-sidedly on the confusing and idealistic demands of students and other urban residents, overlooking their likely impact on the country's economic reform, which was popular among deprived peasants. Thus, the focus on the protests of the 1980s continued to be elitist in nature and largely irrelevant to the demands of the so-called masses at the time and the dynamics among them (Kelliher 1993).

The problem that was identified was seen as a different type of elite-mass conflict, with a visible bias towards urban educated people that has troubled the field of China studies for decades. Even if it has since been accepted that China's reform has caused significant instability while causing a general decline in the authority of the political system, it is analytically mistaken and flawed to generalise too much from protests. This is because a great proportion of the population has been compensated by a better standard of living and chances to achieve upward social mobility. The effort to theorise China's democratic future based on non-Chinese experiences has given rise to several theories of the likely outcomes of democratisation in China, including the danger of incessant upheavals, the formation of opposition and even the collapse of China's present regime (Kelliher 1993; Chen 2001; Ho and Edmonds 2008). It is evident that some of these conclusions are out of proportion to the evidentiary basis, overstretching the nature and significance of some protests. The tendency to overtheorise the protests of the 1980s was modified in various ways in studies undertaken in the 1990s and early 2000s. As noted by Wright (2013), almost no protest since 1990 has been overtly political in nature, despite suggestions in media coverage.

Post-1989 China had achieved greater economic progress than previously due to both the lessons of the 1980s and the new push by reformers. The latter was evidenced by Deng Xiaoping's famous inspection tour of south China in 1992, promoting a de-ideological approach to reform. As noted, deeper reforms have extended the sense of grievance and resentment of many changes from educated students and intellectuals to urban blue-collar workers and rural people. Reforms to urban-based factories were painful, making millions of workers redundant (Cai 2002, 2010; Chen 2009). Grievances were also voiced through the Falun Gong movement (Keith and Lin 2003; Li 2014a). Despite the latter being seen as the most serious crisis facing China since 1989, various accounts of it were put forward by more China studies researchers (Perry 2001; Zhao 2003), and the attention soon turned to widespread and frequent rural protests (Fan et al. 2006; Hsing 2010).

Rural social protests, which have increased in number and scale since the late 1990s, especially since the early 2000s, have been highly regional phenomena, more specific than student protests. These characteristics of rural protests have led researchers to focus on various aspects of the protests themselves and less on their remote ideological causes and effects. Such changes have also been a result of other causes, including the lessons of inadequate theorisations of the events of previous decades. The recent decades have seen an increasing number of specified assumptions and approaches to considering rural protests. These include frameworks formed at micro or meso levels, such as the rightful resistance concept, which views the peasant protests from the perspective of existing Chinese political–legal frameworks (O'Brien and Li 2006). Such focused analyses have expanded to consider rural protests from the identity politics angle, by which identity as a victim of reform measures is weaponised against local management (Hurst 2019). Attention has also been devoted to the changes from being restive campaigners to becoming negotiating citizenry (Ho and Chen 2016) or from being hostile demonstrators to participatory protesters (Wright 2013; Gao and Su 2019).

The tendency to de-ideologicalise protests has helped the field mature significantly, but the focus remains largely on protesters and petitioners. In the process of making the above efforts, two main research focuses have attracted attention. The first is concerned with the rights of individuals and the violations of their economic, social, political and cultural liberties. This focus is related to the previously mentioned notion of rightful resistance and has lately evolved into a very dynamic area of study (Pei 2008; Shambaugh 2008; Woodman 2011; Benney 2013). China has also seen the development of notions of rights defence and the spread of a rights defence movement. As a result, there are more activists in China – including lawyers, investigative journalists, critical researchers and other rights activists – who have helped turn the issue into a political topic.

The second focus is similar to the rights issue in terms of theoretical shifts and turning grassroots protests into a topic of public concern, but it has mainly taken the forms of activism. Just like the rights defence issue, research attention to activism has resulted in new publications, and even given rise to a new subfield of civil society study (Rankin 1986; Ho and Edmonds 2008; Wu et al. 2019). As argued by Yu and Zhou (2012), the civil society concept is useful in understanding the relationship between Chinese civil society and changing societal dynamics in China. However, its actual use has repeated the fate of the rights defence perspective, with the idea being utilised by activists before in-depth studies are undertaken. While these efforts run the risk of overemphasising the importance and nature of adverse responses to social changes, the reactions and actions of the majority of citizens towards social change have remained a significant omission in contemporary China studies.

The absence of the masses and temporal continuity

As noted, almost all research studying present-day China has been focused on either policy changes and their processes at the macro-national level, or the many forms of spontaneous and impermanent protest. Such analytical preferences have created an impression that China consists of two opposing categories: the oppressing ruling class and its angry, oppressed opponents. While such thinking seems to echo Marxist, Leninist and Maoist worldviews, the picture it portrays is also rather different from what has actually happened in the country, leaving many knowledge gaps in the published research. More specifically, what is visibly absent from the research literature on social changes in China is the vast majority of the country's population – or the masses, in an old-fashioned phrase – and their responses to social changes and related actions.

While recognising that a small group of scholars has given attention to the 'everyday people' side of social change, or to relatively large groups of Chinese people involved in certain events or periods of China's ongoing social transformation (Chan 1985; Li 1997; Shi 1997; Gao 1999; Zhou and Hou 1999; Zang 2000; Yan 2003; Zhou 2004; Andreas 2009; Veg 2019a, 2019b), only limited effort has been made to study this largely missing but key element in any understanding of social dynamics in a changing China. Previous researchers' efforts largely comprise two categories of studies: life-course studies looking at societal dynamics and change from both a bottom-up viewpoint and the angle of participants (Li et al. 1999); and oral history studies as an important part of a paradigm shift from structural-institutional analysis to a process-event approach (Xie 2010). This change has even caused debate among Chinese sociologists, helping modify the institution-oriented approach to instead pay attention to ordinary people's experiences in a changing China. The debate has also given rise to a dual perspective on the issue, stressing the need of studying both institutional changes and the experiences of ordinary people (Zhou 2011).

Even with all the earlier efforts, the gaps in the scholarly literature on China's social dynamics and changes have not only remained practically untouched, but have actually widened as academic inertia prevents the needed shift in thinking. After years of focusing on both the ruling elites and institutional changes, the problems in studies of social dynamics and changes in China have become greater than ever. Based on the earlier review, the problem appears to have gradually expanded from one area to the other. This review has identified five interrelated but different aspects of the problem, showing a trajectory of the analytical problems in the research literature, expanding from the two crucial exclusions – of the masses and of the temporal continuity of ordinary people's choices and actions – to three other subsequent problems. These are all worth analysing briefly in this section.

First, as pointed out earlier, the irrational or illogical outcomes of the dominant research focuses in studying China's social changes have left a massive knowledge gap – namely, the perceptible absence of the masses, especially those socially responsive and aspirational non-elitist and non-activist members of the population, and their active role from the research literature. It is true that some researchers have tried to consider numerous changes from perspectives of both certain groups of individuals and some events, including the role of women and minority groups, but their efforts have done little to change the conventional focuses on either political and ideological issues at the macro level or the various categories of protest and unrest at the micro level (Hsu 2007; Yang 2000; Mi 2011; Smith 2012; Bian 2015). On the other hand, it is also true that a long time span is needed to observe changes in society and to understand the role of the aspirants among the masses in driving and shaping social change and politics among elites. The influence of the dominant research culture on China studies has all but precluded the study of the long-term driving forces created by generations of motivated individuals. These issues are worsened by the fact that Chinese activists, as well as many analysts, have not always articulated their demands clearly, separating them from the everyday Chinese who must devote most of their attention and effort to their families' survival and their careers. This study does not advocate the historical materialist viewpoint, but calls for more research emphasis on the importance of historical–sociological and historical–demographic dynamic viewpoints, which may lead to a greater focus on the apolitical but aspirational sections of the Chinese population than previous scholars.

Second, despite several earlier studies on the Chinese participants in some major events and social change processes – such as the Red Guards of the Cultural Revolution (Chan 1985), and the red or communist engineers who once dominated Chinese politics (Andreas 2009) – there is an evident lack of longitudinal or temporal continuity in the research on social dynamics and changes. Earlier studies have examined various scattered events and transient groups that have emerged in recent decades and have analysed various specific but shorter periods of China's recent history (Chan 1985; Tsou 1986; Li 1997; Hua 2001; Liu 2001a). However, the much-needed analysis of the temporality of historical events and life-course factors seems to have succumbed to the pressure of drawing quick conclusions about what has occurred based on incomplete data. Commonly, people's personal and social relationships to time, and other correlated factors, such as age, life course and generation, have been largely ignored (Nolas et al. 2017), depicting China as a country characterised solely by ideological and political conflicts between the two extreme ends of the population. This analytical flaw has also made the temporal continuity of social dynamics and transformation a secondary aspect in many studies. Consequently, most recent academic understandings of China's social dynamics and changes still appear rather patchy and intermittent, although they are still valuable and represent the interpretations from other perspectives.

Third, as a special problem of the absence of temporality in studies of China's social changes, the unique features of collective preferences and choices that drive changes at a specific point of social course remain under-examined and theorised. It is also often the case that changes are observed and defined according to researchers' own perspectives or their need for theoretical creation (Gong 1996; Walder et al. 2000; Liu 2001b; Schubert and Ahlers 2012; Osburg 2013; Heurlin 2017). It is because of such approaches that the references, if not demands, of the non-elite and non-activist but nonetheless aspirational members of society at different stages of social transformation have been defined in a partial manner. Many explanations produced by such approaches have been characterised by biases towards certain people or groups, especially activists, oppressed groups and some other minorities. Students and readers are often informed that the Chinese population is either madly enthusiastic about Maoism or desirous of democratising the nation. Many of these studies seem to have revealed more about the stances of the analyst than the fundamental issues of Chinese society. Because the intentions and motivations of non-elite and non-activist groups or classes, and their general inclinations, are largely absent from existing research, China has become a rather unpredictable country in the eyes of those who rely on Chinese analysts.

Fourth, without a clear understanding of the motivations of different sections of society – and especially the combined effects of different intentions – studies have failed to predict the direction Chinese society is heading, how far it has moved in that direction and why it is headed that way. There are also many changes in course throughout China's recent reforms; reform agendas have been pushed by both the left and the right of the ideological and political spectrum to such a degree that complete reversals can be seen within the short period of a few decades. Many readers are confused by shifts in China's public sentiment: from the enthusiasm for Dengist reform to Mao fever, from post-Mao liberalisation to increasing nationalism and from the worship of anything Western to the growing anti-Western stance. More vital shifts, such as the retreat of the state power and the advance of the private sectors (called *minjin guotui* in Chinese), have been studied only in limited and narrow contexts (Lardy 2014). The turns and directions of China's societal dynamics and change have always been a puzzle for Chinese scholars and observers, who have left it to historians to study.

Finally, and even more vital than the issues raised previously, while also more problematic to observe, there is the absence of a comprehensive and clearer understanding than before of the influence or power of the masses – of socially responsive and aspirational everyday citizens in particular – and its growing intricacy in a fast-changing China. Although this study does not suggest that all Chinese people are equally aspirational and that they have similar aspirations, such knowledge is sorely needed, especially in a broader social context and over a longer time period than offered by earlier studies. The ancient Chinese phrase *boyi* (strategic game-playing) has been lately used in many studies undertaken by Chinese scholars to reflect the existence of complex and multifaceted dynamics and their roles in driving social change in the country (Lee and Zhang 2013; Tang 2014; Gao and Su 2019). However, such academic efforts have not yet been fully reflected in studies carried out by Chinese specialists outside China, delaying the formation and development of new understandings of China's social dynamics or driving forces, let alone the many variations of their spatial and temporal presences. The influence and power of the non-elite, non-activist masses and their complexities sounds like an unfashionable cliché of revolutionary teaching, such as Maoism; however, what is suggested here concerns rather the analytical approach that has been found absent from contemporary China studies. In the eyes of many Chinese scholars, China's domestic politics, political structure and power relationships have all changed significantly. The country has long since entered what is frequently called the era of *boyi* or strategic game-playing, an arena full of socio-economic and socio-political bargaining, tensions and conflicts among numerous interest groups or social forces. This area is a critical omission in the non-Chinese scholarship on China, and the study of these vital aspects will help advance current knowledge of Chinese society.

A New Perspective of Competitive Social Repositioning

This chapter has so far reviewed the research literature on China's recent social dynamics and change. As pointed out earlier, most previous studies of these topics have focused on either elite groups (ruling and non-ruling) and institutional changes or on the various different forms of protest. These efforts have generated a large volume of literature, shedding light on a range of crucial issues that have emerged from China's reform. Such highly focused research attention has also, however, left analytical gaps in the literature, a result of inadequate attention to the various responses and actions of ordinary, but aspirational, people in an ongoing social process and its dynamics – or, in the words of other scholars, the human agents of social change in a long social process (Dwyer and Minnegal 2010). This is a clear gap that has not only existed for decades, but has also become a real problem in understanding Chinese society. Because of these flaws, this analysis has also looked at some other useful concepts and approaches that enable it to deal with the gaps that have been identified.

Just like the adoption of the idea of *boyi* (strategic game-playing) by many Chinese researchers, this review has also prompted a search for an innovative analytical concept and framework to guide the examination of what has been overlooked or under-explored in the existing scholarship. The review in this chapter has suggested a new standpoint on the human agents of social change in a long and continuous social process. It is evident that a new standpoint is needed, given that while many China studies researchers and observers can see the changes in economic opportunities and standards of living in China, few have been able to observe 'the sea changes in social behavior, norms, attitudes, expression, and interests that have occurred as well' (Girard 2018, n.p.).

Based on the extended review of the sociology and social psychology scholarship on social positioning and repositioning, as well competitive repositioning in marketing studies, a new competitive social repositioning perspective has emerged as a novel alternative approach to studying China's societal dynamics. The core ideas of social positioning and competitive repositioning are found to be very helpful in addressing the problems reviewed earlier, focusing attention on the actions of the ordinary, aspirational members of the population in an ongoing social process. This large cohort, in its wide range of temporal and spatial situations, is equivalent to tectonic plates shifting the earth's crust; they are the actual driving forces of many social changes, including what has frequently been reflected at the macro-national and micro-grassroots levels. In other words, this new lens enables this analysis to consider the social reactions and behaviours of ordinary aspirants as a process over a long period of time, escaping the limitations of previous studies. These ideas can be combined and modified into a new and alternative standpoint, which will be called competitive social repositionings in this analysis.

The first source of these analytical ideas is applied sociological and social psychological studies of social positioning or repositioning. The notion of social positioning has been used by researchers since the 1990s in analyses of relations between the self and others, social representations, identities, meanings and human social relations generally (Harré and Langenhove 1991; Elejabarrieta 1994; Aström 2006; Sammut and Gaskell

2010). Although this approach has not attracted as much attention as other ideas, it has not only been deployed as a point of view, but also extended to include multiple aspects of social positioning, such as socio-economic and socio-cultural elements, everyday micro-practices or even meritocratic positioning, which go beyond social class structure analyses (Simon 2018; Neubert 2019). While the concept initially focused on patterns of reasoning in interpersonal interactions or exchanges (Harré et al. 2009), it is now believed to be relevant to a range of societal interactions and even international interactions (Simon 2018). The extension of this analytical notion has also given rise to the idea of social repositioning, emphasising the continuing and dynamic nature of diverse categories of social positioning (Irwin 2005; Wagoner 2010; Anghel et al. 2019). As a result of their focus on individuals and their motivations and the dynamic process, ideas of social positioning and repositioning have been found to have great potential for studying large-scale interactions at the societal level.

The second source of social positioning and repositioning theory is the large number of published studies about competitive repositioning in the field of marketing and business strategy studies. As mentioned by Harré and Langenhove (1991), the notion of social positioning has its origin in marketing studies, where the idea refers to communication strategies that permit a business to replace a certain product among its competitors. It is obvious that the nature of marketing studies enables analysts to pay more attention to dynamics than in studies of social contexts, and the competitiveness of positioning and repositioning, as well as strategies and approaches, has been set forth without much controversy. In marketing studies, competitive positioning and repositioning have become a crucial component of contemporary marketing management to create and sustain superior performance in the market place (Hooley and Saunders 1993; Burke 2011). The competitive and strategic nature revealed in marketing studies reflects real social life situations more accurately, perhaps, than the social science research and can thus overcome the problems and deficiencies of social science studies in studying social positioning and repositioning.

Based on what has been reviewed, it becomes clear that the combination of social positioning and competitive repositioning concepts not only appears to be very similar to what has been observed by many researchers, including myself, in China over the past few decades, but also offers an effective approach to analysing social dynamics, or the reactions and behaviours of the non-radical, active, ordinary citizens in Chinese society, in a continuing social process over a long period of time. Theoretically, this perspective is also based on a few useful ideas taken but modified from the abovementioned two sets of research literature.

First, all members of society have their basic needs, desires and preferences, which constantly drive them to keep repositioning in changing social environments. Consequently, any research approach must reflect this dynamic aspect of human social life. This reflects similar ideas to those of Maslow's positive psychology, focusing on positive qualities in people. This analysis agrees that human life cannot be understood unless basic aspirations are taken into account (Maslow 1954).

Second, although many ordinary people seem to be outwardly inactive or cautious, all at one stage or another will make proactive decisions and take proactive steps to position and reposition themselves according to their changing life circumstances. Many will also be influenced by the periodic 'changes in epistemology and desire' that serve as an engine generating other behavioural changes (LiPuma 2001, xii).

Third, this new analytical point of view considers the positionings and repositionings of the majority of socially ordinary but aspirational citizens as ongoing social processes. This reflects the fact that despite being driven by different needs, they all must continuously position and reposition themselves in their social settings in order to successfully cope with the changes caused by other social members' reactions and actions, and to achieve what they want to realise in their lives.

Fourth, because of the ongoing nature of this repositioning, this approach considers various social dynamics and changes to be the responses to the reactions and actions made by a proportion of the masses, if not a very large majority, in terms of what the others prefer and what actions they take to cope with a challenging situation. In such processes, people's actions and reactions are often the start of a chain social reaction that leads to a critical mass of people being made aware of the situation and subsequently mobilised. This new analytical perspective would overcome the limitation of previous studies and put the masses back into analyses of social change.

Fifth, competitive social repositioning as a reactive social process can be closely linked to politics dominated by elites and their discourses, but can also be separated from them. The latter approach has been largely ignored by researchers, with much of the literature being written and produced to advance various political agenda. Since the mid-twentieth century, China has published a huge number of studies extolling its political choices and leadership, while those published in the West have often focused on their problems. These publications and their findings have resulted in an imperfect understanding of present-day China, which can be portrayed as lacking any non-politicised form of life, discourse and logic.

Lastly, this new perspective can also help understand various zigzag changes and patterns in the life cycle of a society, making possible the observation and analysis of overall trends in social change over long periods. Overall, this study argues that the perspective of competitive social repositioning can be used to deal with analytical issues in the existing research literature on China's social dynamics and will allow researchers to analyse how the majority of China's population has reacted to the numerous changes in society over time, their deep-rooted dynamics and changing trends. Given the profound changes in China in recent decades, it has become more pressing than ever to consider the use of new analytical perspectives in studying this ever-changing society.

Methodologically, the application of this novel perspective in this analysis has been aided by a multi-method approach. Specifically, this study is based on information drawn from the published personal memoirs of many people who lived through the decades from the 1960s through to the 2000s, and other published non-academic accounts, online and in print, as well as information gathered through many in-depth interviews. This study has also greatly benefitted from numerous social media outlets, including various WeChat groups, WeChat-based magazines, newsletters and other online and mobile-based publications. For example, the WeChat-based 'New Three-Year Grades' or 'New Three Classes' (*Xinsanjie*) magazine has in recent years published and circulated a large member of personal histories and short memoirs. The WeChat groups built by the author's old school contacts alone have provided hundreds of links providing a diversity of views. This study thus relies on a combination of three different but complementary research methods: quantitative content or textual analysis of documentary sources and visual or audio-visual materials; in-depth interviews with no fewer than fifty people, both in groups and individually; and my own earlier observations of and participation in various events. However, information assembled through the first method, textual analysis, forms the primary source for this analysis with interviews and personal observations providing context.

Organisation of the Book

This chapter has outlined the historical context of this analysis and the connection between this study and the current scholarship on China's social dynamics and change. It is evident that events in China between 1964 and 2000 represent a drastic and fundamental social change in the country and deserve systematic analysis from a new standpoint with the aim of enriching the knowledge of social dynamics of the most populous and rapidly evolving country in the world. The rest of this book will elaborate on how everyday Chinese people passively or actively reacted to the changing societal environment during those decades.

Chapter two, building on information provided in Chapter one, considers the responses of many ordinary but aspirational Chinese to the rebranded communist heir narrative that was widely propagated in 1964 in order to create a hopeful atmosphere in the post-famine years, and their active and aggressive part in the Maoist Cultural Revolution in 1966. The chapter contains three sections. It starts with an analysis of how the communist heir narrative was put forward and rebranded through promoting the 'Red and Expert' idea, which gave rise to a set of new practices in the post-famine years. The second section reviews some of these new practices and trends, especially the growing competitiveness of China's selection processes in schools and universities, which was used as the excuse by Maoists to launch the Cultural Revolution in 1966. The third section looks at the main individual-level reasons for the violent Red Guard movement. This third section also considers the impact of the communist heir narrative on many Red Guards, including their decision to go *shangshan xiaxiang* (up to the mountains and down to villages), and how their pro-Mao, radical left tendency reached its climax.

Chapter three explores how the strategy of sending urban youth out of the cities was recycled and executed in China in late 1967 and 1968 after the most chaotic period of the Maoist Cultural Revolution in 1966 and 1967, and how the sent-down movement reduced the interest of many urban youth in following Maoism. The first section of the chapter revisits the sent-down movement with a new focus on how this policy was articulated by Maoists in order to re-inculcate young urban students with a utopian mindset. The second section discusses a number of early reasons for the de-utopianisation of the Maoist vast land narrative or the rustication theory. This helps understand why unusual channels and patterns of social mobility emerged. The third section explores a divisive episode of Mao's Cultural Revolution, the so-called worker–peasant–soldier university students. This category of university students has been a contentious topic among Chinese scholars, but this study focuses on how it became part of irregular social mobility channels and patterns during the Cultural Revolution. The fourth section examines the so-called sick returnees (*bingtui*) among sent-down youth – those who were forced to use the *bingtui* option and return to their home cities for health reasons. This was an even more unusual strategy than Mao's worker–peasant–soldier students.

Chapter four is concerned with the events after the 'sick returnees' returned to their home cities, with upward social mobility long being impossible and frustrated everyday citizens calling for more and fairer chances at a better life and future. The first section of the chapter offers more information on how job and career opportunities had become not only limited for young Chinese, but also highly restricted during the 1970s, with a focus on how the choices of young, as well as middle-aged, people's social positioning and repositioning became highly abnormal and how social ladders were removed or blocked. This analysis prepares readers to understand why there were large-scale protests in a number of Chinese cities in 1976. The second section focuses attention on the 1976 Tiananmen Incident as a historical effort by the masses to voice demands and what they wanted the ruling CCP to do for them. The third section of this chapter examines what new options and chances became available to ordinary people who wanted to reposition, or position, themselves in society, and what people gained from a series of changes made by the post-Mao leadership. This section also devotes special attention to one of the most welcomed policy changes made by the new leadership of Deng Xiaoping, which was the restoration of non-discriminatory university selection examinations, giving everyone from certain age groups a chance to study at university.

Chapter five extends the analysis to the early years of the post-Mao era, which started in 1978. Over this transition period, more aspirational Chinese started engaging in the open and competitive social environments created by various reform measures, before these reforms ran into their first major trouble in 1985 and 1986. The new changes and competition are discussed in four sections. The first section devotes attention to a special form of societal dynamics, or political push, which non-Chinese journalists and analysts have termed the Xidan Democracy Wall Movement. This movement, which occurred in the very late 1970s, contrasted with the enthusiasm about new opportunities in society, representing instead the continuation of campus and street politics, as well as the new liberal tendency in post-Mao China. This section also serves as helpful background for discussions in other sections. The second section looks at what happened to peasants and workers as their life was profoundly disrupted by some reform policies. Indeed, the first cohort of new business operators and owners in post-Mao China was mostly from these two big social groups. The third section considers the new university students; while well regarded by the general public, their liberal inclinations, or objections to aspects of China's politics and ideology, gradually made them less favoured by some conservatives. This was first signified during attempts at campus-based elections in the early 1980s; these provoked a strong reaction from CCP conservatives, who criticised these students for being politically unreliable. The final section turns attention to how the worker–peasant–soldier university students were treated by the post-Mao leadership, as they were seen as direct rivals to post-Mao university students for various leadership positions in China.

Chapter six seeks to re-analyse events in China in the second half of the 1980s from the competitive social repositioning angle to reveal how reform-generated changes in job prospects, wealth distribution, perceptions of social status and mobility influenced the attitudes and behaviours of many ordinary Chinese people. This was an important but unstable period of reform, and many of the existing accounts of this period are highly speculative and influenced by the discontents of some activists. However, it was during this period that many Chinese identified new opportunities for themselves and became involved in competitive social repositionings and positionings. The first section reviews social structural changes across the main sectors of Chinese society. The second section examines what may be called a ladder of *qinlao zhifu* (enriching one's life through diligence) and explores the winners and losers of the reforms of the mid- and late 1980s. The third section studies what is called a ladder of *xiahai jingshang* (jumping into the sea of business), which was already popular among those working in the party-state-controlled organisations but became more widely known in the 1990s. The fourth section compares two famous large-scale demonstrations in Tiananmen Square: the 1976 Tiananmen Incident and the 1989 protest, and discusses those who found no other opportunity or access to upward social mobility except partaking in protests to demand political changes.

Chapter seven analyses what happened to many bureaucrats and other professionals and educated Chinese people at mid- and grassroots levels in post-1989 years, focusing on the impact of the Tiananmen crackdown on their positions and their opportunities for social mobility. The period covered in this analysis overlaps that explored in Chapter eight, but these two chapters analyse different aspects of the post-1989 changes. There are three sections in this chapter. The first starts with the post-1989 official campaign to remove active participants in the 1989 protests from the party-state system, forcing many people to seek employment elsewhere. This gloomy situation started to reverse when Deng Xiaoping made his inspection tour in early 1992. The second section continues with an evaluation of the impact of Deng's inspection tour on the depressed socio-political atmosphere in post-1989 China. This discussion will then focus on a new upsurge in resignations from the party-state system by those trying their fortune in the soon-to-be-booming commercial world. The third section of this chapter offers a preliminary analysis of a vital change to the CCP's cadre training practice, which altered the rules and channels of upward social mobility in the country.

Chapter eight continues the analysis of the most entrepreneurial period in China's recent history of economic reform and examines how motivated Chinese responded to the post-1992 changes. The first section discusses what is called in Chinese *diyitong jin* (the first bucket of gold) as the initial step by many businesspeople to be involved in various businesses. The second section examines laid-off workers and their responses to not only reform of SOEs, but also the changing job market. Special attention will be paid to the Falun Gong issue, as many of its members were victims of the SOE reform and their options were very different from those of the new rural and urban entrepreneurs. The third section returns to a topic explored in Chapter seven, namely the various institutional changes to the talent training and selection systems. These changes were welcomed by some, but they also escalated the changes to the generally recognised rules and patterns of social mobility. The final section offers an analysis of the shifting dynamics in Chinese society towards the end of the 1990s and the logic of Jiang Zemin's Three-Represents theory in 2000.

Chapter nine, the concluding chapter, offers some theoretical insights into how China's social dynamics and transformation can be better understood than they are at present, and what practical lessons may be drawn from this analysis of China's recent past. Special attention is to be given to the importance of both the Three-Represents theory in bettering China's ruling political ideology and the competitive social repositioning perspective in understanding societal dynamics and change. The first part of the chapter summarises the key points in earlier chapters and emphasises the importance of the competitive social repositioning perspective in studying social dynamics and transformation. This discussion pays special attention to the theoretical implication of the findings, emphasising the need to improve analysis in order to understand not only a rapidly transforming China, but also the manner in which social dynamics are created among citizens and how they interact with each other. The second section explores the practical implications of this study, including a brief discussion of the fate of Jiang Zemin's Three-Represents theory in the past two decades. Some suggestions for future research are also to be offered in this chapter with the aim of promoting the importance of adopting a competitive social repositioning approach in future studies.

Notes

1. This old saying is expressed in Chinese as *shui ke zaizhou, yi ke fuzhou* (water can carry a boat, but it can also overturn it), which can also be articulated as *shui neng zaizhou, yi neng fuzhou*. In some books, it has also been written as *shui ke zai zhou, yi ke fu zhou*, or *shui neng zai zhou, yi neng fu zhou*, which are not strictly based on the rules of Chinese *pinyin* (Romanised phonetic system). In his book, *In the Red: On Contemporary Chinese Culture*, Geremie Barmé also mentions that this ancient Chinese political saying was originally from the 'System of the Ruler' chapter of the pre-Qin philosophical work *Xunzi* (Barmé 2000, 426). Xunzi (also spelt as Hsün-tzu, or Hsün-tze), born in 300 BCE, was a Confucian philosopher. He recorded something similar to the above saying, but the current popular vision was frequently used by Emperor Taizong of Tang, Li Shimin (598–649 CE), the second emperor of the Tang Dynasty (618–907 CE). Li Shimin has been regarded as one the greatest emperors in Chinese history, and this philosophical saying has, therefore, also become very popular. For more information about this saying and its meaning, readers are referred to Gries (2004), Lewis (2012) and Li (2015).
2. I draw readers' attention to historical stories of Lushan or Mount Lu. It is in the northern part of Jiangxi province in southeastern central China and situated directly south of China's famous Yangtze River. Lushan was a summer resort for Western missionaries in China in the early twentieth century, but acquired political significance as it was favoured by the leading figures of both the Nationalist Party (Kuomintang (KMT)) and the Communist Party. Mao Zedong held several key political conferences there to combat two famous military marshals-turned national leaders, Peng Dehuai in 1959 and Lin Biao in 1970. The latter will be discussed in Chapters two to four of this book. Because of these events, Lushan was once seen by some politically minded Chinese as a politically 'spooky' mountain resort.
3. Liu Shaoqi was a long-time loyal follower of Mao from the 1920s, and they were also from the same region in Hunan province. Liu made Mao a thinker in the 1940s through creating and promoting the concept of Mao Zedong Thought. Liu was chosen to be the second president of the PRC in 1959 to take over administrative duties from Mao as a result of a political

compromise reached at the Lushan Conference of 1959. To the casual eye, Mao seemed to be a victor of the Lushan Conference of 1959, but his governmental role was reduced – or, more accurately, he was sidelined. Historically, Liu became Mao's number-one enemy for multiple reasons, one of which was Liu's speech at the Seven-Thousand Cadres Conference in January 1962, asserting that 70 per cent of all the mistakes in 1958 and the subsequent famine were due to human error and only 30 per cent was due to natural disasters (Davin 2013). Liu's strong words about the man-made disaster *(renhuo)* made Mao visibly angry in front of the conference participants, several thousand officials from provincial, regional and county levels (Dikötter 2010). It was at that moment, according to numerous Chinese publications, that Mao decided to get rid of Liu. In addition to the abovementioned books, interested readers can also read Yang (1996) and Dittmer (2015).

4. There are many publications about Jiang Zemin's Three-Represents *(Sange daibiao)* theory, and many researchers have put forward their own translations of the theory as I did in the main text of this chapter. The CCP's website has translated it in the following way: 'Three Represents refers to what the Communist Party of China [*sic*] currently stands for. That is: It represents the development of trends of [China's] advanced productive forces. It represents the orientations of an advanced [Chinese] culture. It represents the fundamental interests of the overwhelming majority of the people of China' (china.org.cn, n.p.). Interested readers can use the index of this book to see how it may have been explained by other researchers, or read Dickson (2003), Wong (2005) and Kuhn (2011) for more information.

Chapter Two

REBRANDING THE COMMUNIST HEIR NARRATIVE AND THE CULTURAL REVOLUTION

One of many sets of confusing, illogical and self-contradictory discourses in contemporary China is that, although in the post-Mao period there had been some efforts to change, the ruling party has almost always defined itself as a revolutionary party (Dickson 1997; Zhao 2006). The insistence on defining itself as a revolutionary party may serve the CCP's political need for reminding everyone that they established the PRC – the new state power – at the cost of the lives of millions of its supporters, and that they own the state power. This political understanding in Chinese is called *da tianxia*, *zuo tianxia* or *da jiangshan, zuo jiangshan* (those who fought to win the state power rule the country) (Watson 1992; Huang 2000). It is historically true that this thinking has been part of the traditional Chinese political logic regarding the dynastic changes over a couple of thousand years. However, the new leaders, if not rulers, have failed to understand that there are hardly any intelligent rulers of past dynasties who would back and advocate a rebellious spirit and discourse after seizing the ruling state power. For several generations after the late Qing Dynasty (1644–1911), Chinese left-wing intellectual and political elites have acted differently, paying excessive attention to revolutionary ideas, including imported Marxism. They have hardly pondered upon why the rulers of the Han Dynasty (206 BCE–220 CE), a far more successful state system than almost all the other later nation-states, decided as early as in 136 BCE to relinquish all other schools of thought but maintain and venerate Confucianism only (Yao 2003).[1] The latter had been endorsed by all later Chinese dynasties to generate and uphold a non-rebellious socio-political order after dynastic changes.

What was worse in the case of China in the 1960s was that the whole society was not only confused by the numerous new sets of revolutionary discourse but also devastatingly troubled by its post-revolution internal fight. As noted in Chapter one, the internal fight within the CCP erupted in 1959, which was followed by the nationwide famine from 1959 to 1961. This was a disastrous start of the second decade of the PRC's rule, which was very different from the 1950s and its socio-political order introduced after 1949, following the nationwide armed revolution of a few decades. The devastating famine and its subsequent widespread malnutrition issue had held off the intraparty conflict until 1962, when the Seven-Thousand Cadres Conference – aiming to soothe internal tensions – turned out to be the start of what Mao Zedong called the struggle of two-lines in terms of the leadership and the ruling strategies. It was under such circumstances that everyday Chinese people started to form and utilise a set of different approaches from that of the 1950s – to cope with the various new challenges in their lives in the second decade of the PRC. Many CCP leaders might be unable to adjust themselves quickly and properly to this second post-revolution decade, but everyday people had somewhat worked out how to handle the political ideological contradictions under the CCP.

While the immediate years after the peasant-based armed revolution, the 1950s, should be considered differently from peacetime social conditions, norms and practices, China in the 1960s was also characterised by the pressing issue of nurturing and satisfying those who were born in the so-called new China after 1949. The CCP created a label in the early 1950s to define them as being 'born in New China, growing up under the red flag' (*shengzai xin Zhongguo, zhangzai hongqixia*). These cohorts of people were seen by the new ruling class as the sons and daughters of new China, and various special attentions have since been given to them (Chen 1963). By the early 1960s, this label had evolved into a narrative to show the high hopes of the new regime for the loyalty and support of these new cohorts. At the same time, this narrative had also introduced a few sets of politically compromised and self-contradictory new narratives in motion, such as the communist heir narrative and the 'Red and Expert' ideal, which were read and construed in a very utilitarian fashion.

One aspect of Chinese socio-political life emerged in the early 1960s, which is worth revealing before the discussion in each section. This was a perceptible change in people's attitudes, by which more people could live with political and ideological contradictions, ambiguities and confusions, despite the fact that many of them would normally wish to live in a rational, or less self-contradictory, social condition. Of course, certain pragmatic tactics and skills are required for living in and through such difficult times. What happened in China in the years after the famine is a typical case of such social realities and processes, in which ordinary people had found their own ways of finding some hope for themselves and pursuing their aspirations. To a certain extent, this approach was similar to what Maslow once defined as positive psychology of focusing on potentials, achievable aspirations and other optimal human experiences (Maslow 1954). Many optimistic Chinese saw some hope in the words of successor, or heir, and expert contained in these new narratives, while quietly brushing aside the parallel requirements of being communist and revolutionary.

The discussion in this chapter considers the responses of many ordinary but aspirational Chinese to the rebranded communist successor narrative that was widely propagated in 1964 in order to create a hopeful atmosphere in the post-famine years and to actively take part in the Cultural Revolution in 1966. The chapter covers two successive periods: the first period was the late stage of the post-famine economic recovery, and the second period was the early years of the Cultural Revolution. All these are discussed in three sections. The first section examines how the communist successor narrative was set forth and rebranded. The second section reviews new social practices and trends, especially the increasing competition in school and university selections as a response to the 'Red and Expert' push. The third section looks at the individual-level reasons behind the formation of Red Guard groups. It is argued this was a politicised reaction to the intensified competitive social repositioning, including how the successor narrative influenced those who opted to leave urban centres as sent-down youth. This third section reveals how the pro-Mao radical left tendency reached its peak at the time and how the first round of competitive social repositionings of the 1960s was concluded.

Rebranding the Communist Successor Narrative

The analytical perspective of the communist heir narrative is based on a peculiar social and political situation in the second decade of the PRC's history. Mao, as the sidelined figurehead of the CCP, put forward his new idea about the leadership successor issue some months after his retreat to the second line of the party-state management, in early 1962, after the Seven-Thousand Cadres Conference. The actual target of his successor topic was to attack Liu Shaoqi who blamed Mao publicly for the three-year famine after 1959. The top leadership circle was aware of the purpose behind the successor issue, still the party-state apparatus had tried very hard to rebrand the narrative, and turned it into a positive spin or a nationwide propaganda topic. Among a large group of senior officeholders, especially those who were somewhat educated or experienced, there seemed to be a blurred consensus on how the stability of the new PRC regime could be achieved and sustained, and how the new society was run. Their ideas became a little clearer than that of the 1950s after a series of disastrous political and economic campaigns. This was part of the political realities of post-famine China in the early 1960s, characterised by the coexistence of the re-emerging tension between the leaderships in front line and second line and the strong push by pragmatic frontline leaders for a speedy socio-economic recovery.

Along with these incompatible realities, there were also numerous people's positive survival attitude and approach,, which became essential in sustaining not only a positive social mood but also a promising course out of predicaments. In the case of the public reading of Mao's communist successor remark, it was evident that ambitious people were somewhat enthusiastic about the successor part of the remark, giving the pragmatic frontline leaders a clue on how to make use of its suggestion effect.

In fact, Mao first raised the successor issue in a shyly puzzled fashion. He Yunfeng, a Chinese specialist on Mao Zedong studies, once wrote the following in one of his research papers:

> The five requirements for [selecting] the successors that were raised by Mao Zedong in June 1964 were both general and specific. In the latter case, he aimed at his successor Liu Shaoqi. Mao Zedong [used the topic to] in fact indirectly sound an alarm bell to Liu Shaoqi. But Liu Shaoqi disregarded the real intention of Mao's speeches, keeping doing things in his own way. (He 2007, 95)

Mao started hinting his new political tactic for returning to the CCP's top leadership role through making use of what the then Soviet Union leader, Khrushchev (1894–1971), did to Stalin in the Soviet Union. Khrushchev's strong denouncement of many Stalinist policies and practices was known as 'revisionism'. To mobilise the support from his comrades, Mao politicised his concern as a grave issue of whether the political colour of China's new socio-political system could be maintained without change. Through this politicisation, the personal fate and future of many senior CCP members and their families were tied up with the existing socio-political system. In a sense, an internal fear-mongering operation was undertaken before making the successor issue a public topic.

The published version of Mao's five-point conditions for training the future successors was also articulated in reference to the revisionist mistakes of Khrushchev, who was deposed in October 1964. Evidently, Mao was not confident at the time to win sufficient support for his return and he had to draw on geopolitics.[2] This was why he once described himself as having both the tiger spirit and the monkey spirit, confessing that he also had to play tricks (Lu 2017). In addition to stating that revolutionary successors must not be like Khrushchev, Mao listed the next five-point appointment criteria: they must be genuine Marxist-Leninists, they must be revolutionaries who wholeheartedly serve the majority of people, they must be proletarian national leaders capable of uniting and working with the overwhelming majority, they must be models in complying the CCP's democratic centralism and they must be modest and prudent and guard against arrogance and impetuosity and filled with the spirit of self-criticism spirit (Barnett 1967, 193).

To make it attractive to wider interpretation, the published version of the selection criteria for successors also included the following message, advising that the selection was a mass-based process and everyone could have a chance to be considered as long as they closely followed the party line and took active part in their activities:

> Successors to the proletariat revolutionary cause are coming from mass struggles and are tempered and matured in the great storms of revolution. It is essential to test and identify cadres, as well as select and train successors in the long course of mass struggles. (*People's Daily* and *Red Flag* 14 July 1964, n.p.)

Despite the strong and clear hints from Mao of new prospects of training and selecting more future leaders, and despite the influence that Mao had in the 1960s, the dissemination of his new idea was still governed by the party-state apparatus before reaching ordinary people. It was at this point that gaps began to emerge among officials of different institutions and levels, as well as between the party-state and the masses. In reality, they were all also able to fill these gaps. At first glance, all the CCP divisions and all the government departments had to involve themselves in a range of activities within their organisational structure to promote this new political idea. Among them, however, three sets of the party-state institutions have been found to have played a more important role in rebranding and promoting the successor narrative than many other institutions. Precisely, they were the CCYL or the Youth League system, departments of education at several levels as well as the People's Liberation Army (PLA). In terms of their approach to the promotion of Mao's new narrative, the PLA was apparently different from the CCYL and the education system, and it emphasised the loyalty to the CCP and Mao.

The decision of starting this book-length analysis of non-activist and non-elitist members of the Chinese population from the year 1964 is also because so many other nationwide top-down campaigns were initiated or started in the same year to help promote and rebrand the communist heir narrative. Of course, Maoists focused their attention on ideology and dangerous people, like Khrushchev, 'nestling beside us' without following Marxism–Leninism (Gary 2002, 338), while other pragmatists wanted to turn the pessimistic societal mood around. Therefore, 1964 was a stormy year on many fronts for both the ruling CCP and the suffering citizens in terms of launching so many seemingly positive and constructive national campaigns. Almost all of them were rather different from the oppressive campaigns of the 1950s, various themes of which have also set tunes for China's political culture in the coming decades.

Because of these coordinated campaigns, 1964 was one of the several turning points in the history of post-1949 China, but more importantly, it was also almost the first time in the PRC history that China started to see various spontaneous and voluntary competitive activities at the grassroots level. Although this optimistic public mood was short-lived and brutally disrupted by the Maoist Cultural Revolution in mid-1966, China in 1964 started to be driven by new sets of social dynamics, including bottom-up pushes or non-confrontational demands. Part of the latter had, of course, contributed greatly to grassroots support for the Cultural Revolution, but the new social mood had originally aroused fairly enthusiastic responses among people from different sectors.

Apart from the anti-Khrushchev propaganda, the promotion of Mao's communist successor narrative was also accompanied by other top-down campaigns including *Gongye xue Daqing* (industries learn from Daqing), *Nongye xue Dazhai* (the agricultural sector learns from Dazhai) and a third – and very different – one, *Quanguo renmin xue Jiefangjun* (the whole country learns from the PLA). This last one revealed Mao's real political intention and strategy in preparing for a long and difficult fight.[3] Despite Mao's intention in making use of the 'learn from the PLA' drive (Gittings 1964; Powell 1965), the effect of the PLA's activities before the Cultural Revolution was still confined to those within the PLA or associated with armies. What are these days often mentioned in memoirs, biographies and autobiographies is the memory of what CCYL branches and schools had done in the wider society. Importantly, both the CCYL and the education system had developed and taken what may be called a pro-establishment constructive approach, making their effort to rebrand what Mao had said and fit it into the mainstream narratives of the time. Their approach was different from the radical leftist interpretation that had then emerged as a result of Mao's further push to attack Liu Shaoqi and his colleagues.

This externalisation process was the key mechanism to understanding how Mao's new successor narrative spread out in post-famine years from the inner political circle to the wider society; how it was rebranded by the pragmatic, or revisionist in Mao's word, frontline leaders and bureaucrats; how numerous ordinary but motivated Chinese reacted to the narrative in those desperate years and how new practices and patterns of competitive social repositionings were created and used during the mid-1960s.

As hinted, there were at least three sets of sub-narrative corresponding to the communist heir narrative. Published memoirs and interviews have all revealed how widespread and prevailing both the Red and Expert slogan and the learning from the PLA had been in the years leading to the Cultural Revolution. Some other interviewees have also recalled the *Bi Xue Gan Bang Chao* campaign (The push to emulate, learn from and catch up with the advanced, help the less advanced and overtake the advanced) in 1964 (Huang 2004; Chen 2018b). The third narrative was largely related to the initiative of encouraging industries, including service sectors, to learn from Daqing. Because of its sectoral focus, this push for the high effectiveness in workplace or productivity was not as widely impactful and memorable as the other two sets of narrative. Therefore, it has not only evidently skipped attention of non-Chinese scholars but has also appeared less often in lately published memoirs.

Leaving aside both the PLA's role and the productivity initiative as a result of their incomplete impact on the wider society, the CCYL and the education system nation-wide had not only joined the many other sectors that were pushed to learn from Daqing's industrial practise and Dazhai's experiences in agricultural production, but had also developed their own narratives and practices according to Mao's new successor narrative, or precisely without offending Mao's leadership. In other words, there had been a modification and reworking effort, in which Mao's unhelpful and destructive threat to the first-line leadership and the post-famine recovery was cunningly concealed and reworked into a much more optimistic and hopeful sentiment, which attracted a large proportion of ordinary people into what many observers have recently called 'the successor dream'.

The CCYL as the CCP's youth wing started making its effort in 1963 through launching a youth education campaign to learn from Lei Feng, a PLA soldier. He was set up as a model of learning Mao's works in 1960, soon after the political fight at the Lushan Conference of 1959, but died in an accident in 1962. In early 1963, as part of Mao's push to learn from the PLA and to win the military support, Mao wrote 'Learn from Comrade Lei Feng' for *Chinese Youth*, the CCYL's institutional journal. This was a major shift in the CCP's style of conducting the propaganda, different from fighting with one group of adversaries after another in the 1950s. The party-state apparatus had finally learned and taken a positive approach to the issue through showing people what the party-state would like to see. To a large extent, this was an epistemological progress, if not maturity, which resulted from the CCP's ruling experiences in the 1950s and the severe famine under its rule. More party-state officials learned to devote attention to the positive aspects of society than they did, or in the words of Maslow, not treat people as a bag of symptoms (Maslow 1954). Of course, this did not reflect in Mao's epistemological level as his main political idea was still based on class struggles, believing that 'once class struggle is stressed, every problem will be solved' (*jieji douzheng yizhua jiuling*) (He 2001, 200). His inscription of learning from Lei Feng was a reflection of his monkey spirit, which is outside the scope of this book.

Regardless of whether it was well planned or accidental, a thin bright light was seen among a few parallel national campaigns. This had finally generated a much-needed optimism, or a relief that there would be more learning from good examples than fighting against various categories of enemies, which often meant many active people themselves according to the campaign experiences of the 1950s. It is worth noting that this short-lived optimism was also based on the change generated by the education system by deploying the political paradox of both Red and Expert, which will be considered in the second section. What was also ironic about this narrative is that it had finally become handily summarised, and therefore, clearly articulated by a popular children's song called 'We are the heirs of communism'.[4] This was initially the theme song of a children's film, but became widespread since it was not only part of the learn-from-the PLA campaign, but had also echoed exactly with Mao's successor concern. Of course, the CCYL played a hands-on role in promoting it among school-aged children nation-wide in the early 1960s through its massive network and turning it into the de facto organisational song of the Chinese Young Pioneers. The latter is the children's branch of the CCYL, and its members are often seen wearing a red scarf. The song was for-mally ratified as the organisational song of the Chinese Young Pioneers in late 1978, a couple of years after Mao's death, which shows how popular this song has been among post-1949 Chinese. The current widespread joke about the successor dream is largely because of the popularity of this song among those born in post-1949 China.

Even to date, there are still more grown-up Chinese people talking or cracking jokes about that they were 'the heirs of communism' before the Cultural Revolution in 1966 than recollecting the party-political context. This collective societal memory reveals how effective and influential the effort of 1963 and 1964 to rebrand Mao's suc-cessor narrative had been. It also clearly reveals that there was a stirred enthusiasm among many Chinese people for being given more opportunities in terms of studies, jobs and promotions, though the latter had to be articulated in the words China used in the 1960s.

A contributor to *Wuyou Zhixiang (Utopia)*, one of China's famous and notorious pro-Mao blogging website, recalls what she thought of the mid-1960s as follows:

> My deepest impression of that era is that the whole society, from Chairman Mao to ordi-nary individuals, were all unselfish and fair-minded and serving the people wholeheartedly. The interests of the country and the people were above anything else. Besides, slogans were everywhere, making people high-spirited all the time. [...] In such social circumstances, as long as one did not have a jackal heart, who would not study hard? Teachers advised us that the red scarf [of the Chinese Young Pioneers] was a corner of the [national] red flag and that it was tinted with the blood of the martyrs. We must treasure this hard-won happy life and 'study hard and make progress every day', preparing ourselves for continuing the revo-lutionary cause. That was China's industrial development era, emphasising the importance of sciences but less on humanities and social sciences while promoting the idea and belief to accept that one would have no obstacle to go wherever they would like to go if studying maths, physics and chemistry well. (Song 2008a, n.p.)

The abovementioned high-spiritedness of the mid-1960s is a contentious comment in today's China, which may upset many who were mistreated and tortured then. On the other hand, it was also true that the rebranding process and its suggestion effect had indeed turned Mao's revolutionary heir concern into a new political symbolism, by which people from non-revolutionary families seemed to be allowed to share some opportunities. At the time, many Chinese had also reacted positively to the fresh social atmosphere, which was in fact partially related to the reality that China's median age in 1964 was only 20.2 years old as revealed in Figure 1.1.

This fresh and hopeful social atmosphere, or imaginary, in 1964 was also felt by those from non-communist families. Chen Danqing, a leading liberal public intellectual, once wrote the following:

> There were two melody lines in education at that time. The first was the main theme, which was the communist successor education. All the teaching materials were revolutionised, and the songs they sang were also revolutionary, such as 'We are the heirs of communism', and so on. [...] In those years, composers knew better about melodies than they do now, and they knew how to stir up people's emotions. Little kids could not understand these, just sang along. [...] There was another theme, or a 'secondary melody', which was about education: Students had to be ambitious, studying harder and growing up with goals and aspirations. The grown-ups at that time often remarked on whether one kid was ambitious or not. There were the values of the era. (Chen 2014, 7)

Both of the above quotes have touched upon the second important step of rebranding the successor topic, which was how the new narrative had been made attractive to many ordinary families who were practically desperate for new opportunities after the many rounds of purges of those from non-communist family backgrounds in much of the 1950s and early 1960s as a result of the CCP's new class classification. As noted, China's education system had made very practical contributions to the creation of new social norms and practices in post-famine China through a choice of measures introduced under the Red and Expert slogan. As also noted, the Red and Expert politics, and the responses to it by privileged groups and numerous aspirational people as well, will be considered in the following section. However, as a systematic analysis of this exceptional rebranding effort, it is necessary to mention a couple of differences between the CCYL's effort and what the education system did then. This seems to be more than necessary since the role of the Red and Expert push in lighting up people's lives in the mid-1960s was largely overlooked from the early years of its application (Bridgham 1967).

In comparison with the political promotion undertaken by the CCYL, what was originated and deployed by the education system as part of the efforts by the administrative apparatus of the Chinese state had made an apparently greater and more practical impact on ordinary people than the CCYL did. In pre-Cultural Revolution years, China was in a transitional mode of governance, or political control in a critical term, because of the dynastic change in 1949. Therefore, more attention was paid to political control, eliminations and suppressions than making constructive and accommodating social mechanisms to provide everyday people with opportunities to have a normal and hopeful life. Having been shielded by the political paradox of the Red and Expert idea, a range of new school education practices were introduced with an emphasis on cultivating more experts for its nation-building endeavours and strategies. This new focus had two socio-political implications.

On the one hand, it had made the effect of the class-struggle thinking and talking less dominant in the PRC's second decade. Specifically, new practices in education at all levels had essentially added something more motivating and hopeful to social life nationally than political fights with each other among people themselves. These new educational practices in both urban and rural settings had attracted a great deal of attention within just a couple of years. The social optimism caused by these practices had greatly reduced people's interest in Mao's ideas of class struggle. On the other hand, the emergence, as well as the public acceptance, of the many new educational practices was eventually also a formation of new social mobility mechanism. In 1964, such new mechanisms might not yet be in everyone's sight, but their formation was a great challenge, if not a threat, to what was introduced and used by the new ruling class in the 1950s, the 10 years under Mao.

More theoretically, the impact of the new educational practices or the influence of what the education system did in the early 1960s was in fact reflective of the fundamental problem that China faced at that time. This was the social structural pressure caused by the incompatible relationship between the large young population and the very limited opportunities for young people to achieve upward social mobility. The CCP had, in the 1950s, provided almost all benefits and privileges to its followers, and economic difficulties in the early 1960s had also made them unable to do anything different while the population was exploding. The typical example of the latter was that there was no pay increase for more than fifteen years (or even longer in many regions and sectors), after the start of the famine in 1959 (Liang 2019). The significant majority of the population who were provided no actual benefits or hope was all, therefore, actively searching for anything hopeful. This was particularly true for the rapidly expanding families with many young children. At the time, many people from non-communist backgrounds were far too scared to be dreaming of becoming an heir of the Chinese communist cause, but the second half of the Red and Expert slogan was seen as an auspicious sign. Of course, this likelihood of sharing the benefits of new society with a wider population was soon seen by Maoists and vested interest groups as the restoration of capitalism (*zibenzhuyi fubi*) in an old Maoist phrase, laying a conceptual foundation for the Maoist Cultural Revolution, which will be analysed in the third section of this chapter.

New Social Practices Driven by the Red and Expert Ideal

Although the Red and Expert slogan was heavily and extensively used in the years ahead of the Cultural Revolution of 1966, it was invented in the 1950s as one of the many new phrases created by the CCP, such as Great Leap Forward. As documented in numerous publications, both academic and otherwise, the phrase Red and Expert was first mentioned in Mao's closing speech to a plenum of the CCP's Central Committee in late 1957 (Baum 1964; Feurtado 1986). Mao used the phrase as a further idiomatic explanation of his abstract talk on the relationships between politics and various sectoral duties that were equivocally defined as *yewu* in Chinese, referring to managerial, commercial, professional and technical work in different types of organisations, sectors and industries. Among the many politically savvy readers of Mao's speech was Jiang Nanxiang, the then president of Tsinghua University.

Jiang Nanxiang was the university president from 1952 to June 1966, when the Cultural Revolution broke out, turning him into one of China's most famous Capitalist Roaders. The latter name was invented by Mao's supporters to attack the CCP's then second-line leadership. Almost at the same period of time, Jiang was also the secretary of the CCP's Tsinghua University Committee from 1956 until his removal in 1966. It was due to his dual role in this key university that his reading of the Red and Expert idea and implementation responses had taken the idiomatic expression further beyond what the CCYL could do with it.

In present-day Chinese discourse, the Red and Expert notion has been more closely associated with Jiang Nanxiang besides Mao because of his success in implementing the Red and Expert idea and expanding it to the so-called Tsinghua Model or the red-engineer model. This model and its appealing and inspiring impact on young Chinese had worked in concert with the CCYL's promotion of the idea through establishing and presenting a clear route to be both Red and Expert. Because of these real-world contributions to China's post-famine recovery, Jiang was promoted to be the Minister for Higher Education in early 1965, more than a year before the Cultural Revolution. As educated and highly sophisticated officeholders, Jiang and his colleagues had, until China had long entered its Dengist reform era in the 1980s, kept stressing the importance of the political component in the Red and Expert formula, including many political education practices designed and introduced by Jiang and his team. However, the social responses of the early 1960s and the collective memories of those living through the period were different. Many inspired people were not only thinking highly of the new focus on training more specialists, but were also largely attracted to this new idea and its various programmes as well.

Therefore, there were a few key steps the Red and Expert idea took to turn this colloquial expression into something actionable and well functioning in China's nation-building effort and process. In addition to the role played by the CCYL and its Young Pioneers division in primary schools, the so-called capitalist roaders in the education system had made various efforts to make the Tsinghua model first before making use of it to guide the secondary school system. It was after the emergence of the Tsinghua model and its spread to secondary schools that the Red and Expert notion had firmly rooted in both the public discourse and people's minds, which had also been gradually evolved into a fresh ideal in many people's lives and imaginations. Of course, as will be discussed later, ordinary families were more interested in the second part of this idea than the first.

The function of the Red and Expert ideal and its attraction to ordinary people were not clearly understood until fairly recently, when researchers, both Chinese and foreign, were permitted to do real fieldwork and Chinese people could freely comment on their past experiences without restrictions and without too much emotions about that era. In his widely praised book, *Rise of the Red Engineers*, Joel Andreas provides readers with a different explanation about the logic of the Red and Expert question and suggests the following way to consider it:

> All communist leaders, including Mao Zedong, had reason to embrace the Red and Expert logic. In order to consolidate Communist power and reduce their dependence on nonparty experts, it was necessary to train a new generation of experts who were committed to the Communist project and loyal to the party. It was easy to extend the Red and Expert logic

to make it the foundation of a grand technocratic version – that the New China should be run by Red Experts. (Andreas 2009, 80)

Because of its elitist orientation, the rational awareness discovered by Andreas was not fully understood and accepted by everyone in the 1950s and early 1960s. This was because the attention to such question and further debates about them would indicate, or lead to, new changes to the newly formed and settled social class structure and relations. In China in those decades, politics, and the interest of newly appeared vested interest groups, was considered far more important than the logic and wisdom of any new policy initiatives. This was once vaguely called the politics-first awareness and attitude. In the case of the Red and Expert approach, there had been fairly intense debates over its actual meaning and utilisation for years after the phrase was invented. A CCP historian once reviewed how the slogan was understood before the Tsinghua model became influential. The debates, and the following interpretations as well, had made the new catchphrase very popular:

> Since then to early 1958, it had become a major theme of debate for intellectuals, especially young students, about how to deal with the 'Red-Expert' relations. At that time, the typical views that appeared included the 'Expert first and Red second', 'more Expertise and less Red', 'Red-Expert work division' and so on. [...] To participate in the debate about 'Red first and Expert second', *China Youth Daily* even published an editorial on 17 January 1958, entitled 'The "Red and Expert" Debate is a Struggle between Two Roads'. It argued for that those who advocate this [Red first and Expert second] relationship attach importance to the thought reform of educated youth, which is good. But we must not overlook the need of 'Expert', and not lessen the effort of delving into skills development. (Li 2012, 68)

These above two quoted passages, one is from a foreign researcher and the other is from a Chinese historian, indicate that despite the dominance of Maoism, there was a practical and pragmatic thinking in China about the nation-building process in the case of the late 1950s and the post-famine recovery and progress in the early 1960s. As noted, this was obviously a pro-establishment constructive approach, but one of the big omissions in understanding this idea is how the masses were influenced by this notion and related debates, or in which way ordinary people were attracted to it. The answers to these questions are necessary in view of that no clear and full understanding was reached after a few years of active debate prior to the Cultural Revolution. In reality, it was before the Cultural Revolution that many discussions of the Red and Expert idea were already criticised and politicised as the 'white expert road' (White 1989, 203).

In present-day jargon, also from the constructive perspective, the Red and Expert discussions were pushed along by two types of forces. On the one side, there was a strong pulling force from the demand side, resulting from China's industrialisation or ambitious strategies for rapid industrial development. The latter was further agitated and provoked by the rapidly deteriorating Sino-Soviet relations in the early 1960s. The withdrawal of Soviet experts from China was, therefore, a dark shadow behind the Red and Expert debates (Li and Xia 2018). On the other side, there was also a strong pushing force from the supply side. This was caused by the social structural tension that I noted above, which is the obscured contradiction between the big young population and the limited upward social mobility opportunities. The discussion of Red and Expert relations sounded rather abstract and senseless, but it contained a hopeful element.

The second aspect above is the main concern of this study. Figure 2.1 shows the contradiction, revealing that China's gross enrolment ratio in higher education was very low in the 1960s. The ratio refers to the higher education enrolment, regardless of age, expressed as a percentage of the population in the five-year age group following upper secondary education. The popularity of the Red and Expert debate in the early 1960s was largely a reflection of people's interest in, if not demand for, new opportunities for themselves.

As pointed out, the Tsinghua model was a breakthrough point for the CCP's first-line leadership to go beyond the abstract debates of the Red–Expert relationship and put both the key elements into practice. After the abovementioned debates, a central government document entitled 'Sixty Articles on Higher Education' (*Gaojiao liushitiao*) was drafted and soon also adopted by the CCP's central work conference in late 1961 (Seybolt 2018). Through drafting the Sixty Articles, which was involved by Jiang Nanxiang of Tsinghua University, the Tsinghua model was reinforced as the best possible practice for answering the Red and Expert questions.

At first sight, as numerous publications recorded, the Tsinghua model became famous as a result of its focus on the Red or political component, such as introducing the class-based political counsellor or tutor practices. Some media headlines have even suggested that Tsinghua's success was due to its implementation of politics-first approach or *zhengzhi guashuai* (politics in command) in Mao's phrase (Sun 2013). In fact, a large number of recent and social-media publications have revealed otherwise. Tsinghua seemed to have creatively and adeptly harmonised both the Red politics and

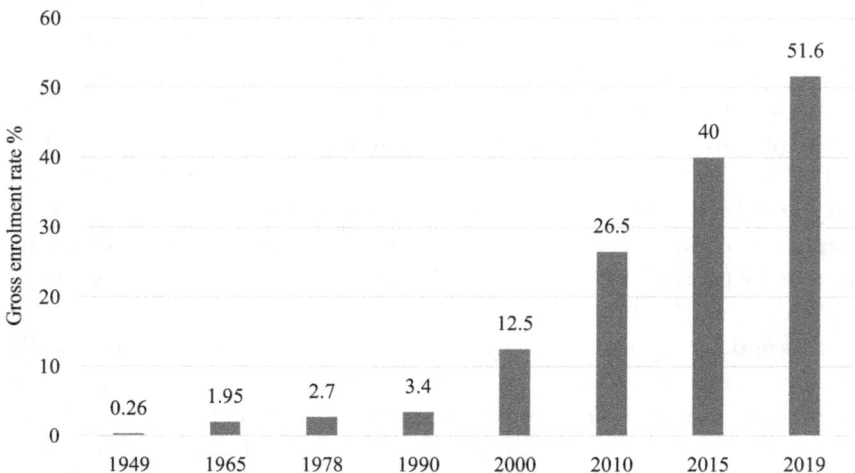

Figure 2.1 China's gross enrolment ratio in higher education, 1949–2019. *Source*: Created by the author using data from Ministry of Education (2020).

the demands for Experts in practice and set up the exemplary practice of what Maoists and many observers defined as 'waving the red flag to oppose the red flag' (Liu 1998, 52; Leese 2011, 151).

Many new memoirs and other publications have tended to accept that the Tsinghua model had skilfully wrapped up their practices for the very left-wing atmosphere of the early 1960s. However, regardless of whether the red flag was waved as a cover-up of Tsinghua's new practices, or the 'White Expert Road', as it was strongly criticised by aggressive Maoists, the true story could only be told in more recent times. Now, more people accept that the actual attractiveness of the Tsinghua model to many everyday Chinese families and school-aged youth in the first half of the 1960s was not its political exercise, but the opportunities to be trained as experts. It was in those years that the popular Chinese aphorism, xuehao shulihua, *zoubian tianxia dou bu pa* (When maths, science and chemistry you know, fear nothing under heaven wherever you go), quickly became the most familiar expression of aspirational families and children in both urban and rural settings.

In a short memoir published in *Beijing Youth Daily* in 2009, a former Tsinghua University High School student, who passed a set of exams for admission into this highest scored school in Beijing in 1964, recalled the following:

> That was the time when the national economy was in the process of recovery from the three-year disaster, and the national sentiment was soaring. [...] At the time, Tsinghua High School that was located in an isolated western suburb and under the headship of Wan Bangru was carrying out a vibrant education reform: [it had developed] the 'one-stop' strategic plan to quickly train first-class talents while aiming at completing the 'triple jumps' within a few years, and accomplishing the goal to be a world-class middle school. (Yan 2009, n.p.)

The new practice applied in universities had also spread across sectors to push many secondary, as well as primary, schools into action. It was, in essence, the start of what I would call competitive social repositioning in the PRC. This could only take place after possible new paths for upward social mobility, especially going to work in cities for rural residents, had been created and opened up to more citizens than those from communist clusters. Moreover, this could only be thinkable in the PRC's second 10 years when the new ruling class had learned many lessons from their first 10 years in holding the ruling power.

Many primary schools were even dragged into the increasingly fierce competition generated by the Red and Expert push in the early 1960s. Of course, their focus was on sending more graduates to locally well-known secondary schools. In 1998, He Xin, one famous and controversial researcher of the Chinese Academy of Social Sciences (CASS), brought his mind back to 1963, when he attended the secondary school admission exams in Beijing. His memories of 1963's primary and secondary school education are insightful, and part of this personal recollection proves that 'the secondary school entrance examinations [partaken by primary school students] had in fact already escalated to become an occasion for ruthless competition and elimination' (He 2012, n.p.).

His following observations on what was then occurring in wider Chinese society are of some help in considering China's societal dynamics in the post-famine years, and pre-Cultural Revolution conditions as well:

> In the 1960s, middle schools in Beijing implemented the so-called 'dual-track education': One track was to introduce general education to teach manual workers and the other focused on elitist education to educate intellectual workers. All the middle schools were at the time divided into four types [...] which was in reality a combination of the modern Western elitist education system and the traditional Chinese social stratification practices. [...] Through the inflexible examination process, the selection process would then take place at each layer of the pyramid of primary, secondary, and tertiary education to pick up 'talents' and eliminate 'mediocres'. (He 1998, 297)

Among numerous memoir writers, He Xin did not seem to be among the high-achieving students in scoring superb marks for attending one of the best secondary schools in Beijing. Maybe because of this experience, he formed a different understanding from other authors about the escalating competitiveness of the education system prior to the Cultural Revolution. Such competitions have always been one of the most functional pushing social forces in China as it has long been influenced by its *keju* (imperial examination) system. Moreover, these published memoirs have recorded various responses to the changes created by the Red and Expert strategy, ranging from positive, neutral, to negative.

From a positive perspective, the attention to training more talents and the career paths outlined by the Tsinghua model and some other regional examples were unprecedented in the PRC's history and did indeed bring fresh hope to millions of people and their families. This is not a denial of the fact there were deep divisions within the CCP at that time, as well as many forms of oppression and resistance at the grassroots level. It is also true that from the 1960s to present day, there have not been many people who are able to distinguish how Mao's successor narrative and the Red–Expert initiative had reset public expectations and sentiment in the post-famine years. Specifically, regardless of the real intentions, the objective effects of the successor narrative alone had created an upbeat atmosphere among many aspirational, but politically trouble-free, young and middle-aged Chinese. The Red and Expert ideal had helped outline in detail how personal goals could be achieved. Despite the indistinct understanding of what had helped them cope with post-famine difficulties, this short-lived optimism before the Cultural Revolution of 1966 helped many start their upward social mobility through education and other policy opportunities. Therefore, among those who are positive about post-famine China in the mid-1960s, there are at least two types of people. Some understand what they benefitted from while others remain confused. The confusion of the utilitarian and constructive approach implemented by the CCP's second-line leadership with Maoist ideals has long been behind the existence of pro-Mao sentiment in post-Mao China.

A special positive outcome of the competitive school education in the early and mid-1960s has made a long-lasting impression on China's post-1949 baby boomers. One interviewee remembers the following impact of the Red and Expert push on China's school system:

> There were few dozen well-known high schools nationwide [in China], located in major provinces and cities. Apart from some that became famous in the 1920s and 1930s, before the [Second World] War, and apart also from some old reputable missionary schools, all the other well-known secondary schools became well-known in the Jiang Nanxiang era through their higher-than-usual passing rates in the university entrance exam. This competition [in school rankings] has lasted until now, and it was even not altered by Mao's Cultural Revolution. (Interviewee 16 2019)

The negative social reactions to the changes generated by the Red–Expert strategy were primarily from the new privileged or revolutionary social class, if not classes or groups. This is partially also because of the reality that the people from privileged groups are presently still able to publicise their discontent over the increasing competition in their school life in the early and mid-1960s. Significantly, many of such unhappy students even became organised with the support from Mao himself and his supporters. This was the so-called Red Guard movement, the name of which reveals that they would stand guard over Mao's ideological line and fight against the capitalist or revisionist roaders in the school system.

The Red Guards as Responses to Increasing Competitions

The first group of Red Guards was formed by Tsinghua University High School students in late May 1966 (Bu 2009a), which is logical in view of that the most prevailing and influential change at the societal level at the time resulted from the Tsinghua model. It was because of the model that Tsinghua High School was dragged into the politics of drastic changes in the early and mid-1960s. As stated by one of the initiators of the first Red Guard group in the preceding section, there had been a vibrant education reform at Tsinghua High (Yan 2009). The comment made by Yan Yangsheng seems to be moderate, indirectly pointing out where the problem was. Luo Xiaohai, fellow initiator of the first Red Guard group, has from time to time been more critical and open than the others in commenting on what took place at Tsinghua High in the years from 1963 to mid-1966. In his widely circulated talk of commemorating the 40th anniversary of the formation of the first Red Guard group, Luo mentioned the following reasons for their actions:

> I tell this story to show that there was a reason behind the creation of the Red Guard group at Tsinghua High School. The reason, in a nutshell, was the discontent with the school system and the various traditional practices implemented in the education sector. This disappointment stemmed [partially] from a childish sense of justice, but it lacked an awareness of inner-Party struggles and so-called two-line struggles, which sowed seeds of various naive conducts or behaviours at later stages. (Luo 2009, n.p.)

In the eyes of many observers and analysts, Luo's reflection was still not very clear, other than admitting discontent and anger. He was also very defensive about what the

Red Guards had done as they know that more people now consider their movement as the main contributing force to the destabilisation of the post-famine recovery process and the then emerged post-revolutionary order. As time goes on, especially as more people have lately developed a clear awareness of the existence of certain privileged social classes and ruling elites, there have been an increasing interest among the general public to ponder why Red Guards acted in such a rebellious way. Two general questions have been raised about their past actions. One is straightforward while the other has given rise to more recent debates.

What is believed to be relatively trivial in these issues is whether they were used by Maoists or volunteered themselves for the intraparty fight. Almost all the initiators or instigators of the first Red Guard group were from the so-called revolutionary cadre families, lower-senior and senior-middle ranks. Therefore, they were under huge pressure by the Tsinghua model, but they had also acted on certain insider information due to their family contacts. The question is why these Red Guards did not support the political ideas and plans of the first-line leadership if they knew something about the intraparty tensions. For a long time, the question was discussed and answered along with the position set out by Maoists, blaming the first-line leadership for directing the education system into a capitalist or revisionist way. This stance was well represented, for example, by a major newspaper article produced by 'Liang Xiao', a pen name of the infamous writing team formed by Mao's loyal literati from both Peking University and Tsinghua University in the mid-1970s (MacFarquhar and Schoenhals 2006, 368). Liang Xiao set the tone for explaining why the disruptive changes were made to the popular practices in the education system in two ways.

First, Liu Shaoqi and his followers were criticised for opposing Mao's revolutionary line by putting forward a revisionist line of education. The latter was considered to be the recycle, if not restoration, of the pre-1949 education system and practices without new improvements. The Maoists also politicised the many practices in schools and universities in the post-famine years as nothing more than an anti-revolutionary combination of feudalism, capitalism and revisionism. Second, they were also intensely concerned about that because of the revisionist line of education, schools and universities did not train successors for the proletariat causes, but for that of the bourgeoisie. The minds of young people might be polluted by many 'landlord and bourgeois ideas', such as 'to study for personal fame and career' and 'to put intellectual education first' (Liang 1976, n.p.).

Later on, more people have taken a step back, focusing the queries on what the Red Guards were dissatisfied with. Such query has been seen as being very rational considering that the post-1978 leadership of the CCP reinstated what was called by Maoists 'the Liu-Deng revisionist line' after Mao's death in 1976, despite being without former president Liu Shaoqi, who was tortured to death in 1969 (Jakobson 1998). The most influential political proposal put forward by Deng Xiaoping in the late 1970s was to *Boluan Fanzheng* (restore order from chaos and return to the right path). Deng's new political strategy in the late 1970s was to turn the politically left-leaning tendency generated by Maoists and supported by young Red Guards around, reintroducing what was abandoned in 1966.

In his recent book, Yang Jisheng, a renowned journalist and author in writing the Mao's era and the three-year famine in the early 1960s, who was also a student at Tsinghua University from 1960 to 1966, mentioned the following changes that took place in China's education system in the first half of the 1960s:

> After the Seven-Thousand Cadres Conference, […] when universities enroled new students in 1962 to 1963, the bias of emphasising family political backgrounds was [partly] rectified, and more attention was given to exam scores. Many students from [politically] problematic family backgrounds could also go to Tsinghua University as long as they scored high marks. Some reputable secondary schools could also enrol students from [politically] problematic families (typically from [former] capitalist and senior intellectual families). There was then a noticeable separation between the students from cadre families and intellectual families. The former had a very superior attitude, looking down upon those from the latter group. But the latter was also very proud with their academic results, disdaining those from the former group without good academic performance. The issue was that many teachers usually like students with good academic performance and results. (Yang 2018, 280–81)

As a result of the availability of new evidence, there have been more researchers and analysts who go beyond the direct reading of what some Red Guards have said or written about their radical actions in the early years of the Cultural Revolution. This has gradually freed observers and analysts from the influence of the CCP's ideological excuses and big political topics on observing real social experiences and identifying societal dynamics among citizens. A better understanding of some sorts of competition in society has then started to emerge.

The study conducted by Anita Chan in the early 1980s was one of the earliest analyses of the Red Guard movement from a sociological stance. This study found that most of the Red Guards misunderstood the real meaning of Mao's new successor idea. More importantly, Chan's survey also clearly showed that the 'political competition' among students in the years before 1966 'was not only intense; it was calculating' (Chan 1985, 92). That is, although many Red Guards have been wrapping their unruly actions in ideological debates and rebranding them as part of the Cultural Revolution, the actual reasons were rather different from what they have publicly stated.

According to Yang's eyewitness accounts and Chan's study, the Red Guard movement has since been considered less as a political competition as defined by Chan than a competitive social positioning of the masses of society. Of course, it takes more reading, evidence and analysis to reach this level of understanding, which is hardly obtainable with conventional research methods, such as flying in and out to interview a few people for limited hours. The relatively relaxed political climate in post-Mao China has also been very helpful in tolerating more people to speak out of their observations and allowing analysts to consider the topic more freely. For example, He Xin, as introduced above, as an active researcher within the Chinese system, has emphasised the influence of the student population change in the early and mid-1960s and the subsequent competitive study environment. In He's eyes, the Red Guards' extreme reactions were predominantly caused and driven by 'the strong hostility and jealousy of children from good [revolutionary family] backgrounds' (He 1998, 302). The students from non-revolutionary, or poor, family backgrounds were found to have a much stronger motivation to study hard than those from politically good families. What was also disturbing was that the students without revolutionary parents accounted for a considerable proportion of the number of students admitted to well-known schools and universities. This change had then become 'an important psychological factor in their "revolutionary" fanaticism' in forming Red Guard groups and rebelling against the education system when they were alluded by some seemingly more influential leaders, such as Mao (He 1998, 302).

In other words, the excessive politicisation of what had taken place in the early 1960s and the radical and intense reactions of many Red Guard students were a superficial appearance, and their reactions have since the 1980s been more considered as a type of a competitive social positioning among people than previously. Such an explanation is not something that has only been shared by both local Beijing residents and pro-government people. Li Weidong, a young scholar from Heilongjiang province, carried out a PhD project on *The Class of 1963 at Tsinghua High School*. Zheng Yefu, one of Li's supervisors and a liberal-minded social scientist, wrote the preface for Li's published thesis and mentioned the following:

> Li's thesis does not have any extravagant hopes to reveal the reason for the emergence of the Red Guards, but only seeks to learn certain characteristics of the Tsinghua High before the Cultural Revolution that were different from other middle schools. What has he found? More eye-catching things were found than the differences we knew. Many cadres' children studying at Tsinghua High were actually in a very awkward situation. On the one hand, the students from ordinary [non-cadre] families were academically better than them, while the school also enroled many students from Tsinghua teachers' families, who were undeniably armed with cultural capital. On the other hand, the ratio of cadre-children at Tsinghua High was slightly lower than that of Beijing Sizhong, Beijing Experimental, and Beijing Bazhong. The official ranks of their parents were also lower than that of those schools. [...] Thus, the cadre-children at Tsinghua High were irritated by the lack of care from the school, so they were inclined to take the position of defending the Party's class line. (Zheng 2018, n.p.)

Besides the focus on the student population change, numerous observers, analysts and published memoirs have also been trying to understand the historical reasons for the strong and rebellious responses of Red Guards. This is in part because now young people believe that what the students experienced in schools before the Cultural Revolution was not unusual in comparison to the increasingly fierce academic competition in schools in recent decades. In the words of several interviewees living through those turbulent years, they have also felt the need to find out why many people from their generation had reacted so ridiculously and outrageously if not attributing it to the famine-related malnutrition or the problem caused by malnutrition. Having experienced a cycle of Maoist internal fighting and Dengist pragmatic economic reforms, more Chinese have become aware that a society is an intricate system, and regardless of its ideological and geopolitical label, one of its own laws and patterns is more decisive than other causes, which is that people have in fact kept making their effort to put themselves in ideal and expected positions. When those in privileged positions feel threatened, they can behave insanely.

Among the various new understandings of the Red Guard movement, there are three points worth noting. First, after the many campaigns in the 1950s and the famine in particular, non-communist members of Chinese society had become less outspoken and more sophisticated, if not wily or matured as some interviewees have labelled. There were increasingly less people who openly criticised the party-state system, but more who turned attention to policy gaps and took advantages of various favourable policy settings. In general, these new attention and effort had then made schools, as well as workplaces, increasingly competitive in terms of academic study and skills learning in workplaces. The latter was carried out through the abovementioned *Bi Xue Gan Bang Chao* drive (the push to emulate, learn from and catch up with the advanced, help the less advanced). As a result, while many other narrow-focused and slow-adapting people were blindly following the direct and shallow meanings of various official slogans and subsequent social trends, some had become more strategic and calculated than before in their actions.

Second, many CCP leaders appeared to have also learned from the political campaigns that their leadership launched one after another in the 1950s. In post-famine years, many rectification measures were introduced despite keeping its loud political talk, such as the Anti-right Opportunist Campaign. Among the new policy approaches or measures, they had, to some extent, relaxed its stance on sharing opportunities with those from non-communist groups. The relaxed policy of letting students from the latter group attend better schools and universities was a source of social tension all over the 1960s before universities and schools were shut down in mid-1966.

Third, under such political circumstances, one unique social structural issue of post-revolution China was laid bare, which was the less capacity and competitiveness of a large proportion of students from revolutionary families than those from previously established families. The majority of the first and second generations of Chinese revolutionaries were peasants, and they were less familiar with China's *keju* (the imperial examination selection) tradition and practices than those from the traditional families. However, they had a clearer and stronger sense of defending and keeping their newly gained socio-political privileges than non-revolutionaries. Of course, many observers believe what the children of revolutionaries were suffering was their attitude, too proud without sufficient effort.

No matter how many reasons people can now identify, young students from revolutionary cadre families had then responded angrily to not only the increasing fierce competitive pressures from schools, but even more strongly to those from non-communist cadre families, disadvantaged social groups, who created a great momentum through better academic results for overtaking and overpowering them as the proud citizens of the nation. This was supported by Yan Yangsheng's analysis, who points out another layer of rivalry between different groups of cadre children as exemplified by Tsinghua High and Beijing Sizhong. The latter had more boy students from more senior-leader families, whose superior positions made them slower in forming Red Guard groups than Tsinghua High students who faced serious challenges from those from intellectual families (Yan 2021).

This was why the Red Guard students supported Maoists' criticism of what occurred in schools and universities before the Cultural Revolution, despite the popular acceptance of new education practices by many from non-cadre families. As noted, the new educational approaches introduced by the first-line leadership were then defined as the capitalist reactionary line or revisionism in the education system in abstract words. These odd terms not only created a politicised excuse for their unruly actions in the early weeks of the Cultural Revolution, but also reflected the rage of new privileged groups over the changing social conditions. Nowadays, almost no one still believes that those rebellious students were worried about the future of China, but regards their actions as either the passive reaction of the cadre children to the actual risk of losing their privilege in new open competitions or the overbearing demonstration of their dominance as the sons and daughters of the Chinese communist revolutionaries. Up to this point, it has to be mentioned that their actions caused the death of many hundreds in Beijing alone (Wang 2004; Song 2006).

In addition, there were also two additional types of responses that may help better understand the desperate efforts made by many students, both non-Red Guards and Red Guards, to adjust themselves to the rapidly and radically changing socio-political conditions. First, despite being openly accused of filial sons and daughters or grandchildren of various counter-revolutionary social classes, many students from non-cadre, or politically problematic, families were also found to have made their effort to reform themselves, in the phrase of the time, in order to be recognised as part of the revolutionary team, or to reposition themselves if considering it from the viewpoint of this study. According to the people living through those turbulent years, many of so-called non-revolutionary elements of society had actually made such effort that was defined by themselves as sinful or evil conduct against their consciences. A former editor who grew up in a politically problematic family of artists in Beijing, but has been living in Australia since the mid-1980s, wrote the following in her memoirs to file what she did as a rightist's daughter:

> At the start of the [Cultural] Revolution, I, like other classmates, wrote big-character posters at school all day and night, exposing the school's capitalist education line, and dedicated myself to defending Chairman Mao. At that time, the prevalence of suspicion overthrew everything, and often seized a trivial issue to politicise it. I remember that at that time, a few classmates and I decided to write a big-character posters [...] [because] most of us come from intellectual families, and I am also a daughter of a rightist. If we didn't follow the Red Guards, we would be assumed of protecting the capitalist education line. (Xin 2021, n.p.)

This was one of the numerous cases taking place when the whole society took a sudden left turn after only a few years of post-famine recovery. A variety of policies and practices that were just introduced as a more open and fairer social benefit distribution system or procedure than that of the 1950s were criticised as the restoration of pre-revolutionary, or pre-1949, practices in the eyes of the newly privileged, and therefore disrupted and dumped. Since the short-lived hopefulness and optimism to many young people who did not have revolutionary parents had suddenly evaporated, many students from the unprivileged section of society had to adopt new strategies to cope with the radical turn.

In the course of this change, the lofty ideal and model of training more Red–Expert talents were trashed by Maoist Red Guards, who felt to have regained their privileged status and even misused it to harm many people from previously established classes before these Red Guards themselves were cruelly dumped by the Maoist leadership, which will be analysed in Chapter three. In addition to the people from non-revolutionary or politically problematic families, the ones who most suffered were those from families that were politically identified as 'five black categories', including landlords, rich peasants, counter-revolutionaries, bad elements and rightists (Schrift 2001, 49). Many from these bad social class categories tried to adapt themselves to the changing life situations, which had also taken different forms at different stages. However, their responses have frequently been observed and explained from two standpoints. Culturally speaking, some critically consider it as a traditional Chinese approach of *nilai shunshou*, meekly submitting to hostile treatment and adversity (Wang 1991). From the Chinese political perspective, these humiliating reactions were called *sixiang gaizao* (thought reform) (Cheek 1997; Fewsmith 2001). In fact, such responses were one of the limited options for desperate people during a hopeless time. They were largely a proactive approach to their unfavourable social conditions, through which some of them hoped to be able to reposition themselves in a new socio-political order. These tactics have been well documented in both oral history collections and formally and informally published sources.

Second, a large proportion of sent-down youth are also found to have still been dreaming of their opportunities to be a revolutionary successor when they were about to be sent out of urban centres. As will be detailed further in Chapter three, a group of national leaders including some from the PLA publicly opposed the Cultural Revolution in 1967, first in February and then in July of 1967. Maoists were forced to keep a distance from the trouble-making Red Guards. Some highly spirited students from both Shanghai and Beijing found a rather innovative way to demonstrate their stronger determination than many others to be a revolutionary successor. They decided to voluntarily go to the countryside to learn from peasants. According to Mi Hedu, a veteran researcher and a participant observer of the Red Guard campaign, these students seemed to seek to practice what Mao did in the 1920s and 'pursue a new dream in the new era' (Mi 1993, n.p.). That is, this action had its strategic use and could at least show that they were more revolutionary than others, seeking to put themselves in a better position to evidence their loyalty to the communist cause and their readiness for being a revolutionary successor. Historically, the pro-Mao, ultra-leftist, tendency reached its peak during the sent-down youth drive; however, the momentum of the superficially leftist but purposefully rebranded logic was not only maintained, allowing many to act in certain abnormal manners to place themselves in competitive positions but also utilised in the sent-down movement.

Notes

1. The original expression of this ancient Chinese governance and political strategy is that *Bachu baijia duzun Rushu*, or *Feichu baijia, duzun Rushu*. According to Yao (2003), the phrase is

a latter dynasty summary of a famous political strategy and approach adopted and implemented by emperor of Wu, the 17th emperor of the Han Dynasty (206 BCE–220 CE). It has been translated into a few slightly different versions, but predominantly means that 'abolishing and dismissing the hundred schools [of ideas], venerating only Confucian arts' (Yao 2003, 198). This idea was systematically developed by Dong Zhongshu (179–104 BCE), a leading thinker of the Han Dynasty, who played a vital role in promoting Confucianism as the official ideology of imperial China, which was criticised by intellectual and political elites after the collapse of the Qing Dynasty in 1911. Apart from Yao (2003), interested readers are referred to Hardy and Kinney (2005) and Loewe (2011).

2. Readers may need to be aware of two pieces of background information in relation to Mao's use of geopolitics. Before his death in 1976, he also used the geopolitical lever to turn nationwide critical attention away from his failure in dealing with his second, but widely promoted, successor Lin Biao, who died while escaping to the Soviet Union on 13 September 1971. After the Lin Biao incident, Mao used the visit of Richard Nixon to China in early 1972 to keep his political leader image. In the case of what occurred in 1964, many analysts believed that Mao had a big ambition to be the leader of the socialist bloc, which may be one side of the story. On the other hand, it is worth mentioning that Mao was one of a small group of CCP leaders who did not receive any training by the Comintern and the Soviet Union. For a long time of his political career, he was often disregarded, and even sidelined, by those associated with the Comintern as a foreign force. This is a very interesting research topic, and so is the link between the Comintern and the CCP. Interested readers are referred to MacMillan (2007) and Walker (2012) for more information about Nixon's visit to China, and McDermott and Agnew (1996) and Shen (2020) for more information about the second case.

3 .There are many publications about these national campaigns. Daqing was an oil field in the western region of Heilongjiang province, a northeastern province in China, neighbouring with Russia. Oil reserves were discovered in the region in 1959, which was soon developed into China's largest. According to the Chinese state media, Daqing achieved its great success, contributing to the country's energy supply and self-sufficiency when the Soviet Union stopped oil sales to China in the early 1960s. Because of its economic and political importance, Mao called on all industrial sectors in 1964 to learn from Daqing. Interested readers are referred to Hou (2018) and Mao (2019). Dazhai is a poor mountainous village in the middle-eastern region of Shanxi province. When China was suffering from agricultural problems in the early 1960s, Dazhai became famous due to its persistence in Mao's People's Commune system and collective farming practices in harsh conditions. For more information about Dazhai and the so-called Dazhai experience, see Tsou (1986) and Teiwes and Sun (2016). Mao's campaign of learning from the PLA was a typical case of revealing his deep and long connection with and influence in the army, which could date back to the mid-1920s, when he led an armed uprising called the Autumn Harvest Uprising in his home region in Hunan province. His new campaign in 1964 rallied the support of the PLA to prepare a showdown with Liu Shaoqi, who had no strong ties with the armed forces. For more information, interested readers are referred to Teiwes and Sun (1996) and Li (2007).

4. This song became very popular in 1961, and it was even mentioned in Mao's chat with the visiting retired British field marshal Bernard Montgomery in September 1961. Through the interpreters, Mao realised the differences of English words of heir and successor, and said that this [heir] word was not correct as he had no land, no real estate and no funds in the bank. Mao ended with a rhetorical expression: 'and what do you inherit from me'? (Liu and Li 2003, 157). Of course, Mao made some rare remarks about his successors at his meeting with Bernard Montgomery. This story revealed how serious the successor issue had become in the early 1960s, and how the issue was transformed from a top political topic to a new nationwide narrative among ordinary people. For more information about Montgomery's visit, interested readers are referred to Gardner (1982) and (Bo 2007).

Chapter Three

TEARING THE UTOPIAN VEIL DOWN
BY THE SENT-DOWN YOUTH

It has been widely accepted that the Cultural Revolution was the negation of the post-famine recovery approaches and actions if the personality politics between Mao and his first-line leaders can be set aside. Up to mid-1966, almost all of the newly implemented open and fair social mechanisms were criticised and rejected as the revisionist line defined by Mao and his followers. Chinese politics were once again pushed strongly by Maoists, aided by radical students, to turn to the left of the ideological spectrum. Mao's caution to never forget class struggle and to prevent the restoration of pre-1949 capitalist system unified his followers, making them realise the need to guard their interests and their social status, which they had achieved through the revolution. This was partially the reason why the radical and rebellious student group – initially formed by Tsinghua High School students – was called Red Guards. As a consequence of such political impetuses, the connection between politics and personal behaviour that was already separated to some degree in the post-famine years was once again closely connected. Many confused students had then staged violent acts of destruction in several cities, which was once proudly called the Red Terror (Chan 1982; Unger 1982).

Having demonstrated their mad political shows all over the country from the early summer to the early winter of 1966, the start of another process of negation in post-1949 Chinese history came into view. An internet writer who attended Mao's eighth grand reception of the Red Guards in Beijing wrote the following reflection:[1] in 1967, Mao 'had clearly disliked the Red Guards and turned to rely on various Workers' Rebel Command Headquarters to continue with' his Cultural Revolution (Zhu 2006, n.p.). On the other hand, an online memoir records the following vivid scene at the famous Beijing Railway Station:

> I left [Beijing] at the end of December 1968, and my parents did not go to see me off. The atmosphere at the railway station that day was rather sad and miserable. In the summer of 1968, when the campaign to go to the mountains and the countryside first started, a large team of our classmates opted to go to the Great Northern Wilderness [in Heilongjiang province], and they were highly spirited, feeling like going on a revolutionary journey. Later on, every time I went to this railway station to see people off, I felt that people's mood was getting low and depressed. Just when we were about to leave [Beijing] in large numbers, [Mao's] instruction of 're-education of intellectual youth' was publicised [in a tardy manner]. The drums and gongs were so loud at the station, bustling with noise, but in actual fact many people felt helpless. The general social trend then was that there was no longer a choice if you wanted to go to the countryside. (Ye and Ma 2019, n.p.)

As a person who went to the same railway station to see off one brother, one sister and a few relatives and family friends throughout 1968, I do not only concur with this account of the changing scenes of the station, but can also remember what many parents and grandparents were anxiously and worriedly talking about after such farewells. The latter was a very different type of experience from those sent-down youth, which had then expanded the issue into a wider social problem and anxiety. Specifically, the issues of both Red Guards and sent-down youth were not simply the problems that affected the young students themselves, but the enormous worries and uncertainties of tens of millions of families, including those with younger ones. They started to worry about the same forced downward mobility and banishment (Singer 1971; Bernstein 1977).

This last viewpoint is noted now because of an evolving historical nihilism about the issues of the Red Guards and the sent-down youth, especially the latter. In recent decades, there are many people who have not only regarded them as one or two trivial aspects of the changing Chinese society, but have also praised the campaign to send urban youth out of the cities as an opportunity to let young people obtain more social experiences. It seems to be predictable that one day younger generations, including researchers, may well be challenged by the hesitation over the importance of both issues in public policy and governance. Many people have already mixed up the gain of personal experiences with the societal provision of an open and fair social mobility and its related policy issues (Rene 2013; Deng 2015; Xu 2016). More theoretically, positionings and repositionings of society members are found to exist in the downward social mobility trend. Although the sent-down push showed the radical Maoist tendency peaked at this moment, the original round of competitive social repositionings of the 1960s was not completed yet.

This chapter is concerned with how the tactic of sending urban school leavers out of the cities to the countryside was recycled and developed in late 1967 and 1968 after the most rebellious and disruptive months of the Cultural Revolution, and how the sent-down campaign had then changed the mood of sent-down youth and their families, especially their interests and passion in following Maoism, driving more people into different types of competitive repositionings to cope with the powerful downward trend of social mobility. All this will be analysed in four sections. The first section revisits the sent-down campaign focusing on how the policy was articulated by Maoists in order to keep young urban students in a utopian state of thinking. The second section discusses a number of early steps or reasons behind the de-utopianisation of the Maoist vast land narrative or the rustication theory. This would help comprehend why various unusual channels and patterns of social mobility emerged and were put into use by politically advantaged or well-connected families. The third section devotes attention to a divisive episode of the Cultural Revolution, which was the so-called worker–peasant–soldier university students. The issue of this unusual category of university students has been a contentious theme among Chinese people, but this study focuses on how it became part of irregular social mobility channels and patterns during the Cultural Revolution. The fourth section of this chapter examines hundreds of thousands of the so-called sick returnees among sent-down youth, who were forced to use the *bingtui* option, leaving the rural areas due to medical reasons. This was a far more unusual method than the Maoist university students.

Before the End of the Revolutionary Romanticism

Post-1949 China had been full of new catchphrases and novel narratives, except during the famine years. This had made a large portion of the population brim with some sort of revolutionary romanticism until so many urban families nationwide saw their children being sent out to rural and border region one train after another, as described above (Leung 1994; Yang 2000; Liu 2009). Behind all this, there was a strong push to end student-led revolts and rebellious actions. The pressure had already evolved into a political threat to the regime so that, in late July 1968, Mao and his circles sent tens of thousands of militia workers from major state-owned factories to suppress students-led violent and factional fights. Tsinghua University was once again among the targets and completely encircled by the workers backed by PLA soldiers (Han 2006).[2]

The Cultural Revolution and Mao's leadership started to be seriously challenged after the second half of 1966, during which Mao paraded his dominance through the Red Guards and the PLA. In January 1967, the party-state system was deeply shocked by Shanghai's 'January Storm', and the Cultural Revolution entered its 'seizing power' phase (MacFarquhar and Schoenhals 2006, 155, 170).[3] In February 1967, several PLA marshals and vice-premiers met in Beijing to articulate their worries over the instability, which was furiously criticised by Mao as the *Eryue niliu* (the February adverse current or counter-current).[4] On 20 July 1967, Mao himself was almost detained in Wuhan by the local rebellious forces (Robinson 1971; Wang 2017c).[5] After this event, the conservative revolutionary veterans once again called for restoring law and order. One of the major reversals of the Maoist approach was to condemn and remove a few junior members of the widely unpopular Central Cultural Revolution Leading Group (see note 5 of this chapter), who were then causing too much trouble, especially instigating Cultural Revolutionary activities within the PLA system, and threatening the stability and solidarity of the Chinese military forces.

To achieve the goal of keeping stability, Mao's old self-contradictory catchphrase *Zhua geming, Cu shengchan* (focusing on revolution, hastening production) – proposed in the early 1960s – reappeared in various places, including the front pages and the headlines of newspapers nationwide. At the same time, the Maoist leadership was also under great pressure to deal with the troubles caused by the Red Guards. In late 1966, the Red Guards had formed several inter-school bodies, and by 1967 their radical activism was spreading beyond schools and university campuses. Together with the efforts of the 'seizing power' push in provinces, China was fast descending into a state of anarchy in much of the country. After the Wuhan Incident, the Red Guard activism had slowly become the new target of the top-down push for reinstating societal order and resuming production activities. Various memoirs mention Mao's old mates – who had been following him since the Autumn Harvest uprising in 1927 – urging him to do so. This was also why Mao became impatient and said that 'now is the teenager's turn to make a mistake' in July 1968, implying that it was the time to reprimand unruly Red Guards (Han 2006, n.p.).

While top-level leaders were busy adjusting their political and policy positions at their level, many young students – including Red Guards – and their families were anxiously thinking about what to do without any hopes of resuming normal school life and routines. Just two or so months after the Wuhan Incident of July 1967, voluntary actions were taken by a handful of group of Red Guard students in Shanghai and Beijing, making the sent-down movement take place quietly in early October 1967 (Chen 1999c; Bonnin 2016). This happened more than a year earlier than Mao's famous directive publicised on 21 December 1968, in which Mao argued that it became absolutely necessary for educated urban youth to go to the countryside to be re-educated by the poor peasants (Hawkins 1974; Unger 1979). Of course, most academic publications have overlooked this time difference between the actions of some students in October 1967 and the directive of Mao in December 1968 and regarded the latter as the start of the sent-down youth drive (Rene 2013; Honig and Zhao 2019). The voluntary nature of the actions of some students before Mao's directive and the purposes and calculations of early groups of self-imposed sent-down youth should not be overlooked.

According to numerous offline and online non-academic publications, during this time gap – and before the sent-down had become increasingly involuntary – many students were still vastly inspired by the revolutionary heir narrative. Their high spirits in leaving for the rural areas and border regions were evidenced by numerous accounts and stories from all over the country. A pre-Cultural Revolution catchphrase extracted from Mao's old instructions was also charmingly re-articulated, portraying the countryside and border regions as *guangkuo tiandi, dayou zuowei* (vast land and great accomplishment) (Pan 2003). The phrase hinted that the dream of being a communist heir could be realised there.

There are two types of documentary evidence that can help show that the sent-down youth movement was, in some measure, initiated by active Red Grad students. The following is a non-official account accessible on the *Shanghai Zhiqing* (sent-down youth) *Forum* website:

> From October 1967 to April 1968, the problem of student graduation became the core issue of education revolution. Based on the available historical data, there were several plans for allocating school students who did not graduate for years. A 'four-directions' plan seemed to be the first option and was also announced publicly. [...] [However,] just before the resumption of classes in 1967, the Red Guards in Beijing once again took the lead in initiating the movement of 'Going to the Mountains and the Villages' as they did in launching the Red Guard movement in 1966. They even contacted Zhou Enlai and demanded support to go to the countryside. They even gained the support from Chen Boda and Qi Benyu [Mao's political secretaries], the leaders of the Central Working Group of the Cultural Revolution, who published an article to praise the revolutionary actions of these students in the *People's Daily*. (Shan 2018, n.p.)

Apart from the above non-official account, the sent-down movement partially initiated – in 1967, as well as in early 1968 – by some highly motivated and spirited Red Guard students has lately been studied by researchers within China's state-party system. An analysis conducted by a senior researcher from the CCP's Central Committee's Party History Research Office, who obviously also went through the entire Cultural

Revolution, including the sent-down campaign, as a high school-aged student, offers the following explanation in an article published in the CCP's research journal:

> In October 1967, in the climax of the Cultural Revolution's seizing-[local governing] power stage, Qu Zhe and other educated youth in Beijing carried forward the pre-1966 traditional practice of going to the Mountains and the Villages, and voluntarily asked to go to the pastoral areas of Inner Mongolia. This opened the prelude to the sent-down youth movement during the Cultural Revolution. Their actions received a positive response from a group of passionate and idealistic youths, and were supported by the Revolutionary Committee and the Military Management Committee at the time. This kind of voluntary action by a small group of students was soon replaced by an ordered mobilisation of the state. (Zheng 2013, 43)

It is not clear whether some explanatory efforts have been made to blame some Red Guard students for the sent-down youth movement, one of the most hated parts of the Cultural Revolution. It is in some way suspicious given the fact that some publications mention Mao's initial disagreement with the idea. In either case, one aspect of the sent-down drive was fairly clear; that, in 1967 and much of 1968, many Red Guard students were still seeking to put themselves in a better position to show their loyalty to the CCP's cause and their readiness for being a communist successor.

In one of his widely circulated memoirs, Liu Xiaomeng, a former sent-down student from Beijing and a senior research fellow of the CASS, provides two more perspectives on the motivations and calculations of some pioneering sent-down youth. One was the internal competition among Red Guard groups and the other was to explore a new path for the revolutionary undertaking:

> The establishment of a cross-school and cross-regional 'Secondary School Red Guard Congress' marked the collective regeneration and replacement of the student leaders from the 'Old Three-Year Grades' [Year 1966, 1967 and 1968]. However, no matter if they were the old Red Guards or the new Red Guards, also regardless of whether they were the so-called 'conservatives' or 'rebels', they were more or less the same in terms of political orientation and ideological ideas. The sent-down movement started in Beijing in September 1967, and it was organised by the leaders of the pushy 'rebel' Red Guard groups. They naively believed that they were launching a new Long March to 'continue the revolution'. [...] [In addition] through criticising and condemning the 'capitalist education line', many students from the 'Old Three-Year Grades' had developed a profound aversion to the education system of the previous 17 years, hoping to go to the villages and border regions to engage in a vigorous and large-scale undertaking in the process of exploring the road of revolution. (Liu 2006, n.p.)

Similar explanations about the high level of revolutionary ambitions and spirits of many Red Guard students, especially some of the leaders, were also mentioned by most former sent-down youth in the interviews. At the same time, almost all of them want to point out one driving force behind their own decisions to leave for the countryside, which is fairly similar to what was called the conformity behaviour of the everyday

Chinese. They mostly insist that while many activist students were politically motivated and even calculated adopting bubbly approaches to new actions, most of them were essentially driven by a wish of catching-up or not-falling-behind from the others. This latter approach was the strategy used by many to reposition themselves in a competitive social condition. This was needed in view of the high level of politicisation and mobilisation of the campaign all over the country, including the promotion of the CCP's propaganda apparatus, such as the *People's Daily* (Hu 2018). As a result, the number of urban students leaving for rural areas in 1967 and 1968, as listed in Table 3.1, was greater than the total of the previous five years.

As also shown in Table 3.1, a significant majority of sent-down youth were sent to the villages. The next section will discuss how bad their working and living conditions were and why the parent community as a whole strongly and negatively reacted to this policy so quickly. While the latter was happening in their home cities, a big proportion of the early groups of young urban students were, at the start, still enjoying their home-away experiences, and dreaming of their future according to the narrative of the vast land with great potential. There are many published personal history accounts, documenting that some sent-down students did not only submit their requests for undertaking dirty and laborious works right after arrival, but also handed in the applications for joining the CCP (Wang 1998b; Ding 2006). What they hoped by doing all these was to have decent sent-down experiences in rural areas to qualify as acceptable candidates to be future leaders. This thinking and actions sounded very naive and idealistic to most sent-down students, except to those with helpful social connections and family backgrounds.

Among those who were actively seeking a membership of the CCP at the time while being sent down to rural areas was China's current leader, Xi Jinping; his experiences represent one type of such cases. In mid-January 1969, at the age of 15, he went to a poor village in Northern Shaanxi province from Beijing. China's official media has reported he handed in his applications for joining the CCYL eight times and ten times for the CCP before he was recommended for attending Tsinghua University in Beijing in 1976, as one of the very last group of the so-called worker–peasant–soldier university students (CCTV 2021). Of course, his family background makes his case atypical or rare, apart from the times he handed in his applications to local CCYL and CCP branches.

Table 3.1 The numbers and categories of sent-down youth, 1962–72.

Year	Total Numbers	Sent to the Villages	Per cent	Sent to the Bingtuan*	Per cent
1962–66	1,292,800	870,600	67.3	422,200	32.7
1967–68	1,996,800	1,659,600	83.1	337,200	16.9
1969	2,673,800	2,204,400	82.4	469,400	17.6
1970	1,064,000	749,900	70.5	314,100	29.5
1971	748,300	502,100	67.1	246,200	32.9
1972	673,900	502,600	74.6	171,300	25.4
1969–72	5,160,000	3,959,000	73.7	1,201,000	26.3

Note: *Bingtuan* refers to the quasi-military farms in the border regions.
Sources: Compiled by the author based on Bonnin (2005) and NBSC (2009).

The De-utopianisation of the Rustication Push

There were several documented turning points in the Cultural Revolution, and fewer of them originated from the people side of the process than the CCP's internal politics, such as the political interventions by the PLA leaders (see note 5). One turning point caused by the people's attitudes and actions was the slow end of the sent-down campaign (Jiang and Ashley 2000; Pan 2003; Gao 2021). The Cultural Revolution was disruptive to the lives of everyday Chinese citizens, but the information we have about it has been mostly confined to the official discourses of that historical period and the academic debate over its theoretical significances. In recent decades, more non-academic publications on the sent-down history appeared, but they tend to either glorify or condemn the decision and practice, concealing some meaningful aspects of these past experiences by doing so. All this has obscured the de-utopianisation of the vast land narrative. This core idea of Maoist urban youth employment strategy and the actual sent-down push were once called the rustication campaign (Unger 1982).

Due to this focus and the fact that there are numerous publications on this chaotic period in Chinese history, this analysis focuses on the socio-economic and socio-political conditions that led to a rather fast and clear realisation of what the vast land would mean for them and a shift in their understanding of the sent-down practices and their own lives and future. Specifically speaking, China has been full of contradictions, the latter of which had once reached a ridiculous level before and during the Cultural Revolution. Among many sets of contradictions, one set of them had not only resulted in the formation and implementation of the strategy to send urban youth out of cities or *shangshan xiaxiang* (the 'up to the mountains and down to the villages' movement) (Singer 1971; Bernstein 1977), but had also awakened many sent-down youth from their idealistic dream of accomplishing what they were told, *guangkuo tiandi, dayou zuowei* (vast land, and great accomplishment) (Bennett and Montaperto 1972; Bonnin 2013; Kor 2016). This set of paradoxes was caused by the inconsistency between China's deteriorating socio-economic conditions after mid-1966 and the extreme idealism of Maoists.

As Table 3.1 shows, most of the early groups of sent-down youth were sent to the villages, not to *bingtuan* – a shortened phrase for *shengchan jianshe bingtuan* – quasi-military agricultural farms. These farms were controlled by the state authorities, both central and local, and their workers were paid low wages. The villages in China in the 1960s and 1970s were very different, and they were poor and impoverished.

Consequently, the first reaction of most sent-down youth to the life in the rural areas was a shock. Apart from those whose families maintained close and regular contacts with their rural extended families and relatives, many urban students were not very familiar with the low living standards and poor conditions in rural areas. They were shocked when they saw and realised how poor the living standards and conditions of the villages were. Importantly, they started asking themselves if they could cope with such living and working conditions.

Economically, despite the noisy self-proclaimed greatness and success by Maoists, the chaos in 1966 had sent China's economy into another tailspin after a brief economic recovery in 1964 and 1965 from the post-1959 famine, which was also termed as the three-year Natural Disaster in China's official discourses. Many analyses record that

China's economy contracted by 5.7 per cent in 1966, 9.6 per cent in 1967 and further 4.2 per cent in 1968 (Zheng and Lin 2009; Wang 2014b; Zhao 2014). The official statistics also show that the total industrial output declined by 15.1 per cent in 1967 and 8.2 per cent in 1968 (NBSC 2009). The economic deterioration reduced state revenue by over 30 per cent, substantially limited the state's capacity to provide millions of school graduates or leavers with jobs in factories, production lines and other forms of urban-based workplaces, except making other arrangements for them, letting them make a living elsewhere. The nationwide anarchy also made it impossible to effectively utilise the administrative mechanism of China's planned economy in arranging normal economic activities at the time. In 1967, the chaotic situation saw rare suspensions of both China's regular annual planning processes and its national planning gatherings at every level of the state system, creating a policy vacuum in which short-sighted, casual and even politicised ideas were put in practice.

Under such macro-political and macro-economic circumstances, all the sent-down urban students had also finally seen their future living and working conditions at the micro level. There are many accounts and stories of the living conditions of different Chinese regions in the late 1960s and early 1970s. The figures in Table 3.2 are indicative of the seriousness of a big gap between urban and rural areas in terms of income at the time, even if the urban life was also very difficult then.

In addition to the overall situation delineated by the data in Table 3.2, there are many estimates of living standards in China in the mid- and late 1960s, and one of them shows that the average income per capita of rural residents was consistently less than 40 per cent of urban residents (Yang 2016). The real situation was in fact far worse than what was depicted by statistics as most sent-down students were sent to the most impoverished and remote regions. Aside from many details about their life difficulties, including a sudden tailspin in life or an abrupt downward social mobility, this change also excluded them from China's small urbanised population, which was only approximately 15 per cent of its total population – of well above 700 million at the time (NBSC 2011a, 2011b). Despite being short of actual knowledge of rural living conditions, all urban students in the 1960s were rather familiar with the phrase of *yiqiong erbai* (poor and blank) that was officially used to portray how poor China was. What the sent-down youth found after arriving at villages or *bingtuan*, or precisely after their early excitement

Table 3.2 China's rural–urban income divide, 1966–72.

Year	Rural Average Income Per Capita (yuan)	Urban Average Income Per Capita (yuan)	Difference (yuan)
1966	106	244	138
1967	110	251	141
1968	106	250	144
1969	108	255	147
1970	114	261	147
1971	116	267	151
1972	116	294	178

Sources: Compiled by the author based on Yang (2016) and Li et al. (2019).

of being away from home, was an abrupt and better realisation of the factual meaning of poor and blank. Almost all of them realised that the rural villages were not only not as hopeful as propagated by the party-state government, but also far too challenging to settle down for a long time.

Wang Guilan, a model sent-down student who was sent from Beijing, but has since the late 1960s settled down permanently in a country in the middle Shaanxi province, told a reporter the following about their early days in a village:

> On the first night in the village, the hearts of the students went cold. Although the village [committee] gave us their best brick kiln to live in, the cave was equipped with nothing, completely empty. The girls were afraid that the kiln would collapse. On the very first night in the cave, a few female schoolmates cried together for most of the night, and only fell asleep when they became exhausted. At that time, the commune members were all given inadequate food rations, financially struggling, and virtually no supply of non-staple food. Everyone was busy working for their livelihoods all day. (Yao 2005, n.p.)

On top of the dreadful early impression, which was an intuitive process to make the students aware of the rural living conditions in a material sense, the second factor or process to de-idealise the vast land narrative was, in fact, generated by what Maoists theorised as the re-education view itself (Wu and Hong 2016; Grazianzi 2019). To generate happy and supportive social conditions for sending school leavers out of the cities, two sets of official discourses were used: the communist successor narrative (to keep these students inspired in the hopeless social conditions) and the re-education theory (to let them accept the sent-down tactic as a way to train them as future leaders). However, what actually happened to many of these sent-down students was just opposite to what was described by the propaganda messages. Almost all sent-down youth encountered frank local people who did not believe in the existence of any good opportunities in their place to allow the young urban people to accomplish what they were promised. In the words of many former sent-down youth, the Maoist version of re-educating urban youth by peasants quickly evolved into a very different process of debunking the purposely adorned, if not deceitful, blueprint, for the vast land narrative and its idealised nature.

Numerous recent memoirs of sent-down youth, print and online, long and short, have all mentioned the opposite re-education process. Among many anecdotal accounts and stories, hunger and food shortage were the most frequently mentioned part of what was learned from peasants. There were also many other sufferings over this historical period (Rosen 1981; Thurston 1984; Fiskesjo 2018), but the most pervasive theme and fundamental problem confronting these teenagers were the shortage of food and the even severe scarceness of non-staple food supply, such as meat and sugar. Figure 3.1 is a set of evidence to explain why so many anecdotal examples of the opposite re-education process of the sent-down youth all were related to hunger and food supply. Readers need to be aware that the per capita figures of food supply in Figure 3.1 refer to the unprocessed grains, not the amount of actual edible food.

Being poor made many rural residents in China in the 1960s not only feel frustrated, but brave enough to tell some truths. They had nothing to lose. They were at

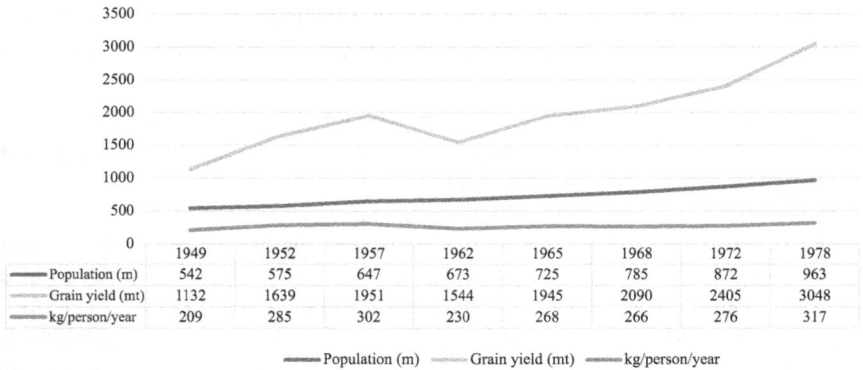

	1949	1952	1957	1962	1965	1968	1972	1978
Population (m)	542	575	647	673	725	785	872	963
Grain yield (mt)	1132	1639	1951	1544	1945	2090	2405	3048
kg/person/year	209	285	302	230	268	266	276	317

Population (m) ——— Grain yield (mt) ——— kg/person/year

Figure 3.1 China's population and food supply per capita, 1949–78. *Sources*: Compiled by the author based on NBSC (2011a, 2011b, 2015), Yang (2016) and Zhao (2016a).

the lowest tier of social hierarchy and had no worry to be dumped further. It is also worth noting that many parents were involved in this learning – or realisation – process remotely from urban centres as many of them did not only still remember their hungry famine years, but also the fate of tens of millions of workers who were forced to return to their rural home regions during the famine. In such a real-life re-education environment, the sent-down youth became less influenced by the theories or notions created by urban theorists or officials, and more by impecunious peasants with first-hand evidence. Significantly, the latter was not only seen by the students themselves but, as several former students put it, also felt in their always starving stomachs. Such real-life stories display how persuasive the opposite re-education was for these teenagers during their years of taking their future seriously. Consequently, the Maoist practice of re-educating urban youth by peasants had resulted in various long-term impacts. More young people had learned about how wide the urban and rural divide was and how backward the rural economies were. The effect of the latter was enormous, playing a vital role in the subsequent social changes.

Third, more significantly, their real re-education learning from peasants soon led to the awareness of their massive and irreversible drop in terms of social status. Almost all of them were told by poor peasants that the villages had no potential for them to accomplish anything promised in the rustication notion. Such a common feeling of hopelessness and despair became stronger and more widespread day by day. This was only worsened by the shared worry of their parents. The idealisation of the social status decline and the anguish over seeing no future had troubled many sent-down students profoundly. One former sent-down student can still recall the suffering as follows:

> In my dreams, there was always a feeling of drowning, [in which] I saw somethings that could pull me out [of the water], such as recruiting workers, promoting cadres, attending universities, but they were always taken away by someone else. It was a nightmare to be in that kind of drowning and sinking, and not being able to catch anything out of it. [...]

Originally, none of us knew what was called the road of uniting with workers and peasants and the meaning of great accomplishment. When we were in the countryside, we all realised that this path was leading to nowhere. (Interviewee 23 2020)

The stress and anxiety suffered by many students evolved into a strong wish to leave the villages. This realisation and the final resolve were the sign of the end of this previous round of idealistic social repositionings based on Mao's vast land narrative and the beginning of a fresh round of competitive repositionings of many sent-down youth. The social conditions behind this new process were that widespread negative responses to the destitution in rural areas from sent-down youth and their families, as well as no follow-up plans, made the urban youth issue remain a central concern of almost the entire population. According to one former sent-down high school student, the future of children from each household became the main melody of that era, as an outcome of sending them out of the cities. From a family life viewpoint, it became a far more central concern than what Maoists would like people to be worried about, such as the emergence of revisionism within the CCP. Consequently, the process of people's social repositionings started to enter a new phase.

The Evaporation of Hopes for Fair Opportunities

Despite the strong desire to leave the countryside, most sent-down youth came across great difficulties in finding a justification and an acceptable way to leave, except those from families with power and connections. It was not only because of the Cultural Revolution as a macro-level reason, but also because some abnormal channels and patterns of social mobility emerged, which were also put into use by those politically privileged and well-connected families. Such circumstances made the next round of repositionings more tactical and competitive, and even take some peculiar forms in the effort of sent-down youth and their families in selecting and utilising the chances and methods to leave the countryside. This includes *bingtui* – returning to the home cities because of health reasons. Besides some genuine cases in which sent-down students were suffering from various health problems, many other students opted to claim health problems because they found no other opportunities, as will be discussed in the next section. This section looks at why many sent-down youth and their families were forced to falsify their own medical conditions, as an unusual way of competing with those from politically privileged families.

In general, the resistance of many sent-down students, as well as their families, to the rustication scheme emerged as soon as they arrived in the countryside. Many recent biographies or memoirs show that this started happening as soon as months, if not weeks, after these students arrived at villages and *bingtuan* (Rene 2013; Honig and Zhao 2019); but from 1970, their reactions quietly developed into a range of countermeasures against the sending-down strategy. This process then evolved into a very proactive and strategic stage, where many sent-down youth no longer believed in the promise of being trained as the heir to communism or candidates for the future leadership. Instead, the students from politically privileged and other well-connected families made the first move, starting to use the contacts of their families and relatives to transfer themselves away from the assigned rural areas, if not return to the home cities. Their actions disturbed almost all sent-down students and their parent communities one after another. Those who were socio-politically underprivileged and from economically vulnerable backgrounds had also, at the same time, started planning or plotting their own approaches to achieve what could be readily achieved by those from politically privileged families. Theoretically, this implies that there are also competitive social repositionings in a downward social mobility process. What is different from a normal process is that various actions may be more depressed and desperate than normal, and that some partakers could act unscrupulously.

Researchers have identified four main channels through which sent-down youth could leave their assigned rural villages or *bingtuan*: being recruited as a worker, being recruited as a university student, joining the army and making use of the excuse of medical conditions (Yang 2000). Various recent non-academic publications and oral history accounts suggest two key points. First, these channels were not evenly utilised by the students in the early 1970s. Second, and more importantly from the angle of competitive repositionings, the time sequence of identifying and using these channels has actually clearly confirmed the competitive nature of this whole failing process of the rustication movement.

The first move by those from politically privileged or well-connected families was pivotal in this round of social repositioning. It had activated what many people have termed as chain reactions in a social setting. In a memoir entitled 'The Rivalry between the Peasants and the Students over Worker Recruitment', Jing Wen, a former sent-down student to Northern Shaanxi province from Beijing, recalls the following in his village:

> Less than half a year after settling down in the village, we heard that someone had left using the back door to join the army. Later, a few more people left the countryside through various other channels, for example, joining their parent or parents to go to the 'May 7th' Cadre School,[6] or joining them in the Third-Line [factories].[7] My family had no such connections to help me jump out of the village, so we could only take root in the countryside and undertake the re-education with our heart and soul. [...] In May 1970, a newspaper in Yan'an published an article written by a student from Beijing, expressing the resolution called one-red-heart and two-preparations in treating the opportunity of being hired as workers. This was the first time that many sent-down students from Beijing heard about the recruitment of workers from our groups. Only then I realised that I did not have to work my entire life in the countryside. (Jing 2021, n.p.)

Apparently, the first move that might easily then be accused of a sabotage of Mao's Cultural Revolutionary line and deployment could only be made by those politically privileged and well-connected families. Their tactics included: joining the PLA and its non-combatant services or subsidiaries, and being transferred to the cadre schools affiliated to the institutions that their parents worked. All these were soon furiously denounced by Mao as *zou houmen* (taking or going through the back door), which was not only the sign of the weakening support for Mao's policies, but also the evident indication of cadre corruption issues at the time (Lü 2000).

This strategy to escape the villages created a different type of pressure, if not a driving force, additional to the rural socio-economic conditions themselves. A couple of former students reported that some later actions were caused by the initial actions of other fellow students, more than the hardship itself. Many former sent-down youth still believe that if no one made the first move, the sent-down arrangement could well be prolonged for a few more months or even a couple of years. In other words, there was also a process factor in this round of repositioning, which was secondary to the fundamental causes, but very decisive in terms of the time sequence of a competitive social process. That is, the dynamics of their return from the countryside was not as simple as generally thought due to the hardship in the countryside, but an outcome of the combination of the rural hardship and the actions taken by some families to relocate their daughters or sons. The rural life hardship was regarded as the reality facing everyone at the time, which is why more former students now believe that their choice to leave was predominantly a result of the fact that many had not only kept talking about it, but were also found to depart one after another.

Because of the focus of analysts on the departure of sent-down urban youth from the countryside as an ending process of the sent-down drive, several local policy measures of assigning sent-down students' local non-physical jobs have been ignored in many analyses. For example, *minban jiaoshi* (village- or commune-appointed teaching positions) and *chijiao yisheng* (barefoot doctors). These arrangements were long viewed as promotions, or the reward for political loyalty and excellent performance, which were therefore documented in different types of publications. It is true that these local appointments could be used as evidence that a small group of sent-down youth held out the hope of being re-educated by poor peasants longer than others, and therefore being a communist successor. However, it can also be considered a factor or step from the competitive social repositioning perspective. To a large degree, these local promotions had also changed the mood of the communities, and just like the effect of the first move by those from well-connected families, they had also caused a sequence of reactions of more students to their possibly disadvantageous positions in relation to the others.

These local arrangements for some sent-down youth to undertake non-physical work had also provoked the desire of some local rural families, and many local youth were also dragged into the resettlement process, or precisely, taking advantages of some of the new chances intended for the sent-down urban students. Therefore, this was another additional local factor pushing the repositionings of the sent-down youth, on top of the local socio-economic conditions and local promotions or appointments. In the above-mentioned memoir, Jing Wen points out that the urban youth were sometimes unable to compete with some well-connected local young people. To send their own children to factories, some village cadres even made use of their political power to disqualify the sent-down youth from being considered for factory jobs. Jing records the following example:

This bunch of village cadres went to the commune [office] to check the dossiers and family backgrounds of the sent-down youths, and they knew that one student's grandpa was [politically classified as] a landlord. They therefore wanted to take this opportunity to pick him up as a soft persimmon [as a less competitive nominee] and pair him up with their candidates. These local monsters wanted to show their power and dominance and scare the sent-down [youth] off from the [worker recruitment] scheme. While the village cadres kept making some excuses without using violence, a head of village militia once threatened to tie the grandson of a landlord up. (Jing 2021, n.p.)

As discussed, the way of many sent-down youth to leave the countryside was in earlier stages at least largely decided by their family backgrounds and connections. While the role of the latter is nothing new, this position can help understand not only how *buzheng zhifeng* (evil and unprincipled conducts or practices) had widely spread among the cadres and networks, which had then mushroomed into wider society, but also how vulnerable and powerless families were forced into desperation, leading to the wide use of health-related excuses that will be detailed in the next section.

The unhealthy social trend, especially *zou houmen* (getting things done using connections), has been discussed in an enormous amount of publications, but all of these analyses are undertaken from either an institutional or an oppositional perspective (Yang 2018). From the second half of 1969 and 1970, the *zou houmen* issue was so widespread that Mao himself became very worried, forcing him to act in 1971 and 1972, ordering to clampdown the practice (Lü 2000). However, there were many forms of unprincipled abnormal social conducts at the time. Besides *zou houmen* – that was soon also widely tried by more families without access to the back doors – a new institutionalised abnormal policy measure of selecting and enrolling university students through recommendations of local CCP branches provided socio-politically privileged groups with more opportunities and powers. This has been a very divisive issue for Chinese people, but when the practice was first introduced, it made more people feel politically and socially deprived, supercharging competitive social repositionings.

This unfair and divisive policy measure or socio-political experiment refers to the Maoist Cultural Revolutionary chapter known as the worker–peasant–soldier university student issue. This was trialled in a handful of leading universities in 1970 and then continued for six years. As listed in Table 3.3, the initial selection and enrolment processes lasted until 1971, and it was then carried out as a new revolutionary practice from 1972.

Although the total student number listed on the left-hand side of Table 3.3 was not as big as those on its right-hand side, it was the students who were selected through recommendation without examinations, which was therefore sufficient to provoke strong negative social responses. Without the examination component, the policy measure of recruiting the worker–peasant–soldier university students was unpopular among the majority of average Chinese from the very beginning. They had at least two intuitive judgements. First, it was an unscrupulous violation of China's traditional practice of many centuries of selecting the talented people through open, fair and non-discriminatory examinations. Because of this negativity, this group of university students has commonly been called *Gong-nong-bing xueyuan* (worker–peasant–soldier trainees) in Chinese (Li 2006a, 2006b), seldom being seen as university students, as the English translation of the phrase does.

Table 3.3 The total numbers of two types of Chinese university students before and after 1976.

Year	Number (k)	Year	Number (k)
1970	90	1977	270
1971	N/A*	1978	402
1972	130	1979	284
1973	153	1980	280
1974	165	1981	280
1975	190	1982	320
1976	217	1983	390
Total	945	Total	2,226

Note: *This year's number was included in the 1970 figure.
Sources: Compiled by the author based on Zhou (1999), Yang (2006), Zhao (2016b), NBSC (2009) and Ministry of Education (2020).

Second, this policy choice and practice were also considered to be the institutionalisation of various irregular practices that had been employed over the Cultural Revolution. It was a political effort to legitimise what Maoists had done in those years, to fixate social class divisions of the time, and to monopolise for revolutionaries and supporters all the benefits of founding the new political system. This measure was also different from what occurred from 1966 to 1969, when radicals were smashing the old system. The new university system restructured in 1970 and 1971 was the new system that would more directly affect what people could do and achieve within this radically changed socio-political setting. This new policy seemed to many people from non-revolutionary backgrounds to be equivalent to a strong statement that the whole world belonged to them. According to Mi Hedu's analysis of the Red Guards or *hong erdai* (Second Red Generation), this university strategy and design institutionalised the privileged status of those believing that 'the country was founded by our parents' generation, and we are the offspring of this state, standing in the first hereditary line as the children of first families' (Mi 2014, n.p.).

What was more disappointing to those being politically considered as non-revolutionaries was that the historical mission of those new students was to completely revolutionise China's higher education system. At the time, the Maoist leadership decided to not only abolish the examinations but also develop and execute a new recruitment method. The new method combined local CCP branch or committee recommendations, approvals by higher-level leadership and university reviews. The principal tasks of these carefully chosen workers, peasants and soldiers were then also defined as to 'go to university, govern the university, and transform the university with Mao Zedong Thought' (Gan and Li 2004, 70).

These revolutionary objectives informed the vast majority of families without political privileges and contacts that the higher education system would be completely transformed, being kept for those who were born to communist revolutionary families or trusted working-class families. The young people from non-revolutionary families strongly felt that they had been left without a future or hope. A few former sent-down youth thought that the ridiculousness of governing ideas and the hopelessness of the politically and economically underprivileged people had all reached their climax. Social mobility channels and patterns in China became deformed and distorted, blocking the chances of what were then called 'alien class elements' (*jieji yiji fenzi*), of achieving anything they would like to reach (Womack 1982, 149). Therefore, a large number of underprivileged sent-down urban students had no choice but to rely on different irregular tactics – including making use of medical reasons for leaving the countryside – to achieve what those from privileged and connected families could easily achieve.

Being a Sick Returnee as the Only Hope

A range of social practices and related behaviours that were disdained or despised by most urban residents either resurfaced from disconsolate quarters of society or were attempted by the sent-down students and their families who were powerless to help their children. From 1970 onwards, the sent-down youth from ordinary or politically problematic families only had two options for applying for returning to the cities: *kuntui* (family hardships, including a small number of single-child families) and *bingtui* (health reasons) (Shi 1995; Gao 2012). *Kuntui* was very clear so that only few sent-down youth could make use of it because of at least two reasons. First, many families in destitutions were unable to afford the returning of their children, while those being able to afford it were unable to meet the *kuntui* conditions. Second, seeking the return through *kuntui* categories could be a risky path as they had to rely on the documents from their parents' work units or neighbourhood committees, while *bingtui* had no such strict requirements except for doctor certificates. Therefore, many former sent-down youth believe that almost all their fellow students had tried *bingtui*, turning themselves into sick returnees (Xie 2016).

Therefore, the Chinese phrase *bingtui* refers to some of those 17 or so million sent-down youth who, from as early as 1970 but largely from 1972 onwards, were allowed to return to their home cities if they were 'proven medically unfit' (Kor 2016, n.p.). As mentioned, *bingtui* was the practice and experience of the first cohort of sent-down youth, but it was not only their joint resistance to the rustication push, but also their strategic use of various excuses for breaking the limits imposed by the Maoist leadership and gaining similar rights and opportunities as those advantaged to leave the countryside. As recorded in many non-academic Chinese publications, *bingtui* was also regarded as a huge but apparently inverse shift in public sentiment about many aspects of Maoism. The realities of being forced to move down the social ladder to go to the countryside and being provided less chances than the privileged few made it no longer possible to keep the people to stay in a utopian state of dreaming before being thrown into an even deeper confusion than they were in.

It was true that there were a small percentage of sent-down urban students suffering legitimate health problems, but a vast majority of them regarded and used *bingtui* as an opportunity and channel to return to the cities. On the *Hunan Zhiqing* (sent-down youth) website, a former female student from Changsha, the provincial capital city of Hunan, wrote the following:

Bingtui, as a phrase, was created in a special era. It is an expression coated with blood, saturated with tears and burnt with scars. [...] *Bingtui* was the special policy initiated to allow the sent-down students with serious illnesses and being unable to take care of themselves to return to the cities, but it evolved into the means the sent-down students with no other choice used to return to their cities of origin. The prerequisites for applying for *bingtui* were serious health issues affecting independent living, which implied that diagnosis certificates from hospitals were needed. The sent-down youth who were unable to return to the cities because of family backgrounds and other objective reasons had to rack their brains to get an illness in order to get doctor certificates. (Li 2018, 1)

Another Hunan sent-down youth also recalled how upset and annoyed he was when he was unable to show he was suffering from phthisis, hepatitis or heart problems, and that his successful try to become a kidney disease patient after a failed claim of chronic post-surgical pain (Le 2017). As an angry former sent-down student put it, all these illness claims and tactics relied on cheating and falsifying something (Xie 2016). One of such cases was a Wuhan student, who pretended to be a psychiatric patient for more than a year until his urban resident permit was re-registered in the city of Wuhan (Wang 2019). He formed this crazy idea after missing all the other chances due to his problematic family background. He read several books and learned how to pretend to be mad; he even learned, from a successful sick returnee, to take an abandoned malaria drug to turn his skin yellowy green colour. He kept this a secret from his parents too. Of course, the worsening crisis over the CCP's leadership, as symbolised by the Lin Biao incident of 13 September 1971 (the details of which can be found in note 5 in this chapter and Chapter four), provided many sent-down urban youth with a sympathetic social atmosphere for seeking the return to the cities of origin. At the time, the zealous and unwavering loyalty to Mao and his radical ideas started fading and the bureaucrats or cadres at the middle and lower levels were changing their minds on some issues. One of the significant changes was that many cadres started using the power in their hands to seek personal gains, including receiving gifts and whatever valuable, even chunks of pork or a few kilos of wheat flour because of the widespread shortages of basic goods (Xu 2012).

A careful analysis of all the *bingtui*-related memoirs, both written and spoken, reveals that sent-down youth seemed to have acted in three main different ways based on their own family circumstances, all intended to get doctor certificates for *bingtui*. The first approach was used by the families who were not politically influential or those in trouble over the Cultural Revolution years, with non-political contacts beyond the Maoist revolutionary politics or class divides. Even if they did not know any people working in hospitals directly, they were able to dig out at least one contact. They would give gifts to contacts and the people entrusted to assist with certificates, but the process was not originated by gift-giving. Even with usable social connections, most of the certificates issued by doctors were also about tuberculosis, hepatitis, chronic enteritis, chronic gastritis, duodenal ulcer and kidney and heart diseases (Shi 1995; Xie 2008; Li 2018; Zhang 2018a; Honing and Zhao 2019).

The second tactic was to use numerous types of gifts, money power and other alternative exchanges. It is worth reminding that the cultural meaning of gifts and their value were very different from the current understanding. In the late 1960s and early 1970s, the income of ordinary families was so low that a carton of cigarettes, a bottle of Chinese spirits, a metre or so of fabric or even a large piece of meat was all rather precious to the low-rank cadres holding decision-making positions. A former sent-down student from Shanghai to the Ningbo region, Zhejiang province, spent as high as 300–400 yuan through relatives on obtaining the permission to leave the region (Yun 2008). There were even some go-betweens emerging in many cities, large and small, when *bingtui* became widespread (Xie 2008; Xu 2012).

The third method was very much a barehanded approach deployed by those who neither had usable networks for finding doctor certificates and approvals nor money to spend on forming working networks. These sent-down students are believed to be the largest group of *bingtui* seekers. Many former sent-down youth argue that the income of ordinary households was so little in the early 1970s that they were reluctant, if not unable, to use any money on obtaining doctor certificates. Accordingly, there were many efforts and manoeuvres in trying self-created strategies, shrewd and stupid, but mostly in identifying where and how to make the *bingtui* seeking process less problematic and more accessible than it was (Li 2018; Wang 2019). There were even a very small number of students relying on a self-reliance strategy, a right barehanded tactic. Examples of these include a wide range of conducts, such as obtaining, if not stealing, blank certificate papers from hospitals, forging signatures of consultants. Official stamps were even forged for stamping self-produced certificates (Du and Li 2017).

The widespread use of *bingtui* by millions of sent-down students was the powerful sign of the end of Maoist idealism at the grassroots level. It had indeed greatly altered moral standards and social norms in a national scale, but it had created the chance for underprivileged people to partially achieve what children from politically privileged families could achieve. From the perspective of competitive social repositionings, the emergence and utilisation of *bingtui* and its tactics had unquestionably expanded the channels for disadvantaged sent-down students to engage in competition with those revolutionary families or networks. A folk belief in something similar to the phrase 'every dog has its day' has come into people's minds, boosting the competitive mentality of disadvantaged people.

This shift in both mentality and social conduct at the grassroots levels or, more accurately, among politically underprivileged social groups, was then characterised by the surge and prominence of two sets of social attitudes and behaviours or conducts. These include the resurrection of gift-giving practices and the utilitarian use of identity performance. The first one has since become very visible to the Chinese general public while the second one has remained unclear. They were all very destructive to social norms from the position of cultural conservatism or institutionalism, but helpful from the stance of disadvantaged people and groups.

Although the gift-giving was long used by the Chinese people, it had been largely abandoned until the coming of the sent-down youth issue. A Chinese American lawyer, who was a Shanghai student to Yunnan, also witnessed the influences of the practices on social behaviours and ethos, recalling that more people started giving out gifts and knocking on back doors to seek help beyond what their families and networks could reach (Feng 2004). After many sent-down youth had left the countryside, these practices had become even more popular because of three reasons. First, those left-behind in countryside had to repeat what earlier returnees did because the practices of obtaining sick leave certificates were open secrets to almost all the urban population. Second, those earlier returnees also had to make use of contacts and gifts for their resettlement in their home cities, especially for finding jobs (Xu 2012). In fact, third, the gift-giving practices were believed to have also been employed by many sick returnees in seeking further job changes or even promotions in the home cities. Although many sent-down youth and their families were originally reluctant to spend too much on gaining health certificates for *bingtui*, the process of seeking the return, and their resettlement in cities, had shown them that asking contacts for assistance and gift-giving was, likely, a way of overcoming the hurdles in their life, especially compensating for their deprived social status caused by Maoist class-based discriminations (Xu 2016; Fan 2016). Many of such practices have since been judged by many to be morally incorrect, but through them, many former sent-down youth did in part regain the power deprived by Maoist politics and break up the monopoly of power by new privileged groups.

At the same time, the utilitarian use of identity performance has since also become a very essential but less visible part of what has been called changing social ethos. This was done through using various forms of gift-giving practices, opening up a different social space from that gripped by the new ruling classes. The process of finding their own chances to leave rural areas led sent-down students and other people to develop their own version of political courage and conduct, which was in part similar to the Maoist revolutionary spirit. In terms of this, the Cultural Revolution had seen that more Chinese started using what they learned from Maoism in their own way, resulting in the realisation that certain aspects of their identity could be performed, especially when they can empower needy people. If leaving the countryside of sent-down students has to be seen as a turning point, one of the main attitudinal and behavioural traits of the era must be the widespread use of identity performance (Jin 2014). It was because of its wide use that the identity performance issue has also been part of the recent debate over the Cultural Revolution and the sent-down campaign, which have all recently been complicated by new politics (Bonnin 2016). Among the competing memories of the sent-down episode, a professional writer and former student to a farming area in Heilongjiang region confirms the role of *bingtui* in the sent-down history and the understanding of attitudinal and behavioural changes in China:

> *Bingtui? Bingtui!* they had somehow all become patients and returned to home cities as sufferers. [...] Is there anything more ridiculous than that lively sent-down urban youth had to return to home cities as sick people? I have been wondering if there was no other way to let sent-down students return to the cities in a proper way? [...] If it was forced to do so at the time, no other choices, does it deserve an explanation afterwards? [...] Sent-down students were allowed to return because of illness, the reason of which was then used to support that the sent-down movement was not wrong, except that *bingtui* was overused. Is there sufficient evidence for this? If they cannot be forgotten, the first task is to have authentic records. (Shen 2017, n.p.)

Obviously, the deep impact of *bingtui* on people's attitudes and conducts has not only been felt across generations, but also one which has been politicised in the polarised public discourses in China regarding the Cultural Revolution and Maoism. However, the debate about this has largely been confined to non-academic groups. The long-term impacts of *bingtui* practice on present-day Chinese identity performance have not yet been adequately considered in the scholarly literature. In fact, the *bingtui* practice was a decisive push for, if not the real beginning of, the strategic identity performance by more Chinese in a very utilitarian manner in the contemporary Chinese history.

Leaving aside the identity performance issue, the *bingtui* practice has been identified by some researchers to be one of the few original ways of enabling some sent-down youth to return to their home cities. As pointed out, the resistance of many sent-down youth to the sent-down push in the early 1970s was quietly developed into various countermeasures against the sent-down policy. Those from politically disadvantaged families had found the excuses of medical reasons to challenge the limits placed upon them and to use them to achieve the goals that could be easily reached by those from privileged families. As an early form of bottom-up resistance against the Maoist Cultural Revolution, the *bingtui* practice was not only the action taken by the sent-down urban students and families to fight for their own rights and interest, but has also altered the way people think of the dominant socio-political norms and handle the difficulties created by them. Their miseries had also, since the early 1970s, made many Chinese people realise that nothing about socio-political attitude and identity could not be performed and acted. As a result, the growing intricacy of Chinese people's attitudes and conducts started taking their shape as early as during the Cultural Revolution years, when Mao's social class politics divided the population and triggered different responses to social repositioning (Lin 1991).

Since the wide use of *bingtui* options in the early 1970s, the profound unhappiness of many sent-down youth who were unable to obtain factory jobs or to enrol into any university was mitigated slightly for a short time. Many had either returned to their home cities or had found ways of returning. For a short period of time, many of those sent-down youth even felt that they had achieved something equivalent to what children of revolutionary, or other fortunate, families had obtained. However, Maoist class-based discriminations were still rampant, placing young people from different social class background at actually different competitive levels and conditions in society. Since many young people, including former Red Guards, had all become so different from who they were in 1966 and 1967, especially many had then become fairly sceptical about Maoist approaches, many young Chinese people had remained in a competitive mode. These were exemplified by the gift-giving practices used in seeking the resettlement in home cities or in changing a better position (Jin 2015). Towards the mid-1970s, young people's hopes and demands for better career prospects and life opportunities had slowly contained more political elements. As Chapter four will examine, the governing approaches adopted by the Maoist leadership were found to be deeply problematic, offering young people with less or no opportunity to achieve their aspirations, while keeping finding new political enemies to focus every attention on political fights inside and outside the new ruling political party.

Notes

1. From 18 August 1966 to 26 November 1966, Mao attended the grand receptions or large-scale mass rallies of tens of millions of Red Guards in Beijing for eight times, setting an unprecedented record for revolutionary madness and mass mobilisation. The young students attending these rallies were transported without fee or charge of any kind from different cities and regions nationwide to Beijing, which was called *da chuanlian* (the great link-ups). These link-ups were the massive-scale exchanges of unruly and rebellious experiences, but was also defined as a journey of youths to revolutionary sites and the countryside (Mittler 2012), According to *Beijing Review*, as many as a total of 11 million of 'Mighty Cultural Revolutionary Army' had been inspected by Mao in those eight mass rallies (*Beijing Review* 1966, 6). Because of the students were told 'to rebel is justified', a nationwide devastation called 'destroy the four olds' was then conducted in the second half of 1966 (Jian et al. 2009, 237). In addition to Mittler (2012) and Jian et al. (2009), interested readers are referred to MacFarquhar (1974), Dittmer (1987) and Leese (2011).
2. This was a turning point in the Cultural Revolution history or the end of the rebel faction during the Cultural Revolution according to Yang Jisheng, a former Xinhua News Agency journalist and author of several influential books on the Maoist era. According to Yang, Mao felt an urgent need to restore social order in 1968 after two years of chaos, but a few student leaders in Beijing did not support the revolutionary committee idea that was backed by Mao. Having failed to stop faction fights after issuing a few directives, Mao had lost his patience with the rebel faction leaders and decided to send more than 30,000 workers and PLA soldiers to Tsinghua University on 27 July 1968 to take over the control of the university. At the same time, Mao and the key figures of his leadership team held a meeting from the midnight of 27 July 1968 to meet the so-called five great rebel leaders from five Beijing-based universities. This lengthy overnight meeting that lasted until the early morning of 28 July 1968 marked the end of Mao's political utilisation of rebellious students. For more information, readers can read the English translation of Yang's book (2018), and Jian et al. (2009) and Dittmer (2015).
3. This was also called Shanghai's *Yiyue Fengbao* (the January Storm) or even the January Revolution. In the original Cultural Revolutionary expression, it was also called *duoquan* (grabbing or seizing power) by the Maoist rebel groups in January 1967. It was supported by Mao and his loyal followers and had then rapidly spread to other provinces, resulting in that many local governments were replaced by new Revolutionary Committees, while the rebel faction fights for influence were going on in many regions. The Shanghai Storm marked that the Cultural Revolution had entered its 'seizing power' stage. Ironically, Wang Hongwen, one of the leaders of Shanghai worker rebel groups, was quickly elevated to be Mao's new successor, at the age of 37, after the Lin Biao incident on 13 September 1971. In addition to MacFarquhar and Schoenhals (2006), interested readers are referred to MacFarquhar (1974), Teiwes and Sun (1996) and Dittmer (2015).
4. This was the very first collective opposition that a group of senior leaders of the CCP's central leadership had staged in February 1967 against the seizing power activities outlined above in note 3, as well as the various Cultural Revolutionary policies. This refers to a few meetings at which three vice-premiers and four PLA marshals had heated arguments with Mao's followers about the PLA's stability, the nationwide seizing power activities and general law and order issues. The debates had posted direct and serious challenges to Mao's Cultural Revolutionary strategy, making him so angry that he named the meetings as the adverse or counter-current. This incident had deeply divided the CCP's central leadership, which has also been used to confirm that Mao had never enjoyed what many would flatteringly call a complete power or authority and that his influence should also be seen in a relative sense. Interested readers are referred to Teiwes and Sun (1996), Huang (2000) and MacFarquhar and Schoenhals (2006).
5. After 1949, Mao's governing ideas and his leadership had from time to time been challenged or restricted by the Chinese military leaders for at least four times. This includes: (1) In 1959, Marshal Peng Dehuai, who was then minister for defence, put forward his criticism of the Great Leap Forward at the 1959 Lushan Conference as discussed in Chapter one and its notes 2 and 3; (2) in February 1967, as noted above in note 4, four marshals jointly opposed

various Cultural Revolutionary approaches; (3) in July 1967, Commander General Chen Zaidao of the PLA Wuhan Military Region indirectly expressed the strong dissatisfaction and firm opposition of their generation towards the Cultural Revolution in the Wuhan Incident of 20 July 1967; (4) in September 1971, Marshall Lin Biao, Mao's second but well-documented, or constitutionally designated successor, adopted a running-away strategy and died in an airplane crash on his fleeing to the Soviet Union on 13 September 1971. Among these four incidents, the Wuhan Incident was an understudied topic and its unique aspect was Mao's quick correction to his early judgement within days. This quick public humili-ation to Mao's authority and reputation included the very surprising decision to publicly denounce and arrest three junior but active and loyal members of the Central Cultural Revolution Leading Group, Wang Li, Guan Feng and Qi Benyu, who were involved in the talks before the incident with Wuhan-based rebel groups. They were first treated as revolu-tionary heroes and even welcomed back to Beijing at a mass rally in the Tiananmen Square. But to everyone's surprise, they were defined as troublemakers after days, and obviously Mao had to give in to the pressure from some veteran PLA leaders. Apart from Robinson (1971) and Wang (2017c), interested readers are referred to Oksenberg et al. (1968) and MacFarquhar and Schoenhals (2006).

6. The so-called 'May 7th Cadre School' was created according to the main ideas of Mao's let-ter written to Lin Biao after reading a report from the PLA's General Logistic Department on 7 May 1966. The report was about how the PLA divisions organised soldiers to par-ticipate in agricultural and agriproducts productions. This helped Mao to develop a set of idealist ideas over what workers, peasants, students, and officials should do, which was then praised as 'May 7 directive'. To implement Mao's directive, all the government departments at the central and provincial levels set up their agricultural farms in rural regions under the name of 'May 7th Cadre School' in order to send their staff members and dependents to work on farm. This was also part of Maoist re-education effort. However, some people have also used 'May 7th Cadre School' to indicate their family backgrounds as all these schools were associated with China's central and provincial party-state system. For more information, interested readers are referred to Starr (1979) and Pieke (2009).

7. This type of factories, as well as research and development institutions, was set up as part of China's 'third-line' or 'third-front' strategy, which was developed in the mid-1960s after its split with the Soviet Union, but before the Cultural Revolution. This has been called 'third-front construction', or *sanxian jianshe* in Chinese, refers to the national industrial distribu-tion strategy, but predominantly about its military industrial distribution and development that the CCP leadership under Mao Zedong developed in the mid-1960s. The key idea of 'third-front' strategy was to construct and locate, or relocate, various nationally and strategi-cally important industries in China's 'third-line' areas in southwest and northwest regions, away from the first-line or first-front regions (coastal provinces, northeastern provinces, and Xinjiang) and the second-line or second-front regions (middle-strip regions, between coastal provinces and the Beijing-Guangzhou railway), because they could be targets of foreign invasions. Readers can find more information about these in Bramall (2007), as well as in Naughton (1988), and Wang and Hu (1999).

Chapter Four

CRYING OUT FOR CHANGES IN THE
SECOND HALF OF THE 1970s

Since the time when Mao was alive and leading the Cultural Revolution, a widely used narrative suggests that Mao was fighting for his political legacy in Chinese history. This was based on his own logic and the example of the then Soviet Union's leader, Nikita Khrushchev. After taking over leadership of the Soviet Union, Khrushchev had strongly condemned Stalin's wrongdoings. Stalin's embalmed remains were even removed and buried elsewhere. This story was awful in the eyes of the Chinese culture of Mao's generation. Mao made strategic use of this case and cautioned his followers of the real danger of China's Khrushchev: Liu Shaoqi, Mao's first successor, who openly criticised Mao for the famine at the 1962 Seven-Thousand Cadres Conference. Obviously, Mao's efforts in his last 10 or so years were not only to place himself in history in the fashion he would have wanted, but also to fight against any form of revisionism or attempt to modify his anticipated position in history. This was a form of competitive repositioning – even if at a different level – aiming at positioning his revolutionary legacy in the world.

Mao had clearly overplayed his repositioning efforts, running against what he would wish to be remembered for. Having put a break to the faction fights between student rebel groups in July 1968, the CCP's Ninth National Congress was finally held in April 1969, almost thirteen years after its Eighth National Congress held in 1956. At the Ninth National Congress, Lin Biao was formally designated as Mao's successor. Mao could in fact stop at this point and avoid more damage to his historical position, but he was offended by Lin's proposal to reinstate the position of the PRC's president at the Lushan Conference held in early autumn 1970.[1]

Lin Biao must have felt deceived by Mao after the 1970 Lushan Conference, so he started to show part of his military man's nature. He had since kept a long distance from Mao for a year, before opting to run away from China on 13 September 1971. His plane crashed in Mongolia on the way to the Soviet Union.[2] The 'September 13 Incident' – or the 9/13 Incident as it is called in Chinese – was therefore a conclusion of Lin Biao's historical repositioning. His not-so-glorious relationship with Mao in much of the 1960s ended with his fleeing China and subsequent death. His death earned him a position in Chinese history. As time goes on, more and more well-educated and middle-class people in China seem to consider Lin – who was once seen as a disgraceful flatterer – to be some sort of historical hero, who put an actual end to Mao's Cultural Revolution and his personality cult.

These political repositionings, if not fights, for historic legacy among top leaders have further worsened the societal conditions for ordinary inhabitants' social positioning and repositioning. If the previous stage was characterised by the positionings and reposition-ings of society members in the enormous downward social mobility trend, the post-9/13 years were very much a standstill period, during which the entire country was witness-ing Mao's final show and failing health. A vast majority of people in the country were driven to see the real reasons for what had happened to their life and future after many political campaigns. Basically, they were given no economic incentives, while being restricted to limited opportunities and resources by the class-category policy and prac-tice. There were almost no people still talking about being a communist successor – the notion of which was once again confirmed to be farcical by the 9/13 – after the sent-down campaign. There were no social ladders to climb in such an immobile society. Therefore, more people were becoming rather political as an effect of their deprived feeling, focusing on more essential issues in society. This seems to be the obvious char-acteristic of the social positionings or repositionings of an immobile population in a motionless society.

As will be analysed next, there was nothing else in the early 1970s as critical and systematic as a synopsis known as *571 Gongcheng Jiyao* (the 'Outline of Project 571'), allegedly drafted by Lin Biao's co-conspirators, in terms of criticising Mao's wrongdo-ings. The Outline of Project 571 is also translated as the '571 Military Coup Plan' as the enunciation of 571 sounds close to the broken Chinese expression of armed insur-gency. The outline was publicised as part of the campaign to denounce Lin Biao, but Maoists misread the attitudes and needs, if not aspirations, of tens of millions of Chinese people, who actually agreed with the outline. For example, the document criticised the decision to send young school leavers out of the urban centres as a disguised form of labour re-education camps. Such anger or resentment over Maoist policies was wide-spread among officials, military and civil, at medium and senior levels. It created an accommodating atmosphere for the return of sent-down youth to urban centres and the expression of critical questions about Maoist policies. Frustrated people – despairing young people in particular – were waiting for opportunities to voice their concerns and strong demands for real changes in society. The death of Zhou Enlai, the then premier, in January 1976 finally provided them with the chances to gather in mass and march on streets. Their last mass gathering in Beijing during the Qingming (Tomb Sweeping Day) Festival in April 1976 was furiously condemned by Mao as an anti-revolutionary riot. However, the protest had demonstrated future leaders what they were supposed to do.

This chapter is, therefore, concerned with what happened after a large number of sick returnees came back to urban centres. In the cities, social mobility was also impossible unless it was downward. Numerous frustrated ordinary Chinese cried out for more and fairer opportunities to have a better life and future. This chapter is structured in three sections. The first one details how job and career opportunities had become limited and highly restricted for young Chinese during the 1970s. This section focuses on how the choices of young, as well as middle-aged, people's social positioning and repositioning became rather deviant and how the social ladders were removed or totally blocked. This analysis prepares readers to understand why there were large-scale protests in several large Chinese cities in 1976. The second section analyses the 1976 Tiananmen Incident as a historical effort by the masses to voice their demands and inform what they wanted the ruling CCP to do for them. The third section examines what new chances were available to the people who wanted to reposition themselves differently in post-Mao China. This third section also devotes special attention to one of the most welcomed policy changes introduced under Deng Xiaoping's leadership, which was the restoration of the non-discriminatory university selection examination policy.

After the Fleeing of Mao's Chosen Successor

The popular enthusiasm for Mao's Cultural Revolution, as well as for his personality cult, largely vanished after the sent-down urban youth campaign was pushed on. However, the 9/13 Incident was the most decisive turning point in terminating the Cultural Revolution, while it also made Mao's health deteriorate badly (Wu 2015). His originally problematic capability to make judgements was further weakened, if not impaired. He was still making the effort to maintain his leadership position, but his new ideas to guide the party-state system and the masses towards adjusting to the post-9/13 situation revealed flaws and limitations in thinking. Two cases have been seen as evidence of the problems Mao and his followers had developing new convincing and effective narratives. First, when the campaign against Lin Biao was launched, it was weirdly linked with Confucius. Lin Biao and Confucius were about two thousand years away from each other, hardly sharing any similarity with each other, except Maoists' miscalculation of utilising the damaged reputation of Confucius to demonise Lin Biao. Second, maybe even more senseless still, was the call for 'Ping *Shuihu*, Pi Song Jiang' (Critiquing *Water Margin* (a fourteenth-century classic novel) and denouncing Song Jiang (the head of a group of outlaws in the novel)).[3] It was due to this campaign that many less-educated people also found out how ridiculous China's national governance had become.

Zhong Acheng, often known by his pseudonym Ah Cheng, is a 1949-born Chinese author and screenwriter. As a sent-down youth from Beijing to remote Yunnan province, he recalled excitement after the 9/13 in his short memoir, 'Listening to Enemy Radio Broadcasting':

> We heard of the Lin Biao incident in 1971 from overseas broadcasts almost on the same day. This was an important event in the 1970s. The mythical greatness of Mao Zedong collapsed instantaneously. [..] Everyone sat up from the bed and looked at each other, showing an uncontrollable excitement in shock. [...] We knew that the Party branch-secretary was also an enthusiastic listener of enemy radio broadcasting, [...] no one would mention it directly, but teased him by suggesting it was time to go to bed and he shouldn't be worried too much, taking it easy. [...] About a month later, the province sent a special working group to the county to gather local cadres above the [production] brigade level to the county. After the brigade head came back, he was very proud, saying it was ridiculous, and the county had made f-word thing that we already f-word knew so nervous. [...] [The local people of] Yunnan were unable to speak without using the f-bomb. (Ah 2011, 273)

According to Ah Cheng, the party's grassroots members started changing their attitudes and positions in the early 1970s, years before the end of the Cultural Revolution. Ah

Cheng's short piece was part of a memoir collection, *The 1970s*, published by Beijing's Sanlian Publishing House in 2004 and then by Oxford University Press in 2008. A common theme of almost all these memoirs about the 1970s is the influence of the Outline of Project 571 on their understanding of the Cultural Revolution. As recalled by an interviewee, the 9/13 hit the Maoist leadership and the entire society twice. The first direct bash was the 9/13 Incident itself, and the other heavy blow was the systematic criticism of Maoist practices by the Outline of Project 571 (Interviewee 30 2020).

Xu Youyu, a 1947-born former researcher at the CASS and public intellectual, believes that the campaign to send urban students to the countryside altered young people's belief in the political system, and that the 9/13 and the 571 Outline further overturned their understanding of Maoism and the Cultural Revolution (Xu 2013). As mentioned, it was also evident that Mao's leadership team was then unable to accurately read the attitudes of everyday people, and they even wanted to distribute the 571 Outline to demonise Lin Biao. However, many people found in the 571 Outline a systematic summary of what they were angered about. For example, the 571 text condemned: the 'national economy has been stagnated for more than 10 years', and people's 'real standard of living has fallen', and so on (Yin 2009, 350). As listed in Table 4.1, the 571 Outline provided people with terms to talk about China's situation.

The nationwide campaign of analysis and criticism of the 571 Outline was like opening flood gates. A widespread anger was rising everywhere among people outside the CCP – and even a large portion of the rank and file of the CCP – because of the reality partially outlined in Table 4.1. In the case of young people, they did not only feel cheated and exploited by leaders, but were more importantly upset that almost all the opportunities, especially the chances for upward social mobility, were firmly controlled and monopolised by new revolutionary classes or groups according to the Maoist class

Table 4.1 The 'Perilous Crisis' outlined in the Outline of Project 571.

List	Perilous Crisis in the Original Third Section
1	The dictator is becoming increasingly unpopular
2	The ruling group is very unstable, fighting for power [...]
3	The army is under pressure, the military spirit is unstable, senior middle and upper-level cadres are dissatisfied [...]
4	A handful of [Party] literati are aggressive and domineering, making enemies on all sides
5	Senior leaders ostracised and attacked during the long struggle within the Party and the Cultural Revolution dared not speak up
6	Peasants lack food and clothing
7	Young students going to the countryside are tantamount to labour reform in disguise
8	The Red Guards were deceived and exploited in the early stage, [...] but later suppressed and turned into scapegoats
9	Government officials have been streamlined, and going to May 7th Cadre School is equivalent to being unemployed in disguise
10	The freezing of wages of workers (especially young workers) is tantamount to being exploited in disguise

Sources: Compiled by the author based on Teiwes and Sun (1996), Qiu (1999), Yin (2009) and Yang (2018).

theory and practice. At the time, Chinese society as a whole was no longer operating in a way to allow aspirational people to do what they would like to accomplish; this made the Chinese way of life abnormal and poisoned the social ethos of the country.

In addition to the hopelessness felt by the politically underprivileged, the low morale of grassroots officials and the political abandonment of Red Guard students by the Maoists leadership, those who were born and grew up in the so-called new China after 1949 had entered their 20s. They had less illusions then than they had in the mid-1960s but, from the early 1970s, they started to confront actual issues related to their future marriage and setting up their own family. It was on these life issues that these baby boomers further felt the problem illustrated in Figure 4.1.

Figure 4.1 needs to be read in conjunction with Table 3.2, which also provides background information on China's socio-economic conditions during the Cultural Revolution years with a focus on rural–urban income divide of the time. These deterio-rated economic conditions had occurred against a backdrop of fast population growth depicted in Figures 1.1 and 1.2, and the Red Guard generation had reached their mar-riage age as the country's economy had slid into near paralysis. Several interviewees also point out that such a stagnant economy had even made many advantaged revolu-tionary families powerless to assist their grown-up children have a well-waged job or a place to live independently after marriage. Since the per capita housing space has been above 40 square metres (NBSC 2020), many young Chinese are now also unable to completely comprehend the seriousness of the housing situation portrayed in Table 4.2.

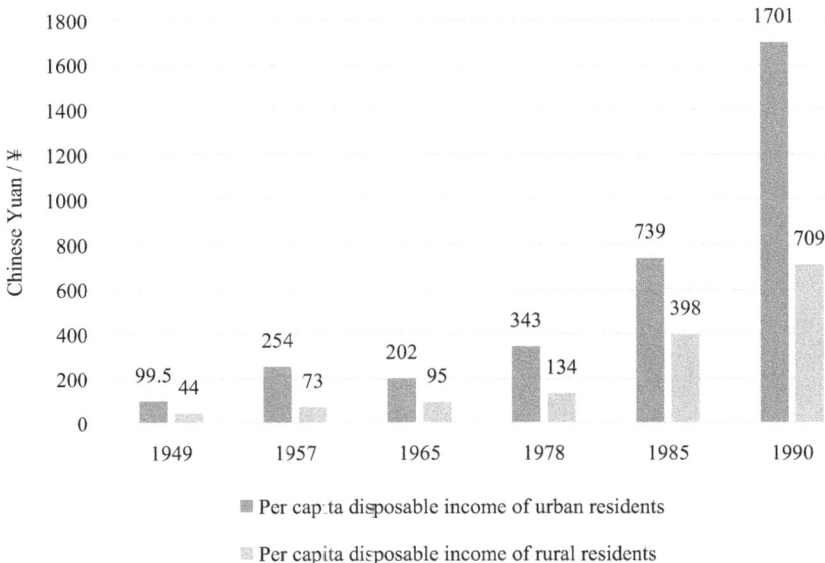

Figure 4.1 Slow growth of disposable income of urban residents per capita in the 1970s. *Sources*: Compiled by the author based on NBSC (1999, 2015, 2020), Zeng (1999), Li (2002) and Cao (2008).

Table 4.2 The deterioration of the urban housing supply in the 1970s.

Year	Housing Space Per Capita in Beijing (m²)	Housing Space Per Capita in Shanghai (m²)
1949	4.9	3.9
1957	3.7	3.1
1960	3.4	3.8
1965	3.7	3.9
1970	4.3	4.4
1976	3.3	-
1978	4.6	4.3
1980	4.8	4.4
1990	7.7	6.6

Sources: Compiled by the author based on *Beijing Local Gazetteers* (2000), Shan and Lu (2002), Sun (2004), Yang (2011), Liu, (2012), Zhao (2015), Li (2017), Wang (2018a), Wang (2018b), Yao (2019).

The figures in Table 4.2 are indicative of the bad housing situation of the Cultural Revolution years, but most of the interviewees feel that they were largely amplified as both Beijing and Shanghai had a big number of privileged households, revolutionary or otherwise. The following may be close to what they remembered:

> In 1976, the per capita living area in urban Beijing was 0.34 square meters lower than that in 1957, which was less than 4 square meters, and it was far less than the 4.9 square meters in 1949. The housing problems were a major headache for Beijing. Apart from the spacious living area of some officials at that time, the housing area of ordinary residents was less than 3 square meters, and numerous working-class families lived in a 14-square-meter old house with five or six people. (*Beijing Local Gazetteers* 2000, 489)

China's shortage economy in the 1970s was not only reflected in the low income and the lack of housing supply, but also in the change of thinking and behaviour across different social groups and classes. A general trend was to abandon idealism, including the revolutionary heir ideal. However, there were different alternatives to fill the vacuum left by the sceptical attitudes towards Maoism. From a neutral or philosophical viewpoint, there was a strong deviation towards pragmatic and realistic, if not utilitarian, thinking. From a social norm stance, many changes in the early and mid-1970s were characterised by the emergence and prominence of two main sets of social attitudes and conducts, which were the resurgence of gift-giving practices and the utilitarian practice of identity performance. The first one was very visible and prominent to the general public, while the other was not directly visible. However, both of them were all used as alternative ways of overcoming various hurdles in people's life and compensating for their powerlessness caused by Maoist class-based discrimination (Gao 2021). As a result, there were also other forms of the so-called *buzheng zhifeng* (unethical conducts) spreading in society, such as *zuo houmen* (to get things done through the back door).

From a critical psychological perspective, these nationwide abnormal social conducts were so widespread and strong that the social ethos also started to change dramatically. What first emerged was an obvious social phenomenon, *nifan xinli* (converse psychology or reverse mentality), by which anything said by the authorities or the media should be considered from an opposite direction (He 2001; Gao 2013a). There was also a strong upsurge in social competitive pressure, which was then called *panbi xinli* ('making invidious comparison') (Hansen 2015, 84). Mi Hedu and Yang Guobin, two active researchers of the Red Guards, identified a strong awareness of the self as an essential change:

> In Mi Hedu's book, *The Red Guard Generation*, he documents the following comment by an interviewee: Many people started to be aware of the existence of the 'I' or the 'self" as a result of the loss of confidence in accomplishing social objectives. They started running their own world, from studying all kinds of scientific and cultural knowledges, navigating in the vast ocean of books, to planning their own future […]; from earning more work points [in rural production brigades] and more money, to finding ways to place themselves in a better position. (Yang 2006, n.p.)

It was due to the realisation of the self and the social competitive pressure that more Chinese people tended to become more attentive to calculating personal loss and gain and less ideological than they were. A former sent-down student named this propensity using a colloquial phrase: *xiao jiujiu*, the sophisticated calculations of personal benefit and cost. In the view of several former sent-down students, the contemporaries – or coevals – of the PRC China (or *Gongheguo tonglingren* in Chinese) were all grown-up in the early 1970s and had all also learned many political and social lessons from their mad and naive support for the Maoist Cultural Revolution. As mature youth, most of them had developed the basic ability to judge their own life conditions, which were not satisfactory. Therefore, they believed that there was nothing incorrect or immoral in calculating their own benefit and loss.

In fact, everyone was seriously calculating their own position in such worsening social conditions, which often took place while reading and condemning the Outline of Project 571. Among the three seemingly loyal supporters of Maoist approaches, the PLA was apparently not fully supportive of various Cultural Revolutionary tactics, but its position was not as bad as the 571 Outline noted. The army was then not only put in a dominant position, but also granted some benefits, such as higher salaries and post-service settlement provisions. Workers and peasants, the second main social class basis of Maoism, were given no real benefits despite being defined as the leading classes of China. At the time, their political halo was no longer glowing. The university students recruited during the Cultural Revolution had been considered as a vested interest group, but they also started reconsidering their positions.

Li Jiangyuan, a 1964-born researcher, interviewed numerous worker–peasant–soldier university students in the late 1990s onwards, one of his interviewees mentioned the following:

> The Lin Biao Incident played a huge role in breaking the political superstition of our generation. Of course, 'three feet of ice were not frozen in one day' [Rome wasn't built in a day], our process of alienating the official political doctrines of the Cultural Revolution began as early as the middle of the movement. Some of us were thinking about this question at the time: Although the slogan of the Cultural Revolution was to 'smash the Four

Olds, and establish the Four News', it actually only touched the surface without altering the feudalism in the culture and thoughts, which was why Lin Biao was chosen to be the heir in the [party] constitution. (Li 2006a, 597)

All these rethinking had first happened separately, and the early effort of many people to reposition themselves in the instant aftermath of the 9/13 was also tried individually. Such a social force had been so powerful that some individuals were even pushed to make their demands for sympathy from the party-state system, creating several different types of individual heroes in the first half of the 1970s. Among the famous examples created by the muddled Maoist leaders through the official media outlets, Zhang Tiesheng became a hero for refusing to answer exam questions (Dittmer 1987). Another hero was Huang Shuai, a primary school student who was furious with a stringent teacher, and her complaint letters were used by Maoists for furthering the education revolution (White 1981). Li Qinglin, a primary school teacher in despair from Fujian province, altered his fortune after sending his complaint to Mao, who instructed to send Li 300 yuan to manage his troubles (Honig and Zhao 2019). All these examples show that individuals were making demanding changes. However, the overall social conditions in China, especially the leadership crisis, were so hopeless that the demands of most of its people were impossible to satisfy.

The people's attention was therefore gradually shifting its focus to the big issues that had prevented them from repositioning themselves in an acceptable way. The individual-based personal calculation of benefits and losses was then elevated to a shared societal concern. As indicated in Table 4.3, what made the bad situation worse was the inclusion of intellectuals in the 'class enemy list' as the 'stinking ninth category' (MacFarquhar and Fairbank 1991, 79; Saich 2001, 168).

The above situation that was once condemned as the expansion of the scale of attack had even compelled Mao to quote a saying from a popular Peking opera, *Taking Tiger Mountain by Strategy*, and warn that the 'Old Nine cannot leave' (Li 1995, 225) or we cannot let the Old Nine leave in 1975 (He 2001). In his final months, Mao seemed to have realised that his followers should not make the enemy list longer and longer, which could reduce the social base of the CCP's rule. However, Mao and his followers as a new generation of revolutionary-turned-ruler gave too much attention to their own success,

Table 4.3 A growing list of politically adversary social classes.

No.	Anti-revolutionary Social Class Category	Time to Introduce
1	Landlords	The late 1940s
2	Rich peasants	The late 1940s
3	Counter-revolutionaries	The 1950s
4	Bad elements	The 1950s
5	Rightists	1957
6	Traitors	1966
7	Enemy agents	1966
8	Capitalist roaders	1966
9	Intellectuals – the ninth stinking category	1968, but mainly in the early 1970s

Sources: Compiled by the author based on NBSC (1999, 2015, 2020) and Li (2002).

with no proper awareness of certain governing rules, especially the risks of removing the ladder for social mobility or placing any ceiling, transparent or otherwise, on aspirational members of society. The political difficulties after the 9/13 had led to the panic use of various irregular measures for promoting new leaders. Apart from the return and subsequent fall of Deng Xiaoping before Mao's death in September 1976, the elevations of Mao's last two successors, namely Wang Hongwen and Hua Guofeng, had also exposed a serious abnormality. The latter became even more irregular in the promotion of quite a few new national leaders from factories, villages and other grassroots work units, including vice-premiers and deputy chairpersons of two rubber-stamp legislative organs. All these had not only profoundly disenchanted many CCP members, but also upset a large number of aspirational young people because the cadre promotion policy had shown no clear pattern. This added yet a new dimension to the brewing fury among the people who felt both hopeless and helpless.

The 1976 Tiananmen Incident as Collective Repositionings

The ongoing collective dissatisfactions with what had happened in China before and after the 9/13 had well prepared the population for a national outburst. Before 1976, Chinese politics was largely performed by few leadership figures, but the disappointed and angry masses were waiting for a chance to stage a showdown with the radical Maoists who had prevented many people from either enjoying a decent life in a materialistic sense or realising what they would like to accomplish in society. This opportunity appeared in January 1976, when Zhou Enlai, the then-esteemed premier, died after a long battle with cancer. His death was spontaneously used as a good excuse for discontented people to gather in public places and voice their dissatisfaction and anger. The difficult and unachievable social positionings, or repositionings, of a vast majority of people started to take the form of collective action.

The 1976 Tiananmen Incident – normally called 'the April 5th Movement' in Chinese – refers to the protests and crackdowns taking place during the Qingming (Tomb Sweeping Day) Festival days in April 1976. The tension between spontaneous demonstrators, police and other forces rapidly intensified to violent clashes in Tiananmen Square on 5 April 1976.[4] Young protesters were so angry at Maoists' condemnation of what occurred in the square that they set on fire cars (and a key security building) near the square. Thousands of furious protesters surrounded and threatened to break into the Great Hall of the People located at the western edge of Tiananmen Square. However, the incident was in reality started by hundreds of thousands of spontaneous mourners within the week after Zhou's death on 8 January 1976. On his cremation day on 11 January 1976, Beijing saw hundreds of thousands of mourners lining up spontaneously along Beijing's Chang'an Avenue, staging a very political scene that has since been depicted as 'the 10-mile long road says farewell to the Premier' (*shili changjie song Zongli*) (Gao 2008; Dikötter 2016). The emotional reactions in those days were a decisive part of the preparation of the 1976 Tiananmen Incident. Zhou's death provided people with a chance to vent their rage towards China's economic situation and endless political infighting. This had once made Zhou Enlai a respectful figure for a few years before more people started seeing him differently (Dillon 2020). However, Mao's last political campaign in February 1976 to attack Deng Xiaoping's 'overall rectification' approach made Zhou's death the only excuse for unhappy people to gather together and express their anger to Maoists (Dong and Walder 2021, 158).

There are at least two main perspectives to explain the mass protests in 1976: a liberal or enlightenment standpoint and a democracy perspective. Despite his book is published by one of China's most official presses, Tong Qinglin's book, *Looking Back at 1978: History Turned Here*, defines the 1976 Tiananmen Incident (or the April 5th Movement) from the liberal or enlightenment stance as follows:

> The 'Tiananmen Incident', also known as the 'April 5th Movement', was in fact a movement to liberate thinking, which awoke the whole nation. The Cultural Revolution that lasted for 10 years had caused serious disasters to China and aroused people's resentment. People initially placed their hopes of restoring social order and executing right policies on some older revolutionaries, such as Zhou Enlai and Deng Xiaoping. But they were treated unfairly, which made people furious at the 'Gang of Four'.[5] The Tiananmen Event was an eruption of love and hatred in people's hearts. In essence, the event supported the Party's correct leadership represented by Deng Xiaoping, showing the common aspiration of the people. (Tong 2008, 9)

The democracy viewpoint has not only been long favoured by democracy activists, but also put into use by many of them since 1976. Chen Ziming, who died of pancreatic cancer in Beijing in 2014 at the age of 62, became one of such activists since the early 1970s, after returning to Beijing as a sent-down student from Inner Mongolia. He had since taken an active part in a series of protests and the formations of a number of organisations outside the party-state system. Because of his direct and deep involvement, Chen Ziming once argued that the significance of what occurred in 1976 lies in the emergence and formation of two additional socio-political forces: the reformist force within the ruling CCP, and the outside-the-system forces. The latter was also commonly called the forces outside the system or the non-institutional forces (Chen 2006b).

Although Chen was punished a few times for creating quite a few non-official groups and big associations in Beijing – and despite his democracy position – he believed that the April 5th Movement of 1976 was more relevant to the new tension between the Dengist governing approach and the Maoist dogmatic stance than to the death of Zhou Enlai. In one of his important writings, Chen offered the following analysis of China's socio-political situations in 1976:

> In 1975, Deng Xiaoping focused attention on – and also energetically carried out – an 'overall rectification', emerging as the centre of public sentiments, policies and influences that were outside [the circle of] Mao Zedong within the party. This freed a substantial number of the people from hesitation or pessimism and despair, and gathered them under the banner of Deng Xiaoping. The mass bases of the Maoists and non-Maoist alliances had then undergone a shift, which was the historical context of the April 5th movement. (Chen 2006c, n.p.)

Just like all founders of new groups or organisations, Chen was obviously good at remembering many names and people's networks, including the names of several of my old acquaintances who took part in the April 5th Movement, but were detained or sent to prison in 1976 and 1977. His long lists of names even included my name as a member of a new editorial committee under the *Twentieth Century Book Series* (*Ershi shiji wenku*) in the 1980s (Chen 2009). His lists, as well as the names mentioned by other researchers (such as Yin Hongbiao), have also established that the 1976 Tiananmen Incident could also be defined as the social repositionings of many individuals, but they had taken a politicised approach to their difficult social repositionings or positionings at the time (Chen 2006c; Yin 2009).

At the intersection of individual ambition and political uncertainty, if not public resentment, the city of Beijing alone saw at least hundreds of young people detained, arrested and then sent to prison. There were even more who were denounced in the workplace for their participation in the demonstrations in Tiananmen Square or for sharing some rumours about what had happened at the top leadership level. The strong anger of many individuals was also spread all over the country, including many faraway regions and counties. In *Secret Archives about the Cultural Revolution in Guangxi*, compiled by Song Yongyi, more than one hundred and thirty local people living in the county of Long'an in the remote Guangxi region were found to have spread rumours about what had happened in Beijing after the April 5th Movement (Song 2016). All these records have clearly proved that people's attention had shifted significantly and focused on the crucial issues blocking many of them from positioning or repositioning themselves in society in anticipated fashions. This specific situation had resulted in the convergence of protests of many individuals with a hope to eliminate the common obstacles that had made their progress in private life and career difficult or even impossible to achieve.

There are numerous personal recollections and anecdotes of everyday people's life in the mid-1970s. These include those who have since 1977 and 1978 established themselves in different fields and in different ways. Liu Chuanzhi, the founder of China's Lenovo Group, made the following comments, focusing on the impact of the Cultural Revolution on people:

> Some people believe that the 'Cultural Revolution' attacked those in power, and they are wrong! The 'mass movement' is actually the fooling and using the masses. The masses were foolishly stirred up, and they themselves became the most miserable of sufferers. Why did so many people go to Tiananmen Square, like a volcanic eruption, during the April 5th Movement to commemorate Premier Zhou in 1976? This was because they couldn't find any other better ways to survive. (Liu 2012, n.p.)

Wang Juntao, who was detained because of his participation in the April 5th Movement and has, since the early 1990s, exiled in the United States, believes that individuals shared the following views:

> In fact, almost all or the vast majority of people in Beijing at that time were opposed to the Gang of Four and Mao Zedong. You didn't need to have any sophisticated consciousness

about it, as everyone thought and talked about [the situation] like that. I therefore believe that the Lin Biao Incident was a turning point, and in 1975 the discontent had reached its peak. (Wang 2014a, n.p.)

In actual life, the sent-down youth issue was still alive in 1976, while the worker–peasant–soldier university students were still chosen based on the recommendations of CCP's local branches. These two key issues had also acted behind the people's growing discontent as these key problems were representative of the hated inequality between the privileged members of society and the underprivileged groups. Despite the tolerance of frontline officials towards the sent-down youth who still lived in rural areas (Shen 2017), doctor certificates for seeking to return to the cities of origin were still required, while many had no choice but to remain in rural areas. The April 5th Movement was partly fuelled by the widespread anger over the above two issues, as well as the resettlement problems confronted by the sick returnees of sent-down students in their home cities (McLaren 1979; Gold 1980; Harmel and Yeh 2016).

As noted, the sent-down drive and the quiet and slow departure of the party-state systems at different levels from the Maoist approach to allow many sent-down urban students to return to their places of origin had not only drastically altered the dynamics of the sent-down campaign, but had also started a long trend of suspecting and distrusting official information, ideas and publicities. In the eyes of some people who went through those unhappy years, the attitudes of China's population as a whole have since become both cynical and critical of any new claims and promises, which have helped dispel the blind faith in not only Mao as the great leader, but of the party as a leading force, and the political system as the only option.

While people's political tastes and desires were rapidly changing, the effects of which were reflected in their conversation topics, attitudes and behaviours towards a range of key issues, there were not, however, many options on China's political menu at the time. The whole population was once again forced to partake in a new nationwide campaign as they were repeatedly in the previous decade from 1966, which had eventually made the different stances of both sides of the new political campaign the only options for the public to choose from. This fresh intraparty political fight was formally called the campaign to criticise Deng Xiaoping and counter the Right-deviationist trend to reverse the verdicts reached by the Maoist leadership (MacFarquhar and Schoenhals 2006; Dikötter 2016). The long name of this campaign had once again shown the conceptual inability of Maoists to read the people's minds and articulate their stance believably. Instead, the campaign launched in early February 1976, directly after the funeral of Zhou Enlai, was to criticise and eliminate Deng Xiaoping, the newly reinstated frontline leader, from the central leadership. More stupid than removing Deng was to blame him for rectifying a wide range of apparent economic problems. Deng's option to rectify various problems was in fact welcomed and supported by people from almost all walks of life in the mid-1970s.

As a result, a high percentage of the population was united in anger at placing the national economy and their livelihoods second, behind Mao's personal reputation. In terms of this change, Chen Ziming was right to state that the Chinese people were then united 'under the banner of Deng Xiaoping' (Chen 2006c, n.p.). Specifically, Mao and his followers found Deng's approach, which was summarised as *Yi sanxiang zhishi weigang* (Taking the three directives as the guideline), dishonest and problematic. They regarded Deng's real tactics as a revision of what Mao had opted to do in the past. However, as shown in the quotation below, Deng's actual focus on economic development had won the popular support:

> Comrade Mao Zedong has recently given us three crucial directives. First, study theories and combat and prevent revisionism. Second, achieve stability and unity. Third, boost the economy. These three directives, being related to one another, form an organic whole and none of them should be left out. They form the key guideline for our work for the present period. [...] We have a lot to do. There are many aspects of the international struggle that demand attention, and there are also a lot to do domestically, especially to improve the national economy. (Deng 1975, n.p.)

The above final point was overwhelmingly welcomed since Mao's worry about revisionism was not a concern of almost the entire population after the 9/13. People were not pleased at all with the living conditions and the national economy. In the words of one interviewee, the discontent became so strong in the mind of the general public that the prevailing mindset of *panbi xinli*, to do or to achieve whatever others do, was found impossible to operate. 'We became all so stretched financially that nobody could make you feel jealous or envious. There was only one nemesis that had made it impossible to focus on the improvements of our living conditions and our future' (Interviewee 5 2020). That nemesis was publicly referred to as the Gang of Four, Mao's ideological believers; but everyone, including Mao, knew that the storm of public outrage aimed at Mao and his governance approach (Lu 2010; Weng 2015). This is why a large group of scholars have agreed that the essence of the April 5th Movement was a mass revolt against the ultra-left policy of the Cultural Revolution (Yang 2006).

   The above understanding of the April 5th Movement is apparently an underestimation of its political–historical significance. All the strong and stormy social reactions in the first half of 1976 had also demonstrated an assortment of ideas and opinions about what was wrong in the country's politics and what should be done in addition to articulating anger to what had happened then. It would be even more critical than the revolt against the Cultural Revolution if considering that the April 5th Movement was a nationwide movement, such as the protests in Nanjing. A set of the most frequently and widely used expressions at the time was *minxin*, or *minyi* (the hearts of the people and the public opinion). Not only did the young activists from outside the party-state system believed that the 1976 Tiananmen Incident had clearly revealed the hearts of the people, but many working within the CCP and the PLA had also seen the people's demands of change, as pointed out by Chen Ziming (2006b). Since the late 1990s, a large number of books and articles have been published by those working in China, but focusing on the changes from 1976 to 1978. For example, *The Great Turning Point* by Zhang Shujun (1998), *Looking Back at 1978* by Tong Qinglin (2008) and *Deng Xiaoping Changed China* by Ye Yonglie (2008). These have all recognised and praised the helpful role of the 1976 Tiananmen Incident in forming a new nationwide political consensus on what to rectify and how to rectify in post-Mao China.

The constructive role of what took place in 1976 was put another way by a few interviewees. Specifically, what people had held back had burst out of their silence and the explosion of public anger had brought to light fresh and helpful ideas, revealing what was described as *minxin, dangxin* and *junxin* (the hearts of the people, the CCP members, and soldiers and PLA leaders). Among the many positive outcomes, at least the following points are worth mentioning as they are helpful in understanding why the 1976 Tiananmen Incident should be seen as collective repositionings.

First, there was indeed an emergence of different socio-political forces in China from its extremely rigid social structure that was once described in Chinese as 'a solid iron board'. The utopian nature of the CCP's governance ideas and practices, as well as their length of time and the radicalisation tendency, had alienated a big proportion of the general population, especially those faithful supporters of the CCP's ideals. Even though this point was often advocated by some political activists, such as Chen Ziming (2006b), it was not only a true change in society, but also a very useful clue to understanding what has taken place in China since the mid-1970s. At a micro social level, the emergence of new socio-political forces seemed to be nothing more than the aggregation of many personal preferences and choices that had emerged in their social positionings and repositionings.

In my conversations with some interviewees, the newly emerged forces, especially activists, were regarded as a mixture of those who calculated their individual benefit and loss first, and then decided to undertake a big calculation at a societal level. In other words, there was a transference from personal social repositionings to collective ones in the minds of aspirational people. Because of the analytical usefulness of this point, more will be discussed in later sections and chapters. For example, the period after the incident and the death of Mao had seen the easing of social class lines, or the clear decrease in the strictness of class structures and the fictitious dominance of the worker–peasant–soldier alliance. This change will be considered in detail shortly in the last and third section of this chapter.

Second, the mass rallies and protests throughout the first half of 1976 were believed to be an affirmation of both Deng Xiaoping's rectification strategy, which was put in practice in 1975, and its focus on the economy. Within the days from late March to early April 1976, numerous wreaths, big-character posters and banners were placed in Tiananmen Square and surrounding areas. Among them, a very large number of posters directed their condemnation at the Gang of Four, such as, down with Jiang Qing, Yao Wenyuan and Zhang Chunqiao, Mao's most trusted radicals. There were also posters referring to Mao himself and his leadership in a way of criticising Qin Shihuang, the first ruler of a united China. The posters and fuming speeches did not only call for the end of Qin Shihuang's style of rule – which was identical to what was mentioned in the 571 Outline – but also openly praised Deng Xiaoping. In his book, Tong Qinglin mentioned the following story: 11 years later, when Deng talked about the 1976 event with foreign visitors, he said that when the people mourned Premier Zhou, many also supported him. 'It proves that the reforms from 1974 to 1975 were popular and reflected the people's wishes' (Tong 2008, 9).

Third, the public support for Deng's rectification policies in 1975 had also helped develop clear reform strategies to guide the changes adopted after Mao's death in September 1976. Dengist reform was not a result of sudden revelation or enlightenment. Instead, Dengist pragmatic view was extracted, or refined, from the past experience of the 1950s and 1960s and what reformers tried to rectify in 1974 and 1975. The latter effort alone was a comprehensive strategy, covering a range of new and bold decisions to rectify agricultural issues, major industries, science and technology institutions, culture and education sectors, and personnel and leadership issues of both the CCP and the PLA. Cheng Zhongyuan, a specialist in CCP history, defines the 1975 rectification as an experiment for China's post-Mao reform. This understanding is shared by Jiang Zemin, who also pointed out that 'the essence of this [1975] rectification was an experiment for the later reform. […] The success of the rectification and the strength of Deng's determination in the rectification had won the hearts of the party, the military and the people, laying a broad mass basis for crushing the Gang of Four' (cited in Cheng 2015, 26).

Among a range of strategies executed by Deng Xiaoping in 1975, the rectification of education system might well benefit young people, which heartened young aspirational people to support the changes advocated by Deng. In the eyes of those who lived through those years, the education rectification did in fact imply a set of likely changes to rectify commonly disliked policies, including the class status of intellectuals, the procedure and criteria of selecting university students and the effect of family class status on young people's education and career opportunities. At this point, it becomes clear that Deng was supported because his policies met the needs of social positionings or repositionings of many individuals. In the Nanjing University Chronicle, three key changes in 1975 are identified: strengthening teaching and research, implementing the CCP's policy on intellectuals and restoring normal university activities (History Museum 2020). In her long memoir published 2013, Deng Rong, Deng's youngest daughter, discussed that Deng's stance on intellectuals was one of the key reasons her father became a focus of the April 5th Movement of commemorating Zhou Enlai. Deng was accused of intentionally spreading Mao's comments incorrectly: the 'Old Nine cannot leave' (Deng 2013). This was, in fact, hailed by almost all educated people and those hoping for the changes to the CCP's social class classification system.

Restoring the University Entrance Examination

The people who supported Deng Xiaoping's rectifications and demanded his return to leadership were soon rewarded with a string of sweeping changes. One of the most profound changes that have been celebrated by several generations of everyday Chinese citizens over the recent decades was the decision to restore the university entrance examination system in September 1977, just one year after Mao's death. This change was a significant decision for numerous reasons. In terms of societal functionality, the re-establishment of the university entrance examination practice re-activated individual-based competitive positionings and repositionings in society, bringing more normal practices and social orders than Maoist utopian ideas and practices back into Chinese

society. Of course, it occurred and enabled many other changes, including the reintroduction of the notion that intellectuals are part of the working class and the abolition of
the social class classification system.

Deng Xiaoping returned to his previous leadership role in July 1977, and within days
after his return, he initiated and led a national working forum on science and education development. It was at this multi-days working forum that the university entrance
examination system was decided to be reintroduced in 1977, and the 16-character guiding principle for selecting university students was discussed, but revised by Deng. The
original 16-character guiding principle that was proposed in June 1977 included four
main steps or measures: voluntary application, approval by the leader, strict examination and selection based on merit. At the working forum, Deng suggested to remove the
second phrase, a key measure of placing the CCP in control. In Deng's eyes, studying
at university is the right of each young person and, if they could pass exams, everyone
should be given an opportunity to study at university (Liu 2007; Wen 2007).

The prioritisation of the reintroduction of the entrance examination into China's
higher education system was not simply the policy answer required to deal with the
educational stagnation, but the political answer to a series of mistakes made by Mao's
leadership since at least the early 1960s.

Cui Weiping, a female sent-down student who passed the entrance exam in Jiangsu
in late 1977 and went to study at Nanjing University, and since then became a professor and a famed social critic while teaching at Beijing Film Academy, once argued that
what took place in 1977 had a political dimension, which had touched upon almost
everyone in China. She lately offered the following explanation about it:

> In just one or two years, the ropes that had tied numerous people up for so many years
> were unknotted. Thousands of people who were deported to invisible corners could finally
> walk under the sun and enjoy the same blue sky as others. [...] Efforts to politically restore
> the equal status of citizens were also reflected in the reinstitution of the university entrance
> examination in 1977. The exclusion of young people from certain family backgrounds from
> attending university started before the Cultural Revolution. When the students of years
> 1977 and 1978 with a vast age difference enroled at universities, university teaching was
> resumed, and the dignities of teachers and knowledge were also recreated. [...] It was a
> thawing moment, [...] and driven by [a goal of] 'political reconciliation', the reconciliation
> [of the CCP] with intellectuals could be seen as an important step in its reconciliation with
> the entire society. (Cui 2008, n.p.)

As a political priority in the immediate aftermath of the return of Deng Xiaoping to
leadership, the second national working conference on university admission was held
after the above top-level forum. Despite the reluctance from some officials promoted
under Mao's leadership, the decision that the university entrance examination would be
held nationwide over the month from late November to late December was made and
announced in late October 1977. As partly revealed in Table 3.3, there were over 5.7
million young people nationwide taking part in the examination in 1977, and 270,000
of them were admitted to university (Liu 2007; Ye 2008). Despite that a vast majority
of young people were unable to meet the university entrance requirements, the action

of running open examinations was both socially and politically meaningful for reviving people's confidence in society.

The political reconciliation, as Cui Weiping calls it, seems to refer to the three changes frequently mentioned and applauded by many Chinese in recent decades.

First, the procedure of selecting and enrolling the so-called worker–peasant–soldier students to university was commonly seen as an unfair practice. This was largely because they were granted this benefit without appropriate examinations and relying only on the approval and endorsement of the local leadership. This practice made the chances of studying at university being widely believed to have grasped and shared among their own networks. Many memoirs recorded that, at one meeting to discuss the university issues, Deng even angrily warned that 'we also need to pay attention to social fairness' (cited in Jiang and Tang 2014, n.p.). According to two researchers from the CCP's Party History and Documents Research Office, Deng was cited to have also said the following:

> No matter how many university students will be recruited, they must take the exam, and we cannot enrol them if they fail the exam. No matter whose children they are, even those from the families [of some senior leaders] we cannot enrol them [without passing the exam], and they cannot go through the back door. (Cited in Long and Zhang 2016, n.p.)

Deng even said that his own children should not be given the chance to attend university if failing the exam. His warning on the importance of blocking the back door indirectly implied Mao, who admitted helping several young people enrol in universities on a few occasions (Chen 2011). In the eyes of Deng, the university entrance examination was not simply a decision about the exam, but a correct response to the demands of the general public for social fairness.

Second, the reintroduction of the university entrance examination had also resulted in the bold policy initiatives of dismantling the social class classification system that had long been imposed by Mao's generation on many Chinese people. This social class labelling system had been one of the most divisive social control measures in post-1949 China, which had momentarily aided those who partook in revolution to be advantageously positioned in a changing social environment. The system was radicalised through the Maoist class struggle politics, and it was also cruelly used by many from new advantaged groups – in the 1960s and part of the 1970s – to uphold their dominance in an increasing social competition. Specifically, the new ruling elites had used the social class classification system as the political and mental shackles to restrain the competitors or rivals so as to dominate or even monopolise social resources and the distributions. As a medium- or long-term outcome of the self-interested use of the system by some privileged, a much more serious challenge emerged: fewer people believed in the utopian ideals that the new ruling elites promoted.

The gradual declining of faith in the regime could be deteriorated to a point where the new PRC would sink into a deeper crisis. For the sake of the regime, a compromise had to be devised, even sacrificing the interests of some privileged groups. According to Long Pingping from the CCP's Party History and Documents Research Office and his co-workers, in 1977 Deng also criticised *chengfen lun* (the bloodline theory or the theory of social class origins) as follows:

> In the past few years, we have set so many strict restrictions on the evaluation of people, among which the most absurd is the Bloodline Theory and the Class Origin Theory. [...] Changing the requirements of the political examinations is to break shackles imposed on the educable [or reformable] young people because of their family origins and social connections, and give them equal opportunities to compete. [...] There are two main criteria for selecting [university] students: the first is their own good performance, and the second is merit. Not only the university enrolment needs to be like this, but in the future, it should gradually expand to all recruitment: soldiers, workers, promotions, and so on. (Cited in Long et al. 2014, Chapters 44 and 45)

These reformists were correct in seeing the coming of a legitimacy crisis, which was then called the crisis of belief and faith. Many Maoist ideas sounded utopian, but they were in reality very divisive, favouring their own supporters by depriving others from their rights. The reform to the university admission system softened the negative impact of the faith crisis on the recovery of the late 1970s.

Third, the restoration of the university entrance examination also meant the reconciliation with intellectuals, or the right step and action of revising the Maoist understanding and policies regarding intellectuals. As commented by Cui Weiping at the start of this section, the reconciliation with intellectuals – who were ridiculed as the stinking nine in the ninth category of class enemies – was the important step in the ruling elites' reconciliation with the entire society. From the social mobility perspective, this was one of the main steps to restore some sense of normality in people's life. China has long been a society that relies on the *keju* (imperial examination system) to allow some aspirational young people from a lower socio-economic status or background to position themselves in a higher or better social position. Under rule of the PRC, the university entrance examination, as a contemporary version of the old *keju* system, was considered to be almost the only social ladder to allow the young people from non-revolutionary or politically problematic family backgrounds to position themselves in a relatively and moderately better position than they would otherwise be able to climb. What was more disturbing to educated people, or people who wanted to be educated, than the importance of university entrance examination was that more education would degrade them to the ninth category of social reactionaries. Therefore, Maoist anti-intellectualism had created a contradiction in society, precisely in people's lives, where many people would like to be educated and climb to, or stay at, higher social places, but once they were educated, they would be alienated by anti-intellectualism and the politics of social classes.

Such an irrational thinking and its subsequent irrational social norm had fundamentally overturned people's existing beliefs and confidence, leading to the blockage of upward social mobility of many aspirational people. One of the most likely resolutions to such a social impasse would have been the overthrowing of the existing rule and the ruling class behind it. A Chinese saying warns that the water can carry a boat, but it can also overturn it. This was China's situation in the mid-1970s, which was why the new leadership had to act decisively to put a stop to anti-intellectualism and restore normality back into society.

Because of such swift and sweeping policy changes, people's views and approaches to their own social position and repositionings had also started recurring and converting along with the trends and dynamics in post-Mao China. In addition to the above political reconciliation stance, the most fundamental change from the competitive social repositioning point of view should be the resurgence and revitalisation of individual-based social positionings or repositionings. The latter was seen to have swiftly resumed its previous form and status that were widely observed during the years leading up to the Cultural Revolution.

As an outcome, these new rounds of social repositionings were less characterised by the utopian ideals and practices portrayed by Maoists, such as showing a great enthusiasm for being a CCYL or CCP member, or performing in an obsequious or flattering manner towards anyone in leadership. Driven by the anger towards the despotism and suppression suffered during the previous 10 years, young people who had never before displayed growing individualism and strong confidence in themselves started changing their values and beliefs, as well as attitudes and behaviours of almost every aspirational Chinese citizen.

A few interviewees pointed out that while many able and ambitious young people were devoting attention to the new university selection policy and practice, the attention of many urban factory workers was drawn to the bonuses that they had never earned before. Many rural families were, at the same time, immersed in the cheerfulness and eagerness of having their rights of using the newly decollectivised land and the chance to undertake other moneymaking activities. The interest and attention of people were not only attracted by the new policies but, more importantly, by the efforts of many other people to reposition themselves in the new social reality. What was abandoned was a set of social conducts that were encouraged in Mao's years. One interviewee noted the following:

> If you could dig out more statistics, you would definitely see that in the two or three years [after 1976], there were fewer people who wanted to join the party, and fewer students writing and submitting applications for membership in the Youth League [than many did]. It seemed that no one had heard of anyone mentioning these things anymore. Not only was there a resentment that everyone had stopped doing those things, but everyone was striving to do something very different. People were vying for university entrance exams, trying to return to home cities as sick returnees from rural villages, or looking for better jobs. It was also no longer popular for people from cadre families to join the army, and it once again became a way-out for rural youth. (Interviewee 41 2019)

One has to admit the reformed university system put many young people from the so-called problematic family backgrounds in an advantageous position over those from families with less experience in education or with less intellectual capital. According to Zheng Ruoling, a professor at Xiamen University, a large proportion of those who passed the university entrance examinations in 1977 and 1978 were from the families in the so-called academic circles, accounting for more than 25 per cent and 23 per cent, respectively (Zheng 2007). Many people can still remember that local cadres had responded to this fine-tuning more strongly and negatively than others. This seems to be because they not only disagreed with the change to the class-based university selection, but also hated to see their authority to decide who could study at university deprived. What these low-ranking cadres did not realise was that there was always an adjustment and adaptation process or interaction between the ruling elites and the vast majority of general public. When the regime was under threat by the latter, their status and power of influence had to be constrained as a sacrifice to the survival of the regime.

While low-ranking cadres were not happy, it was surprising that many young people who had partaken in the university entrance exams and failed in 1977 onwards did not respond to the new policy as strongly and negatively as many cadres or officials at grass-roots levels. This resulted from two factors according to several interviewees. One factor seemed to be their basic respect to the fairness of the reinstated examination practice, while the other was that many of them had already foreseen the rise of other new opportunities and chosen to reposition themselves in society through other means. The former existed at the time partly because of the overwhelming support by the general public for the new university entrance practice. The latter was new in the late 1970s, and these fresh options will be analysed in Chapter five.

Towards the late autumn of 1978, the second group of new university students had completed their enrolment and started their long-anticipated university life on campus, except those who were later admitted into new university campuses through the enrolment expansion plan (Wang 2017a; Zhang 2019). While a large number of young people, students and those who graduated earlier, were busy in preparing for the next round of university entrance exams, there were various other social positionings taking place among the less academically inclined young people and families. That is, after a couple of years of excitement, the late 1970s and early 1980s saw not only the opening of higher education for young people from different backgrounds and the abolition of the CCP's old class policy, but also the positioning effort of those who were unable or unwilling to be part of the new social order, including seeking new business opportunities in newly opening markets.

Notes

1. There are some general information about this famous summer mountain resort in note 2 of Chapter one. This particular Lushan Conference held in late August and early September 1970 is also called the Second Plenum of the Ninth CCP Central Committee. This was the last nationally significant conference that ever held in this mountain resort because of the disastrous consequences of two conferences held there in both 1959 and 1970. At the 1970 Lushan conference, the main divisive issue was Lin Biao's support to reinstate the president's position of the PRC, but he and his supporters overlooked Mao's seeming reluctance. The Chinese phrase for the state presidency is *Zhuxi* (Chairman), which was exactly same as Mao's title of the chairman of the CCP's Central Committee. Of course, Lin Biao was not directly criticised during the Lushan conference, nor were his supporters from the PLA, but his non-military supporters, for example, Chen Boda, and a set of topics raised by Chen at the conference were strongly denounced, staging a political showdown that is described in Chinese as *qiaoshan zhenhu* (hitting the mountain to warn the tiger). This was the start of the

open rivalry between Mao and Lin. Interested readers are referred to Teiwes and Sun (1996), Qiu (1999) and Mao (2017).

2. There have been different accounts about this 9/13 incident, including assassination speculations, but most analyses show that Lin Biao refused to admit mistakes after the 1970 Lushan conference while Maoists, supported by Zhou Enlai, launched a new nationwide campaign to criticise Chen Boda in late 1970 and the first half of 1971. As a result, Lin Biao openly embarrassed Mao by arriving late to the 1971 May Day celebration in Tiananmen Square and leaving early without a word. Mao decided to have another southern inspection tour from early August 1971 to do the preparation for removing Lin Biao. Although Lin's supporters had also prepared a set of countermeasures, Lin and his wife and son eventually opted to flee by plane. The 9/13 incident was a big wake-up call to most Chinese people and the end of the myth of Mao. For more information, readers are referred to Teiwes and Sun (1996), Qiu (1999) and MacFarquhar and Schoenhals (2006).

3. This novel was also translated as *Outlaws of the Marsh, All Men are Brothers*, and its original name in Chinese is *Shuihu Zhuan*. Mostly written by Shi Nai'an in an early form of vernacular Chinese in the fourteenth century, this novel has been regarded as one of the four great classical novels in Chinese. It is a story about a group of 108 bandits who gather at Mount Liang during the late Song Dynasty (960–1279) and form a sizeable army to rebel. Because the story is about outlaws and rebellions, an old and famous Chinese saying warns that the young people should not read *Water Margin* (while the old should not read *Romance of the Three Kingdoms*). For more general information, interested readers are referred to McMahon (1988) and Ge (2001). Interested readers can also read the English translation of the novel.

4. It seems to me to be necessary to point out that 1976 was a leap year and the Tomb Sweeping Day of that particular year was on 4 April, not on 5 April as the Tomb Sweeping Day, or Qingming Jie in Chinese, is normally on. This was why the 1976 Tiananmen Movement was initially called the Qingming Movement, but later on, more people call it the April 5th Movement in order to accurately record and reflect what happened in Tiananmen Square on 5 April 1976.

5. The so-called Gang of Four (*Siren Bang*) refers to four radical Maoists who were used by Mao during the Cultural Revolution to execute his political ideas and tactics in order to achieve his political goals. The group was headed by Jiang Qing, Mao's last wife; Zhang Chunqiao; Yao Wenyuan and Wang Hongwen. The last three had all worked in Shanghai before being promoted to the central leadership in Beijing. Because Jiang Qing was once also living in Shanghai when she was an actress, the group was, therefore, originally called *Shanghai Bang* (the Gang of Shanghai, the Shanghai Clique or the Shanghai Faction) among veteran leaders including Mao himself. The Gang of Four was in fact nothing more than Mao's attacking dogs in the words of Jiang Qing (Qiu 1999, 148). They were so unpopular and widely hated that the final end of Mao's Cultural Revolution was eventually marked by the arrest of them within a month of Mao's death. Because of their evil reputation in Chinese politics, there are many publications about them and their conducts. In addition to Qiu (1999), readers are also referred to MacFarquhar and Fairbank (1991), (Huang 2000) and Yang (2018).

Chapter Five

BATTLING FOR THE ADVANTAGES UNDER THE DENGIST POLITICAL ALLIANCES

The social consequence of the change to the central leadership in certain authoritarian systems is, to a great extent, similar to that of regime change. Both could lead to the abrogation of power and privileges of some people and the creation of new opportunities for others. As pointed out in Chapter four, a number of political obstacles were swiftly removed in response to the demands made by hundreds of thousands of people in the 1976 Tiananmen Incident. Apart from a small group of radical leftists, including the Gang of Four, who were politically dumped or punished, the vast majority of people were happy to see a time for changes both in their personal life and in society more generally. The latter was clearly seen in rural villages, where the rigid rule of organising rural production was relaxed, with the politically incorrect activities of selling and buying surplus agricultural produces. In the cities, as analysed in Chapter four, many people's attention was drawn to the renewed university entrance system, which not only provided young people with a chance to study at university, but also relaxed some related restrictions.

These new social dynamics slowly transformed the rest of the late 1970s and early 1980s into a situation where more people from different backgrounds or political persuasions were allowed to try to position, or reposition, themselves in their anticipated places in society, but also to conduct it in their own ways and capabilities. Such new massive-scale social repositionings, in turn, transformed the conditions of social actions and performances of individuals, and the dynamics of their social positionings as well. The latter was characterised by an increasing number of highly motivated citizens and their attempts for the advantages under the Dengist leadership.

This chapter analyses to these changes and people's new repositioning efforts in the early years of China's post-Mao reform and opening up, which started in 1978. To help readers understand the social conditions of people's repositioning, a few more general changes need to be taken into consideration. Within the first few years, numerous Chinese had opted to throw themselves in the new, open and competitive societal environment generated by many new measures before reforms run into their first momentous trouble in the mid-1980s, which was a small but meaningful turning point in our examination. China entered the second main stage of the rural reform in 1985, which was characterised by the bold decision to end the state monopoly over the purchasing of key agricultural produces, with the strategic determination of permitting more money to flow to the agricultural sector. This desirable policy to lift price controls contributed significantly to a sudden and huge rise in inflation.

However, before the inflation issue was politicised, in the second half of the 1980s, China had rapidly evolved into a society that was full of competitions and inspired citizens. Two forms of political partnership, if not social class alliance, were formed between the reformist ruling elites and both the intellectuals and the rural residents, respectively. At the same time, in spite of the loud claims by the new leadership with regard to the elimination of dangerous militant radical leftists from the party-state system, many Mao's devoted followers at the grassroots level, especially those so-called *sanzhong ren* (three categories of Cultural Revolutionary radical activists), were in fact not treated in a retaliatory way. These people had not only survived the purge, but soon also contributed to the complexities of the post-1978 socio-political life. Although these Maoists were unable to return to politics, their orthodox leftist views were shared by those who were better off before 1978 than after that. The situation had eventually safeguarded, if not created an ideological battlefront which was not only different from the reformist stance, but had also kept Maoism alive in a reforming China.

These changes and people's repositioning efforts will be discussed in the following four sections. The first section considers a special aspect of the social dynamics or political activism, which non-Chinese journalists and observers have called 'the Xidan Democracy Wall Movement'. The movement took place in the very late 1970s and was not in tune with the general enthusiasm about new opportunities in society. However, the push represented the continuation of popular street politics, as well as the strong liberal tendency in post-Mao China. The second section looks at what occurred to peasants and workers as their life was profoundly changed by various reform policies; many of their social repositioning efforts have been commonly regarded as a start of the new entrepreneurialism in China. In fact, China's first cohort of new business owners and operators was mostly from these two portions of the population. The third section examines the crucial issue of the new university students, who were seemingly the most hopeful group of citizens in post-Mao China and also well regarded by the general public, but their liberal leanings, or objections to the various aspects of China's politics and long-existing ideology, gradually made them less favoured by an increasing number of conservative party-state leaders. This change was first shown in the campus-based election attempted by some students in the early 1980s, which caused a strong reaction from CCP conservatives, criticising the university students for being politically unreliable or untrustworthy. The fourth and final section turns attention to how the worker–peasant–soldier university students were treated by the post-Mao leadership as they were seen as direct competitors of post-Mao university students for leadership positions in China.

Devoting to a New but Less Popular Activism

Certain ideas or schools of thought that are favoured and shared by some members of a society are often called ideological or social trends of thought. An analysis may be needed to observe the overall social trend and situation, but the problem has been that many have always observed and examined Chinese society from a macro-level perspective, or precisely, according to abstract notions. This has long been an epistemological trap in the study of social changes in China, resulting in an analytical deviation, if not bias, that is exactly opposite to the problem of being unable to see the forest for the trees. In the case of post-1978 China, any social trends, including ideological ones, seemed to have been all based on the options that many people preferred to have and their subsequent actions to positioning themselves accordingly in an actual social situation. Therefore, the various trends of ideas could be regarded as abstract summaries of people's different ideological preferences or options, as well as their repositioning efforts in a changing society. Before a trend becomes clear and popular, it starts as the changes that are generated by people's new preferences, life choices and their subsequent repositionings.

The Xidan Democracy Wall Movement happening in Beijing in 1978 and 1979 was the first case of this nature in post-Mao China. It has long been regarded as an important democracy movement in the history of the PRC. Partakers and some foreign journalists working in China in the late 1970s helped to make this episode of youth activism well known globally. Inspired by an emerging and widespread interest in liberal ideas and the long-anticipated freedom as a strong and retaliatory reaction to the Maoist political control before 1976, several different groups of young people chose to devote their time, energies and talents to activism. They would give kerbside speeches and put up posters in a small area outside the wall of the then Xidan Sportsground, which was only a couple of hundred metres away from Zhongnanhai, the garden compound for the headquarters of China's central leadership. The movement occurred while a large proportion of young Chinese were focusing on preparing for the university entrance examination or coping with their study of new university courses in the case of those who already passed the university entrance exams and were enrolled at universities.

Table 5.1 reveals a parallel focus of societal interest generated by the newly restored university entrance examination policy and practice at the same time as some activists flocked to and gathered in streets near Xidan, Beijing. Of course, this table should be read along with Table 3.3 despite some repetitions.

Table 5.1 The total number of people taking the university entrance exam, 1977–87.

Year	Number of Universities	Number of Exam Participants (k)	Number of Enrolled (k)	Enrolment Rate (%)
1977	404	5,700	273	4.8
1978	598	6,100	402	6.6
1979	633	4,680	280	5.9
1980	675	3,330	280	8.4
1981	704	2,590	280	10.8
1982	715	1,370	320	17.1
1983	805	1,670	390	23.4
1984	902	1,640	480	29.3
1985	1,016	1,760	619	35.2
1986	1,054	1,910	570	29.8
1987	1,063	2,280	620	27.2
Total		33,530	4,514	

Sources: Compiled by the author based on NBSC (1999), Zhao (2016b), Ministry of Education (2020) and Tencent.com (2021).

Because of the general public's attention to the university entrance policy changes, as well as many other available new opportunities in 1978 and 1979, this streetside mass movement attracted far fewer people than the 1976 Tiananmen Incident, but it was still a major draw of public attention and it fascinated many young bystanders. Importantly, this short-lived campaign sowed some seeds of liberal idealism and democratic expectations, inserting them as a core issue into China's social change in the decades afterwards. As will be analysed later, this movement also influenced many university students who did not only flock to streets near Xidan, but later also repeated similar ideas and actions. However, this whole episode was rather controversial from the outset. One of the earliest remarks was that these activists seemed to be a group of youth who might have failed to pass the university entrance examination in December 1977 or those who were no confident in taking the next round of exam in July 1978. Such a negative remark sounds like gossip, but it was not only widespread in the late 1970s, but also considered to be partly factual in terms of time coincidence and the drawing power of the restored university entrance system as indicated in Table 5.1. The table confirms that over those two years alone, there were many millions of young people who had focused on trying the chance of going to study at universities.

Despite these negative comments, what happened in Xidan in 1978 and 1979 was still the life choice option, or the career activist path, that interested many ambitious young and middle-aged people. This was also not a mass-gathering action by Beijing residents only; in fact, it was initiated by a few young people from the remote Guizhou province, who came to Beijing in October 1978 in order to promote their new self-published periodical. Therefore, this whole movement was an effort of some politically ambitious people to take advantage of this period of relaxed political controls in the mid-1970s. Many documentary accounts of the campaign do not reflect this aspect, sounding nothing but the fact they were spreading and advancing freedom or liberty and democracy. In reality, it also revealed some other career advancement options or ladders that some people found convenient for themselves to position themselves in a rapidly restructuring society.

The key elements of these activists' efforts as new options seemed to have at least included three approaches: forming their own groups or organisations, promoting their own publications and spreading their own political views.

First, the creation and expansion of their own groups or organisations clearly characterised this movement, which had therefore made itself very different from what happened in Beijing in 1976. Through their self-published materials and big-character posters, some bystanders had from the beginning sensed that some activists were promoting not only various new ideas and opinions, but also their new organisations or groups (Chen 2006a; Hu 2004). The latter was the key difference between this political campaign and the 1976 Tiananmen Incident, which had even made many liberal-minded citizens feel alert and alarmed. Many urban Chinese, especially educated ones, have long leaned towards democracy and liberal ideas over many elements of Chinese political traditions since the May Fourth Movement in 1919,[1] but many had also learned their lessons before the end of Mao's era in 1976; one of them being political taboos that they should never contemplate establishing any organised groups outside the current

ruling elite circles or taking any organised actions without approvals. The relaxed political climate of post-Mao years made some people forget many political taboos, but focus
on pursuing what they would like to do. There were more than a dozen self-organised
associations and groups that have been documented in different memoirs and articles,
including some with plans to form their own political party (Qian 2012; Weng 2016;
Zhang 2016).

The reason why this campaign did not actually attract more partakers than the
1976 movement, apart from the other emerging opportunities, is that China was changing and becoming different from its 1919 version. Not only was there a rising revolution
fatigue, or campaign fatigue, since the early 1970s, but this fresh general realisation was
also leading a big number of liberal-minded people to become less sympathetic to some
political conducts. This is why a few interviewees who were interested in certain ideas
of the movement now believe that these Xidan campaigners seemed to wish to repeat
what young Chinese communist revolutionaries did in the 1920s and what Red Guards
did in the 1960s. The interviewees do not think that the failure of the Xidan campaign
can be fully explained by the crackdown by the ruling party; they accept that its fate
was also due to the outdated pursuit and actions taken by Xidan activists, who seemed
to have been largely influenced by China's century-old liberal leftist idea of enlightenment and salvation. The ruling elites under Deng's leadership at the time had, however,
just picked up another century-old approach from the past, which was the pragmatic
approach of national salvation through education and industry. It was also at that time
that the second pragmatic thinking was also rephrased as modernisation in a new popular narrative, which sounded more realistic and attractive to politically fatigued people,
than asking them to accept another set of unproven ideas.

Second, as part of the influence of the century-old enlightenment and salvation idea
and practice, the running and promotion of their own self-published periodicals and
other publications were also preferred by these Democracy Wall activists. According
to Chen Yan, a France-based Chinese analyst, more than fifty privately owned periodicals appeared in Beijing over those couple of years, and more were published and
circulated in other major urban centres (Chen 2006a). Running their own magazines
and other publications was helpful to these activists in quite a few ways, including the
formation of their own networks, the promotion of their own views and the possible
income from running self-published periodicals. Of course, there are not many people,
including those who partook in some activities in 1978 and 1979, who are now able
to recall the names of those publications, except those associated with a few leading
campaigners, such as *Beijing Spring* and Chen Ziming and Wang Juntao, *Today* and Bei
Dao (Zhao Zhenkai) and Mang Ke (Jiang Shiwei), and *Exploration* and Wei Jingsheng.
While the first and third publications were instrumental in helping the founders position themselves as leaders of a new social movement, the second one almost became a
self-reliant business. As the main publication of the so-called misty poetry school, or
obscure poetry school (*Menglong shi*), the second issue of *Today* already had around a
thousand subscribers nationwide, at a fairly high subscription fee. E Fuming, one of the
operators of the magazine, documented in his online memoir how their new adventure
quickly expanded before the government declared it illegal (E 2015).

The person who recommended me to read E Fuming's memoir joked that the *Today* people were actually very entrepreneurial in setting up the business, but they were selling a politically incorrect product at a wrong time. This remark makes sense if comparing the fortune of this magazine business to many rural residents who were then allowed into cities to sell their produce.

Some Xidan activists were also believed to be in a fairly advantageous position compared to that of other partakers in terms of their access to resources and connections with existing elite circles. The access to resources and information is typically defined as social capital, but it can also be utilised as political, or even intellectual, capital. In this case, these asset issues clearly influenced the option of positioning and repositioning efforts of many people. It was due to their assets, and related attitudes as well, that some Xidan activists seemed to have chosen to do something different from the rest of society. One interviewee who defines himself as a casual participant of the Xidan movement offers the following explanations:

> Apart from personal aspiration, which does not always mean good, resources are a decisive factor in determining a person's choices of action. [...] In fact, a high ratio of the Xidan [activist] people were so-called cadres' children, similar to the situation of the Red Guards in 1966. Outsiders might not have noticed their family backgrounds, so they have kept wondering why many Chinese did not join them to fight for freedom and democracy. [...] The family's social status and backgrounds of many Xidan [activist] people provided them with confidence and skills, and their familiarity with politics gave them courage and opportunities. To a great degree, what they did to create organisations and publish publications was exactly the same as what the elder generation did in the 1920s. They did what Chen Duxiu did in publishing *La Jeunesse* (*New Youth*), Mao Zedong did in printing *Xiangjiang Review* and the Red Guards did in 1966. Their resources and networks helped them become active [democracy] fighters, but deterred those without them from partaking. (Interviewee 37 2020)

Third, the most widely used strategy for positioning to be a leading voice and a recognised opinion leader was to spread one's own ideas as unique and as wide as possible. During the Xidan campaign, there were so many people who were not only from different regions and age groups, but also confident they could guide society. Within these competitive social repositioning efforts, there was also a competitive tension that placed pressures on campaigners. Unique views were needed to separate these ambitious protesters. Wei Jingsheng is believed to be one example of such typical cases. He posted an essay on the Xidan wall to promote political democracy as the fifth modernisation, to be added to the ruling party's four modernisation narrative. To promote his opinions, he also started running the magazine *Exploration*. Because of his revolutionary family background, he was not experienced about, and therefore not feared by, frequent contacts with foreign reporters. The latter contacts were then used by the government as the basis for sentencing him to 14-year jail term. He was deported to the United States in 1997.

From a democracy promotion point of view, Wei was a brave person, but from a career ladder standpoint, what Wei did in 1978, as well as the others did then, is regarded by some Chinese as a repeat of the *Gongche shangshu* strategy (writing to the

ruler to enunciate a concern and obtain recognition).[2] It is a long-used method to petition in Chinese history, which has also helped some people achieve their career ambitions. This career shortcut to climb the social ladder has long existed, and it has been
attempted at times by those who prefer to count on one idea or one act, without doing
what is described in Chinese as *shinian hanchuang* (10 years of rigorous study by a cold
window). The latter once again became a preferred social ladder in 1977 and onwards,
which greatly affected people's appreciation and understanding of street activism. In
the eyes of many Chinese people, these campaigners should try to study at university
first or focus on their university study in the case of those enrolled at university. As
revealed in Table 5.1, it was not easy to pass the university entrance examinations in
1977 and onwards, but almost everyone at the time thought it was highly acceptable to
make every effort to take part in it. A few interviewees pointed out that there was a special policy arrangement for those unable to score high in entrance examinations, which
was the creation of many university *fenxiao* (branch campuses) in major cities (Zhang
2019). This approach provided urban youth, many of whom were from families like that
of some Xidan activists, with an additional opportunity to attend university. However,
just like many Red Guards in the mid-1960s, some Xidan activists were believed to be
less gifted in academic work because they were from the families with less intellectual
capital.

There have been at least two big misunderstandings of the movement. The first
misunderstanding is that despite its importance, this was not a large-scale movement,
and its importance was in reality partly decided by what had then taken place in China.
Second, this activist push was closely related to certain ideological options under discussion within the central circles of the CCP. Wu Wei, a former researcher of the CCP's
Political Reform Office, once commented on this as follows:

> In the beginning, some comments appeared on the Xidan Democracy Wall were supported
> by CCP leaders, such as Deng Xiaoping and Ye Jianying. Many of its expressions were
> surprisingly similar to many speeches made at the [CCP] Theoretical Work Conference,
> showing that the people inside and outside the CCP, or inside and outside the Conference,
> shared the same understandings. They were interlinked, responding to, and promoting each
> other. [...] As the debate deepened, the Democracy Wall activists had also become dissatis-
> fied with just posting big-character posters and giving speeches and they started to establish
> organisations, publish publications, organise various forms of gathering. (Wu 2014, n.p.)

While the above remark could also be used to elaborate the role of some activists' family
background in their activism, it is evident that the whole nation was then reflecting on
how to correct or revise Maoist policies and how to turn the sluggish economic situation
around. When searching for the solution, people were divided into different groups.

As noted in Chapter one, these Xidan activists focused on liberalisation and democratisation, and their strong demands sounded flawless to some educated urban residents,
but failed to fascinate economically struggling peasants, who made up more than 80 per
cent of the population at the time. As discussed, this specific political movement also
failed to attract the direct involvement of many other aspirational urban youth, whose
attention had been drawn to a range of new opportunities emerged over the years after

1976, especially the restored university entrance examination from 1977. Because of the other two strong social interests and processes, the Xidan campaign was well known to many people, but less attractive; still, as will be examined in the third section, people cannot deny it as a reality and its potential influence on certain groups of people. In fact, it was not only the new start of Chinese liberalism, but has also been a carrier, or a history marker, to keep liberalism afloat in the process of China's recent social transformation. Its core ideas may have never been appreciated by the masses who were busy making a living, but they have definitely been favoured by many educated individuals, both properly educated and those self-confident in their own knowledge.

Emerging Entrepreneurialism among Peasants and Workers

As hinted out earlier, what had happened in rural China in the immediate years after the end of the Cultural Revolution is a very fascinating topic, clearly characterised by economic liberalism. Together with the reforms made to various industry sectors, the emergence or re-emergence of entrepreneurialism and a large number of entrepreneurs in both rural and urban China is a very big topic that goes well beyond the scope of this section. This analysis is, therefore, made here for the purpose of outlining a fuller picture of how widespread people's social repositioning efforts were in the second half of the 1970s. Through this brief examination, readers should be able to understand that social repositionings are not a luxury or indigence for urban middle class and petit bourgeoisie, and they also take place among rural residents and urban blue-collar workers at a very basic level.

Although the urban bourgeoisie, especially intellectuals and officials, had turned the many changes in their life into a central theme of China's recent social transformation, the crucial changes and powerful dynamics were actually generated in rural China. In 1977, China's total population reached about nine hundred and fifty million, more than eight hundred million of which lived in rural villages. Therefore, apart from poverty, there was also a serious imbalance between rural population and the size of arable land. In the words of an analyst of the CCP's Party History and Documents Research Office, 'there was a serious labour surplus' (Li 2013, n.p.), which deteriorated after the production responsibility system was introduced.

Before the late early 1980s when clearer ideas about how to deal with the rural labour surplus issue had formed, the late 1970s witnessed a few simple but effective policy measures that allowed poor peasants earn additional income elsewhere than from the land to increase their earnings. This was the start of a new socio-economic process that has given rise to two more significant transformations, namely the agricultural production reform and the rural industrialisation. However, as reviewed in Chapter one, the importance of this process has been overshadowed by the attention to both the political and policy changes and the many forms of spontaneous social protest and resistance. Without exaggeration, the latter focuses are actually just the reflections of the various demands made by rural people and what they had been doing then.

From the viewpoint of social positionings of individual peasants, they were all given three types of fresh opportunities to make better earnings, which included selling and buying agricultural produces in rural markets, finding jobs outside their villages or regions and working for or running their own TVEs. Despite these humble beginnings, it is worth noting that the first cohort of new business owners and operators (or 'new riches' as some of them are jealously labelled lately) in post-Mao China was mostly from the peasants who tried to use one or more of these opportunities, especially those running TVEs.

The first new and most accessible opportunity for village residents to earn extra income was the policy relaxation over the control of selling or buying agricultural produces in rural markets or any other outlet. These were illegal in the late 1970s and judged to be a capitalist behaviour in ideological terms, not based on local rules. Among the numerous illegal peasant traders, a well-known case was the man behind the new brand called *Shazi Guazi* (Simpleton's (cooked sunflower) seeds) (Young 2015; deLisle and Goldstein 2019). A local government in Anhui province regarded it as capitalist trading, and it was famously overturned by Deng Xiaoping in order to protect his open market policy. Trading activities in streets alone helped many rural residents become millionaires or even billionaires. One of the often mentioned examples are the Liu Brothers, who ranked as the richest people in China for nearly a decade in the 1990s and 2000s. They started selling quails in small towns and found more business ideas from a streetside repair stall.

Feng Lun, one of China's well-known scholars-turned-developers, recently wrote the following in his WeChat-based periodical to show the past small-good trading experiences of a few Chinese billionaires though they were not typical peasants or workers:

If looking around, you may find that many Chinese entrepreneurs had set up street stalls in the past. Their road to success can be described as bumpy and fascinating. For example, Liu Chuanzhi once pulled a flatbed cart in Zhongguancun to sell sportswear, electronic watches, roller skates, and refrigerators. Ma Yun carried sacks on his shoulder to city of Yiwu to procure flowers, flashlights, underwear, socks, and handicrafts in bulk and peddled them on the streets of Hangzhou; Ren Zhengfei peddled weight-loss products and fire alarms. Often wearing a straw hat and pedalling a flatbed cart, Zong Qinghou drove through small lanes and main streets to sell popsicles and stationeries.[3] (Feng 2020, n.p.)

The data in Table 5.2 show overall socio-economic conditions in the late 1970s and early 1980s, and demystifies why many Chinese people reacted so readily to the many changes that various actions were taken to reposition themselves in a changing social order. This table should be read together with Table 3.2, outlining the rural–urban income divide over much of the Cultural Revolution, and Figure 4.1, displaying in part a general trend of increasing disposable income based on the data of 1978, 1985 and 1990. These figures explain not only why many rural households welcomed the policy of selling and buying agricultural produces, but also why many of them decided to try the next opportunity, earning income elsewhere.

The second opportunity many rural people used was to join what has long been negatively portrayed by urban people as *mangliu renkou* (floating population) to find job opportunities outside their home regions. In more recent years, they have been called *nongmingong* (rural migrant workers or more literally peasant works), but the new

Table 5.2 China's economic growth in GDP and income, 1977–85.

Year	GDP Growth (%)	Urban Annual Income Per Capita (yuan)	Rural Annual Income Per Capita (yuan)
1977	7.57	305	117
1978	11.3	524	220
1979	7.59	612	263
1980	7.83	695	306
1981	5.11	712	349
1982	9.02	753	414
1983	10.8	792	467
1984	15.2	900	522
1985	13.4	1,022	593

Sources: Compiled by the author based on NBSC (1999), Zeng (1999), Fan et al. (2002), Wang (2018b, 2018c) and Li et al. (2019).

phrase has still kept the label to indicate their rural residential status. According to a researcher of the Development Research Centre of China's State Council, the total number of rural migrant workers 'rose from a few million in the 1970s to 30 million in the 1980s' (Zhang 2008c, n.p.). These numbers are believed to be lower than the actual figures, but they are enough to show that these workers have not only played a very significant part in China's recent industrialisation, but have also contributed greatly to urbanisation. What is more significant is that migration and interregional employment have, at the same time, been a decisive step towards achieving numerous goals, including accumulating capital for running their own business and learning the markets. There is a rather large amount of publications, both online and in print, that have documented the life experiences of migrant workers from rural villages. Their numbers have been so substantial that almost all grown-ups in China can tell some stories about them, let alone senior citizens. Many interviewees I have spoken to went to university in 1977 and 1978, and they can still recall the first sighting of new cleaners and gardeners working on campuses from rural areas. While there are so many sad stories in contemporary discourses, many of these workers are rather satisfied with what they benefitted from working away from home, such as the Liu Brothers and many entrepreneurs (Tomba 2011; Sun 2020).

Despite the negativity over rural migrant workers, their earlier groups have been regarded by many researchers as efforts to make use of new chances and to cope with the changing patterns of wealth distribution. Li Qiang, one of my former colleagues at Renmin University of China, and then the head of social sciences at Tsinghua University, once defined the floating population of the late 1970s and 1980s as a category of informal employment and saw the following two positive functions of them:

Informal employment has been the main form of employment for hundreds of millions of rural migrant workers who flow to Chinese cities. We should clearly appreciate the positive social function of informal employment. [...] [In addition,] there is also an existence of low-level elites among rural migrant workers. It would be unfair to adopt a policy of total exclusion for them. (Li 2004, 3)

The third and most recognised new opportunity that emerged in the late mid-1970s was the establishment and development of rural enterprises, which have long been called commune and village workshops and factories, but have lately been named TVEs. Different from the simplified explanation that TVEs were the reform policy to 'let some people get rich first' in the words of Deng Xiaoping, it was in fact first used to take care of the rural labour surplus issue. This focus was handily summarised as the policy to keep peasants stay where they lived, which included two objectives: leaving the land without leaving the countryside (*litu bu lixiang*) and entering the workshops or factories without entering the cities (*jinchang bu jincheng*). This important component of China's reform is now generally defined as China's rural industrialisation, which had not only helped resolve quite a few rural issues, especially poverty and surplus labour, but also provided the reformist leadership with much needed experience and confidence for restructuring state-owned factories or enterprises. From a macro-economic perspective, TVEs accommodated as high as 50 per cent of the rural surplus labour before the mid-1980s according to a general estimate mentioned by Deng Xiaoping (1994, 251). Many famous examples had emerged during those earlier years, such as those in Huaxi Village in the southern part of Jiangsu province as the richest village in China (Tsai 2007; Hou 2013). Several new models of local economic development, if not simply rural industrialisation, had also emerged and were branded in time, including the so-called Sunan model (the South Jiangsu model) and the Wenzhou model (Byrd and Liu 1990). Table 5.3 sketches the general development of China's rural enterprises from 1977 to 1985.

What Table 5.3 cannot demonstrate is the controversy concerning the expansion of TVEs. In addition to numerous unadventurous cadres at the township and village level, who knew nothing except farming, many had become worried about the strains caused by the strategy to develop more TVEs. Of course, there were almost no open concerns over if TVEs were capitalist tails as claimed by Maoists in the late 1960s. That view was pushed aside or silenced by the pressing concern about widespread poverty in the 1970s. According to a researcher from the Shanghai Party School, the expansion of TVEs was questioned because there were 'four competitions' emerging between TVEs

Table 5.3 The emergence and growth of China's rural enterprises, 1977–85.

Year	Number of Rural Enterprises (k)	Number of Rural People Employed (m)	Share of Non-farm Employment in Total Rural Labour Force (%)*
1977	–	≈ 28.00	4.7
1978	1,524	28.27	10.0
1979	1,480	29.09	–
1980	1,425	30.00	10.3
1981	1,338	29.70	10.0
1982	1,362	31.13	10.0
1983	1,346	32.35	10.4
1984	6,065*	52.08	16.9
1985	12,225*	69.70	22.4

Note: *These figures vary slightly in MARA (2009), Zhong (2011), Liu (2014), Chen (2019a) and Li et al. (2019).
Sources: Compiled by the author based on Zhou (1997) and NBSC (2005).

and big urban-based SOEs. These competitions included 'raw materials, energy, market, and capital', based on which some serious fervent believers in economic planning had demanded the closure of, and the restrictions on, the development of TVEs (Ding 2020, n.p.). From the stance of individual peasants, they all could feel new competitive pushes, but people had reacted to the new socio-economic conditions differently. Such difference did not, however, substantiate the claim that rural people had lower aspirations than urban residents.

From the position of rural individuals, they felt more tension between their aspirations and the reality than many urban individuals. That is, the aspirations of the rural people were also high, or at least as high as urban individuals as documented in various publications and other sources, but their actual expectations were to some extent different from that of many urban people. A significant majority of them had seen TVEs either as an opportunity to earn additional earnings or a chance to stop doing the hard farming work on the land. These views seem to be very realistic if taking the poverty of the late 1970s into consideration as most rural households were struggling financially at that point. There was only a small group of them, however, able to find a balance between aspirations and expectations and also put their aspirations into action. The formation and development of TVEs provided them with brilliant opportunities, like never before. Among the most mentioned cases is Cao Dewang, whose career started as a purchaser of a glass factory in his hometown in the late mid-1970s and then as a contractor to manage the business a few years later in the early 1980s. Since then, he has owned and advanced his production lines into one of the world's largest glass manufacturers. His decision to set up several factories in the United States during the Trump years has made him known globally, but with some controversy (Zhu 2017).

Urban blue-collar workers were also pushed into accepting some new policies and rules resulting from reform initiatives, despite the reality that many urban-based factory workers had responded to the various changes less eagerly, and also much slower, than many peasants and those taking part in the reinstated university entrance exams. Nowadays, many people often mention two general reasons behind the tardy reactions of workers towards new social repositioning chances in the late 1970s.

First, manufacturing workers, as well as many other factory workers, had long been politicised as the leading class and the societal mainstay in post-1949 China. According to Wang Xiaolu, a leading economic expert, almost all the economic sectors outside agriculture were eventually state owned before 1978. When China started implementing its reform policies, SOEs accounted for as high as 77 per cent in 1977 while the rest were collectively owned (Wang 2018c). As I mentioned in the preface of this book, urban-based collective-owned factories were the unfinished business of China's initial socialist construction, and since the economic crisis in late 1950s, these factories were mainly used to absorb urban jobless people. Because of their ideological and political standing, urban-based workers were portrayed as *guojia zhuren* (the masters of the nation), although there were hardly any actual benefits for many of them. The state master narrative had, however, made many workers become so proud and privileged that they were less motivated than rural residents to not only be proactive in terms of creating and trying their own initiatives, but also be responsible to the many changes that had already emerged or had been slowly put forwards then.

Second, the ruling elites were also rather slow in forming their views and strategies on handling this ideologised and politicised section of the population. In addition to the political complications, it was also difficult for the ruling elites to imagine anything beyond the old Soviet models of managing industrial sectors, while paying most of their attention to rural issues. Of course, a traditional approach was deployed in August 1977 to show the different focus of the new leadership from Mao's period, which was the first wage increase for many urban blue-collar workers since the late 1950s. In most cases, this long anticipated increase simply meant an additional five Chinese yuan per month per worker, but as high as 60 per cent of urban blue-collar workers nationwide had finally seen more take-home money (Song 2008b). For multiple reasons, the so-called urban reform was not the main political spectacle before the early 1980s, making many urban workers feel less pressure to reflect on the imminent changes and their own chances to reposition accordingly.

What was noted above is, however, by no means a complete denial of the motivated and proactive efforts made by some urban workers, which seemed to have happened on two fronts: outside and inside the system in which they were then positioned. The former implies those who opted to leave the highly praised industrial labour force and sought the chances to reposition themselves elsewhere, such as endeavouring to take part in the new university entrance examination or transferring to other professions. The latter, or the second type of efforts, refers to those who tried new chances within their enterprises or factories that they were familiar with.

On the latter front, urban workers could also feel a greater pressure to become competitive than before (as early as 1977), when a new workplace reward system was gradually introduced. The new system was moderate, focusing on encouraging hard work, without any measures to manage the widespread slack attitude towards work and performance. This moderate workplace reward system included three policies measure: performance-based monthly bonus, position-related supplemental pay and some pilot schemes of selectively promoting diligent and competent workers. These measures seemed less bold and decisive than those executed in the early 1980s as part of the SOE reform strategy, but they were sufficient at the time to disturb the stagnant workplace culture and routine. The latter was once colloquially depicted as *chi daguofan* (eating from one big pot) and the policy to fix the problem was, therefore, described as *dapo tiefanwan* (smashing the iron rice bowl). Before the early 1980s, in the words of an interviewee, the situation was not yet worsened to the extent of smashing everyone's bowl, but serving more rice to those some working diligently (Interviewee 18 2019).

Since there are not many people from these groups who enjoy writing about their past, there are less written records about them, except clues in the conversations with those going through the changes. My old contacts from one urban collective-owned factory and a Beijing-based major SOE have been hugely helpful, reminding me of the fact that some workers who were ambitious, forward-looking and able to put their ideas into action had not only sensed the change, but had also seen some new opportunities to improve their own lives. The person quoted above was one of such cases, who had not only received bonuses every year and a promotion, but had also taken over the leadership of his factory soon after, in 1980. In other words, some blue-collar workers had also made their efforts to reposition in the late 1970s.

Proud University Students in a Changing China

This discussion looks at those who passed the university entrance exams and became a unique group of new front-runners in social positionings in the eyes of a vast majority of the Chinese population in the late 1970s. As revealed in Table 5.1, more than fifteen million young people enrolled in university courses before 1980 when the university entrance examination system and practice returned to normal. The most distinct difference between the pre- and post-1980 cohorts was the considerable decrease in the number of the so-called non-current school leavers, or graduates, who had finished their secondary or high school education, or simply reached the age to leave schools, during the Cultural Revolution years from 1966 and 1976. Consequently, the new university students enrolled in the three years before 1980 were very much a generation affected by the Cultural Revolution, which had led to certain interest, attitudes and behaviours. It was also because of their achievements and future potential that they had since been driven by the combination of their traumatised experience and rising confidence in their own societal competitiveness, the joint force of which had then put them in a competitive relationship with other groups, especially with the worker–peasant–soldier university students. Of course, the pre-1980 cohort was commonly regarded as the most hopeful group with almost no controversy over their intellectual capacities in post-Mao China. Comparatively speaking, they were also not as radical as the new street campaigners as analysed in this chapter's first section, but far more ambitious than peasants and urban workers, who were struggling to make better earnings within the circles in which they were positioned before or during the Cultural Revolution.

These new university students did not, however, live in a competition-free society; even if the official discourse claimed that people were equal and that the university students were future leaders of the country. While these students were enjoying their advantageous position in China's post-1978 social structure, their ideological and political orientation soon gave rise to a reconsideration of their political loyalty to the ruling CCP and dependability by some conservative state leaders. Competitive social repositionings are such processes where the triumph, or an advantageous positioning, without a basic degree of prudence may well be the start of a loss of advantage. In the words of one interviewee, there were numerous disgruntled people waiting for the mistakes that the new students were to make in the late 1970s and early 1980s (Interviewee 6 2019).

Over the course of these ongoing repositionings, there were two main incidents that affected the thinking and attitudes of decision-makers, both conservative and reformist, towards this cohort of new students and their political inclination.

The first major protest incident took place from early to mid-October 1979 among thousands of students of Renmin University of China. As I explained in this book's preface, I was then a second-year student at this university, which is normally called Renda in Chinese. In October 1979, when a new group of students enrolled, Renda encountered teaching and accommodation space issues as a large part of the campus had, since the Cultural Revolution, been allocated to the PLA's *Erpao* (the new Second Artillery Corps) after Renda was disbanded in 1970. Since the university was reinstituted in 1977, the tension was brewing between Renda and the *Erpao* institutes on the campus. In October 1979, students took an active role through their associations in regaining more campus spaces for their new fellow students, who arrived at the campus without dining spaces.

To the casual eye, this was an isolated incident that was only relevant to Renda and its students. In actual fact, the decision by student unions and groups to hold a demonstration in Tiananmen Square and at the front gate of Zhongnanhai (the compound for China's central leadership) disturbed the central leadership profoundly as they had just resolved the crisis triggered by the Xidan democratic movement. Therefore, the new leadership disliked any signs of new activism, and street activism was the thing they hated most to see. What was equally important was the significance of Renda as a special educational institution in the politics of both the CCP and the PRC. As the first university established by the CCP during World War II years, Renda had long been seen as a politically trustworthy education and training institution of China's new ruling class. This campus dispute thus involved two powerful institutions of China: *Erpao* (a new and modern section of the PLA) and Renda, the university of the party-state system (until this privilege was weakened badly by this seemingly trivial event). In other words, Renda students not only placed themselves in a power jostle between two big institutions, but also clearly irritated the new central leadership, leading some to pondering and reflecting on university-related issues other than the restoration of university entrance exams.

Some Renda students were well connected in Beijing, and quite a few versions of remarks from the central leadership and other influential people soon spread out, criticising the university leadership for their failure to stop students from marching out of the campus. Young students were also criticised, for being disobedient and for lacking a political consciousness over the entire societal situation of the country. As recalled by Zhang Jinfeng, the then chair of Renda's student association, the protest was commented by people from the following two points of view:

> During this period, people from outside the university kept coming to visit us. For example, some people said to us that they understood our actions very well and that they also felt anxious for us all, that the reason why not many people partook in the demonstration was because we did not shout the slogans such as democracy and freedom that many people cared about. [...] After the resumption of classes, some teachers approached us to say that the news media had now adopted a policy of blocking the university. No Renda news was allowed to be reported, and articles by teachers could not even be published. If this went on, it would be very harmful to the university's development. They wanted us to take this situation into account. (Zhang 2008a, n.p.)

To a great degree, the protest was only the observable portion of the new societal tensions that resulted from the large-scale social repositionings or the many changes to the relationships of different social groups or classes within the shifting social structure.

As pointed out, these seemingly hopeful university students were well regarded by the general public, but their liberal inclinations were also widespread and became apparent after the street protest by Renda students. The latter as a special group was not only seen as the best students countrywide, but their attitudes and actions were also regarded as a benchmark in the political arena in the late 1970s. In the eyes of the CCP's followers, these students appeared to give little, if any, credence to many parts and aspects of China's political system and culture, especially ideology and discourses. This feeling appeared among local CCP branch leaders before spreading out across much of the party-state and into a sense of frustration. This was a start of what the students had become less favoured by the CCP's conservatives. This thinking was further substantiated by the passionate participation of many students in the campus-based election campaign in 1980, giving the conservatives more evidence to cast a doubt on their trustworthiness.

The second key reason why new university students started losing their competitive edge in the early process of societal repositionings was, therefore, the abovementioned campus-based election. China revised and adopted its new election law in 1979, providing voters with 'some choices of candidates as early as 1980' (Jacobs 1991, 171). The new law allowed 'direct elections at the local level', including the district in urban centres and the county in rural areas (Bedeski 1986, 154). As an exciting element of this set of Dengist reform ideas, the nomination of candidates opened up a little, allowing non-CCP residents with an endorsement from as little as 10 voters to participate in the election. This legislative change led to a sudden rise of interest in elections, but the related concept of democracy that the CCP used was different from the understanding of a large number of young intellectuals. As Andrew Nathan once mentioned: 'what the leaders did not foresee was that the democrats would view the election as an opportunity to try to put their own ideas of democracy into effect' (Nathan 1985, 193).

The university-based district elections attracted different types of student candidates, turning this specific legislative change into a possible career opportunity to allow some students who were more ambitious than others to distinguish themselves from the crowds. Unquestionably, many candidates wanted to devote to reforming China's politics, but this whole episode also revealed self-contradictory ideas in the CCP's political ideology, which has long been typified by its democratic centralism. The campus-based district election had even made a group of professional activists outside the higher education system very excited about it. A few had even named the 1980 local elections as *Gengshen Bianfa* (*Gengshen Reforms*) according to a Chinese revolutionary tradition of naming a key socio-political change (Dittmer 1987; Baum 1994).[4] Among the students at universities, prospective and nominated candidates were also from very different political spectrums, including some activists, such as Wang Juntao at Peking University and Chen Ziming at Graduate School, University of Science and Technology of China. Remember that both Chen and Wang were very active in the 1976 Tiananmen Incident. At Beijing-based universities alone, a few hundreds of students put hands up for the district elections in 1980. Table 5.4 reveals the distribution of the student candidates who passed the nomination process and went into the election. There were as many as 11 students elected at the end, including activists.

Table 5.4 The number of student candidates partaking in the district elections in Beijing, 1980.

University	Number of Candidates
Peking University	18
Tsinghua University	13
Renmin University of China	6
Beijing Normal University	14
Graduate School, University of Science and Technology of China	1
Beijing Institute of Aeronautics and Astronautics*	6
Central Institute for Nationalities*	5
Beijing Institute of Iron and Steel*	4
Beijing Medical College*	1
Beijing Institute of Commerce*	3
Beijing Normal College*	7
Beijing Institute of Economics*	3
Peking University No. 1 Branch Campus*	2
Renmin University of China No. 1 Branch Campus*	3
Total number	*86*

Note: *The name of this university has changed.
Sources: Compiled by the author based on Li and Song (1992), Yang and Yan (1997), Qian (2008) and Yu (2011).

Such a high level of enthusiasm for the district election resulted from both the relatively relaxed political climates of the time and the changing conditions of people's social repositioning. An American researcher who was teaching English in China at the time noted the following changes to the campus life in Chinese universities:

All of these changes had a profound effect on university students – on their values, expectations, and behavior. Because so many change-oriented young people were concentrated on campuses where they enjoyed a bit of autonomy, students found the opportunity to build types of relationships that were not directly controlled by the state. Not only did students became more involved in non-political activities and informal, uncontrolled groups, but they also became more critical of and detached from the state and Party. (Englesberg 1992, 232–33)

In addition to the participation of several activists in the election, another case that has fascinated the populace for decades was the involvement of Liu Yuan, the son of former PRC president Liu Shaoqi, in the same socio-political attempt. He was then studying at Beijing Normal College, today known as Capital Normal University. As his first political move after the Cultural Revolution, during which his family was harshly persecuted, his election statement was obviously influenced by a strong demand for reforming China's political system, including his following words:

China needs democracy, and it must achieve it! Each of us must work hard for democracy, and I am even more responsible. I am willing to fight this charge, and declare war on the remnants of feudalism and all societal evils, and break with privilege. Only when we all play a part can China's future be bright! Otherwise, it would be unthinkable. (Liu 2020, n.p.)

The involvement of Liu in the election was indicative of another front of the social positioning of the late 1970s and early 1980s. It might just be a topic for gossip keeping many ordinary people entertained, but some close observers and participants realised as early as 1980 that many partaking in the 1980 election were not only still driven by the successor dream (though no one mentioned the prefixed adjective of communist, or revolutionary, at that time), but a large proportion of them were also from cadre families. Almost all partakers were talking about many democratic ideas, which had prompted a strong reaction of the CCP's conservatives, criticising the students as a whole for being politically disloyal. However, other students had seen the involvement of students from cadres' families differently, which have also been explained differently. This observation has lately evolved into a new theory that many from the third echelon of communist successors partook in the election as a strategy to manage the possible loss of their privileged position or the competition caused by the reform ideas (He and Gao 1996). Of course, many party elders could not see the utilitarian use of this new approach.

Another trend to emerge at the same time as the 1980 district election went on was the formation of various types of coterie as networks to help some position or reposition in changing social structures and relations. In Beijing, a number of small inner circles established and carried out a range of activities. Cai Xiaopeng, an active participant in some of these, lately penned what he observed among Renda students and depicted two main clusters. The first one was the so-called rural development research group, which was associated with some central decision-makers, and the second group was originally called employment research group before it was expanded into three subgroups. Interestingly, the latter had actually existed between the Xidan democratic activists and the institute affiliated with two central organisations (Cai 2017). Another observer believed, as quoted below, that there were more than these two networks and they all became division lines among new university students in Beijing:

> There were more small circles in Beijing than those formed by the envious students who were all one way or another connected with someone in power. You can now also read memoirs about reading groups in the university district, circles of cultural critics and editors in the east of the city. You can safely imagine that all the ambitious students had their own circles. [...] Some seemed to have acted based on the idea: you should set up your own circle if you were unable to occupy the commanding heights elsewhere. (Interviewee 11 2019)

The above observer also added that, after a few decades, it was clear that the students who made whatever efforts in the early 1980 to position themselves on the commanding heights of career ladders had apparently benefitted from their circles. However, their effective repositionings have been achieved at the cost of rising wariness of new university students as many of their actions were well beyond the comprehension of the CCP's conservatives. As a consequence, some decision-makers and party elders started reconsidering how future leaders were to be selected.

Shifting Ideas about Heirs and Changes to Social Ladders

Both the Renda student protest and the campus election had all happened under the eyes of China's top leaders and officials, and some participants were even connected to this circle of decision-makers. New repositioning efforts by some young pushy people had created a new focus of attention, and as mentioned at the start of this present chapter, it had given rise to a long pondering over the successor echelon issue of the CCP's succession politics. The process of pondering had begun among a small group of top official advisors and ideological specialists in the early 1980s, which has since continued until now. Parts of the latter will be discussed in coming chapters due to the effect of the issue on the political conditions of social repositioning or positioning of individuals. In the early 1980s, there were three major groups of young and middle-aged people within the attention range of some CCP's ideological workers and advisors. In addition to the new university student group, the other two main groups included the so-called *sanzhong ren* (three categories of Cultural Revolutionary activists) and the worker–peasant–soldier university students. The two latter groups were products of the Cultural Revolution, and therefore not well accepted by the general public at the time, especially those who felt alienated by Maoist policies and practices before 1978.

According to one version of the account, the tracking and removal of Cultural Revolutionary extremists, or *sanzhong ren*, from the leadership team at every level were strongly advocated by Chen Yun, another CCP heavyweight parallel to Deng Xiaoping. The sidelining of the worker–peasant–soldier students was supported by Deng Xiaoping since the first half of the 1970s when he was restored to the leadership. These two CCP elders supported each other on these two issues, thinking that these tactics were necessary for preventing the recurrence of the Cultural Revolution, while anticipating the new students to be the pillar of China's reform. A general feeling was that the upwards career path for the other two groups into leadership seemed to have been blocked.

Since the campaign to eliminate the three types of people from the CCP's leadership circles was a quite separate process from reconsidering the other two groups of university graduates and students, this discussion starts with this line of reassessment first.

The three categories of Cultural Revolutionary activists refer to those who were followers of the clique of Lin Biao and the Gang of Four; who were seriously factionalist in political motivations; and those who were involved in beating, smashing and looting during the early Cultural Revolution years (Unger 2007). As stated, the campaign to track down and eliminate them was initiated by Chen Yun, who raised it among a small group of people close to him first in 1980, and then widely to the provincial level in 1981. Chen believed that these people were potentially dangerous to the party's future, and he made use of his position as the first secretary of the CCP's Central Commission for Discipline Inspection to push this political tactic further on to Deng Xiaoping and other centre leaders in 1982.

Despite the strong push from the top, this political campaign, and the concern behind it as well, was somewhat short-lived compared with the problem concerning the worker–peasant–soldier university students. This was due to two reasons (or two defences, in the words of one interviewee). The first one was to defend Mao's political reputation and standing as so many accused people argued that they were followers of Mao, not of the Lin Biao clique or the Gang of Four. This claim led to the revision of the definition of the first category of Cultural Revolutionary activists, which has since been expressed as those who rose to high levels through rebels. The second defence was to protect a large number of former Red Guard leaders or student rebel team leaders who were from the families of senior cadres, including the families of several national leaders (Interviewee 9 2020). In his three volumes on the history of the Cultural Revolution, Yang Jisheng documents how the double standards of the leadership over separating the very active Red Guards from the families of senior cadres from the other radicals without such backgrounds had been created. A couple of former active Red Guards from senior cadre families wrote to Chen Yun, making Chen realise that there is a political difference between them and us. The following details and comments are from Yang's book:

> On 27 February 1984, Chen Yun gave the following instruction: [...] these Red Guards do not belong to the 'three types of people'. The good ones among them should instead be identified and selected for the third echelon [of the leadership teams]. Cleaning up the 'three types of people' is a political struggle, and it is necessary to prevent some from disturbing the muddy water. [...] In the process of cleaning up the 'three types of people', it was because of the interests of the ruling bureaucratic groups that the legal net had to be left open little for the children of veteran leaders and other senior cadres. The final winner of the Cultural Revolution is these ruling groups, and these two types of people had, therefore, to be protected. The [grassroots] rebels were then pushed [to the front] to take a responsibility of the Cultural Revolution. (Yang 2018, 1048–49)

The political waters remained muddy, if they did not become even muddier than it was after Chen's instructions, due to the strong liberal atmosphere nationwide over those years and people's active attitudes and approaches to the new prospects of repositioning themselves in society. However, a visible line loomed out of the murky political waters in front of many young Chinese from the early 1980s, reminding them that there were different politically privileged groups in society. In reality, one of the two former Red Guard activists who wrote the letter to Chen in 1983 to argue for their cases and many of those behind the lobbying were all lately promoted to relatively senior positions, which is well documented in various publications.

The campaign to hunt down the three types of Cultural Revolutionary activists had since come to a quiet end. According to Zhang Shu, another specialist from the CCP's Party History and Documents Research Office, this campaign had, in the end, identified and eliminated as little as 5,449 people nationally except the complicated case of the Guangxi region (Zhang 2015). That is why many people have ridiculed the campaign as grabbing some low-level scapegoats to bear the responsibility of the disaster of the Cultural Revolution. This had made many people profoundly confused in spite of the fact that the CCP passed a resolution in 1981, criticising Mao for launching the terrible Cultural Revolution. However, what was really exposed by this particular elimination campaign was a trigger for making the CCP's top decision-makers realise once again the importance of their two political foundations for the CCP in the midst of overheated political atmosphere of what was publicly called 'thought liberation', or 'ideological emancipation', in the early 1980s. Two distinct political red lines for new CCP politics have re-emerged into the public eye and consciousness: one was to uphold Mao's political legacy and historical status while the other was to treat the children of veteran revolutionaries and senior cadres in a different way from those without such backgrounds.

As a result, many ambitious young people who were immersed in the enthusiasm for relaxed socio-political atmosphere and new opportunities had seen the looming boundary of their domain of societal existence and positioning. At the same time, some privileged revolutionary groups had started once again gaining the privileged rights to access some resources, including new social ladders to climb. From a social structural viewpoint, this realisation by many young people from non-cadre families implied a crack in the new political partnership, or class alliance, between the post-1978 leadership and the intellectuals and other grassroots classes. From a political–ideological view, many Cultural Revolutionary activists had not only survived from the elimination from the party-state system, but soon also contributed to the growing complexities in politic, although many of them were not able to stay in the political arena, nor promoted further. Their fundamentalist leftist stances and beliefs have since been shared by those who benefitted more before the end of the Cultural Revolution than after that. This situation has kept an old ideological front line alive up to now, posing ongoing challenges to the Chinese reformers.

The second major group who has until very recently been driving the rethinking of which types of young people are appropriate for the CCP's future leadership at different levels is the worker–peasant–soldier student group. The existence and effect of this key issue have lately been further evidenced by the team composition of the Xi Jinping leadership, many of them are from the worker–peasant–soldier student group, which has been used by many to explain what has since happened in China.

As introduced, this particular group of students studied at universities during the second half of the Cultural Revolution. Since they were chosen through the recommendation of local or sectoral officials, without proper exams, they have long suffered from a reputation problem among a large proportion of educated and urban citizens. Before their major competitor group, which is those studying at universities after 1977, had been found less politically dependable by more decision-makers and influential party elders, the worker–peasant–soldier students had as a whole suffered badly from the infuriated public sentiment against the Cultural Revolution and other prior political campaigns as well. Many reformists, including party elders, believed that their 'education level is too low, and many have not achieved the technical secondary school level at graduation' (Chen 2021, n.p.). They were, however, on the radar of the future leadership selection process of the ruling CCP due to a Dengist political strategy to reform or modernise the makeup of future leadership team.

Since 1980, Deng had vigorously advocated what has been called the four modernisations of cadres, *ganbu sihua*, which have in practice been specified as the four criteria for appointing cadres: revolutionary, young, educated and expertise in a field. Obviously, apart from the first one as a political prefix and the second one as a rigorous prerequisite, the last two requirements are all tied up with educational qualifications. Having been confined by the age requirement, there were only two groups of educated people who were eligible for being considered for promotion: the worker–peasant–soldier students and the students of Deng's era. As a result, these two groups have been put in a competitive relationship, if not a collision course, which has then affected the social positioning or repositioning of people from these groups.

Because the worker–peasant–soldier student group was not popular by the social standards of the time, most of them had behaved in a quiet and unassuming manner, letting the post-1977 university students enjoy their moment of glory. For a number of years, they were in a passive situation, although many jointly tried to demand for the official recognition of their tertiary education qualifications, which is indicative of the bad situation they were in. In addition to the reputation issue of these students, there were many institutions, both academic and otherwise, that had also tried to transfer them to less-challenging positions, such as labs, libraries or other managerial posts. A very small number of academically capable graduates had attempted to take postgraduate courses in order to distance themselves from this group and its identity.

As another piece of evidence to show how competitive these people's repositioning efforts were, a small proportion of these students had even tried to study abroad, which became increasingly popular in China in the early 1980s, resulting in a higher percentage of them studying at Western universities and institutes than they were in China before the mid-1990s. This phenomenon has not been fully analysed yet, especially the fact that many of them have since stayed on in the West, living and working there for decades. In fact, the whole issue regarding these students did not also draw enough research attention from analysts in China before the present central leadership team took office in late 2012, or more recently when a range of different approaches from the pre-reform leadership have been brought forwards and put into operation. This change has reminded many observers of the early experiences of the new leaders and the likely links between their backgrounds, early work and education experiences, and their levels of thinking and governance capacities.

Despite the unexpected success of the worker–peasant–soldier student group in gaining some advantage over its rival group after the late 1980s, and despite the fact that many of them had also made their great effort to reposition themselves in post-Mao China, it is not unreasonable to claim that most of them had still been under enormous pressure of the ongoing reform processes and the competitive social conditions over the period of time under examination. One of the last groups of worker–peasant–soldier students at Shanghai's Fudan University said the following to a journalist about their student identity:

> Many of us have tried our best to hide ourselves over the years, as the hat of a worker-peasant-soldier student still leaves a shadow in our hearts, hurting us from time to time. A quiet number of years ago, many places had even had their policies restricting employment [of us] in the processes of selecting and promoting new cadres. (Mei 2006, 9)

It has to be emphasised that the final changes to the relative advantage of each of the above three groups in future career progression in general, or official promotion in particular, were neither because of what the 'three types of people' (*sanzhong ren*) did, nor due to what the worker–peasant–soldier students did in seeking for qualification recognition. In the case of the post-1977 university students, their clear advantages in the late 1970s and most of the 1980s had been slowly depleted by years of political and ideological activism. As will be further analysed in Chapters six and seven, the post-1977 student group had for years been heavily affected by a type of new modernisation romanticism, which had made them disengaged from the reality of Chinese society and people. A former Hangzhou University student enrolled in 1977 recently wrote the following comments:

> Most of the students from classes 1977 and 1978 were idealistic, to some extent. They were more able to think independently, but were not willing to agree with other people. There was quite a bit of arrogance in the heart, seeming to see 'no hero in the world except themselves'. With such characteristics, they could take advantage of the situation and bring their talents into play when having open-minded leaders. They would be given tight shoes to wear when encountering jealous superiors. Most of these graduates, as well as the class of 1979 and those after that, were assigned to the party-state systems. They were all able to not only work cooperatively with others, but also compete with each other. On some special occasions, they could even quarrel so ferociously that no one was willing to be convinced by each other. (Chen 2019b, n p.)

Of course, various other socio-cultural factors had also contributed to the slow but apparent decrease in the social favourability towards post-1977 university students. These factors ranged from the growing popularity of Western music, dance parties, clothes and various fashion accessories to the reading topics and the topics of their discussions. These were not the new interests that were only shared and enjoyed among the population of post-1977 university students, but different types of anti-reform forces or conservatives had somehow linked these new popular trends emerging in wider society to liberal leaning university students. Several interviewees have also mentioned that the new student population might actually have suffered from what they call 'the honeymoon effect' from the early 1980s. While the latter will be further examined in the subsequent chapters, it is sufficient to assume that societal attitudes towards the above three major groups had started shifting as early as in the early 1980s. Although many aspects of such competitions had occurred in a barely perceptible way, it was the start of a general shift in the relative advantages of each of these three groups in their social repositionings.

Notes

1. The May Fourth Movement or May 4th Movement took place in Beijing on 4 May 1919, triggered by the Treaty of Versailles to allow Japan to control some territories on China's Shandong peninsula after World War I. The movement has long been considered a significant turning point in modern Chinese history, characterised by the upsurge of Chinese nationalism, the cultural nihilism that it sadly generated and spread and the birth of modern Chinese intellectualism. Of course, apart from the accompanying efforts of the movement to evaluate Chinese cultural and institutional traditions, such as Confucianism, the movement also led to widespread political radicalisation and extremism among educated and

less-educated youth in China. These young Chinese, as well as some middle-aged erudite people, were seen as responsible for the spread of anarchism in the early twentieth century and for the later move towards communism. This is why the movement has been highly praised by the CCP that was formed consequently in 1921 as the patriotic movement and the start of China's bourgeois-democratic revolution against imperialism and feudalism. For more information, interested readers are referred to Schwarcz (1986), Hu (1991) and Mitter (2004).

2. *Gongche shangshu* has been a long tradition among literate Chinese of participating in top-level public policy activities or politics since the Han Dynasty (206 BCE–220 CE), and it has since become an allusion to describe the practice of writing to the top ruler to express a concern and obtaining recognition and position to serve the ruling class. From a public opinion perspective, it may be considered a supplementary but abnormal communication alternative between the grassroots people and the state in authoritarian regimes. As an option for individuals, the term carries certain negative meanings, implying realising ambition through quick access. The most famous case of applying this political strategy was the so-called *Gongche Shangshu* Movement in 1895 during the late Qing Dynasty (1644–1911), when Kang Youwei from a county in remote Guangdong province produced a 10,000 word petition to the Qing emperor to recommend a strong approach to Japan after the First Sino-Japanese War of 1894–95. Since then, China entered a long period of civil unrest and turmoil, and *Gongche shangshu* has become a popular option for politically ambitious people in China. Interested readers can find more information about this period and tactic in Chang (2013), Haggard and Kang (2020) and Wan (2021).

3. Because these people, including Feng Lun himself, have been well known in China in recent decades for their entrepreneurial success, a brief note is needed here to help readers understand why this quotation is used in this discussion. Liu Chuanzhi is the founder of Lenovo, one of the world's largest computer (desktop and laptop) makers. Ma Yun is the founder of Alibaba Group, China's largest e-commerce conglomerate running Taobao, Tmall and other platforms. Ren Zhengfei is the founder of Huawei Technologies, one of the world's largest manufacturers of telecommunications equipment and mobile phones. Zong Qinghou, less well known outside of China than the other four entrepreneurs, is the founder of Wahaha Group, China's leading beverage company. He was ranked as the richest person in China for more years than many other famous entrepreneurs. Feng Lun was a lecturer at the CCP's Central Party School and involved in various policy-oriented research projects before jointly founding Vantone Group, one of China's earliest private real estate companies. Feng has therefore become one of the country's best known academic/official turned entrepreneurs since the early 1990s (Gao 2013b).

4. This phrase is another example to reveal the heavy influence of China's century-long radical political culture on the young Chinese people in the 1970s and 1980s, some of them would like to do something with a strong historical identity. The expression pattern of *Gengshen Bianfa* (*Gengshen Reforms*) is the same as that of *Wuxu Bianfa* (*Wuxu Reforms*), referring to what Kang Youwei and his followers did in 1898 after their efforts of doing *Gongche shangshu* (see note 2 above). *Wuxu* is the designation for 1898 in the traditional Chinese 60-year cycle for counting years (Karl and Zarrow 2002). The *Wuxu Reforms* are also called the Hundred Days Reforms, when the young Guangxu emperor was influenced by Kang Youwei and Liang Qichao in 1898 to decide to undertake a wide range of reforms. The effort was crushed by the powerful forces loyal to Empress Dowager Cixi. Apart from Karl and Zarrow (2002), interested readers are referred to Kwong (1984) and Karl (2002).

Chapter Six

CLIMBING DIFFERENT SOCIAL LADDERS FROM THE MID-1980s

In recent years, the decade of the 1980s in China has attracted research interest among researchers old and new. Like all nostalgic views of the past, which often reflect present discontents and apprehensions about existing social conditions, this new interest among some Chinese seems to be based on a comparison of the current decade to the first decade of reform – especially the differences in official discourses, if not ideological tendencies, policy re-alignments and socio-political climates. Several cultural critics have even called for a 'return to the 80s' (Hong and Cheng 2009). Although such discussions have mostly taken place within the fields of literary and cultural studies, the notion of returning to the 1980s has various connotations and denotations, making the topic more socio-political than literary.

A number of researchers have explored why the 1980s, in particular, has become the focus of nostalgia. In the words of Zhang and Zhang (2011), in an early analysis of the topic, this nostalgia is a condensed representation of the sentiments of many critics and writers. They argue there are three types of publications that can be regarded as part of the push for a return to the 1980s. Besides the pure academic literature, such as various journal articles and textbooks, there is a sizeable body of memoirs, biographies, autobiographies and other records that are historical or semi-historical rather than purely literary works; and, finally, there are numerous literary depictions of the 1980s, generally portraying it as a decade full of passion, ideals and changes. Reflecting these depictions, the phrase 'emotional memory' has been used to explain the attraction to the 1980s.

Under the influence of some earlier publications, as well as the unquantifiable oral histories of 1980s in China, new cohorts of writers produced a large number of inspirational works for China's huge book market. New titles about the 1980s are often associated with optimistic, positive and inspirational narratives or depictions, invoking the era's supposed opportunities for new careers, entrepreneurship, becoming rich, living an exciting life – even becoming a straight-A student, as many are assumed to have been in the 1980s. Perhaps due to the political taboo of using history to allude to current situations in politics, however, or because of China's modern intellectual tradition, researchers and critics largely describe the changes of the 1980s solely through macro-level and abstract concepts, with frequently used terms including individual liberty, the rights of personal wealth, freedom of expression or thought, the legal rights of citizens, civil and human rights (Zhang and Xu 2012).

The abovementioned difference between academic and non-academic literature suggests that nostalgia for the 1980s has been conceptualised by scholars in a manner very different from what many non-academic people might have heard or read about the decade. Of course, there are also some more philosophical reflections that are only understandable and meaningful to those who are familiar with the 1980s and aware of what was taking place at a societal level at that time. Zhang Xudong, a pioneer scholar of China's 1980s, once described the appeal of the 1980s as follows:

> Looking back at the 1980s, we would see that everything was being explored at that time, and everything was possible at least at the level of imagination and theory. This kind of imagination and theoretical thinking was not only the core of social life, but also the political life of the country, as well as the essence of what everyone cared about, thought about together, and what they felt that they shared weal and woe. The key point here was to have a national orientation. Everyone felt that China was then moving forward, exploring a better and more reasonable society, and that everyone should and could be an active participant [in the process]. (Zhang and Xu 2012, 98)

Obviously, what is needed in addition to the general social climate of the 1980s is an analysis of the decade at the intersections of social changes, personal motivations and people's opportunities to adjust and reposition. This chapter looks at events in China in the second half of the 1980s from the social repositioning perspective and exposes how reform-generated changes in job opportunities and prospects, wealth distribution and perceptions of social status and mobility influenced the attitudes and behaviours of many Chinese.

There are four sections in this chapter. The first provides an overview of social structural changes across the key sectors of Chinese society or key segments of its population, and social reactions to the changes. As stated, many previous studies have focused excessively on the outcries of those who felt marginalised and alienated by various reform policies, and of young and idealistic university students, and other youth. A different point of view is needed for real insight. The second section examines what could be called the new social ladder of *qinlao zhifu* (enriching one's life through diligence), with a focus on who were the winners and who the losers from the reform programmes of the mid- and late 1980s. Over those years, many diligent and able peasants, as well as many conscientious laid-off urban workers, accumulated both experience and investment capital. New privately owned and run businesses emerged all over China, while the early stage of the so-called rural industrialisation was well underway. This was to some extent an effect of Deng Xiaoping's tactic 'to let some people get rich first', but it also created a perception among many others that they were being treated unfairly. The third section considers the social ladder of what has been proverbially known as *xiahai*, or *xiahai jingshang* (jumping into the sea of business), which was becoming widespread at the time among low-ranking officers and white-collar professionals, before becoming broadly recognised by more everyday people and China observers in the West in the first half of the 1990s. The fourth and final section is a brief comparative analysis of two large-scale demonstrations in Beijing in 1976 and 1989. The latter provided a controversial end to the decade to which many now wish to return, making it an unavoidable topic for this chapter. The focus of this discussion is on young people's experiences in seeking new opportunities and climbing social ladders, and this analysis argues that the 1976 Tiananmen Incident was a more significant milestone in China's modernisation than the 1989 protest.

A Time of Rapid and Aberrant Repositionings

The 1980s was the most important decade of China's reform, but only a few years in, problems and negativity began to surface. As a result, there have been at least two polarised discourses of the 1980s. On the one hand are more educated people, both within China and around the world, who look back fondly on the 1980s and support the call for a returning to the era. On the other hand, there is the widespread memory of China in 1989, specifically of 4 June, in the Western media and press. Obviously, the 1980s has been seen and conceptualised quite differently by different individuals at different times of their lives. The turning point of this process was 1985, when – as noted at the start of Chapter five – the price reform for agricultural products was implemented. Given the obvious benefits to peasants, and also because the reform started with what has been called 'the dual-track system' (Hua 2005, 22; Zhang 2018b, 215),[1] this process of freeing up the prices of non-staple food was not in itself sufficient to trigger negative responses. Soaring prices for vegetables, meat, poultry and eggs, fruits and aquatic products affected the costs of meals at universities, and angry students at Peking University even held demonstrations, but it was held in the name of condemning Japanese prime minister's visit to a war-related memorial shrine. This is why this campus protest was called at the time the 'new September 18 Incident' or the 'new 9/18 Incident' (Huang 2003, 85),[2] setting the precedent of Peking University's manner of magnifying discontent in a political way for the rest of China's reform period.

The above approach taken by students to the price reform was not the only divergence observed between their general claim of sympathising with impoverished peasants and supporting systematic reform and their actual reactions to the partial impact of the price liberalisation. Two other, more general dichotomies also emerged between the reality of fast-changing socio-economic conditions and the responses of a large proportion of the population.

The first appeared to be more cultured and refined and was characterised by students voicing their opposing views using a range of politicised and theoretical claims. This may be called the dissociation between their feeling of falling behind in positionings and the ideological or politicised expression of their dissatisfaction with increasingly intense repositioning situations. In the eyes of several interviewees, the discontent of some people over their personal life circumstances was often expressed through elegant and highly abstract concepts that were either too wide ranging to be implemented or too advanced for the time. Many people not only maintained the tradition of 'not speaking candidly', but were also used to practising the 'Cultural Revolutionary approach of *shanggang shangxian*' to either politicise or ideologise certain issues in daily life (Interviewee 21 2020). Therefore, their 'demands were never made clear, but instead caused many people to be anxious' over their own position in society (Interviewee 5 2019).

This particular dissociation has long been overlooked by analysts and researchers from within China, partly due to modern Chinese intellectual tradition and practice. Some have even made the mixture of societal issues more ambiguous and abstract than the political and ideological claims. A number of Chinese researchers have considered these public responses to social changes from a cultural and historical point of view, seeing them as prevalent social trends in ideas. These include liberalism, neo-authoritarianism, New Leftism, new nationalism, neo-Confucianism and others (Li 2015). Among these researchers, Xiao Gongqin identifies six main trends in post-Mao China, while Ma Licheng counts eight (Xiao 2009; Ma 2011). Other scholars have focused only on four or five general trends (Zhang 2012; Zhu 2012). There are many problems with such analyses, but the key issue is that they are too general and abstract to reveal the actual needs of the majority of the population or to explain how these general tendencies affected people's repositioning efforts in reforming society. At most, these trends confirm that people's attention was drawn in different directions, but the summaries of the social trends are largely a mixture of temporal vertical axes of these directions. People's efforts to explore directions and paths of social change as part of their social repositioning have been obscured by such scholarly analyses.

Another dissociation that emerged in the mid-1980s was rather more direct and uncomplicated, without being wrapped in any abstractions, and was characterised by the odd combination of support for reform and dislike of the resulting changes to the existing rules and patterns of income and benefit distribution. All these odd social psychological responses originated from a widespread anxiety over rapid social transformation and the growing competitiveness caused by various reform programmes in the social repositioning of individuals. These were once generally called *nifan xinli* (reverse mentality),[3] a widespread social psychological approach in the 1980s of reacting to positive developments in a negative way as a consequence of anxiety over being left behind in a changing social environment.

From a comparative perspective, these anxiety-driven responses differed from the previously noted attempt to politicise or ideologise concerns over change. One interviewee used the ancient Chinese expressions *yangchun baixue* (white snow in spring sunlight, a lofty musical-poetic piece few understand, referring to highbrow culture) and *xiali baren* (tunes of the rustic poor, referring to grassroots culture) to draw parallels between the two main types of social reactions in China in the 1980s (Interviewee 26 2020).

The same interviewee expressed the view that the widespread anxiety in the 1980s was not sparked simply by price reforms and inflation, as wage earners all over the country had enjoyed several wage rises since the late 1970s following more than two decades of stagnating incomes. He argued that their anxieties were, in fact, triggered by a 'choice phobia' in a new phrase. Such worries, if not fears, about choices largely related to two aspects of changing social conditions: what path to select and what risks one might face after making a choice. These concerns were also driven by another prevalent social mindset that saw every new opportunity as a final chance. This outlook – the fear of 'missing the last bus' – remains prevalent in China now and generates a variety of impulses that drive social processes.

On top of the complex socio-psychological processes that were discussed earlier, positioning at the time was also affected by changes that saw more people freed from various restrictions and became competitors in positionings along with increasingly large numbers of university students and rural residents working in cities. Table 6.1 lists several main developments that allowed more people to take part in social repositioning.

Some of the changes mentioned in Table 6.1 had additional connotations for those who went through the 1980s, which signified that more talented people from families with more cultural or educational capital were finally allowed to become involved in societal competition. This seemed to be a stereotype, but it was correct that young people from politically troubled family backgrounds had demonstrated a high level of competitiveness. For example, young and middle-aged rural people from landlord and rich peasant families were more likely than others to master the growing of crops or the running of small businesses. Many urban people from rightist or other politically marginalised families were also likely to perform well in academic or intellectual activities than in the mid-1960s (see Chapter two).

The divergent social reactions at the general public level gave rise to two frequently mentioned social phenomena in Chinese society in the mid-1980s: twisting Deng Xiaoping's call to look forward into a negative catchphrase of always thinking of money (*yiqie xiang qian kan*), and criticising new developments in society while enjoying a manifestly improved lifestyle (*duanqiwan chirou, fangxiawan maniang*). Such abnormal social reactions were driving factors in people's social repositionings and are worth analysing further.

Table 6.1 Major steps to remove policy restrictions on people's social repositionings.

Year	Major Removals of Restrictive Policies
1979	Removal of the 'class hat' (*zhaimao*) of landlords, rich peasants and their children
1980	Completion of removing the 'rightist hat' of more than a half a million rightists punished in 1957 and afterwards
1980	Rehabilitations of Liu Shaoqi and many other former senior leaders and officials punished in the Mao era
1981	Official end of the 'sent-down youth' policy, allowing those affected to return to their cities of origin
1982	Institutionalisation of the retirement of ageing officials and bureaucrats in order to open up positions for young people
1984	Establishment of 14 new special economic zones (SEZs) in coastal regions after the original four SEZs
1984	Nationwide extension of the enterprise autonomy policy to more SOEs
1985	The price reform discussed in the text allocated more resources to peasants
1986	Formal adoption of the labour or employment contract system in enterprises, as well as enterprise leasing and contracting systems
1988	Pilot trial on the new housing reform officially launched, reducing people's dependence on the state system

Sources: Complied by the author based on Lin et al. (2001), Dittmer (2015), Wang (2017b), Kleinberg (2018), Xiao (2019) and Wemheuer (2019).

The popular catchphrase *yiqie xiang qian kan* (putting money first in everything or always thinking of money) was a twisted version of Deng Xiaoping's call to put aside past sorrows and resentments, and to instead focus on the future. The last sections of the topic of Deng's historic December 1978 speech, 'Emancipate the mind, seek truth from facts and unite as one in looking to the future', was mocked by some Maoists, and reworded to create a new popular phrase – 'always thinking of money' – playing on the pronunciation of the last few words. According to one reformist (quoted below), this reflected the divisions in the top leadership, but also partly reflected many people's wish to get rich as soon as possible:

> 'Always thinking of money' is no stranger to me. In the 1980s, it was used as a target [of criticism] and caused a quite big farce. This farce was not trivial because the background was extraordinary and it was launched by four high-level heavyweights of the CCP at the prime time of the CCTV [China Central Television]. Of course, it was also unable to be bigger than that as it was unable to be carried out and evolved into a kind of [political] climate in wide society, including academic circles of economics. (Reformdata 2004, n.p.)

The prevalent and strong desire of most Chinese to 'become rich first' in Deng's catchphrase not only effectively blunted calls for ideological purification – reducing the so-called Anti-Spiritual Pollution Campaign of the mid-1980s to a subject of government-controlled publications and academic debates – but also eventually generated a pushy societal mentality of 'not missing the last bus'. This widespread grassroots mentality was part of the typical Chinese mindset in the 1980s; it has since been called *panbi xinli*, or simply *panbi*, a psychological tendency of 'comparing with and outperforming others' (Lam and Huang 2012, 118). The key point in this mentality was to compare and catch up with what others had achieved (Gore 1998; You 1998). This desire was so strong that many people experienced anxiety, even widespread stress and panic attacks. Because of this social psychological phenomenon, the behaviours of many people at the time were frequently influenced by the *panbi* push in order to avoid missing any opportunities to improve their social position emerging out of policy changes.

According to several people who went through this period, the efforts of Maoists and other leftists to depict the Dengist focus on the economy as a mistake of encouraging people always think of money were a major contributor to the mentality of not missing the last chance. Open debate over ideological issues led many to infer that reforms might be one-off and short-lived, and that they should therefore grasp any chance that came their way while the CCP was 'confused' (*fan hutu*). The suspicion that the CCP might at some point cease or reverse reforms led many people to act in panic mode, seeing every chance as their last. This *mobanche* (last-bus) mentality created an environment in which individuals identified different forms of opportunity over this period and became involved in competitive social repositionings and positionings.

The second unusual phenomenon was prevalent among both rural and urban residents, and both advantaged and disadvantaged groups. This was the previously mentioned reaction of criticising new developments while enjoying improved lifestyles. This key social phenomenon of the 1980s has received an academic sobriquet, but it commonly referred to by its colloquial name: *duanqiwan, chirou, fangxiawan maniang* (literally, holding up the bowl to have meat, and cursing the mother (i.e., the authorities) once putting the bowl down) (Yue 1999). A slightly different explanation of this vivid expression is 'cursing between mouthfuls' (Lee 2000, 23). Leaving aside the accuracy of the translation, this phrase is an accurate representation of a prevalent social phenomenon of the 1980s.

The contradictions expressed in the phenomenon's colloquial name have never been clearly understood from a materialist viewpoint. Many reformers were puzzled by the question of why hunger-free people still felt unhappy and even more upset than before. Nor was it well explained by new viewpoints, such as the viewpoint of opportunity resources proposed by Sun Liping (one of the author's former disciplinary colleagues in Beijing in the 1980s). According to Sun, the 1980s saw the emergence of 'freely flowing resources' and 'free activity spaces' (Sun 1993, 66). These were new opportunities for many citizens, but they also caused a weakening of the existing social structure, as well as disruption to social functioning. Clearly, the focus of Sun's analysis was the structural functional aspects of China's social change. What was ignored was social changes as processes of interactions between people, in which people became more concerned with the possibility of missing opportunities, and with their own possible disadvantages in social positionings, than with the opportunities themselves. The resulting widespread criticism had an enormous influence on young and naive youths, which will be analysed in the last section of this chapter.

One interviewee compared the social responses to the situations in the mid-1980s to the reactions of individuals to gambling:

> At that time, there were so many new policies that were introduced one after another to rectify previous mistakes made from the early 1950s to the end of the Cultural Revolution. One new policy would often liberate and help one group of people. Doing this repeatedly was a lot like a Lotto draw. Those who won celebrated quickly, and those who did not win were disappointed because of both the win of others and the celebration of others. Throughout the 1980s, it was like one lottery draw, or horse race, after another. People seemed to have lived in constant joy and frustration. (Interviewee 21 2020)

Comments such as the one made by this particular interviewee contradict various politicised and ideologised readings of developments in the 1980s and suggest that these social responses should be seen as a process of people reacting eagerly to new opportunities and involving themselves in increasingly competitive social repositionings.

Achieving Wealth and Recognition through Diligence

Looking back from the 2020s at what happened in China in the 1980s, it is clear that no other class of people were more underrated in various ways, yet also benefitted more from reform measures, than the peasants and some urban workers and jobless citizens. Chinese society in the 1980s was influenced by many ideological and moral prescriptions or exhortations. Many of these looked good on paper, or in theory – whether officially endorsed communism or liberal democracy – but most adherents of these views were prejudiced in real life against peasants and urban workers and those out of work. This was part of what has been called the rural–urban divide and the social class divide. It was because of these prejudices that peasants seeking paid work outside their villages, and urban residents running small business, were demonised as either *mangliu renkou* (floating population) or *getihu* (individual business operators).[4] As hinted at in Chapter five, these terms were originally used negatively by stably employed urban workers and relatively well-salaried professionals. However, the lessons of the past – and especially the understanding of the direct correlation between long-term poverty and destructive revolution – coloured the outlook of the Chinese leadership, leading them to resolutely pursue a strategy of allowing some people to become rich first in order to avoid social instability.

Of course, there were also hard feelings and simmering resentments among rural residents and urban blue-collar workers, but they did not have the luxury of acting like many university students, nor could they advance any appealing slogans or convincing ideas to guide new movements for social changes. Keeping themselves and their families fed was a more urgent task than thinking about big-picture issues. Their circumstances forced them to focus on making a living, while letting students and intellectuals vent dissatisfactions on their behalf.

As indicated, the discussion in this section is a continuation of the analysis in the second section of Chapter five and should be considered in conjunction with that section. In the second half of the 1980s, the first policy adjustment mentioned in Chapter five – letting rural people make a living from selling and buying agricultural produce – was no longer as attractive as two new chances: moving to where new opportunities existed, and working in TVEs. These new opportunities not only remained popular throughout the second half of the 1980s but also helped many working-class people achieve more advantaged positions.

Therefore, the widely welcomed development strategy of allowing some Chinese to get rich first was not only liked by poor peasants and workers, especially rural people, but was also used immediately on a national scale. In practical terms, the most visible response was the huge number of peasants who started flowing into cities or small urban centres to look for work. For a long time, this phenomenon was explained in general terms, emphasising the correctness of reform measures and the positive reaction from rural residents. In fact, there were also economic structural reasons – more specifically, labour market reason – that made a floating labour force not only permissible but also necessary in some regions. Economic reform had stimulated economic activities at a national level, which had the effect of shrinking the labour pool in many urban centres within a few years, and also generated strong demand for labour. According to the official statistics, China's urban unemployment rate reached 5.4 per cent in 1979, partly because of the return of many sent-down youth to their home cities. This figure fell to 3.2 per cent in 1982 and then to 1.9 per cent in 1984 (NBSC 2018). This was a situation that China had not seen since the late 1950s, when its Great Leap Forward failed, and it served as a pull factor, attracting labourers to those places where economic activities were greater. As shown in Figure 6.1, millions of rural people were attracted to areas offering paid jobs.

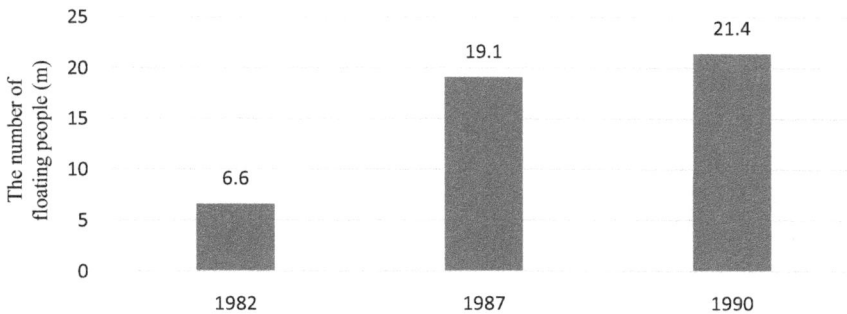

Figure 6.1 Flow of rural people to areas with new opportunities. *Sources*: Compiled by the author based on NBSC (1999, 2009).

At the same time, the expansion of TVEs, and rural industrialisation in general, had also entered a new phase, making them not only an essential sector of the national economy but also far more autonomous than SOEs. These advances are summarised in the quotation below:

> In 1984, the No. 4 document of the Central Committee officially changed the name of commune and brigade enterprises to township and village enterprises [TVEs], which fully and timely affirmed the official recognition of family-run and joint-household-run enterprises. The state also adopted a policy of offering these TVEs more support, allowing them to have greater autonomy [than SOEs] in organising production and product sales. TVEs entered the peak period of their first all-round expansion. In 1986 and 1987, it only took them two years to complete the output target of the Seventh Five-Year Plan. By 1988, the number of TVEs reached 18.88 million, employing 95.46 million people. (NBSC 1999, n.p.)

One key point not revealed in both the figure and the quotation is the connection between the floating rural population and TVEs. In practice, the connection created two types of benefit for rural people. In the case of first-time floating rural labourers, many of them acquired knowledge (including an understanding of market conditions) and skills through working in other regions before returning home to set up their own workshop or factory. The second type of benefit was the money accumulated by those who started as floating workers earlier. These diligent and able peasants had completed their initial accumulation of capital by the mid-1980s, and as a result new privately owned and operated workshops and factories emerged everywhere in China in what has been described as the early stage of the so-called rural industrialisation. Thus, floating was a key part of the social repositioning efforts of many rural residents. This also made possible the expansion of TVEs throughout the 1980s (Figure 6.2).

All these developments provided new social ladders in addition to the commonly used ones (such as attending university) for aspirational peasants, as well as some urban residents. Despite being looked down on all the while, hundreds of thousands – if not millions – earned a fortune through their endeavours and become the first or second

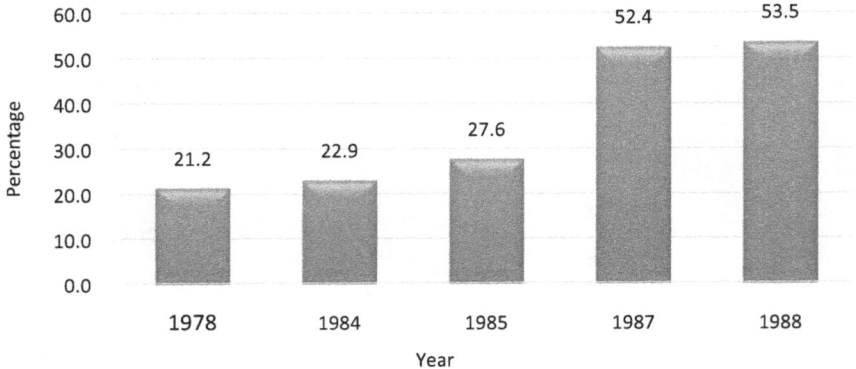

Figure 6.2 A growing proportion of the output of TVEs in the total rural output, 1978–88. *Sources*: Compiled by the author based on Huang (1990), He (1991) and NBSC (1999, 2009).

generation of entrepreneurs in the PRC's history. Because there are so many new entrepreneurs, a careful selection has been made for this analysis. A relatively short list of 146 entrepreneurial cases compiled by Feng Lun, a researcher-turned-developer already introduced in Chapter five, is useful for the purpose of this discussion. Table 6.2 is a list of typical peasants- and workers-turned-entrepreneurs based on Feng's list.

Feng's list seems to have been updated at a fairly leisurely pace, and Table 6.2 is updated to the end of February 2022. It is also worth stating that Table 6.2, like Table 6.3 in the next section, does not include the entrepreneurial cases discussed in Chapter five and its note 3. Another important point is that all 146 entrepreneurs on Feng's list have listed their businesses on the stock markets in China, Hong Kong or overseas, and each of the 21 peasants- and workers-turned-entrepreneurs listed in Table 6.2 has over the past few decades accumulated millions or billions of Chinese yuan in personal or family wealth.

As mentioned, there were winners and losers in the early stages of reform, during which numerous hardworking and competent peasants, as well as some urban workers and jobless people, made use of relaxed policies to explore new opportunities. By the mid- and late 1980s, there were many anecdotes and stories – such as *Shazi Guazi* (Simpleton's (cooked sunflower) seeds) mentioned in Chapter five – that were changing people's understanding not only of Deng's policy to 'let some people get rich first', but also of the new mobilisation slogan of *qinlao zhifu* (enriching one's life through diligence). Those listed in Table 6.2 are examples who were reacting to the changes in society and starting their own endeavours predominantly in the second half of the 1980s. Some of their experiences offer more meaningful examples of the social repositioning efforts made in those rapidly changing years than how much they earned.

The case of Wang Yusuo seems a perfect example of how a person who failed the university entrance exams several times in the mid-1980s could find other avenues to establish himself by venturing out into a range of small businesses. There are other entrepreneurs among the 146 who also made efforts to sit the university entrance examinations, but Wang failed it three times as a new school leaver, which made him feel

Table 6.2 Peasants- and workers-turned-entrepreneurs who started in the 1980s.

Name*	Place of Origin	Job in the 1980s	Business Established
Wang Gang	Sichuan	Kitchenhand in Beijing	Restaurant chain of Meizhou Dongpo Group
Su Zengfu	Zhejiang	Salesman of a county factory	Supor cookware business
Wang Zhentao	Zhejiang	Carpenter in Wuhan	Aokang shoes and Kanghua bioproducts
Wang Yusuo	Hebei	Salesman of a small factory	ENN Energy Group
Cai Zuming	Zhejiang	Peasant and bean curd maker	Soy products and food
Shi Jubin	Henan	Peasant selling dried jujube	Haoxiangni health food
Ren Jianhua	Zhejiang	Peasant	Hangzhou Robam appliances
Yuan Qinshan	Shanxi	Peasant trading motorbike	Dayun motorbike
Lu Youzhong	Chongqing	Cook	Youyou snack foods
Chen Keming	Hunan	Carpenter	Keming noodle and food
Liang Qingde	Guangdong	TVE worker	Galanz Enterprises
Deng Yingzhong	Guangdong	Peasant	C&C Paper Co
Li Shuirong	Zhejiang	Rural carpenter	Zhejiang Rongsheng Holding
Zheng Jianjiang	Zhejiang	Rural labourer	AUX Home Appliances
Chen Shiliang	Zhejiang	Villager	Tongkun (Polyester Fibre) Group
Li Xianyi	Fujian	Tractor driver	Xinyi Glass
Yao Juhuo	Shanxi	Village head	Meijin Energy Group
Zhu Guangcheng	Jiangsu	TVE head	Funing Rare Earth Industrial
Li Hongxin	Shandong	Factory worker	Sun Paper Group producing paper products
Tang Guohai	Zhejiang	Sent-down youth	Leadsun solar light manufacturer
Tu Jianhua	Chongqing	Miner	Loncin Motor Co Ltd

Note: *Names are listed according to the original order of 146 cases in Feng (2022).
Source: Compiled by the author based on Feng (2022).

more disheartened than those being experienced in tackling difficulties, such as going through the Cultural Revolution. This sense of depression must have been overwhelming in the mid-1980s, given that Wang grew up in a small town in northern China, where people were heavily influenced by the *keju* tradition of taking part in the official examinations and finding a position within the state system.

Prevented from following the traditional path of advancement, and faced with the strongly competitive social atmosphere of the mid-1980s, Wang Yusuo had to pick from different options from those popular among urban youth at the time. He had to find

Table 6.3 Officials- and professionals-turned-entrepreneurs who started in the 1980s.

Name*	Place of Origin	Job before Xiahai	Business Established
Li Xiting	Wuhan	Researcher in physics	Medical device of Mindray
Liu Hanyuan	Sichuan	Technical officer	Aquatic and fodder products of Tongwei
Guan Yanbin	Heilongjiang	Youth league branch head	Pharmaceutical group called Sunflower
Huang Hongsheng	Hainan	Office-based engineer	Skyworth group and Skywell Automobile
Liang Wengen	Hunan	Officer of a SOE	Sany Group producing heavy equipment
Chen Jiancheng	Zhejiang	Factory head	Wolong Electric producing motors and generators
Wang Jianxin	Zhejiang	Post office officer	Futong Group producing optical fibre
Li Jianquan	Hubei	Team leader	Zhuhai Winner Medical Products
Chen Baohua	Zhejiang	Head of lab	Zhejiang Huahai Pharmaceutical
Hu Baifan	Zhejiang	School teacher	Zhejiang NHU making nutrition products
Zhou Mingyan	Hubei	Teacher	Hubei Lianle Group

Note: *Names are listed according to the original order of 146 cases in Feng (2022).
Source: Compiled by the author based on Feng (2022).

a livelihood first, rather than engaging in debates over which ideological position was right for China as many university students were doing. As a result, Wang took a series of low-paid casual jobs, selling small goods and driving a delivery van, before spotting a market gap between the demand for gas cylinders and the supply. This was part of China's urbanisation process, in which there were numerous undeveloped industries and services. Wang was lucky to grow up near several large urban centres, where he took a physically demanding job delivering gas bottles. It was through this work that he found himself in a market where not only were there no service and bureaucratic structure in place, but products were also in short supply. To make the product attractive, he opted to manufacture both gas stoves and gas cylinders, an approach that made his upfront payment scheme very successful when he had no money to run the business. By 1989, when China was profoundly disturbed by political turmoil, he was already financially positioned to establish his ENN Energy Group for further business growth. His business soon expanded through contracts to operate gas wells in the oil fields, which helped the company become not only the gas supplier in a few small urban centres, but also part of national gas pipeline projects. ENN Group was listed in Hong Kong in 2001, and over the decades it has been one of largest privately established and owned energy companies in China. One interviewee familiar with this business asked rhetorically on one occasion: 'Successful? Would you like to dig for gas pipelines of many thousand kilometres before seeing a few billions of bucks?' (Interviewee 39 2019).

The case of Chen Shiliang is another example of how a villager, this time in Zhejiang, adjusted to failing the university entrance examination in the late 1970s and repositioned himself, first as a rural casual teacher and then as a worker in a village factory. This took place during the second wave of rural industrialisation in southern China, in the second half of the 1980s, before his fellow workers elected him to manage the factory. There are numerous private factory owners or operators who have emerged from rural Zhejiang since the late 1970s and early 1980s; examples include Lu Guanqiu, who was famous for taking over rural factories and creating a new shareholding system for TVEs in the early 1980s, and the more recent case of Jack Ma Yun of Alibaba Group (although the latter is, of course, an urban case). The uniqueness of the case of Chen Shiliang is his continuing efforts to reposition himself in response to shifting social conditions. This trait was not only apparent before he became a worker, but also after he took over the factory management.

The formation and development of TVEs in Zhejiang has been the focus of considerable research (Wang 2012; Fu 2021). The so-called Zhejiang model that formed through the mid- and late 1980s attracted scepticism from the Maoists and other leftists, who were more concerned with the ideological representation – or the nature of work units, in the old words – of production organisation than the actual productivity and output. The Zhejiang model was developed based on the Wenzhou model mentioned in Chapter five and was believed to be different from the Sunan model used in southern Jiangsu province. While TVEs in southern Jiangsu were developed based on the old factories owned by the brigades and communes and were kept under different forms of collective ownership, the TVEs in Zhejiang were largely privately or family-owned. The operation was thus characterised by not only self-organising processes but also by niche economies (Huang 2010a; Herrmann-Pillath 2017). These last two characteristics drove factory owners and operators to keep adjusting to reflect shifts in the markets. Such adjustments, or efforts to reposition, seem to be a normal part of enterprise behaviour or operation, but they are also in essence part of human behaviour. In Chen Shiliang's case, although his business has focused on the production of chemical fibres, it has seen numerous and ongoing repositioning efforts to turn it into a globally dominant polyester producer. That is why he is believed to have earned his wealth from two traits, diligence and perseverance.

The First Cohort to Jump into the Sea of Business

The abovementioned mentality of *panbi* – comparing oneself with and seeking to outperform others – and the competition in social positioning it triggered or reinforced were constrained by the social circumstances of each individual and their groups. Their social positioning efforts were, therefore, also characterised by differences in social existence or class division. While rural residents made use of more tolerant policies allowing them to work outside their home region, as well as to carry out industrial activities, many sections of the urban population were less restricted than peasants in a relative sense and chose to reposition themselves differently. The university students of the 1980s are remembered for their active involvement in several democratic demonstrations, and some of those who were working within the party-state system chose to exit it and start climbing the ladder of *xiahai jingshang* (jumping into the sea of business).

The option of *xiahai jingshang* or *xiahai* (jumping into the sea of business) had become widely known in the mid-1980s among low-ranked officers and white-collar profession- als, despite only becoming more broadly recognised among more ordinary people in China and by China observers in the West in the first half of the 1990s. In general, two types of white-collar professionals were attracted to this non-mainstream option. The first category was those who felt the strong push of the new politics from within the party-state system – for example, the radicals during the Cultural Revolution (*san- zhong ren*, three categories of Maoist Cultural Revolutionaries) and the like, and the worker–peasant–soldier university students. These two categories were discussed in Chapters four and five. The second, larger, category comprised those who felt that, for whatever reason, they could not be promoted through the work unit or the system they had worked in. There were numerous reasons for such career stagnation, ranging from personal or interpersonal causes to institutional limits. However, these reasons all had a similar impact on some people, driving them away from their work units.

By the mid-1980s, the pull factor to adjust one's career plan and path had also become stronger – a fact largely obscured in intentionally constructed narratives ascrib- ing change to people being encouraged by the great cause of reform or being disturbed by revisionist policies. The new businesses of electronics parts and repair in Beijing's Zhongguancun generated a great deal of enthusiasm, and the financial ability of many Zhongguancun operators to buy private cars and other consumer goods before the mid- 1980s was a common topic of discussion – particularly among professionals and officers in those years.

In addition to the points that have been discussed, which are useful in understand- ing the rise of the first cohort of officials- and professionals-turned-entrepreneurs, two other factors emerged in interviews. First, from the perspective of individuals, societal circumstances after the late 1970s changed the social and political capital possessed by many people. This occurred in a positive way in many cases, but at the same time some people's advantages were reduced. Liang Xiaosheng, a novelist of the reform era, describes this in his novel *In the World*:

> The 'Cultural Revolution' was over, and the fate of many people had also changed. Some people were honoured or even gained additional capital unexpectedly. Having been perse- cuted by the 'Gang of Four' had become a sympathy capital of attracting wide support, and if one had acted unyieldingly [during the Cultural Revolution], it would become the respect capital to attract more respect. (Liang 2019, 450)

From the perspective of social order, some basic approaches and rules of the social benefits distribution system had also radically changed due to a range of new policies – for example, selecting university students without considering family background. As mentioned, these shifts were decisive because they subsequently changed the paths of upward social mobility, opening them up to ambitious and capable individuals. While some felt strongly about the devaluation of the social and political capital they had acquired in earlier times, and the reduction of the privileges they enjoyed, many others responded positively to the changes, embracing various career-building and money-earning opportunities that had emerged during the 1980s. As a result, people's perceptions of social status and social mobility also began to evolve in a similar direction, making some of them enthusiastic and bold enough to disengage from the party-state system.

Table 6.3 is similar to Table 6.2, and it is also based on the list published in Feng Lun's WeChat bulletin. Among the 146 entrepreneurs identified by Feng, there are 11 who can be used as examples of the first cohort of officials- and professionals-turned-entrepreneurs.

The case of Liu Hanyuan shows how far the disengagement process spread across the country. Liu grew up in a region of Sichuan province, far from where the first signs of disengagement emerged. He studied a vocational course specialising in aquatic products at a Sichuan-based technical and further education institute, and after graduation was assigned to work as a technical officer in a local government bureau. Through his official role helping to manage a local reservoir and its fish farming, he realised how severe the local fish shortage was in the early 1980s. He also soon discovered that several developed countries were introducing fish farming technology that could lower the overall cost and increase the output of aquaculture. Although Liu worked within the government system, the combined factors of the remoteness of the region and the dire poverty suffered by locals, including officials, made his trial of the new technology acceptable. Using borrowed money, he not only proved the new method useful but also achieved an above-average yield in a couple of years. This provided him with solid capital for promotion if he opted to stay within the system.

According to an analysis of one interviewee who is very familiar with the CCP's cadre promotion system and practices, this particular case offers a good example of how some officials and professionals 'assessed the different charisma of sticking to the party-state system and jumping into the [commercial] sea' in the 1980s (Interviewee 5 2019). It was obvious that 'sticking to' the government system was not an option for Liu Hanyuan. At the time, China's public servant salary system still fell behind the changes in the countryside, and the so-called *chi daguofan chi* (eating from one big pot) was still in practice no matter how significant a contribution one had made. This seemingly egalitarian system left many staff members feeling alienated while peasants were permitted to earn more. Liu's family background appeared to be another factor, putting the alleviation of family hardship high on his agenda.

In 1987, using the money earned from fish farming, he decided to set up his own factory after identifying the production of fish fodder as a promising new industry. Since positioning himself upstream of the production chain in the late 1980s, Liu has developed his Tongwei Group into a key manufacturer of not only fish fodder but also other fodder products. The massive scale of his enterprise made further business expansion possible. Since the mid-2010s, Tongwei has expanded into the new energy industry, engaging in solar panel production and utilisation. Due to his success in those industries, Liu has become the richest entrepreneur in Sichuan over the past decades, and one of the richest in China. Despite these, Feng Lun regards him as 'China's most underestimated entrepreneur' (Feng 2022, n.p.). He has on a number of occasions been asked about the secret of his success, and he has always referred to the significance of a cut-through point in positioning.

The case of Liang Wengen is another good example of how some officers and professionals chose between sticking to the party-state system or leaving the system to pursue their own business ventures. In contrast to the case of Liu Hanyuan, Liang had already reached a director-level position in a centrally controlled SOE located in Hunan province before leaving the government system.

Liang had benefitted from the Dengist modernisations of cadres discussed in Chapter five, especially the new requirements concerning tertiary education and *nianqinghua* (the rejuvenation of cadres or appointing young people). On the surface, Liang's decision to leave his post seems to have been driven by the demand for young university-educated people, with the 1980s permeated by the view that knowledge is productivity. This hypothesis was not, however, exactly supported by his early experiences after leaving his SOE post. His decision seemed to have been made on impulse, and he and his collaborators explored a range of business enterprises for a number of years, including selling sheep and liquor for a couple of years. The impulse to strike out on one's own was common among many ambitious Chinese in the second half of the 1980s according to several interviewees, who noted a number of reasons – for example, in the case of Liu Hanyuan, he had identified the product in great demand.

According to the analysis by Feng Lun, who has become an expert in the new entrepreneurship since he retired from the Vantone Group, the impulse among some officers and professionals to leave their posts was often driven by personal circumstances. Feng emphasises Liang's family background, suggesting that his family's protracted financial difficulties seemed to be a factor behind his decision. Of course, in the eyes of several other interviewees who worked in the party-state system in the late 1980s, the other side of the equation was people's expectations about their life and lifestyle. The latter may not be applicable in Liang's case but is worth taking into account more broadly.

The real first step of Liang's Sany Group was taken in 1986, when he and his collaborators positioned themselves in the welding industry based on their university training. Having tried various retail businesses (including selling sheep and liquor) over several years, they realised such ventures not only fell outside their field of expertise but also positioned them in competition with more people. Their new welding operation consciously differentiated them from their competitors by taking on new and difficult jobs that few welders could perform. This new venture in the engineering field was a proper utilisation of their skills, providing them with an advantage in this booming industry. China's large-scale factory construction in the late 1980s and early 1990s, and the nationwide infrastructure development that accelerated soon afterwards, saw them expand into manufacturing machinery, especially heavy equipment. The company is now the third largest heavy equipment manufacturer in the world.

It is worth noting that some commentators, and some researchers, have applied the derogatory term *yuanzui* (original sin) in their analysis of China's new entrepreneurs and other high-income earners, arguing that the new rich have accumulated their wealth through 'improper, unjust, or even illegal' conduct (Zang 2008, 56). This is what is now broadly called the mentality of hating the rich, which is a continuation of hostile attitudes and a derogatory tone towards those who left the state system and domestic rural migrants, the latter of whom were branded as 'blindly floating people'. The stigmatisation of the above two categories of reform participants provided some members of previously privileged groups, as well as anti-reformists, with a chance to show off what they had achieved before those new aspirants, but it has not prevented determined citizens from repositioning themselves in the process of reform. As noted by several interviewees, the individuals denouncing the new rich include a range of groups. Apart from those from the old privileged groups – some of whom are now regularly seen as guests at events held by entrepreneurs – the most interesting group of critics are those who missed out on the opportunity to make a fortune because their attention was drawn to the two main student political movements, which are discussed below.

Those with Lofty Ideals without Practical Strategies

Among the many narratives and recollections of ordinary life of Chinese people in the 1980s, a high proportion contain accounts of interpersonal interactions, gossips and rumours. Endless complaining over many issues has been derogatorily labelled as *popo mama* (literally, 'granny and mommy', female talkativeness), and the level of gossip and rumour was so high that they were described as *mantian fei* (flying all over the sky). These accounts offer an intuitive portrayal of what had happened in China in the 1980s. One suggestion offered by number of interviewees was that there is also a need to look at what people were talking about at the time. As noted earlier in this chapter, the high level of interpersonal interaction shared some similarities in attitude, being critical of any changes in society despite enjoying an improved life because of those changes, typically reflected in the already-quoted saying *duanqiwan chirou, fangxiawan maniang*. This strange mode of social reactions influenced many young people, especially university students, who became increasingly concerned about various adverse social consequences of China's reform.

Throughout the 1980s, the growing sense of the societal responsibility of university students was first displayed in campus-based local election campaigns in the early 1980s. Another major display was in late 1986 and early 1987, when student protests took place in Anhui over a local election issue and then spread to other cities. The demonstrations of this time reached their climax in Shanghai, where the government ended them through both police actions and the institutional control measures. These demonstrations resulted in the resignation of Hu Yaobang, the CCP's general secretary, and the launch of what was then called the anti-bourgeois liberalisation campaign in January 1987, while Jiang Zemin – as the mayor of Shanghai at the time – quite unintentionally amassed significant political capital from his handling of the protests. Jiang was appointed to the CCP's top leadership position after the crackdown following the 1989 protests.

It is difficult for younger readers – those who did not live in urban China throughout the 1980s – to read many available written sources and understand why so many students were involved in the protests from late 1986. Written sources mention the local election issue in Anhui, where the protests were first started, but hardly any other specific reasons were recorded to clearly explain why students in several Shanghai universities were sufficiently angered to march in the streets. Five catchphrases, or key slogans, were found to have been repeatedly used in Shanghai, demanding democracy, freedom and human rights, and calling for action against bureaucracy and corruption. As remarked in earlier chapters, the gap between the idealism of young thinkers and students in the 1980s and the pragmatism upheld by reformists was widening over the course of the decade. Young people were not only regaining the sense of historical mission that previous generations experienced, but also reusing almost all the ideas surfaced in the first half of the twentieth century.

The concept of the generation gap was introduced into China at around this time, and part of its local meaning referred to the fact that young people did not recognise the overly idealistic nature of some old ideas, and the many problems that had arisen when they were implemented. This situation was, of course, mainly because the CCP was unable to discard the ideological baggage it had carried for several decades, while the newly formed reform narratives were unable to fully appease many people. A careful analysis of written sources shows that the protesters in a few Guangzhou universities raised a few more practical issues than the Shanghai students, in addition to repeating the slogans used in Shanghai. These included concern over inflation, but this was expressed as a demand for improved living conditions on campus. The other demand was specific and rather strange: to stop the implementation of the CCP's *disan tidui* (third echelon) leadership strategy. The latter was the strategy of modernising the rules of cadre promotion, clearing the obstacles for younger talents. This particular issue, brought forward by student protesters in late 1986, was so confusing that several interviewees believed it may have been raised by people who were disadvantaged by the third echelon arrangement; this will be discussed at the end of this section.

Although the slogans used in Guangzhou were thus confusing, they were still more intelligible than the demands posed in Shanghai and other cities. Up until the mid-1980s, ordinary people in China were mainly disturbed by two issues, inflation and corruption. The authorities had tried to explain why inflation had occurred by publicising some of the reasons, including the transition effects of the dual-track system and benefits tilted to rural areas. The 'inflation rate frequently hit record highs' (Zhang 2017, 112). In 1985, it passed 10 per cent, reaching 19.2 per cent in 1988. By the time hundreds of thousands of students marched out of their campuses in mid-1989, it had climbed to 28.4 per cent (Luo 1988; Zhang 2017). This issue affected the entire population, especially urban wage earners, and the university students were also suffering from the surging costs of food and other basic goods.

Having been influenced by the customary attitude of the Chinese literati, student leaders and activists moved the focus of their attention away from inflation-related problems. In the 1980s, many educated people still considered the financial or materialistic aspects of social problems a concern for low-born people. While some opted to be part of the 'Tide of Going Abroad' (*chuguo chao*) leaving China in the mid-1980s (Hu 1988; Gao 2013a), many others observed the widespread money-grabbing and misbehaviour among those connected to the decision-makers in the party-state system. These issues then became topics of public conversation and gossip, building up resentment in the wider society. What made the societal reaction even more complicated was that the selfish use of political power and networks by those from privileged groups for private profit primarily disturbed those who themselves wished to climb the social ladder. University students were the largest such group, and their attention was soon drawn to their competitors, those who had both political privileges and social resources. This could well be the reason why students in Guangzhou openly opposed the third echelon leadership arrangement in 1986 and 1987.

The next step in the students' logic was that these problems needed to be resolved through political change. This idea became widespread and was accepted by many individuals anxious over being deprived of opportunity. Of course, few if any activists realised that in doing so they were not only more influenced by anti-reform stances than pro-reform ones, but had also generally aligned themselves with various anti-reform forces. They also overlooked the benefits that many forms of deregulation – such as in the retail and TVE sectors – could bring to the people who were unable to study at university and enter the state-run system.

After the student demonstrations in 1986 and 1987, an unprecedented level of public attention turned to corruption issues. The ideas and strategies of political reform, including freedom of speech and press, and open and democratic election, were seen as solutions to the problems China was experiencing. These ideas were embraced by intellectuals and student activists until early 1989, when the death of Hu Yaobang – the former CCP general secretary removed as a result of the political protests in late 1986 – triggered a fresh wave of protests by university students. These protests continued until early June 1989 when the government decided to put an end to them using the armed forces.

As is widely known, the reform era of the 1980s in China ended with the crackdown on what many have since regarded as the democratic movement of 1989. As there is already ample research on this historical event, this analysis will consider the event according to its own analytical logic, with a focus on why few now consider the 1989 demonstrations as significant in driving China's modernisation process as the 1976 Tiananmen Incident.

Throughout China's transformation decades, beginning in 1976, there were two large-scale mass protests staged in Beijing's Tiananmen Square: the 1976 Tiananmen Incident and the 1989 protest. The latter has been portrayed in the Western media and many other scholarly publications as a far more important event than the former. However, in the eyes of those who lived through those two decades, the 1976 protests seem not only to have been supported by larger numbers of ordinary Chinese than those in 1989, but were also more important in terms of influencing the direction of China's social change. In recent decades, different understandings from the dominant narratives of these Tiananmen protests have slowly revealed themselves, emerging not only from the interviews conducted for this research but also in people's daily conversations. While these analyses recognise the 1980's importance in China's twentieth-century history, and consider the difficulties of reform, two of the decade's effects on people's opportunities to reposition themselves are worth considering from a new viewpoint. The first and obvious consequence was the 1989 Tiananmen student demonstrations;

the second, less obvious but equally crucial to people's opportunities to reposition them-selves, was the political conclusion drawn by China's top ruling circles from the student protests – namely, that only those from revolutionary families were trustworthy.

As noted, many analysts now view the 1989 student demonstrations as less construc-tive and less significant for China's social changes than the 1976 Tiananmen protests. Different opinions emerged from both the interviews and analysis of the documen-tary sources for this research. The followings are some of the key aspects of the new perspective.

In terms of general social conditions, the Tiananmen protests in 1976 helped China achieve a directional change, which the 1989 protests did not. China was progressing during the 1980s, with a wide range of new reform measures allowing more people to make better livings than in 1976. Reformists had even publicly abandoned their original idealist principle of social equality, instead encouraging more people to escape poverty through hard work. This ideological shift sounds prosaic, but it marked a significant discontinuity from the Maoist emphasis on class struggle. More people in the second half of the 1980s had already improved their social and economic position in compari-son to 1976, including most student demonstrators. A large majority of the population preferred to see no sweeping change to the course of reform, while the demands of the student movement were more extreme than many people could countenance, especially the call for a shift in focus from economic and financial improvement to politics. The threat of a possible disruption to the reform process that was well underway by the late 1980s was a factor that led many Chinese to avoid overvaluing the 1989 student movement.

The lesser significance of the 1989 demonstrations (compared to the 1976 protests) was due not only to its clear deviation from the focus on economic growth, but also to the consensus that was formed and shared by people from different walks of life before and during the 1976 Tiananmen protests. The core element of this consensus was the rejection of Maoist class struggle and the desire to focus on improving the material standard of people's lives. This consensus was so widely held throughout the 1980s that it seems student activists and protesters must have been aware of what everyday people wanted to see and achieve. Despite this, the 1989 student protesters focused instead on political changes. This has raised the question of why the 1989 protesters were so deter-mined and persistent in pursuing their own beliefs and objectives. The diversification of people's career paths during the 1980s, and the growing contest for upward mobility over the same period, seems to many people to be causes that have not yet been taken into consideration. Of those people who reacted negatively to the competitive pressure generated by reform policies, one interviewee emphasised the following two types:

> There were many Chinese who believed in radical means to reform China. Apart from the young people who were naive about politics, other two types [of people] were all very active in all the protests in the second half of the 1980s. One type was those using politics [as means] for a speedy ascension, [and this] included those who were ambitious, but unable or unwill-ing to climb up step by step in work units. Another group were those who were very worried about their future because it was getting difficult to compete [with others]. The first type

was a mixture, including those born to *da laocu* [peasant-revolutionary] families. They had therefore less intellectual capital, being not used to usual competitions in peacetime. There were also many from the families of the party's intellectuals, some [of whom] have inherited the rebellious spirit of their parents towards adverse social situations. (Interviewee 26 2020)

More importantly, unlike the 1976 campaign the 1989 student movement had put forward no viable strategy or practical goals regarding what they wanted to achieve. As noted, the former clearly supported the idea of the four modernisations, which was not only seen as relevant to the life of struggling people, but was soon also translated into the new political strategy of China's post-Mao change. Throughout the 1980s, university students and other campaigners had held a string of protests, but their objectives and slogans had shown almost no change. Instead, as discussed in Chapter five, many student activists, and the leading intellectuals behind them, were proud of their role in carrying on the unfinished great cause of earlier revolutionaries. This is evidenced by the interpretation of Li Zehou, a leading Chinese scholar in the 1980s, who considered the 1980s as the 'dual variation of enlightenment and salvation' (Dongen 2019, 8).

Interestingly, this dual variation interpretation was shared not only by many within academic circles and other intelligentsia but also by some from veteran revolutionary families. For instance, Qin Xiao, who was an active factional leader of the Beijing-based Red Guards in 1966 and became one of influential figures of China's *Hong erdai* or second red generation, once not only stated that he agreed with Li Zehou's explanation but also argued that enlightenment has not yet been fully realised (Ma 2010). Epistemologically speaking, all these interpretations were very similar to the problem discussed in previous chapters – namely, an over-reliance on past ways of thinking about the nation and its changes. At the turning point of China's post-Mao reform, new theories and practical approaches were badly needed to deal with the problems arising from the reform process. There were, indeed, many young graduates giving their attention to analysing practical issues as early as the early 1980s. Those taking the dual variation view have since been considered by pragmatists as backwards-looking people, deeply entangled in conceptual jumbles without understanding. One interviewee believed it had the following effects:

Having gone through all these decades, we can now clearly see that almost no backwards-looking [student] leaders and intellectuals [of the 1980s] have then positioned themselves easily in comparison to [the careers of] their competitors of the decade. Many of them were adorable, having a strong sense of historical mission, but they were repeating what previous generations did, without understanding the missteps of the earlier generations. It was easy for young people to repeat those big slogans, such as enlightenment and salvation, but China needed those willing and able to study and deal with the new challenges. In terms of these, many [post-1977] university students were not much different in thinking from the 'democratic' activists outside the university [system]. They were all entangled in the old debates, wandering off the [career] path. (Interviewee 39 2019)

The other effect of the ongoing political activism of the 1980s on people's opportunities to achieve upward social mobility was due to the negative responses of the CCP's inner circles to the surging demands for political reform and democratisation. This cause was long less visible, but it negatively affected many people's opportunities for upward mobility from the late 1980s, and changed the dynamics of the elite–mass relationship, as well as the coalitions of new and old elites.

The frequency of the student demonstrations and the radicalism of the political solutions advocated by activists of the 1980s pushed the top ruling circles to reflect further on their thinking about the CCP's guiding narratives and political approach to promoting young leaders. As mentioned, despite the poor articulation of their demands by student protesters and other democratic campaigners, a considerable amount of their anger was in reality caused by corruption scandals – both real and rumoured – involving avaricious officeholders and their family members and relatives. To a great extent, the corruption issues were more closely related to the individual repositionings of people from the politically privileged groups, or from different groups of vested interests, than many critics had supposed. Those people were seriously challenged by the new social norms in post-Mao China, and the new criteria for climbing up the social ladder – such as exam-based entry to university and qualification-based promotion – led many sons and daughters of leaders to realise that they were not competitive if they followed the same path in life as others. Many therefore took advantage of their family influence and contacts to earn quick and easy fortunes. Thus, the 1989 protests can be seen either as a form of elite–mass conflict or as a rising tension between new and old elites.

As reviewed in Chapter one, an apparent bias favouring the focus on the first type of conflict, as well as on urban educated people, has characterised reports and analyses of the continuing protests in the 1980s for decades. Little attention has been paid to the second issue, the conflict between new and old elites, which was part of social change of the time. In reality, the new tension led to the CCP's inner circles rethinking many of the new policies and approaches used in post-Mao years. One of the most significant changes to equality of social mobility and opportunity was, as revealed earlier, the political conclusion reached and shared among the top decision-makers that only those from revolutionary family backgrounds were more politically reliable than other young people.

The above comment was widely spread among the middle and upper-middle classes in Beijing from the late mid-1980s, but it was only recently recorded in detail, in a book written by two dissident scholars living in the United States. They provide the following historical details of the decisions that narrowed the career paths of young people from non-revolutionary families:

> There is no written record of the CCP elders' attempt to cultivate future successors among the princelings, and up to now, the widely circulated words are Chen Yun's remark: 'our children are reliable'. Because this remark is not recorded in official history, some people may assume that this remark is a fictional view of the outside world on the CCP's high-level power inheritance. As a matter of fact, it is not, and this is a history that can be proved by [recorded] words. [...] He Weiling was an active figure in Beijing's political circles from 1978 to 1989. [...] He died in a car accident on the way to Mexico in 1991, and the manuscript that he left behind has lately been sorted out by his friends and published in Hong

Kong. As an eyewitness to what had occurred in Beijing's political circles in early reform years, he had left precious historical materials in his manuscript. As to the succession by princelings, He Weiling had described many details of it. (He and Cheng 2017, 57)

In the interests of full disclosure, I note that I collaborated with He Weiling in 1985 on translating English texts into Chinese, which were then published in 1986 under the new title, *Culture and Individual* (Gao et al. 1986). Based on our limited contact, I believe that He and Cheng's account is not baseless, and the published manuscript on which their analyses are based is also of great value for understanding the new dynamics of not only the succession politics but also social mobility, as well as the changing relationships between new and old elites in the second half of the 1980s.

Another significant decision was made and quietly implemented following the four modernisations of cadres and the third echelon leadership strategy, which was to consider a number of competent children of senior leaders to be placed in leadership positions. This was not an easy task to undertake in the midst of ongoing anti-corruption campaigns. Based on the details recorded in He Weiling's manuscript, He and Cheng sort out three tactics used to position those reliable 'princelings' in the ruling system (He and Cheng 2017). The first was the 'oil-dripping and -immersing' method – scattering these people in many systems and places and bringing more in once they are established. The second was to use the influence of popular princelings to attract more people to build new networks. And the third tactic was to position these individuals first as aides to current popular leaders and then seek their advancement. These efforts drastically affected the dynamics in society, contributing partly to the Tiananmen protests in 1989. As will be considered in Chapter seven, the options open to ordinary Chinese and their social positioning or repositioning have also changed profoundly since then.

Notes

1. The so-called dual-track system – also called a dual-track economic system or a dual-track economy – refers to an economic system in which the command economy and the market economy can coexist. In such systems, the state controls key economic sectors and other sectors are opened to market actors and competition. However, in this chapter I use the narrow definition of the dual-track concept, referring to the first use of the system in price reform. Under this dual-track pricing strategy, officially controlled prices were on the planned track and free-market prices formed the market track. This mixed system was used to transition to a reduced role for state planning in the economy and to strengthen the function of the market. Of course, this reform strategy was then extended to cover almost all economic sectors including the ownership of enterprises, property and other businesses. Such long transition processes on different forms of dual-track system periodically caused strong public reactions and turbulence in the system, which offers a useful perspective to observe events in China. In addition to Hua (2005) and Zhang (2018b), listed in the text, interested readers are referred to Naughton (2007) and Garnaut et al. (2018).

2. In addition to the 13 September Incident in 1971, or 9/13, discussed in Chapter four, the most famous day in September among young Chinese is 18 September, known in Chinese as the 9/18 Incident, to commemorate the Japanese invasion in China's northeast in 1931. This incident was also called the Mukden Incident or Manchurian Incident. The 9/18 Incident has long been remembered by Chinese as a day of national humiliation, and it has, therefore, been often used for domestic purposes. One of the many examples can be found in one of my co-authored book chapters, analysing how an incident was linked to the 9/18, and it was then

used by grassroots people, both group and individual, to push the governments to play their parts (Pugsley and Gao 2009). Readers interested in the 9/18 Incident in 1931 are referred to Young (1998) and Mitter (2000).

3. There are several ways to translate the phrase *nifan xinli*, including rebellious psyche, reverse mentality or negative mentality, as I explain in my 2013 book (Gao 2013a). Other possible translations include psychology of defiance (Bakken 2000), converse psychology (He 2001) and the contrary frame of mind (Drulhe and Black 2002). It was originally borrowed from the developmental psychology of children, but its early use in applied social sciences in China refers to the suspicion that many Chinese people held towards the media in 1980s and their ways of seeing and interpreting whatever happened from an opposite direction. Interested readers can find more information about this phrase from the publications listed above.

4. It is worth explaining that the English translations of the Chinese phrases *mangliu renkou* (floating population) and *getihu* (individual business operator) do not really reflect the negative and degrading connotations of these original terms. The direct translation of *mangliu renkou* should be 'blindly moving population', as the term emphasises the word *mang* (blind or blindness). This is why this term has lately been modified to *liudong renkou*, which is more neutral. The term *getihu* seems to be less negative than *mangliu renkou*, but throughout the 1980s it denoted not only a direct opposite to collectivism, the officially endorsed and advocated political value, but was also used to indicate people's social status. People who were labelled as *getihu* in the 1980s were outside the state system, and the phrase *getihu* had, therefore, a negative connotation at the time to people who were looking for self-employment opportunities to feed themselves.

Chapter Seven

FILLING IN THE POST-1989 VACUUM
LEFT BY EDUCATED LIBERALS

This chapter begins with a brief explanation of events during the politically turbulent period covered by the second half of Chapter six and the present chapter. Many readers know that this period includes the 1989 Tiananmen protests, which lasted several months before the military crackdown on 4 June 1989. Historically, this was the PRC's third large-scale crackdown on activist members of the urban educated elite. In 1957, the Anti-Rightist Campaign was carried out by the CCP in response to the widespread and strong criticism voiced by many urban citizens during the Hundred Flowers Campaign. Much of this criticism went far beyond what the first generation of PRC leaders were prepared to tolerate, particularly in the aftermath of the Hungarian Revolution of 1956.[1] As many as half a million Chinese people were persecuted according to official figures. The second major assault was the Cultural Revolution from 1966 to 1976; while this impacted on almost every section of the Chinese population, educated people had always been the key target of class struggle. Millions of educated Chinese were abused in one way or another. What occurred in Beijing, as well as in several other cities, in 1989 and the purge that ensures were a third attack on the new educated elites, with tens of thousands ousted from their posts in the party-state system and forced to seek a living elsewhere.

As noted in previous chapters, the analysis in this chapter is based on this third crackdown, but focuses on the understudied aspects of this historical episode, as well as the problem of laid-off (*xiagang*) workers, which worsened around the same time.[2] At first glance, the laid-off worker issue caused by SOE reforms after the mid-1980s, notably in 1994 and 1995, was distinct from the trouble facing educated liberals; however, many of those affected by each sought to reposition themselves in the same employment market.

The 1989 Tiananmen protests have been well documented in English, providing readers with ample details about the event; however, the political and social vacuum left by the crackdown has not been clearly explained. The 1989 clampdown was a sudden turn to the political left, quelling the demonstrations and reintroducing various social control measures. It was soon followed, however, by China's unprecedented economic growth. A very clear and sharp zigzag change of political direction emerged before many people had recovered from their anger and sadness of the crackdown on the student rallies. At the risk of cliché, the 1989 Tiananmen Incident had also created a situation where the old adage 'one person's loss is another person's gain' was applicable. The most obvious example of such losses and gains was the positions vacated by activists, protesters, advocates, sponsors and participants who were either expelled from, or quit, the party-state system, including government offices, universities, media institutions and other subsidiary organisations. Those who left were often competent, ambitious and independent, and their departure was a major loss for both the system and the victims themselves. The vacancies they left behind opened up new chances for others, not to mention new rules and dynamics, which were a gain for those from the other side of politics.

The analysis in this chapter begins what occurred to many participants and supporters of the Tiananmen demonstrations. The across-the-board purge of activists was not only the end of the protest campaign, but also the start of a new politics, in which many positions and opportunities were restructured and redistributed. This redistribution was not as simple as many had expected, because a more fundamental turn to pragmatism, if not to the right, had started even before Deng Xiaoping's famous inspection tour of southern China in early 1992. The sudden zigzag change in politics in 1989 was soon straightened to align with reformist ideas and strategies, creating many new opportunities for people from both sides of politics.

The changes that were discussed, and the impact on people's chances to position or reposition in post-1989 China, will be analysed in three sections. The first section starts with the post-1989 official campaign to purge all active participants in and supporters of the 1989 protests from the party-state system, forcing many educated urban people to reconsider their careers. The CCP leadership adopted a far tougher political stance and methods in punishing the activists and protesters than it did in relation to the *sanzhong ren* (three types of Cultural Revolutionary militant activists). This created a gloomy political atmosphere, threatening the future of China's economic reform and growth. This gloom began to lift once Deng Xiaoping made his inspection tour of southern China in early 1992. The second section continues with a brief analysis of the impact of Deng's inspection tour on the socio-political atmosphere of post-1989 China. This section then turns to a new major wave of *xiahai jingshang*, 'jumping into the ocean', of commerce; this high tide was characterised by political drivers, as well as by the participation of many former officers, public servants, academics and other white-collar professionals. While this change resulted in the loss of hard-earned white-collar positions and 'iron-rice-bowl' jobs in SOEs, it also aided the expansion of some industries that had never had such access to so many well-connected and well-educated people. The third section offers a preliminary analysis of the crucial change aimed at training a large group of young and politically reliable officers or reserve talents through non-academic educational institutions. This was not only aimed at avoiding the return of liberal influence, reducing the reliance on universities for graduates, and filling in the vacancies left by departed or sacked staff members, but was also pushed by many lower-level officials without qualification. The latter was required for further promotion. This change in the cadre training arrangement took many forms, including formal recognition of training courses offered by the CCP's party school system. This consequently changed the rules and conduits for upward social mobility in China significantly.

The Socio-Political Vacuum Caused by the 1989 Crackdown

The depressing political atmosphere and massive social vacuum that followed the 1989 crackdown in China were created by a series of political moves, not simply by one action. Overall, however, two approaches, driven by two types of political correctness since 1989, have prevented the general public from forming a clear understanding of events in China during and after early June 1989. Within China, the 1989 protests were originally defined as anti-CCP, anti-socialism and anti-revolutionary political unrest, and the crackdown was defined as a counter-insurgency action. The words used to define both the incident and the crackdown were later softened to depict the protests as less radical and provocative. This tactic has led to the almost complete disappearance of the event from the official discourse, the reasons for which will be considered later in this section. In contrast, the international media response has continued to view the 1989 demonstrations as a democratic movement and the crackdown as an act of brutality by the communist regime. Any other view is widely seen as pro-CCP or anti-democratic.

Leaving aside the positive and negative aspects of those two approaches, both have politicised and distorted the event, with the public little option but to accept to one set of explanations over another. Conventional wisdom suggests history will reveal the truth, but this seems to be highly conditional on the basis that enough participants and eyewitnesses of an event are still available to provide evidence. This study has benefitted from conversations on the topic with several interviewees who worked throughout the earlier decades of reform. According to them, and to voluminous documentary evidence as well, there were at least six courses of action that helped create the socio-political vacuum in society after the crackdown on 4 June 1989.

These actions were the arrest and detention of campaign leaders, the flight of a huge number of active protesters and leaders from China, an intra-party campaign to expel many members from the CCP, the forced removal of staff from state-controlled institutions and students from universities, the voluntary departures of white-collar professionals and other staff members, and an upsurge in the number of Chinese going abroad.

The first step taken by the Chinese government from the beginning of the crackdown was to arrest and detain the prominent leaders of the 1989 protest campaign and the people behind them. While the total number arrested may never be accurately established, the figures in Table 7.1 are often used to show what occurred before 30 June 1989.

It is worth noting that the figures used in Table 7.1 are from an online book, *Deng Xiaoping's Path in his Final Years*, written by Shui Luzhou, whose real name is Wang Zhonglin, a Hunan-based Maoist and the author of a number of popular books on the Cultural Revolution. Despite his political views, Shui's book on Deng Xiaoping's final years is well regarded by researchers from both sides of politics. Wu Jiaxiang, a public intellectual who was also jailed in Beijing for years after the 1989 crackdown, considers the book as a 'serious academic work' (Wu 2006, n.p.). Bu Weihua, a CCP historian who was recognised as a younger member of the plotters of forming the first Red Guard group at Tsinghua University High School, also speaks highly of this book and its rich data (Bu 2009b). Additionally, the figures listed in Table 7.1 are partly confirmed by other sources (Jiang 2009).

The real situation can also be partly inferred from other documentary evidence. In the yearly report by China's Prosecutor-General to the Third Session of the Seventh

Table 7.1 Estimated numbers of people arrested and groups outlawed by 30 June 1989.

Region	Number of People Arrested	Number of Organisations Outlawed
Beijing	1,103	N/A
Shanghai	273	3
Heilongjiang	176	21
Jilin	98	18
Liaoning	338	35
Shaanxi	254	29
Shanxi	218	9
Inner Mongolia	98	N/A
Sichuan	781	53
Hunan	516	17
Hubei	216	33
Anhui	37	N/A
Jiangsu	113	15

Source: Compiled by the author based on Shui (2004).

National People's Congress in March 1990, Liu Fuzhi revealed an enormous surge in the number of vaguely defined criminal cases in 1989. As quoted below, the percentages of increases in reported criminal cases, numbers of arrested lawbreakers and cases transferred to prosecutors were all significantly higher than the annual rises in other types of criminal activity. According to the same report, the latter's increase percentages ranged from 9 per cent to 15 per cent nationwide in 1989:

> In 1989, our country's public security situation was generally stable, but there were many unstable factors, and the situation was still quite grim. [...] Last year, the procuratorial agencies nationally received an enormous number of requests from public security organs to arrest 632,323 criminals, a surge of 33.9 per cent over the previous year. As many as 548,960 arrests were approved, an increase of 35.8 per cent over the previous year. The number of criminals transferred from the public security organs for prosecution was 604,263, and after review, 520,257 people have been prosecuted, an increase of 36.9 per cent and 36.5 per cent respectively over the previous year. (Liu 1990, n.p.)

The differences between the two sets of figures revealed by Liu show an unusual increase in the number of Chinese dealt with by police and other law enforcement agencies. It is highly likely this increase in supposed criminal cases was related to the crackdown that started in early June 1989.

The second change that contributed to the post-1989 societal vacuum was not directly caused by the authorities but, rather, by activist themselves, and several shadowy groups or organisations that rescued many students and their supporters. The total number of Chinese activists rescued may never be accurately established, particularly as the rescue efforts coincided with a surge in human smuggling activity in the region (Chin 1999; Zhang 2008b) as well as a fresh wave of emigration. Many people in this last category also claimed to be democratic activists or the like when seeking asylum in Western countries, in a pattern of what I call 'strategic identity formation' (Gao 2013a, 22). Of course, the attention of the media and its readers was focused on the rescues. According to some published sources, the major rescue operations were organised and undertaken by groups and organisations in Hong Kong and Taiwan. The one organised in Hong Kong was called Operation Siskin (*Huangque Xingdong*), which for some reason has also been translated as Operation Yellowbird. The latter translation has confused non-Chinese readers as it is identical to the translation given to Taiwan's *Huangniao Jihua* (Plan Yellowbird or Operation Yellowbird), which was directed by an external operations branch of the KMT. According to Xie Xuanjun, who has been exiled from China since the early 1990s, the purpose of the plan was to 'send [about] 400 people involved in the protests to overseas countries for protection by Taiwan' (Xie 2021, 273). In total, the two operations rescued about eight hundred campaign activists from China.

Apart from the several hundred protest organisers and supporters who were rescued from China, the importance of this action was its wider effect on many others who were either in imminent danger of being persecuted or were inevitably disadvantaged in their future careers in the country. The escape of hundreds of protesters, prominent or otherwise, to foreign countries was a strong reminder of the option of leaving China, the effect of which will be analysed later as the sixth step in creating the post-1989 sociopolitical vacuum.

The third key measure implemented by the ruling CCP focused on its own team and members. This was the intra-party campaign to expel party members who were actively involved in, and supported, the student demonstrations from the party. Within a month of the crackdown on 4 June 1989, Jiang Zemin, as China's new leader, declared that a systematic and thorough rectification campaign was urgently required to correct the party's severe ideological and organisational problems (Cao 2019). After Jiang's speech on 1 July 1989, a series of work conferences were held by CCP organs to prepare the campaign. The final decision was promulgated on 7 September 1989 through a CCP circular, *Opinions on the Re-registration of Party Members in Some Units* (Brown 2021). The document clearly stated that through vetting and re-registration the party would resolutely eliminate hostile and anti-party elements and eradicate hidden political dangers and corrupt elements within. The other aim was to persuade unqualified party members to give up their membership in order to maintain the party's purity and advancement and to strengthen its political power. This was widely called *qingcha qingli* (checking-up and cleaning-up), often shortened to double cleansing (*shuangqing*). This was the key measure, affecting more people in the second half of 1989 and 1990 than a range of other actions taken by the CCP to handle the 1989 protests and exceeded only by the voluntary departure of many professionals and public servants, which will be discussed later in this section.

The expulsion campaign in the aftermath of the crackdown was conducted in an extraordinarily political manner, in part because of the typical political behaviour of leftist members in many CCP branches. They used the campaign as a chance to punish their competitors, although many local and institutional branch leaders are believed to have protected some of their colleagues from deregistration and other forms of punishment (Interviewee 15 2019; Interviewee 48 2019). Approximately half a million members of the CCP are believed to have been expelled nationwide. At that time, total party membership was estimated to be around forty-five million (Bian et al. 2008; Yao 2011). This ratio was marginally lower than the number of CCP members who were disciplined at Tsinghua University throughout the rectification campaign, from February to December 1990. Of five thousand members at the university, about eighty were expelled from the CCP according to the university's chronicle (Fang and Zhang 2001, 823).

It is also worth mentioning that in the aftermath of the unprecedented anti-government demonstrations, the CCP's new leadership acted differently from the party's leftist branch members. There was a clear deployment of a carrot-and-stick approach to handle the post-crackdown situation. The preceding two paragraphs mention a few key dates based on clues given by several interviewees, who all vaguely remembered that reconciliatory gestures were made and people-pleasing actions were also taken by the new leadership before executing the re-registration.

The stick approach was to arrest and detain the demonstration leaders and their supporters, the first move that was already discussed. At the same time, but before launching the *qingcha qingli* campaign, a National Work Conference on Higher Education was held from in Beijing in mid-July 1989, reemphasising the importance of education of students rather than reprisals against them. In late July, the CCP politburo published a resolution on 'doing a few things that people care about' or 'dealing with the matters that concern people' (Huang 2003, n.p.). These opened a new front in its effort to deal with the post-crackdown situation, and they were regarded as the 'carrot' aspect of the two-handed approach. This helps understand why the dire situation after the crackdown began to turn around after 1992, and why many reform-minded people survived the purge. In early August 1989, before the announcement on 7 September of the intra-party purge, two important decisions were made to deal with the two major issues that triggered the protests: out-of-control inflation, and corrupt business dealings by children and family members of some senior leaders. The central leadership knew that these two issues were the actual triggers of the protests, despite its narrative of anti-capitalist liberalisation – a typical case of political discrepancy between theory and practice.

Both the issues of inflation and corruption were among several matters raised in central party and state leadership documents, but they were particularly critical in order to reduce public anger and maintain stability. There were numerous work conferences and directives focusing on punishing corruption, cleaning up companies and prohibiting the children of senior leaders from doing business. Thousands of newly established companies were deregistered and closed, and thousands of well-connected people were forced to quit or penalised (Shui 2004). This ultimately generated a new issue for society to worry about, unleashing these well-connected people on society, the impact of which will be examined later in this chapter. However, as shown in Figure 7.1, a more effective outcome than the anti-corruption measure in assuaging public anger was observed on the anti-inflation front.

A fourth key course of action that also led to a vacuum in state-controlled bureaucracies and institutions was the forced removal of some other non-party staff members from their positions within publicly funded institutions and some activist students from universities. Because these people were not organisationally managed by the CCP, the *qingcha qingli* (checking-up and cleaning-up) of these non-party citizens only commenced

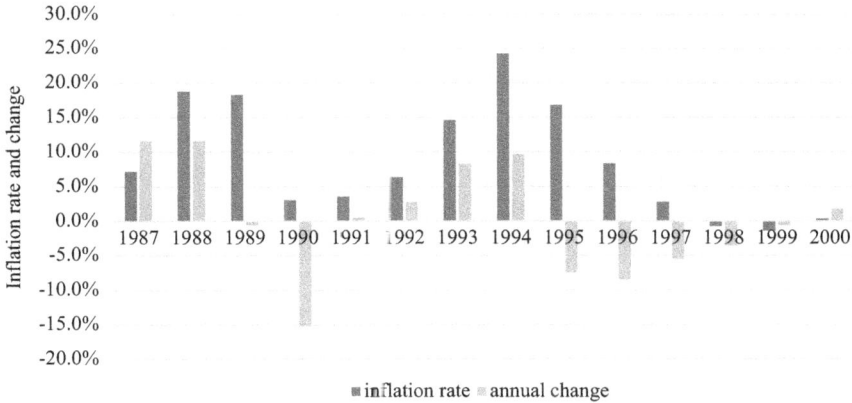

Figure 7.1 China's inflation rate and annual change, 1987–2000. *Note*: The 1988 inflation rate listed above is slightly lower than that used in Chapter six, where the figures are based on Chinese data. *Source:* Compiled by the author based on World Bank (2020).

after the action was taken against corrupt business dealings by some of senior leaders' family members and the runaway inflation issue; it was also conducted in rather ambiguous manner. Of course, the key target was still directed at liberal-minded people, if not educated liberals, and this segment of the campaign also resulted in a huge outflow of many professionals and experienced staff members from the state-controlled bureaucracies. It was estimated that hundreds of thousands of people were victims of this punitive action, contributing to the creation of a societal vacuum after the protests.

A major difficulty in accurately assessing number of people punished under the cleaning-up drive, however, is that a large proportion were penalised indirectly, on grounds other than partaking in the protests or voicing anti-government views. The actions taken by several institutions reveal that direct dismissal was often the last step, especially in the case of those who were not caught by police or wanted by law enforcement agencies. Without external evidence of criminal conduct, or external pressure from law enforcement agencies, many people were typically pressed into voluntary departure from their positions.

Such attempts to fudge the local situation and alter the approaches to local cases were widespread in both 1989 and 1990, as most local leaders still had fresh memories of the Cultural Revolution – including the lesson that overzealous execution of controversial decisions could have personal consequences. This lesson was even reemphasised by Li Ruihuan, one of the seven newly promoted politburo's standing members. As early as mid-August 1989, Li stated:

People who make serious mistakes in the political turmoil should be dealt with as they should. In the case of most others, however, they have to be helped through learning, raising their understanding, but not leaving a dead knot. As I said in Tianjin, we should also 'open windows' and 'build ladders' for them. 'Open the window' is to let him breathe

fresh air, and 'build the ladder' is to give them a step to get themselves out of this situation. (Li 2005b, 612)

The fifth widespread course of action that led to the post-1989 social vacuum was the
voluntary exodus of many white-collar professionals and trained staff members from the
party-state system and its affiliates. These people formed a large cohort of competent
citizens who were angered by the party-state system that they worked for even before the
crackdown in 1989, but who were also confident in their ability and skills to make more
outside the system than they could achieve within it. These people have been observed
from viewpoints of new entrepreneurship and social stratification, which saw them as
the crucial element in the development of China's new generation of business elites and
middle and upper-middle classes. What has been ignored is the socio-political vacuum
left by the departure of so many of them from the party-state system. While more details
about this cohort will be discussed in the next section, it is necessary in this section to
mention that there were numerous reasons some took this ostensibly voluntary option
of leaving their work units, with the pessimistic atmosphere in society at the time a key
push factor. One interviewee reminded me of the following:

> Leaders of many work units did not really want to treat people like what they themselves
> had suffered during Mao's years, and many tried to harm people as little as possible. But
> the whole atmosphere was very scary. The top [leadership] used the tactic of knocking the
> mountain and shaking the tiger, but ordinary citizens did not know how far the Party would
> go. Therefore, the vacuum in terms of the number [of people] eliminated by the 'double
> cleansing' is not the only angle [to consider this]. The vacuum in confidence was really
> strong then. It was just like another saying says, when the tree falls and the monkeys scatter.
> People were in a hurry then to run their separate ways. (Interviewee 15 2019)

The sixth main change contributing to the emergence of the vacuum was the upsurge
in citizens going abroad. To some extent this was similar to the second reason; however,
it was not directly caused by the post-protest crackdown but, rather, by the depressing social climate. Since there are a rather large number of publications on this wave
of cross-border migration, including one of my own books (Gao 2013a), it need only
be mentioned here that the social vacuum in post-1989 China was also caused by the
migratory outflow of young and educated Chinese. This took place at both ends of the
migration flow: while tens of thousands of people were rushing to leave China from
early 1990 onwards, tens of thousands of Chinese who were already overseas chose to
stay on permanently. This choice accelerated the so-called tide of going abroad that first
emerged on a large scale in 1987 (Hu 1988).

   As indicated in the earlier quotation from Li Ruihuan, ideological and political differences within China's central decision-making circles never disappeared, even during the weeks after the crackdown. This was why Deng Xiaoping was pushed to take
a post-retirement tour to inspect southern China in early 1992, more than two years
after the 1989 turmoil and the crackdown. The dismissal of many politically active
researchers, public servants, teachers, professionals and other skilled talents from the
party-state bureaucracies did not simply result in vacant positions. Over those two or

so years, many reform projects were largely put on hold and made almost no progress. Many people who had already benefitted from either economic policy changes or liberal social climates before 1989 felt profoundly depressed and anxious, and a hopeless feeling was once again permeating every tier and section of urban China. While those who were purged from the party-state system were suffering financially, politically and mentally, others aspiring to social advancement were also unable to see any chance or path for their future. All these adversities and distresses led to a new wave of people quitting the party-state system and trying their fortune in the soon-to-be-booming commercial world. This large-scale repositioning by active members of society was a sign of a number of changes, laying the foundation for a major overhaul of China's governing strategy, including the ideological thinking of the ruling party.

A New Wave of Jumping into the Sea of Commerce

To better understand the new social phenomenon of *xiahai*, jumping into the ocean of commerce, it seems useful at the start of this section to look specifically at why Deng Xiaoping chose to make his tour in early 1992. This brief discussion is necessary considering that this new phenomenon contradicts the traditional Chinese career path for ambitious people, who were used to taking the government-organised examinations and seeking a position in state-run bureaucracies.

Apart from the actions mentioned above, there was also a political turn taken by the new post-Tiananmen leadership, seeking to pull China off the reform path and drag it back to the Maoist road, recycling the political strategy of the 1960s of focusing on the struggle against peaceful evolution.[3] There were at least three discernible reverse movements aimed at changing the CCP's post-1978 governing principles of focusing attention on economic construction. First, open debate over the ideological nature of China's economic reform was not only allowed again but was conducted in a more open fashion than in the pre-1989 years. This was considered by many reformists as a re-evaluation of post-1978 reforms. In the words of Zhou Ruijin, the aim of this debate was 'to totally deny the market-oriented reform and opening up' that had been carried out since 1978 (Zhou 2008, 1).[4] Second, the *People's Daily*, the newspaper controlled by the CCP's central committee, published an opinion piece in May 1991, titled 'Build the Great Wall of Steel against the Peaceful Evolution' (Ma 2012; Nan 2014). This political strategy was publicly endorsed by Jiang Zemin on 1 July 1991 during commemoration of the 70th anniversary of the CCP. Third, a rare leadership training scheme, called the Anti-Peaceful Evolution Training Programme, was initiated by the Central Party School. All these were seen as a departure from Deng's strategy of focusing on 'one central task' (economic development) and 'two basic points' (adherence to reform and opening-up, and the four basic principles) (Baum 1994, 218). This governing strategy was at real risk of being replaced by principles opposing peaceful evolution that had been espoused under Mao's leadership in the late 1950s and 1960s.

As documented in numerous publications, Deng Xiaoping was deeply frustrated by the post-1989 developments and made the decision to tour key locations in southern China. During this tour, he criticised any turning aside away from the reform and opening-up strategy that had been developed under his guidance. Among the critical comments made by Deng, the first clear warning was against the drift towards the political left that presented a real threat to China's development. His second point was to openly point out that China could only have one central task to focus on, which was to develop its economy, not battle against liberalisation. The third point made by Deng concerned the pointlessness of ideological debate over the capitalist or socialist nature of China's reform. He strongly urged that China go beyond such pointless debates, stating that 'development is the most essential criterion' (*fazhan caishi ying daoli*) (Jiang 1997, n.p.). More seriously, Deng warned the new leadership, led by Jiang Zemin, that 'whoever does not reform should step down' (Zhang 2010, 168).

Subsequent observers have, of course, interpreted events in China since Deng's tour in early 1992 according to their own viewpoints, giving rise to different accounts of China's post-1989 situation. In general, this tour has been regarded as a turning point in recent Chinese history, and it succeeded in preventing China from being once again dominated by Maoist ideology. Although it did not directly assist those who were expelled from the party-state system, it helped not only revive the national strategy to reform and open up but also expand it to a higher level than the pre-1989 years. The concept of the socialist market economy was formally put forward at the CCP's Fourteenth National Congress in October 1992, providing various reform plans with new ideological and political frameworks. While this new concept may seem confusing, as it still includes the word 'socialist', the inclusion of the reference to the market was definitely progress after a furious decade-long debate between reformists and the adherents of Leninism, Stalinism and Maoism. While there was still a high level of uncertainty in people's minds about how the CCP's central leadership and militant leftist groups would response to Deng's push, the widespread memory of poor living conditions during the Mao period prevailed over utopian rhetoric about the greatness of Mao's ideas and governing practices. As readers may have read elsewhere, China changed gear in its economic management after mid-1992, and its economy had astoundingly gained greater momentum throughout the 1990s than even in the early 1980s. Economically, this was a positive outcome of the ruling CCP's adoption of the concept of market, an alternative word for the utilisation of Western development experiences in the Chinese discourse.

The unanswered question, therefore, is how the recognition of the market's role in the economy was related to individuals, especially their repositioning efforts at the time. One interviewee believes that this change was never a purely theoretical issue, but a political promise to recognise what had been achieved by many people in response to the CCP's call in the 1980s to work hard and get rich, and the many others who desired to make the same effort. The interviewee also offered the following explanation:

> The state introduces the concept of market in order to let market play its role [in economy], [the thinking of] which is far too abstract. The real motivation was to mobilise each enterprise and each person to play active roles in economy. After the late 1980s, the society [also] had a demand for the recognition of the non-public economic sector and individual businesses. [...] With the market's role in the economy, peasants could see the political support to the calls for 'becoming a 10,000-yuan household',[5] 'getting rich first', and running

factories. Those who had already jumped into the sea of commerce could feel legitimately recognised, and those who did not could see one more option in life. (Interviewee 48 2019)

Standing on the shifting ground of social change, hundreds of millions of Chinese, both rural and urban, had continued to reposition themselves in their rapidly changing and increasingly competitive society. They were almost all propelled by various changes and new opportunities, wishing to better their working and living conditions as soon as possible. Among the new chances to emerge at this time was *xiahai*, the possibility of working and earning a better living outside the centrally controlled social structure. Initially, the phrase *xiahai* was used in both a broad and a narrow sense. Even with its broad definition, however, *xiahai* as a new social phenomenon has never been applied to the rural labours who opted, earlier or later, to abandon agricultural activities and participate in the thriving rural industrial and service sectors. For the sake of having a fuller and better picture of the formation of new workforce areas, as well as social groups and classes, in China from the 1980s to the 1990s, it is necessary for this analysis to briefly mention the rural version of *xiahai*, the brave choice of rural people to leave their mandated place in society and seek new opportunities elsewhere. In terms of the total numbers involved, rural job changers actually constituted the largest proportion of those citizens who switched jobs or repositioned themselves over the course of the first two decades of China's reform. Most of these rural job changers first found new means of making a living in TVEs, while others travelled outside their home areas. As noted earlier, the latter was referred to, derogatorily, as the floating population. Table 7.2 outlines the upward trend in peasants repositioning themselves in TVEs and cities.

The exclusion of rural job changers from the popular notion of *xiahai* reflects the rural–urban divide in China. Peasants are not included because they originally had no connection with the party-state-controlled bureaucracies and enterprises that were subconsciously seen as a place of higher social status in the minds of most Chinese. As a result of the same mindset, the exodus from those jobs or social positions was considered to be a downward movement, as implied in the phrase *xiahai*. It is a typical urban bias with Chinese characteristics that changes made by urban people have attracted more attention, and have been better documented, than rural changes. However, the crucial

Table 7.2 More peasants working in TVEs or cities, 1990–97.

Year	Working in TVEs (m)	Migrating to cities (m)
1990	93.7	—
1991	92.7	—
1992	97.0	—
1993	106.5	80.2
1994	123.5	88.5
1995	120.2	93.5
1996	128.5	94.1
1997	135.1	96.1

Sources: Compiled by the author based on Majid (2015) and Wang (2000).

players in the Dengist reform era were in fact the aspirational peasants, who were also the social class basis of the Mao-led revolution before 1949.

What also makes this brief discussion necessary is the fact that the post-1989 political climate also threatened many peasants, especially those who had already repositioned themselves in various TVEs and new rural services, which were seen by pro-planning leaders and thinkers as a non-socialist practice or element that was depicted as a bud of capitalism (Li 2022). The recycled political antipathy to peaceful evolution threatened to not only make all the earlier efforts made by numerous peasants in vain, but also to deny other rural people the chance to become rich as had been encouraged before the 1989 crackdown. Millions of rural aspirants were, therefore, confronting the same challenges as those urban residents exiting the party-state system and its enterprises, but these peasants were excluded from the *xiahai*-related discourses.

To fully depict the large-scale social repositioning in post-1989 China, especially after Deng's political intervention in 1992, the broad definition of *xiahai* seems also to need to include urban blue-collar workers who had left or would leave their jobs within SOEs and the collectively owned urban enterprises. As noted, the gradual reforms to the employment of workers in these two types of urban enterprises began in the late 1970s and early 1980s, but for years there was not even an agreed terminology for such issues, except using phrases such as 'leave without pay' (*tingxin liuzhi*), 'waiting for internal placement' (*changnei daiye*) or 'taking a long break' (*fang changjia*). It was only in 1993 that the government started calculating the total number of *xiagang* (laid-off) workers. Table 7.3 shows an overall, but incomplete, picture of China's urban unemployment situation from 1987, which contributed in part to the student demonstrations in the second half of the 1980s.

The situation outlined in previous paragraphs was also a reason for so many people to change jobs or consider repositioning themselves. As shown in Table 7.3, the laid-off workers' numbers exceeded the numbers of registered jobless urban residents in 1995 and 1996. Analysts have explained this in various ways, including how helpful some reemployment projects were, but the active repositioning efforts made by many

Table 7.3 Urban unemployment situation in China, 1987–96.

Year	Registered Unemployment Rate (%)	Surveyed Unemployment Rate (%)	No. of Registered Unemployed People (m)	No. of Laid-Off Workers (m)
1987	2.0	–	2.77	–
1988	2.0	–	2.96	–
1989	2.6	–	3.78	–
1990	2.5	3.26	3.83	–
1991	2.3	3.32	3.52	–
1992	2.3	3.42	3.94	–
1993	2.6	3.49	4.20	3.00
1994	2.8	3.52	4.76	3.60
1995	2.9	3.98	5.20	5.64
1996	3.0	3.93	5.53	8.91

Sources: Compiled by the author based on Hu (1998), Chen (1999b), Wang (2000) and Cai et al. (2009).

of these people should be seen as one of the key causes. These laid-off people were, in a socially hierarchical sense, different from those who had once worked within the party-state bureaucracies and subdivisions and were then leaving in masse. These latter professionals and bureaucrats are included in the classic and narrow definition of *xiahai*, which will be detailed in the final part of this section. The importance of including the people pushed out of SOEs and the collectively owned urban enterprises in this analysis is also due to the profound impact of the issue on society as a whole from the 1980s to the 2000s. In a widely circulated and lengthy article documenting the lives of the urban workers after their 'iron rice bowls' (jobs in the state sectors) were smashed, Zhao Yunxian notes that 'it was not until the end of the 1990s that the "laid-off" was evolved into a tolerable concept, but the cloud of job security concerns had hung over workers throughout the entire 1990s, which was then dragged on into the early 2000s' (Zhao 2021, n.p.).

The positive aspect of this issue was also important. One interviewee described the laid-off worker issue as both a 'tragic drama of reform' and a 'heroic epic of many rising stars' (Interviewee 11 2020). Both the media and the public attention have for decades been captivated by the former, obscuring the repositioning efforts of many laid-off workers. In a survey undertaken in 1999, Mo and Yue also paid special attention to the pre-laid-off occupational category of the workers. As shown in Table 7.4, these workers were not entirely without skills, which may in part explain why many of them did not register themselves as unemployed.

The same interviewee who saw the laid-off worker question as both tragic drama and the heroic epic also believed that many of these workers with skills, connections and positive attitudes had acted in the same way as those white-collar *xiahai* professionals and officers. Specifically, many workers in the early 1990s had opted to jump from their old work units within the state-controlled system, while the others were forced into unemployment. There have been numerous anecdotal stories about these workers, who were rather different from those who left, or were sacked from, their secure jobs in the early and mid-1980s. What the above interviewee mentioned about the heroic epics of self-employment was true, and many popular stories, such as the *Shazi Guazi* case mentioned in Chapters five and six, were shaping the minds of aspiring workers who hoped

Table 7.4 Pre-laid-off employment positions of laid-off workers.

Category	Ratio (%)
Management	4.9
Professional	4.0
Technical	10.9
Office staff	11.6
Sales personnel in service, shop and marketing	6.4
Agricultural and aquatic worker	0.1
Handicraftsman and related jobs	20.8
Worker, machine operator and assembly worker	33.0
Primary occupation	8.3

Source: Compiled by the author based on Mo and Yue (2001).

to find new opportunities elsewhere for better pay and careers. After a decade of reform, there were more proletarian workers who were once too politically proud to compare themselves with peasants, but then realised that they had become less well off than rural business operators, owners and even backbone workers in some TVEs, let alone the urban *xiahai* people. Therefore, it was in the post-1989 China, especially in the post-1992 era, that China's so-called *chanye dajun* (manufacturing or industrial workforce) was also changing from within.

Externally, as noted by Zhao in the abovementioned article, the government had not only resumed its reform of the state-managed labour forces as mentioned in earlier chapters, but also started adopting some of the following tough measures:

> In the 1990s, the scope of the labour contract system was further expanded, and full-time workers began to transform into contract employments. In 1992, a nationwide campaign of 'new three irons' to break down the 'old three irons' was launched, encouraging to use 'an iron face', 'an iron heart', and 'iron hands' to break 'iron rice bowls' of workers, 'iron chairs' for cadres, and the 'iron wages' of all staff numbers of state-owned enterprises [...] this had gradually transformed state-employed workers under the planned economic system into contract workers, and by 2000, the labour contract system was fully implemented to nationwide labour forces. (Zhao 2021, n.p.)

Of course, there was nothing more prominent in people's minds, or more influential on their intentions to act, in the first half of the 1990s than the mass exodus of bureaucrats and professionals from their hard-won positions within the party-state system and its subdivisions, including major SOEs. This is why the original and narrow definition of *xiahai* was often simply applied to those who jumped, or were pushed, from their jobs within the party-state bureaucracies and their subdivisions. In a country in which more than 80 per cent of the population was still rural, these *xiahai* people were seen, in the eyes of peasants, as privileged urban residents who could *chi huangliang* (eat imperial food). Therefore, their departure from their positions attracted more public attention than it would deserve in normal social contexts. Two narratives have then been formed out of different socio-economic and political circumstances and passed down across generations. Nowadays, the younger generations accept the income-oriented narrative as the truth because many of these former officers and professionals have, since jumping into the sea of commerce in the early 1992, become well off or even wealthy. Leaving aside for later discussion the other narratives about these people, their total number was indeed impressive. In an article analysing a marked shift in public interest from the *xiahai* in the 1990s to the revived enthusiasm for entering the party-state bureaucracies since the 2010s, Xu Hui makes the following comments:

> In the early 1990s, China had a wave of the 'reverse operation' of public servants to jump into the sea of commerce. In the context of Deng Xiaoping's inspection tour and China's transformation from a planned economy to a market economy, around 120,000 public servants resigned in 1992 to work in different businesses, and more than 10 million of those from the [party-state] system had 'taken a leave without pay' (if the new business was unsuccessful, they could return to their institution). They had embraced the market

economy, and openly pursued wealth. Among them, there were also groups of entrepreneurs represented by Chen Dongsheng and Feng Lun, who were later known as the '92 faction'. (Xu 2021, n.p.)

Before the enthusiasm of many university graduates for becoming public servants became evident in the 2010s, there were, in general, three *xiahai* waves among officers, professional and other specialists following the early and mid-1980s (Li et al. 2014). The first wave in the 1980s was analysed in Chapter six, and the third from the late 1990s onwards will be looked at in Chapter eight. What has been discussed here is the second main wave. As noted, this second wave in the early 1990s was far more important than the other two, which has led many to believe that the so-called *xiahai* was simply about the wave occurring after Deng Xiaoping's inspection tour in 1992.

Never before in the history of the PRC had so many people on the public payroll decided to leave their posts. Apart from the abovementioned numbers, the scope of the *xiahai* phenomenon and its impact on the people holding middle and upper-middle positions in the party-state system were also unprecedented. For example, the higher education system in Tianjin lost as many as 1,500 teaching and research staff in 1992. The situation in Shanghai universities was even worse, with more than five hundred senior and associate professors quitting establish their own companies in 1992. The East China Institute of Chemical Technology, a small university in Shanghai, lost over forty senior researchers within a few months in 1992 (Chen 1992). The total number of academics at a famous university in Shanghai fell to fewer than 1,900 in 1996, from the 1989 level of 2,500 (*CPCNews* 2005). The exodus of university academics even happened in Xinjiang, with 351 resigning in 1992 and 482 in 1993 (Li 1995). Almost all provinces saw the departure of many thousands of university academics in 1992 and 1993. The CCP's internal analysis documented that about 395,000 staff members resigned from the higher education system nationwide in 1990, and 391,000 in 1991; it was only in 1993 that this total fell to 388,000 (*CPCNews* 2005).

The impact of this mass exodus also affected many officers who had already been promoted to middle and upper-middle positions within the system. Among those who opted to jump into the commercial world, Bo Xicheng, the head of Beijing's Tourism Bureau, may not be very typical despite being repeatedly mentioned as a cadre *xiahai* case in publications. Bo's family background allowed him to do whatever he wished to, just like his brother Bo Xilai, who has been jailed since 2012 in part as a result of his ambition (Li 2001). Chen Dongsheng, who was mentioned in the above quotation, seemed more typical, although he has lately been rumoured to be in a relationship with Mao's only granddaughter. Before jumping into the commercial world in 1992, Chen was a researcher at the Development Research Centre of the State Council and the deputy chief editor of the Centre's journal, *Management World*. His first business venture was the creation of China's first fine arts auction corporation, from which his venture was expanded into logistics and insurance (Deng 2009).

Partly because of the high educational level of these *xiahai* people, and partly because of readers' interest, one of the characteristics of the so-called 1992 group of entrepreneurs, or the '92 faction', is that their stories have been reported in a huge number of publications since the mid-1990s. A new catchphrase, *shiyi renmin jiuyi shang* (one billion citizens, nine hundred million businessmen), was born and has since encouraged many people to consider their next move. The prominence of this cohort has helped not only the expansion of several industries and business sectors but also, and more importantly, the execution of Deng's strategy of stopping debate over 'isms', making the population increasingly entrepreneurial.

However, as noted, the attention on economic expansion and personal income altered the discourse of urban *xiahai* people, with the income-oriented narrative becoming dominant. As part of the income-oriented narrative, some theorists have even depicted the *xiahai* of specialists and cadres as a strategy of sending skilled people to support TVEs. This certainly occurred, although many in turn also learned from those *xiahai* people how to better re-establish or self-actualise themselves in a new world of the 1980s. It was also true that this cohort was not the largest, but it was influential in unsettling the system and the minds of many citizens, especially young aspirants. This influence was mostly due to the system left behind by *xiahai* people being seen by others as a privileged social structure. What has been clouded by the income-oriented narrative, however, is the question of whether these *xiahai* people jumped or were pushed out of the state-party system. The following remarks were offered by an interviewee who has identified this problem of misinterpretation:

> History has often presented itself in a way of not only allowing people to draw different conclusions, but also making all of them sound true and correct. However, a true [social] process is always detonated by a specific trigger. In the case of the *xiahai* of hundreds of thousands of cadres and specialists, the post-1989 *qingcha qingli* (checking-up and cleaning-up) and the party membership re-registration campaign were the trigger to spark off a chain of jumping off. [...] The historical reality was that workers may be more attracted by money and by what TVEs people had earned than the 1980s, but a high proportion of cadres and other people who could 'eat imperial food' were largely scared by the politics and decided to leave the system. (Interviewee 11 2020)

The political push factors noted by the interviewee took several different forms. A small group of *xiahai* people was in fact politically punished and expelled from the CCP and their positions in publicly funded institutions. Many others were pushed out without harsh punishment. A larger proportion of this group could be defined as *xinhui yileng* (disheartened) by observing the fate of these people or by *sangshi gemin yizhi* (loss of revolutionary spirit) among the leadership of their work units.

Bypassing the Higher Education System for Qualifications

The second wave of *xiahai* was undeniably characterised by political push factors pressing a large number of public servants, specialists and other professionals out of their privileged posts. As implied by the *xiahai* phrase, the sense of downward movement in social position, if not status, was clear from the beginning of the phenomenon, reflecting a common understanding of how social position was measured. An ancient Chinese proverb says that water flows to lower ground, people flow to higher places (*ren wang gaochu zou, shui wang dichu liu*). The *xiahai* trend attracted a certain level of sorrow because of the public perception of the downward movement in social position. It is historically correct that those who were affected helped in the expansion of industries and business sectors, such as the real estate industry, which had never before attracted so many well-trained and well-connected individuals. One of the typical examples is my old undergraduate class in Beijing, from which 4 out of 53 students left prominent positions for sectors unconnected to their education or pre-1989 careers. However, as mentioned, understandings of the second wave of the *xiahai* have been distorted by the dominance of the income-oriented narrative.

This misinterpretation or misunderstanding has arisen both intentionally and unintentionally over the course of the past few decades. At the outset, the party-state system sought to downplay the impact of the post-1989 crackdown and beat the drum of economic reform as loudly as they could. On the other hand, a large number of citizens were deeply influenced by the idea of becoming financially better off by jumping into the commercial world, redirecting almost all of their attention to attaining wealth. As argued, this resulted in the dominance of the income-oriented narrative over the politics-oriented narrative. As the interviewee 11 pointed out, this subsequently obscured not only the political drivers, but also the parallel process of replacing those who left or were ousted during the post-1989 crackdown and the subsequent exodus of liberal-minded skilled urban people from the systems controlled by the CCP and the state. Specifically, the question raised after large-scale *xiahai* was how to fill the void left by *xiahai* people.

As examined in Chapters five and six, the changes in the relationships between different social groups or classes within the changing social structure had generated new social tensions. The tension between reformists and leftists had been going on long before 1989. The liberal tendency of university students and a high proportion of intellectuals were seen by the party conservatives as a target for re-education or other punishments. On the other hand, worker–peasant–soldier university students and others who were unable to acquire tertiary qualifications had been demanding official recognition of their educational qualifications. This theme of societal tensions is never absent from China's socio-political life. In this area of politics, the demand and the official response from the party-state system had focused on the formation of institutional provisions and policies to help some people avoid the competitive higher education system for granting or obtaining qualifications, while allowing liberal-minded people to leave the public sectors without imposing Mao-style political punishments, except in some serious cases. There were some efforts made as early as the first half of the 1980s to introduce various alternative arrangements to manage these ongoing tensions – in particular, to avoid over-dependence on the university-trained liberal-minded graduates, which was examined in Chapters five and six. The 1989 political turmoil, as well as the subsequent exodus of *xiahai* people, gave prominence to the need for the new leadership to train a larger group of young and politically reliable officers or reserve talent through unconventional, or even non-academic, educational institutions. Of course, all these attempts were made in the 1980s in the name of broadening the channels for training and cultivating more talents for China's reform and modernisation endeavours, making the proposed schemes morally sound and politically presentable.

During and since the 1980s, there have been at least three key institutional arrangements or provisions under serious consideration or partially executed, including *zixue kaoshi* (exams for self-paced university course learners), *dangxiao jiaoyu* (the party school education) and *gongwuyuan kaoshi* (public servant recruitment exams).

In practice, the first arrangement, examination opportunities for self-paced university course learners, was open to all young and middle-aged school leavers. The participants came from all walks of life, but they were found to have been characterised by the shortage of socio-political resources and platforms for repositioning themselves. This measure did not, therefore, play an obvious role in bypassing the higher education system, nor in avoiding the return of liberal influences on young people. Liu Daoyu, former president of Wuhan University in the early 1980s and a proactive promoter of the restoration of university entrance examinations in the late 1970s, believes that *zixue kaoshi* was only popular among those middle-aged people who were unable to pass the national examination for attending formal university but who still desired to obtain formal qualifications (He 2009). Therefore, in post-1989 China, the above three institutional provisions evolved into the other three types of actions. Specifically, while the roles of party school education and the public servant examination were being strengthened, the qualifications of worker–peasant–soldier university students were finally recognised.

The first post-1989 action of the CCP in consolidating and improving institutional arrangements for preventing over-reliance on liberal-minded university graduates was to focus on party school education. This was an almost immediate action taken by the new top leadership led by Jiang Zemin, who was urgently called in from his local leadership post in Shanghai and promoted to the top leadership role after the Tiananmen crackdown. A high-level work conference was convened from 9 to 15 June 1989, within a week of the 4 June crackdown, to discuss how to strengthen the role of the CCP's party school system in handling the post-Tiananmen political situation. During the week-long conference, Jiang Zemin delivered a long speech stressing the seriousness of the crisis confronting China and the importance of the CCP's leadership, especially the political awareness and quality of many young and middle-aged cadres. Jiang warned the party that the quality of the leadership team would decide the success or failure of modernisation, the rise and fall of the CCP and the Chinese state, and the fate of China as a nation. Jiang concluded that 'the leadership team training and development are a vital and irreplaceable frontline' (Jiang 1990, n.p.).

After the work conference, a series of changes were made to enhance the CCP's leadership, and two of these changes contributed to a sharp turn in the political climate of the country. First, a formal intra-party notice was issued formally instructing party committees at all levels to reinforce the party's organisational development. It also explicitly required the whole party to advance its organisational improvement and achieve what it called the institutionalisation and standardisation of the party school education of young and middle-aged party leaders (*SinaNews* 2007). The message was clear and authoritative: party school education, then open only to current officials or bureaucrats, would be brought into line with other higher education providers. This has since greatly altered and restructured China's cadre promotion practice and upward social mobility. This unfairly favourable treatment towards people within the party-state system has become more evident and outrageous since the early 2000s than before, granting a renewed privilege to those within the CCP, but adding divisive features to Chinese society.

Second, shortly after the 1989 crackdown the 'university president responsibility system' was replaced by a system called the 'university president responsibility system under the leadership of the party committee' (Han and Guo 2017). The former system had been introduced in the 1980s as a reform measure, reducing the interference of the CCP in university governance. Although the replacement system did not directly affect most ordinary Chinese, it was a clear indicator of how bad the political climate was becoming and the obstacles placed in the way of many aspirational people.

At this point, it is necessary to reflect on whether Deng's inspection tour in southern China in early 1992 had reversed the post-1989 leftward trend in politics. As discussed, Deng's tour largely revived the economy from the damage caused by the turmoil and instability in 1989 and the subsequent crackdown, and sustained the much-needed momentum of TVEs. More significantly, as considered earlier in this chapter, the concept of the market was not only inserted into the official documents of the CCP and the government, but also accepted as the vital mechanism for regulating the economy. However, as indirectly indicated earlier, Deng's inspection was also considered a counterattack against the leftists represented by Chen Yun. Many believe that Deng's political counterattack was successful in defending his economic reform strategy, but it also left various political issues unaddressed (Zhou 2008; Nan 2014; Creaders 2015). The former action created a brilliant opportunity for China to build a very large group of entrepreneurs and expand the middle and upper-middle classes, while the latter still provided ladders for left-minded aspirants to climb. The adverse effect of the latter has become evident and damaging since the mid-2000s.

A critical point behind the preceding analysis is that the 1989 crackdown was a major outbreak of the tension between the political left and right in China, which had been worsening since the late 1970s. The crackdowns in 1989 and 1990 essentially helped the leftists remove their rivals, who had blocked them from being positioned favourably in the social hierarchy. The changes caused by the tensions did not stop there. The proposal to institutionalise and standardise the party school education led to further change in 1995, when the CCP's Central Committee publicised a new set of interim regulations on the work of the party school:

> The party school education is the representation of the academic performance of cadres studying in party schools. The students at party school classes should complete the learning tasks according to the requirements of the teaching plan. Those who pass the assessment should be awarded the party school degree and qualified for certain leadership positions. [...] The students taking long-term courses of more than two years held by the Central Party School and party schools of provinces, autonomous regions, and the central-direct-administered municipalities, and also having completed the compulsory courses and passed the assessment, will be awarded the party school degree and can enjoy the relevant treatment of the corresponding national education degree. (Central Committee 1995, n.p.)

There are two crucial phrases in the quote: party school degree and treatment equivalent to the national education degree. These two new policy items shook the authority of both the established higher education system and the talent promotion pathway, which were broadly accepted by the general public. At an individual level, this action suddenly and severely devalued the education or cultural capital that many hardworking people had earned and accumulated. This change is believed to have contributed in part to the *xiahai* phenomenon. To a large degree, it was the key move to replace liberal-minded people with the CCP's faithful supporters, in the process not only changing the rule-book and pathways of upward social mobility, but also once again giving prominence to what the ruling elites believed or how they defined realities. One former bureaucrat-researcher observed the following tendency from within the system:

> Ideology had slowly become a divisive factor in society, and become part of hidden rules in choosing new leaders, and identifying talents, and even discriminating against someone. It was a bit like in certain religious countries, people wishing to take certain positions could not be from very different churches. [...] Dissidents believed that people staying on in the system were foolishly loyal to a set of notions and following the party wholeheartedly. The truth was that politics was above all else, beyond doctrines and beliefs. After the June 4th [1989], especially after Deng's tour, most people have lost interest in isms, and those who were still talking about ideology became an unpopular minority. (Interviewee 4 2019)

The formal recognition of the on-job training of many officers had a profound negative impact on people's confidence in the higher education system and the ruling party's cadre promotion practice, further details of which will be considered in Chapter eight. To outline the issue briefly here, it is worth noting that those interim regulations on the work of the party school were revised in 2008, dumping the policy of allowing party school training to be treated as equal to the qualifications awarded by the higher education institutions (Wang 2008a). This change was widely welcomed. However, it appeared to have been misinterpreted, according to a reporter of China News Service (CNS), the second largest state news agency in China. The CNS report indicated that the deletion of the formal educational treatment from the regulations did not mean that the party school trainees would never have such special treatment (Wang 2008b). This opinion was also partly due to the fact that since the late 1990s some party schools have expanded into postgraduate education, which will be analysed in Chapter eight.

The second post-1989 political decision made in 1993 was to formally recognise the qualifications of worker–peasant–soldier university students who were selected to study at university or college during the second half of the Cultural Revolution. As discussed, this cohort was discriminated against by the general public after the end of the Mao era but had been campaigning for the recognition of their qualification. As part of party efforts to enlist more loyal and conservative members in place of the new university graduates, who were often liberal, the decision to recognise the qualification of those special students was taken while a large number of liberal-minded professionals and civic servants were departing from their publicly funded positions. Chen Jian, a Beijing-based sociologist-turned policy advisor and university leader, documented the following change:

In 1993, the National Personnel Department and the National Education Commission jointly issued the Circular coded No. 4 [1993]. It was specified that the state recognises the academic qualifications of the university students who studied at state-recognised universities from 1970 to 1976 (at the time, the university courses were normally run for two to three years), who were also issued with the graduation certificate by the university at completion of their study. The students who studied at advanced vocational colleges or institutes during the same period are recognised as vocational institute graduates. (Chen 2021, n.p.)

This policy change brought the worker–peasant–soldier student issue to an end in terms of recognition of educational qualifications, but it has had subsequent ramification for the topic of China's leadership succession at all levels. The latter is one of the most talked about topics in present-day Chinese politics. Many liberal-minded people have engaged in a political identity war based on the issue, given that it has resulted in more leadership posts being occupied by those trained either in the late period of the Cultural Revolution or through the party school system. At the core of the issue, therefore, is the ruling party's political inclination towards young talent and leadership composition, which have undoubtedly affected many people's social positionings in terms of opportunity and competitive strength. While outside the scope of this analysis, it is worth mentioning in this context that Xi Jinping, as one of worker–peasant–soldier university students, is a good example of the tensions discussed above, with many liberal-minded critics using his vacillation between Maoist and Dengist approaches to illustrate the faults in post-1989 Chinese politics.

The third major strategy adopted by the CCP was to establish a separate system for selecting public servants, the ranks of which had hitherto usually been filled by university graduates through gradation assignments. The new proposal – for party-state institutions to recruit new staff members themselves – was initially put forward almost immediately after the nationwide student demonstrations in 1986 and early 1987. The initial idea was considered at the CCP's Thirteenth National Congress in October 1987 and was then adopted at the First Session of the Seventh National People's Congress in April 1988 (Zeng 2005). Clearly, this was highly correlated with the growing concerns of political elders about the political reliability of young university students and graduates. From the very beginning, the scheme was aimed at easing the party-state system's reliance on universities for staffing and avoiding the return of liberal influence. However, what happened in 1989 and the next few years delayed the implementation of the plan until 1993, when the detailed 'Interim Regulations on State Civil Servants' was formally publicised by the State Council. In 1994, the Ministry of Personnel issued the 'Interim Regulations on the Recruitment of National Civil Servants', representing the formal start of the implementation of the new national public servant examination and selection system.

The new public servant recruitment system is different from the party school education. The latter is believed to have been strongly pressed by many lower- and middle-level officials without education qualifications, because these people were already working within the party-state system. Although there is no evidence that the public servant examination system was the result of internal demands, it was designed as an alternative to the higher education system for checking and selecting young candidates based on the criteria and requests of party-state bureaucracies themselves (Zeng 2005). From the viewpoint of social repositioning, this scheme has joined the party school system to alter the conditions in which young and aspiring people seek their own careers and progresses. More importantly, aided by the worker–peasant–soldier student group, these new provisions have since gradually modified the composition of China's ruling groups and factions. Of course, the new civil servant examination system was in a trial-and-error process until 1997. Therefore, it continued to play a more influential role in determining people's social repositioning efforts and processes in the second half of the 1990s than before, which will be further analysed in Chapter eight.

Notes

1. There were three closely related events in Chinese politics from 1956 to 1957. The so-called Hundred Flowers Campaign was launched in late 1956 to allow people to put forward their critical comments and opinions on various public issues, especially the governance of the CCP over the first five or so years after the founding of the PRC. The campaign was named after Mao's call to 'let a hundred flowers bloom and a hundred schools of thought contend'. This short period of political tolerance made many educated urban residents very excited, and many expressed their criticism of various issues. Shortly after the campaign, however, the Hungarian Revolution of 1956 stirred concern among the CCP leaders, especially as the uprising was provoked by a speech of Soviet Leader, Khrushchev, attacking the rule of Stalin. What was more frightening to the new CCP ruling elites was that Hungarian rebels won the first phase of the revolution and started establishing a multiparty political system before it was crushed by Soviet forces. After these events, Mao changed his mind about the Hundred Flowers in mid-1957, and the Anti-Rightist Campaign was soon launched, purging hundreds of thousands of intellectuals on an unprecedented scale. Interested readers are referred to Teiwes and Sun (1999), Li and Xia (2018) and Wemheuer (2019).

2. The original Chinese phrase for laid-off workers is *xiagang zhigong*. In the Chinese narratives of unemployment and job loss, the term 'unemployment' had almost never been used, because it was used to refer to the problems of capitalism. Instead, a few new terms were created, such as *xiagang* (off-post or leaving the job temporarily) and *daiye* (waiting job assignment). Interested readers can find more information in Ezra (1989) and O'Leary (1998).

3. The phrase 'peaceful evolution' has been a highly sensitive expression in Chinese politics because it originated in the United States. It became well known after John Dulles, the hawkish Republican secretary of state (1953–59), turned it into a fundamental concept in American policy towards the new, communist-ruled China after the Korean War. It hoped China could be transformed by spreading Western values and lifestyles and through other non-military means. This peaceful evolution strategy elicited a strong reaction from the CCP top leaders. Mao regarded it as a serious political threat and a deceptive strategy to subvert the new China. Mao was particularly worried that this strategy had pinned its hopes of changing China on the third and fourth generations of Chinese communists. This aspect of the American strategy provided Mao with an excuse to launch a string of political campaigns to consolidate his rule. This may also in part explain why Mao, in his dying years, became more friendly to the United States, even praising the Republican leaders. For more information about the concept, interested readers are referred to Feurtado (1986), MacMillan (2007), Walker (2012) and Li and Xia (2018).

4. The so-called the Huangfu Ping Incident has also incorrectly been called the Huang Fuping Incident as many Chinese did not realise that Huangfu is a rare double-character surname. According to published sources, this pseudonym of Huangfu Ping means that the commentaries were made by people living near the Huangpu River running through Shanghai, who were in fact from the *Liberation Daily*, the newspaper of the CCP Shanghai Municipal Committee. In early 1991, Deng Xiaoping spent his Chinese New Year break in Shanghai,

during which he visited factories and shops. Based on what they had heard from Deng, a few people from the *Liberation Daily*, led by Zhou Ruijin, wrote several commentaries, and published in their newspaper in February and March 1991. Their argument was very bold in the post-1989 China and focused on the importance of Deng's reform and open-door policy. These articles were soon attacked by several Beijing-based newspapers and journals in line with directives from leftist elders. Internal investigations were even conducted, and top-down interference also came from the party's conservatives. This was why the debate was depicted as a political incident. The debate started by Zhou Ruijin and his colleagues lasted over a year and led to Deng's decision to make the famous inspection tour in early 1992. Interested readers are referred to Baum (1994), Goldman (1994), Cherrington (1997) and Wong (2005).

5. The original phrase for becoming a 10,000-yuan household was *Wanyuanhu* or *Wanyuan hu*. In the 1980s, especially in the first half of the 1980s, households with 10,000 Chinese yuan were very rare, and it therefore became a slogan to encourage people to work harder to earn more. The well-known case *Shazi Guazi* (Simpleton's sunflower seeds) discussed in Chapter five was a typical example of capitalist practices, but it was protected by Deng Xiaoping in order to protect the new economic reform policy. Interested readers can read more in Young (2015) and deLisle and Goldstein (2019).

Chapter Eight

SEIZING CHANCES TO BE ENTREPRENEURIAL IN POST-1992 CHINA

This chapter is a continuation of the discussion initiated in Chapter seven, which focused largely on the post-1989 and post-1992 years. The primary focus of this chapter is the second half of the 1990s, although it must be recognised that Chinese society in the 1990s was driven by at least two strong conflicting socio-political forces represented by the post-1989 crackdown and the post-1992 economic liberalisation and their constant tension. This situation could well be envisaged as being overseen by a person holding both the carrot and the stick, in a manner similar to what is known as Deng Xiaoping's 'two-hands approach' (*liangshou zhua*). The aim was, on the one hand, to encourage people to actively engage in more economic activities, while on the other hand tightly controlling 'all kinds of ideological and cultural pollutants from abroad' (Kim 2006, 279). There were two boundary lines between what was expected and what was not tolerated. Such socio-political conditions also shaped people's behaviours, making people more individualistic and utilitarian. The natural human tendency to seek advantage and avoid disadvantage not only propelled more people to make new efforts to reposition themselves but also altered the patterns and characteristics of their social repositioning.

Of course, as noted previously, it is critical to remember that the 1989 Tiananmen protest had almost no direct impact on China's rural population, although it has been praised by many activists for promoting democracy in the country. In the post-1989 years, rural residents were still a significant cohort, forming over 74 per cent of the total population (see Figure 1.2). It was at almost the same time that China's rural industrialisation entered its second stage, offering tens, if not hundreds, of millions of rural citizens employment in TVEs. This not only effectively transferred rural surplus labour from the agricultural sector to industrial and service sectors, but also popularised Deng's idea of 'letting some people get rich first' among peasants. The success of rural industrialisation also inspired the state to utilise what it had learned from the early steps of the rural industrialisation in the restructuring of less efficient SOEs, putting new owners and managers of enterprises in a more advantaged position while making many urban workers jobless. The latter issue worsened in the course of the second half of the 1990s, with a prominent example of the new socio-political tensions being the Falun Gong phenomenon, through which laid-off urban workers and other dissatisfied urban residents could voice their grievances.

Despite these tensions, however, the period covered by this chapter is widely regarded as the most entrepreneurial period, to use a neutral expression – or the most capitalist period, in a politicised phrase – in the modern history of China's economic expansion.

It was a period that saw a huge increase in the number of well-off people in both rural and urban areas as an outcome of various policy changes, especially the development of private enterprises and rapid urbanisation. Driven by the changes in society, many aspiring individuals repositioned or positioned themselves via several parallel processes of economic reform: deregulation of more market sectors, private enterprise, reforms of TVEs and SOEs (or rural industrialisation and urban re-industrialisation), rural–urban migration and urbanisation. Most enticing to financially struggling people was the highly visible emergence of more well-off people and families emerging all over the country. The once-shocking notion of *wanyuan hu* (10,000-yuan households) (see note 5 in Chapter seven) was being superseded by millionaires, or even multi-millionaires, and this exerted a much greater influence on people than idealistic goals.

Readers reliant on media reports produced in either China or the West may struggle to understand how the changes that have been analysed in this study thus far could have come about. Chinese readers were still lectured on the evil of private enterprise and business and the virtue of socialism, while Western readers knew only that China was under the one-party rule, with the implication that nothing could be accomplished under such a political dictatorship and its political brutality. In the real world, however, the materialistic turn described earlier diverted most people's attention from the political events of the late 1980s and early 1990s, turning it instead to catching up with well-off people and social trends. The latter revealed different options and patterns in social positioning from those of the past.

This chapter examines this most entrepreneurial period in modern China's economic expansion and seeks to explain how aspiring Chinese responded to both the post-1989 circumstances and the post-1992 reforms from the competitive social repositioning perspective. The chapter has four discussion sections. The first begins with what is called in Chinese the 'first bucket of gold' (*diyitong jin*) – the first phase that saw many entrepreneurs becoming involved in different business ventures. The analysis will pay attention to how their actions were taken as a move of social positioning and repositioning, the push factors that drove these people and the chances that attracted them to change their life course. The second section focuses on the laid-off workers and their reactions not only to the reform of SOEs, but also to changing employment relations and trends. Special attention will be given to the Falun Gong movement, as many of its followers were victims of the reform of SOEs and responded to reform very differently from both the peasants and the new urban entrepreneurs. The third section continues the analysis of the topic introduced in Chapter seven, namely, the range of institutional changes to the national talent training and selection systems. The pre-existing elites and other interest groups at the time became very adventurous, continually changing institutional rules and creating new opportunities for the people supporting them. These changes were welcomed by some, but they also represent the beginning of changes to the long-established rules and patterns of social mobility, providing some with new chances while narrowing the options of others. The fourth section offers an analysis of the changing dynamics in Chinese society towards the end of the 1990s, analysing how political power, money and various other behind-the-scenes factors made the social mobility of many ordinary Chinese more difficult and competitive than before.

Rushing for the First Bucket of Gold

The first appearance of the phrase 'the first bucket of gold' in state-run media outlets was in early 1997, when the influential Shanghai-based newspaper *Wenhui Daily* carried a feature story written by Sha Yexin, a famous scriptwriter of the 1980s and 1990s. The phrase had, however, been in circulation in everyday conversation before this appearance and the same meaning had been expressed even earlier in officially acceptable phrases, such as an 'initiation fund' or 'jump-start money', equivalent to the start-up fund of today. The expression 'bucket of gold' was seen by CCP conservatives as a capitalist abomination with a strong implication of money worship.

By the time 1996 and 1997 rolled around, the socio-political climate had changed considerably, and a different kind of gold rush – kicked off by Deng Xiaoping's inspection tour in early 1992 – had created new mindsets and attitudes towards the use of a variety of Western notions and ideas in public discourse. Deng's intervention had many positive effects, but the most important and immediate impact was to prevent China from returning to the Maoist era by putting an end to the abstract debate over 'isms' and turning the nation's attention to the economy. This has since made the entire population increasingly entrepreneurial. As a result, the post-1992 socio-political conditions offered more people new chances to compete for better jobs and incomes. The difference between this period and previous ones is that *xiahai*, or venturing out of one's comfort zone to undertake a range of business activities, was no longer new, mysterious and untested. What *was* new was that even more people wanted to make their first pot of gold; this was the start of China's gold rush in the PRC era.

Fortunately, up to the mid-1990s, people could see many examples of how successful businesses were managed and why some businesses were unsuccessful. In the decade in which, according to the humorous description of some well-off citizens, it was difficult to *not* make money, a number of cohorts, if not generations, of new businesspeople had already gained enough experience for new adventurers to learn from. As considered in the second section of Chapter five, many peasants and urban residents, both white-collar people and manual labourers, started their new businesses as early as in the late 1970s and early 1980s. Soon after private businesses began to be encouraged some cases – such as the *Shazi Guazi* (cooked sunflower seeds) example – were known nationwide through the traditional channel of gossip and rumour, while the cases of the Liu Brothers and the founders of Lenovo, Huawei and Wahaha were only known to those living in certain regions or working in certain sectors. All these examples emerged before the career alternative of *xiahai*, or leaving the party-state system for new opportunities, became popular. In turn, this *xiahai* fever brought several categories of Chinese closer to establishing themselves outside the party-state bureaucracy. As detailed in Chapters six and seven, these groups included many peasant–worker–soldier students who had been marginalised in the early years of the post-Mao era. Also included were many liberal-minded citizens who were either willing to reposition themselves outside the bureaucracies or forced to leave the system after the 1989 crackdown.

The most thought-provoking aspect of the developments from the mid-1990s onwards was that the peasants and other rural people – who used to be looked down upon by almost all urban residents – as well as those less-academically gifted people who were unable to pass university entrance examinations earned their fortunes from different business ventures. These phenomena were sensationalised by gossip and in the increasingly active tabloid newspapers and lifestyle magazines. The widespread anecdotes of the emergence and rapid rise of rich entrepreneurs were soon brought to international attention by a young accountant working in Arthur Anderson's Shanghai office in the late 1990s. This was UK-trained Rupert Hoogewerf –also known by his Chinese name, Hurun, in Chinese-speaking regions – whose early report on new companies in China and their owners was published in *Forbes* in 1999, confirming the above thought-provoking reality. There seem to be gradual and quiet transpositions of the previously advantaged urban minority and the disadvantaged rural majority and of the egotistic educated classes and the less educated groups. Table 8.1 lists the first cohort of successful entrepreneurs who appeared at least twice on the initial three Hurun lists, which were dominated by people without tertiary education.

Given some personal scepticism regarding the Hurun lists – since its earlier versions included some already-famous people, such as Rong Yiren and Wang Guangying, two former industrialists-turned national leaders[2] – I have tried to make my own uses of the lists. One such use is to check how many years an entrepreneur is listed, which can help moderate the inaccuracy of the lists. Of course, double-checking is also crucial and useful, especially of information in Chinese-language sources, both official and popular. As commented, despite Table 8.1 being fairly diverse, business people from rural areas and

Table 8.1 New Chinese entrepreneurs appearing twice on the first three Hurun lists, 1999–2001.

Name (female)	Years on List	Age in 1999	Education	Industry
Liu Yonghao (one of Liu Brothers)	3	48	Technical	Animal feed, chicken farm
Li Xiaohua	3	48	Secondary	Real estate, construction
Zhang Hongwei	3	45	Secondary	Construction, trade
Zhang Simin	3	37	University	Health care. travel
Luo Zhongfu	3	48	Secondary	Real estate, construction
Wu Yijian	3	39	Secondary	Real estate, services
Zhang Guoxi	3	47	Secondary	Woodworking, real estate
Chen Jinyi	3	39	Secondary	Food, water, real estate
Zhang Can (F)	3	33	University	Computer, pharmaceutical
Lou Zhongfu	3	44	Secondary	Construction, real estate
Wu Bingxin	2	61	Primary	Health care
Huang Hongsheng	2	43	University	Television sets
Wu Zhijian	2	40	Secondary	Trade, printing, taxi
Gao Feng	2	59	University	Wool, Cashmere
Fang Xiaowen (F)	2	39	Secondary	Farming, breeding
Han Wei	2	45	Secondary	Farming, beverages
Li Yikui	2	48	University	pharmaceutical
Shi Shanlin	2	55	University	Water supply. electronics
Zhang Chaoyang	2	35	MIT PhD	The Internet

Sources: Compiled by the author based on Hurun (1999, 2000, 2001).

small towns accounted for a majority of the new entrepreneurs – not only those listed in Table 8.1 but also in wider society. Therefore, two useful points must be made here in order to deal with two stereotypes about who the new rich are and how they made their 'first bucket of gold'. Since the mid-1980s, many Chinese have formed the view that China's new rich are the children of senior CCP leaders and their associates, and that those princelings made their fortunes through a range of deals. These stereotypes have been circulating in Chinese society for decades, in turn feeding the global media which has spread them far and wide.

It is also worth repeating that these perceptions of China's new rich were one of the reasons for the student protests in the mid-1980s and 1989. However, such views have become less pervasive, in part through the tabloids and magazines mentioned earlier, as well as through more formal research, including that of Hurun. As a result of this media coverage and market research, more Chinese have realised that, while there are indeed many so-called princelings who have become rich through their connections, but they are not a majority of the new rich. This insight has, unfortunately, been largely ignored by the global media, making their readers' knowledge of China's new social classes rather outdated. In fact, China's massive new middle and upper-middle classes have lately developed a type of reverse prejudice against the princelings. One interviewee reminded me of the following phenomenon:

> Apart from [the fact] that some princelings made a fortune in earlier years, it has lately become less obvious who the real winners are. What has been popular is the phenomenon that the second and third red generations attend the events organised by entrepreneurs to earn their appearance fees. Such events often look pitiful. On the surface, these princelings attend the events to help the development of TVEs or old revolutionary base regions, but many of such activities look very embarrassing, looking like begging to me. (Interviewee 42 2019)

In the three years since I recorded this observation, such explanations have not only been accepted by the Chinese students taking my university course on contemporary Chinese society, but have also been confirmed by a number of prominent cases. However, a key point here is that of the 350 or so students who have enrolled in my course over the past three years, more than half hail from entrepreneurial families. Their open affirmations of the phenomenon and the explanations make perfect sense from the perspective of social change or social transposition. Several students have also reminded me of similar remarks made by some of China's high-profile commentators, such as Ma Weidu. His comments in one of his TikTok videos have spread widely on social media. However, such transpositions of social status are only a superficial glimpse of what has happened in Chinese society, which was further transformed by a range of new macro- and micro-level factors that better explain how some entrepreneurial Chinese earned their first bucket of gold in the mid- and late 1990s.

From a macro perspective, the reform of SOEs intensified during this period, despite the early confusion of the post-1989 leaders over priorities, which was discussed in the second section of Chapter seven. As considered there, the new concept of the socialist market economy was accepted by the CCP in 1992. Detailed plans to reform SOEs that were becoming a financial burden on the state were developed one year later, focusing on innovation and restructuring. These plans made SOEs even more difficult to keep afloat, leading to the strategy of *zhuada fangxiao* (keeping the large (SOEs) and letting the small go). The number of workers in SOEs had decreased by over 40 per cent from 1995 to 1999, particularly in 1998 when the state stopped financing most SOEs. The downside of this bold reform was the deterioration of the laid-off worker issue, which will be detailed in the next section, but it also generated a unique structural opportunity for new producers and manufacturers in China's massive goods and service market, from which the state started retreating in terms of finance and management.

The reform of SOEs forced thousands of enterprises to relinquish three key elements of the production systems: workers, market and products. The combination of these key elements and people's desire for better life and career opportunities was the source of vitality in China throughout most of the 1990s. There are numerous sources, both printed and online, that illustrate how newly freed resources were redistributed among and redeployed by different types of citizens while SOEs were being reformed, if not dismantled. The process was, in fact, a take-over battle for production facilities or products, which can be better observed from both the urban and rural perspectives.

In urban settings, the individuals involved in gaining control of many bankrupt or abandoned factories were two types: skilled workers or experienced supervisors who previously worked in factories; and white-collar *xiahai* specialists, professionals or bureaucrats. The first category was less visible in the media, especially the magazines and tabloid newspapers which preferred sensational stories of officials leaving their well-positioned posts and jumping into the sea of business. However, there are still numerous written sources detailing how this first category of risk-takers from within SOEs responded to this targeted reform. This evidence includes Feng Lun's list of entrepreneurs mentioned in Chapter five. A set of new reform strategies and policies was developed and introduced after the actual application of the policy which allowed many SOEs to be leased or contracted out (as recorded in Table 6.1) to suitable individuals or groups. From the mid-1990s onwards, the overhaul of SOEs was characterised by 'a large scale sell-off of loss-making SOEs', which is described by some analysts as 'the largest ever in scale in human history' (Zhang and Freestone 2013, n.p.). At that time, a large proportion of buyers of SOEs were outsiders who had already accumulated their wealth through TVEs or other ventures, enabling them to invest. However, there were also many new owners or managers from within SOEs who obtained ownership through loans from financial institutions or other creditors, and thus also accumulated their first big fortunes from this round of privatisation of state assets.

The second category of people involved in taking over some troubled SOEs was those who are often described as *xiahai* people but who were, in fact, quite different in background and experience. As mentioned in the second section of Chapter seven, there were hundreds of thousands of former university researchers and technical staff members who had left state employment for a wide range of private commercial ventures in the period leading up to the mid-1990s. A similar level of response was also observed from those working in China's multi-layered system of science and technology research institutions. Those leaving the party-state system generated greater levels of gossip, and tabloid coverage, as they were seen by other people as suffering a sudden and significant drop in social status. In fact, these *xiahai* people felt no need to keep their decision secret, as many did before the mid-1990s. Apart from the 10 million or so public servants and the like who took leave without pay in the first half of the 1990s, in the second half of the decade the local government system alone suffered a further decline of more than 2.8 million public servants at the municipal, county and township levels (Wu and Bai 2008).

In rural China, on the other hand, the final phase of SOE reform coincided with a new phase in the development of TVEs. It was at this stage that TVEs became more active in seeking to expand their market presence and find new products or services in pursuit of their goals of growth. As noted, after more than a decade of development, many TVEs had accumulated not only ample capital, but also knowledge and skills in running business activities in an open market. As outlined in Table 7.2, more people had found jobs in TVEs in the second half of the 1990s, even though the number of TVEs experienced little growth from the late 1980s to the early 1990s. Their number started rising again after the mid-1990s, although only moderately. The growing trend in employment in new TVEs is clearer if Table 7.2 is read in conjunction with Table 5.3. Another driver of such employment growth was the absorption of *xiahai* people into various business ventures of TVEs All these factors led to a crucial economic change, which saw the gross output value of TVEs surpass not only that of other rural sectors in the late 1980s (see details in Figure 6.2), but also that of SOEs (Chen 1997). As noted, these results not only increased the reformist leadership's confidence in furthering the reform of TVEs, but also produced many rural entrepreneurs who became wealthy by taking over poorly performing SOEs.

The marketisation of SOEs was the gain of TVEs, enabling not only rural industries but all private businesses to undergo a new round of upgrading and restructuring. More specifically, this process was a new chance for people or teams with skills and capital to venture into new businesses that were able to generate more wealth for them. For this reason, this macro process can be also considered to be a micro process in terms of both accumulation of personal wealth and social positioning. For example, one rural business broker offered the following insight:

> In fact, the [so-called] opportunity at that time was just the product, because labourers and factory equipment were not hard to find by TVEs. [You have to] remember that we all had then run factories for about 15 to 20 years. [...] The market was also not a big worry either because [China] was a shortage economy and there was a market for everything. The key [to earning money] was the product, [which had to be] the one that we believed to be able to sell. Many people's first bucket [of gold] was the product that they found from those squeezed out from SOEs. (Interviewee 27 2020)

As a micro process, the products and markets opened up during this round of industry reform were believed by the interviewee 27 to be the vital factor in the nationwide redistributions of resources and wealth after the mid-1990s. I recently reconnected with the interviewee 27, who helped me in 2006 when I was on study leave in China and visiting some newly emerging businesses in the mid-2000s. I was impressed at that time by the many chain stores and the development of franchise businesses across the nation. It was also during those years that domestic investment and the cross-regional operations of many TVEs saw them develop into the most dynamic forces in the rural industry. At that time, several people told me of their various business experiences in both the 1980s and the 1990s. Among them was the interviewee 27, who in the 1990s introduced a wide range of products that could not be made economically by Beijing- and Tianjin-based SOEs to numerous villages in northern China. This is why he drew attention to the importance of products in producing new entrepreneurs and the connection between specific products that TVEs had salvaged from rubble of the SOEs and the wealth extracted by those rural factory owners and operators.

Evading the Miseries in Pre-industrial Beliefs

The reform of SOEs during the 1980s and 1990s was highly disruptive to the life of the people working within the system. As a consequence of its broad effects, the confidence of the Chinese proletariat in official narratives began to be disturbed or even subverted. Discontent caused by the many reform measures was also growing among state enterprise employees. This not only slowly alienated China's working class from the ruling party – which had always portrayed the workers as the masters of the country – but also evolved into an unusual type of social reaction to the reform measures. For many, the most prominent of such social reactions was the Falun Gong phenomenon. However, what also must be considered is the fact that the spread of *qigong* fever as a type of grassroots social reaction took place some years before the emergence of the Falun Gong in the mid-1990s, and that interest in *qigong* accompanied China's economic reform in the latter's spread from rural areas to urban centres (Palmer 2007).[3]

Apart from the temporal characteristics of the societal craze of *qigong*, it is worth noting the way in which the *qigong* fever, as well as the Falun Gong, has been observed and analysed. There seems to be an analytical tendency to view certain social phenomena in Chinese society, such as the *qigong* fever, from either a cultural or religious viewpoint. One of the overlooked aspects of many *qigong*-related societal crazes and organised activities is the actual motivation of those leading and promoting the mass practices. There are many broad descriptions of the resurgence of *qigong* in the 1980s and 1990s, but there is a clear lack of convincing explanations regarding the motivations of many *qigong* masters and their promoters and followers. To many critical observers, there seems to be an asymmetrical social positioning or repositioning among different types of people involved in different waves of the *qigong* craze. Such uneven social positioning was characterised by the fact that *qigong* enthusiasts were not only driven by different motivations, but also placed differently in the hierarchy of *qigong* groups or networks. Such analyses are especially necessary considering the business interests demonstrated by almost all *qigong* masters and groups. This analysis can, therefore, be carried out along the progress of the *qigong* fever.

Historically, since the early 1980s several dozen *qigong* masters had emerged, one after another, from villages, small towns or even factories, claiming to be able to not

only detect various illnesses but also to cure them without modern medicine and treat-
ments. Such masters existed in China's vast rural regions before the early 1980s, but
they were unable to reach communities beyond their home region due to the strict control measures and political climate. From the early 1980s, however, many *qigong* masters
travelled to local urban centres, driven by the same reason factors that had caused
the floating of population – although an obvious difference between *qigong* masters and
other migrant workers is how they sought to make a living.

Among those popular masters of the 1980s, Zhang Baosheng, a mine worker from
Liaoning province, made himself famous through a few magic tricks. He was even
employed in 1983 by one of China's best military science research institutes. Yan
Xin, a graduate of a local nursing school in Sichuan province, started his practice in
Sichuan and then made himself known through a local newspaper in 1984. One of
his claims was that he could spread psychophysical energies while preaching his *qigong*
theory.[4] Zhang Hongbao, a mining technician in Heilongjiang province, became a
founder of a new set of practices called *Zhonggong* or *Zhong Gong* in 1985. He claimed to
have more than ten million disciples, through whom hundreds of millions of Chinese
yuan were made by selling videos, audiotapes and books. There were more such masters, but these three cases are sufficient to show when they came into view of the
public, where they came from and how they presented themselves to their potential
followers.

Most of these *qigong* masters emerged from grassroots society during a time when the
attention of Chinese people was mostly drawn to their *tuopin* issue (shaking off poverty,
or poverty alleviation). The masters of *qigong* were no exception to this strong social
trend. As hinted, however, they adopted a different approach from that of both many
migrant labourers and aspirants seeking to enter the white-collar workforce. To a large
extent, they all identified *qigong*-style exercises and concepts as their marketable product.
This was the time when people's minds were preoccupied with earning more income
or *chuangshou* (to generate extra revenue or to create additional income streams) in institutional settings. The desire to find additional income sources may explain why many
qigong masters were helped by some urban-based institutions, especially publishers, who
took advantage of this social craze. In terms of this connection, many masters were
rather entrepreneurial or tactical, but positioned themselves within a non-material production sphere using ostensibly traditional means. Of course, this was their way of making a living and positioning in changing social situations, which was very different from
that of their followers at lower hierarchical levels.

Because of these background factors, it would be inaccurate to consider the *qigong*
craze as an indication of any surge in religious interest among ordinary Chinese in the
1980s and 1990s. In fact, almost the entire Chinese population was in the process of
de-ideologicalising themselves and freeing themselves from various forms of imposed
belief systems. Apart from the strong influence of Dengist ideas of *qinlao zhifu* (prosper
through diligence), and people's desire to shake off poverty, the still fresh memory of
semi-religious oppression and semi-feudal control in the Maoist era made improbable
that the *qigong* craze arose from religious convictions. Most Chinese observers believe
that those masters and their high-rank promoters should be considered as a different

type of entrepreneur, while the motivations of their low-level disciples need to be viewed through the lens of social psychology and social behaviour.

As suggested, as well as in note 4 of this current chapter, I met Yan Xin twice in the mid-1980s: once at a public seminar in Beijing and once at a closed-door two-day workshop held outside Beijing. The latter event was held when the *qigong* fever was sweeping urban centres across China, and its socio-political impact became an emerging concern across government and academic institutions. Through such close observations, many of us learned how *qigong* groups were run as businesses. In the case of Yan Xin, his talks were not free of charge. Interestingly, as noted, his preference for large-scale seminars was an effective method to collect more fees. It was at the abovementioned workshop that I first encountered another unique reaction: almost all young and liberal-minded people had a rather negative view of the *qigong* fever, while conservative and left-wing public figures were more sympathetic to the *qigong* masters and their followers. The former supported some control measures, whereas the latter regarded the craze as carrying Chinese tradition into the present. On this issue, there was an unexpected repositioning, or shifting, in people's socio-political opinions. In the words of one participant, the right-wing people move to the left (advocating control measures to keep social order and stability) and the party conservatives shift to the right (allowing people to do what they like). This was a unique asymmetrical match between people's ideological alignments and political positions, revealing the intricacies of the process of social repositioning.

A similar asymmetrical social positioning problem can also be observed in Yan Xin's career trajectory; however, his issue had nothing to do with ideology and politics but, rather, with the gap between his fame and ambition and his skills and intellectual ability. While he seemed to us to be very ambitious, he was less able to express himself effectively. He gave many attendees an impression that his knowledge was not sufficient to support the image he wanted to present to his audience. Like millions of others in this rapidly changing society, he was pursuing a goal that was beyond his abilities. However, also like many, he chose to use what is known in Chinese as the tactic of *yiming jingren* (one speech that surprises all or to impress the world with one brilliant feat). While there were millions of internal migrants making a living through manual work and other skills, many *qigong* masters were making money through claiming special prowess.

In terms of their ideas and the income they accumulated, these *qigong* masters were still entrepreneurial, although they were clearly entrepreneurs of a different type. Their route to earning fortunes was a type of practice called *kongshou dao* or *kongshoudao* (the art of empty hand) (Gao 2015, 2021). This implied a way of earning money without investment or product. Of course, while many *qigong* masters became financially well off, the vast majority of the lower-level followers who paid them did not. Ironically, the further restructuring of SOEs after the mid-1990s produced more disciples for different *qigong* groups than the 1980s and early 1990s.

The second half of the 1990s saw many changes in the *qigong* phenomenon. Among those early mentioned three masters, Zhang Baosheng disappeared from the public eye after having failed in several magic performances. Yan Xin disappeared even earlier than Zhang; according to reports in the tabloids, he relocated to North America in the early 1990s. Two *qigong* groups expanded considerably and become dominant in this field from the mid-1990s. These were *Zhong Gong*, founded by Zhang Hongbao, and the Falun Gong network founded by Li Hongzhi, a former PLA soldier-turned officer of a local municipal bureau, where he worked until 1992. This timing indicates that Li Hongzhi could also be seen as a *xiahai* person, leaving his local government job and focusing on teaching his Falun Gong. As shown in Figure 8.1, the number of people following the Falun Gong, who are called practitioners, increased rapidly from the early 1990s.

These two main groups had shared a range of common characteristics. An obvious but less-discussed similarity between these groups is that the founders of both are from China's northeastern provinces. This region has a distinct vernacular, which is far more vivid, informative and interesting than the way Yan Xin spoke to his audience. This issue could well be behind many fast-fading *qigong* celebrities from other provinces. As my co-author and I argued in one of our research papers, China's anti-Falun Gong campaign had, in fact, also made use of the influence of this regional vernacular to ridicule the Falun Gong due to the effectiveness of the dialect (Gao and Pugsley 2008).

Importantly, a large number of China's SOEs were based in the northeastern provinces. The reform and subsequent privatisation of SOEs after the mid-1990s turned the entire region into a breeding ground for anger and dissatisfaction among its citizens, among whom the new Falun Gong started to spread. As noted, it was also during this period that many motivated people were trying different opportunities in different sectors and areas, such as rural industrial entrepreneurs and *xiahai* people. The latter offered a good example to follow, but many people in northeastern regions were less familiar with private economic activities and the many products wanted by consumers. On the other hand, China's campaign of 'emancipating the mind' (*sixiang jiefang*) had

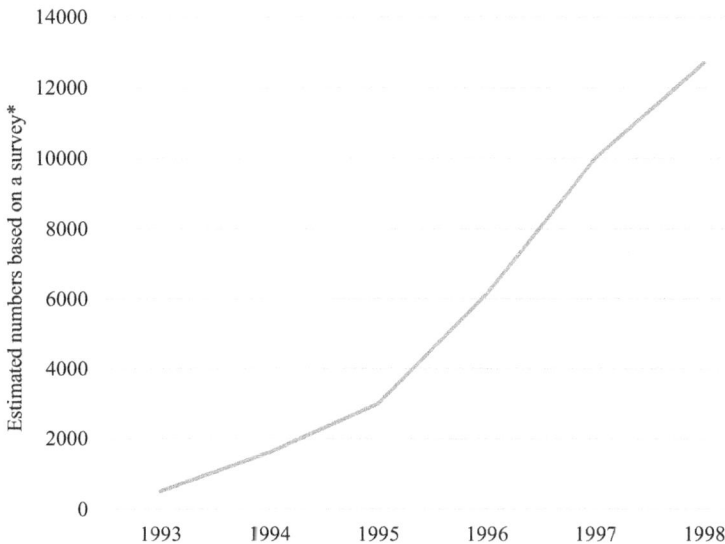

Figure 8.1 Estimated increase in Falun Gong practitionership in the 1990s. *Note*: *Based on a survey of 12,731 people. *Source*: Created by the author based on Minghui.org (1998).

removed many political and ideological constraints on what people could do. Therefore, some people, like Li Hongzhi, turned to non-industrial production activities to earn their fortune. The marketing of this particular cultural product or practice relied on a large group structure, with the Falun Gong starting in Jilin province and then spreading to neighbouring provinces including Liaoning, Heilongjiang and Hebei. As Cheris Chan points out, the number of its disciples 'is in dispute, and probably not even known by the charismatic leader' (Chan 2004, 675). As shown in Figure 8.2, Falun Gong groups seem to be still active in those regions, except Hubei province.

All the large *qigong* groups of the 1980s and 1990s are believed to be operated by the masters and their close disciples. Lu Yunfeng, a sociologist at Peking University, argues that 'entrepreneurial logics play important roles in promoting the birth of new religions', which also 'competed with each other to attract potential customers' (Lu 2005, 174). As noted, they could earn income in several ways, such as coaching fees and product sales. The sale of books, videos and audiotapes was their most profitable business. All these were allowed in China after the mid-1980s. As Benjamin Penny details in his book *The Religion of Falun Gong*, 'many of the controls over what publishers could print and the restrictions on how books and magazines could be sold were lifted' (Penny 2012, 13). As a result, not only did the publishing industry gain more autonomy, but tens of thousands of printing factories were also able to print whatever would earn them a living. This led to numerous unscientific materials being printed and widely circulated in society. What was concerning was that many low-level followers, despite themselves being in financial difficulty, became subjects to be exploited for money by these groups. One interviewee argues that most *qigong* groups were in fact a mixture of activists seeking fame and money in the name of upholding traditional culture, and escapists hiding from rapid social transformations and many challenges in life. As quoted below, this was believed by the interviewee to have led many disciples into an unproductive way of life:

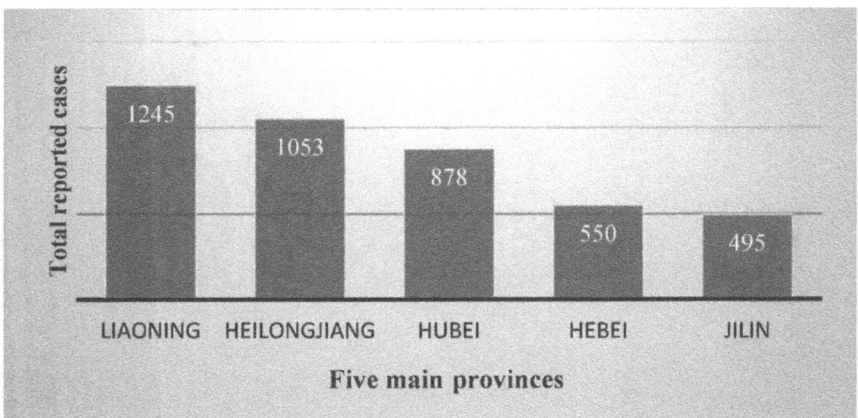

Figure 8.2 The most frequently mentioned active regions of Falun Gong activities in China.* *Note*: *Based on the figures of 2014 and 2016. *Sources*: Created by the author based on Chen (2015) and Gao (2017).

Many of those [*qigong*] masters had become famous and [financially] well-off. They earned their bucket of gold from their learners, but all their [successful] stories were built on the sufferings of the people in troubles. These [masters] people did not care that they had picked up some ancient ideas and practices created well before the modern era, even older than the official political dogmas [...] and that they had offered their followers no skills or ideas in finding new jobs. [...] They may help them adjust psychologically and emotionally, but prevent them from adapting to new social conditions. (Interviewee 35 2019)

The last point is particularly noteworthy considering the unprecedented level of societal repositioning occurring among different classes, groups and people. The Falun Gong and similar *qigong* groups were a type of social response to changes in life, but they offered little real help or benefit to many of their disciples in this regard, making it difficult for them to compete with not only the entrepreneurs in the economic arena, but also the following group within the party-state system.

More Utilitarian Uses of Institutional Resources

The entrepreneurial spirit that permeated Chinese society throughout the 1990s also inspired many bureaucrats working within the party-state system, but the entrepreneurial spirit among institutional adherents has been highly problematic in China since the early 1980s. This worsened as more and more well-off people, especially those *xiahai* people, rural industrialists and small business owners, became visibly better off financially than those staying within the party-state bureaucracies. In a society characterised by a strong sense of comparing and competing with others (*panbi* mentality), the discernible differences in income led those within the system to act. The adoption by the bureaucrats of new and innovative attitudes and strategies was fairly utilitarian at the start. They focused on modifying, or creating in some cases, various institutional arrangements and schemes as a way to protect their privileges and expand their control of the bureaucracies.

According to Chen Jian, a political analyst at the CCP's Party History Research Office, China's ruling classes were challenged on two fronts in the 1990s. Globally, the fall of the Soviet Union left the top CCP leadership worried about the country's political stability. At the same time, they were also confronted with the following challenges:

China's reform and opening up entered a new historical stage [in the 1990s]. [...] There was no doubt that the development of a socialist market economy could liberate and develop productive forces, but it also posed new challenges to the improvement of the discipline of the Party and the fight against corruption. With the gradual expansion of the market economy, the market principle of equivalent exchange had also invaded the Party's life, resulting in more serious corruption such as the use of power for personal gain, favouritism, embezzlement, bribery, and so on. (Chen 2018a, n.p.)

Sun Liping, my disciplinary colleague in Beijing in the 1980s, describes this challenge from a different perspective:

In the survey conducted by the [CCP's] Central Commission for Discipline Inspection for six consecutive years since 1996, the number one issue among the hot social issues was inflation in 1996, corruption from 1997 to 2000, unemployment and employment in 2001, when corruption ranked as the second. According to a survey conducted by the Central Party School, the answers in 2000 focused on five major issues: corruption, SOEs, inequality, unemployment, the burdens of peasants. In 2001, these people still regarded corruption as the number one issue, which topped the list for three years. (Sun 2007, n.p.)

Among various forms of corruption, a range of self-interested changes to existing rules and policies by those within the system are believed in the long run to be the most serious problem. Some of these changes were welcomed by some, but they started altering the long-established rules and patterns of upward social mobility, providing greater opportunities for some cohorts while narrowing options for others. The exploitation of institutional resources can be divided into two main types, involving misuse of power by insiders either in a criminal manner or a political manner. The former has been analysed in many corruption and criminal cases; this analysis focuses on the latter type, looking at the various changes that subsequently affected people's chances of seeking better jobs and greater recognition in society. These were a continuation of the processes analysed in the third section of Chapter seven, but the second half of the 1990s saw many new and fundamental changes to the conditions of people's social positioning.

First, the government decided in 1996 to begin formally implementing the university reform strategy that it planned in 1994, which involved ending its decades-long role in allocating university graduates to jobs across different ministries, bureaus and local governments. In the same year, the new public servant recruitment exam system (*gongwuyuan kaoshi*) was also put into operation after several years of preparation, as detailed in Chapter seven.

The first policy was also regarded as 'smashing the iron rice bowl' of university students, putting an end to the expected career path or social mobility between the university entrance exam and employment. This new policy was put in place along with some other measures, such as the introduction of university fees and the partial elimination of the planning system to control the annual university student intake. The latter was the start of an endless loop of the so-called *kuoda zhaosheng* (increase in university intake), allowing universities to enrol more students. This strategy opened the system up to more people, which sounded fair and inspiring, but it devalued hard-earned tertiary qualifications in the eyes of many university graduates and their parents. Even more disturbing to them was the second change, which was the implementation of the new public servant recruitment exam system to replace the job allocation approach, shutting many educated people out of the party-state system.

The year 1996 has been seen as a watershed moment in the PRC's history of higher education, but it was also a turning point in the history of cadre team construction in a Chinese phrase, or, to use a modern expression, the history of public servant management. As hinted in Chapter seven, the second change was partly driven by the concerns of a group of communist veterans over the likely destabilising political influence of liberal-minded university graduates and other intellectuals on the regime's stability. Their concerns affected not only the political atmosphere, making it favourable to loyal follow-ers of the CCP, but also the various governing mechanisms. One of the latter was to run the cadre selection system separately from the higher education system. Other than the political consideration, the new civil servant recruitment examination system has also been described by some as a power grab. In one analogy, the allocation of jobs within China's party-state institutions dividing a cake, the people in power certainly would like to seize a large slice to gain the associated benefits or to redistribute to their networks.

While the conservative establishment of the CCP was trying to establish this new cadre selection system as a crucial mechanism in selecting trustworthy people, its dis-advantages for university graduates became very evident from the start of the new scheme. In fact, according to a report in *Beijing Daily*, many people noticed an unex-pected phenomenon one year before the formal implementation of the system. In 1995, during a trial of the new system, the new exam arrangement attracted more graduates from technical colleges and secondary technical schools than from universities. Among 5,087 participants in that year, the proportions of postgraduates, undergraduates, tech-nical college students and those attended secondary technical schools were 5 per cent, 42 per cent, 21 per cent and 32 per cent, respectively (Li 2005a, 3). With 53 per cent of participants coming from the last two categories, the general public was surprised by these reports and their distrust of the new system became even stronger. This was also because the above figures contradicted not only the Chinese examination tradition, but also the education criterion for the so-called four moderations of cadres as detailed in Chapters five and six.

The participation in the earlier rounds of the civil servant recruitment exam by more people with lower education qualifications had revived, if not strengthened, the decades-old perception that some people from the new ruling classes were exploiting their families' political position to turn the situation in their favour. This was evident in the mid-1960s before the Cultural Revolution, when some young students from commu-nist evolutionary families advocated a series of changes to the education system as they found it difficult to adapt to the practice. As noted in Chapter two, their push became one of the excuses for Mao to embark on the Cultural Revolution. In the 1990s, these people worked with several other groups to set up the new civil servant exam system, separating this function from the higher education system.

Second, as examined in Chapter seven, from the late 1990s the CCP's party school system expanded into postgraduate education by running courses at master's level. Initially, the Central Party School was the only party school in the country to offer postgraduate courses, in order to train leaders and teaching staff members for the party schools at the provincial and prefectural levels. As a result of the top-down push to strengthen the role of party schools, which was detailed in Chapter seven, a bottom-up push emerged from the party schools at the provincial level and from numerous low- and middle-level bureaucrats seeking education qualifications. Of course, this bottom-up demand was wrapped up brilliantly in what the central leadership wanted to institutionalise and standardise the party school education. The latter excuse was utilised by several provinces, such as Jilin, Sichuan and Beijing, in the first half of the 1990s. In the mid-1990s, Zhejiang, Guangdong and Shaanxi started their own schemes, followed by Jiangsu and Heilongjiang in 1998. What was more controversial than these schemes themselves was that all these courses were formally authorised by the State Council's Academic Degree Commission to award master's degrees to their trainees.

These programmes run by the party school system have since become one of the most contentious issues in China, because they are all run as internal tailor-made courses available to those without required qualifications, but only those working within the party-state system. In other words, in comparison to the university entrance examination system, these party school degree courses are seen as an alternative route for bureaucrats and officers to obtain education qualifications to meet the CCP's requirements for cadre four moderations. The use of the party school system in this way 'has led to the confusion of the higher education system and the personnel management system that is based on the former system' (Gao 2005, n.p.). This is why, as shown in Chapter seven, there have always been very sensitive and critical social responses to the issue (Wang 2008a; Wang 2008b). For this reason, some schemes run by the party school system are now seen as part of what is widely known in China as *xueli fubai* (qualification corruption, or corruption in obtaining education qualifications) (Li 2014b, n.p.).

It is worth mentioning two points that may help understand the issue better. First, the institutionalisation and standardisation of party school education has been carried out in a clandestine manner due to negative public responses to such self-serving schemes. As hinted, these programmes have been challenged for their lack of entrance examinations, which have always been highly valued by the Chinese people, and for excluding participants from the wider society. Second, this new development and the one to be considered next (the new policies on the tenure of official appointments) are reversed a little bit in chronological order, but considering the intricacy of the third development, it is placed after this discussion as the third main form of utilisation of institutional resources in the latter half of the 1990s. Readers can take the chronological order of these new social phenomena into account, figuring out how tough and intricate all the repositioning or positioning efforts were in the 1990s.

Among the many consequences of permitting the party schools to offer more courses and provide education qualifications, many critics are particularly concerned with its damaging impact on the general quality of those cadres staying with or entering the party-state system, especially their socio-political attitudes, manners and behavioural dispositions. As explained below by an interviewee, some of these new policies and practices are not simply an issue of those officers and bureaucrats, but more significantly about the societal conditions that affect the social repositionings of other citizens:

[All these tricks] have created and nurtured a category of people with what I would call 'party school quality' and 'civil servant quality'. They are equivalent to the cadres of workers and peasants in the past. They are foolishly loyal, but have little thinking ability and also lack skills for work, not to mention the ability to reform and innovate. But they could do immoral things, crowding out other capable people to other sectors. [...] A large number of such people have appeared at all levels [of the Chinese leadership], disturbing social norms and other people's career paths. (Interviewee 46 2020)

At the other end of the spectrum, however, the ruling party seems to have benefitted from such self-serving practices. Table 8.2 shows an increase in the number of CCP members in the 1990s.

The rise in CCP membership in the 1990s is believed to be closely related to the advantages membership provided in enabling many members to be more competitive in climbing the social ladder. In many cases, it may simply have been a modest compensation for inherited disadvantages. Because of the large-scale rural–urban migration and subsequent urbanisation, this rise has since the early 2000s become more apparent than in the 1990s. Many studies observe that the 'CCP membership has become a hotly sought after credential for university graduates to differentiate themselves from fellow job seekers' (Cooke 2012, 94). This is the start of a new phase or a new social process; while this is outside the scope of this study, the fundamental drivers remain the same – namely, the advantages associated with party membership. Although this trend might sound selfish, corrupt practices extended beyond the previous uses of institutional resources, which were efforts by a fairly large number of cadres to make use of the newly established and implemented cadre tenure system (renqizhi).

Third, as pointed out, a side effect of the new policies on the tenure of official appointments produced new drivers and opportunities for people within the party-state system to take advantage of institutional resources. This has also significantly influenced the way people position themselves in society in terms of options, rules and patterns. Because of the severe consequences of Mao's unrestricted lifetime leadership role, the CCP's central leaders since Mao's death had started exploring the tenure system. After entering the 1990s, more efforts were made to develop and implement this system. At the Fourth Plenary Session of the Fourteenth Central Committee of the CCP in September 1994, a major decision was made on issues around strengthening party-building. In 1995, the CCP followed up on the resolution and issued the 'interim regulations on the selection and appointment of leading cadres of the party and the state' (Fewsmith 2010, 2). These regulations sought to create a standard decision-making process for selecting and

Table 8.2 Increase in the number of CCP members, 1969–2002.

Year	Number of CCP Members (m)	China's Population in the Year (m)	CCP Members in the Population (%)
1969[1]	22.00	796	2.8
1973[2]	28.00	881	3.2
1977	35.00	943	3.7
1982	39.66	1,001	4.0
1987	46.00	1,084	4.2
1992	52.00	1,165	4.5
1997	60.42	1,230	4.9
2002	66.94	1,280	5.2

Notes: [1] The CCP's ninth Congress was held in 1969 after 12 years without one.
[2] The 10th Congress was held earlier after the Lin Biao incident.
Sources: Compiled by the author based on Sun (2009), Li (2021) and World Bank (2022).

appointing cadres, but the core element was the establishment of time limits for leadership appointments. Some of these ideas had already been trialled in several regions from the late 1980s to the mid-1990s, and the CCP had gained some experience in the use of a tenure system for local party and government leaders.

However, the latter half of the 1990s was markedly different from the preceding years, and the local trials of the new policy and practices were also different from their nationwide implementation. Generally speaking, limited terms for government officials sound sensible, putting an end to the lifelong tenure of many official appointments and opening up opportunities for younger people to enter the system or change roles. In practice, however, it led to changes in the behaviours of many party and government officials. Chinese analysts have cautiously described these new issues as the 'short-term behavior of governance' (Cao et al. 2018, 92). Additionally, they also identify a number of negative consequences. For example, fixed-term tenures may be one reason many leadership teams are unstable, as their attention is diverted to promotion or reappointment. Stringent age restrictions on promotion have been an open secret among Chinese for decades, allowing everyone to predict who is most likely to be promoted and who will step down. On China's centrally controlled media platform alone there is a huge amount of information about such issues. In 2007, Gong Weibin, a researcher at China National School of Administration, published an article on *People's Forum*, an online forum run by the *People's Daily*, analysing a phenomenon he terms 'frustration in officialdom' among cadres. According to his analysis, the so-called 59 phenomenon, 39 phenomenon and frequent incidents of 'officials stumbling each other' are among many forms of corruption closely related to the frustration among cadres (Zhang 2007).

The '59 phenomenon' refers to 'officials who commit graft around the age of 59 when they are about to retire' or give up leadership roles in the case of low- and middle-ranking officials (Lin 2010, n.p.). The so-called 39 phenomenon refers to those 'rushing up the stairs' of promotion around the age of 39 and attempting different ruses to get promoted (Tao 2006, n.p.). Among the ruses used by these bureaucratic ladder climbers, many are involved in *maiguan maiguan* (buying and selling of official positions). Shi Shujun, a contributor to *People's Forum*, believes that the reasons for such corrupt behaviours are as follows:

> Since entering the 1990s, the selection of cadres in some regions has undergone 'qualitative' changes. Due to the influence of 'money worship', 'chasing for an official post and buying an official position' have become widespread. Initially, people hated this phenomenon very much. Slowly, some people with good jobs have also resolutely joined the team of those 'chasing for an official post and buying an official position', after realising that they became vulnerable. As a result, 'chasing for an official post and buying an official position' have spread like a plague. The phenomenon of 'reverse elimination' has risen from 'hidden rules' to 'perceptible rules'. (Shi 2004, n.p.)

Leaving aside the impact of corruption on the CCP, which is beyond the scope of this analysis, these emerging practices have also impacted on the opportunities, and effort required, for many ordinary people, including the CCP's grassroots members, to position themselves in this changing society. China's officially controlled media have reported many corruption cases since the latter half of the 1990s; one of the most notorious cases clearly reveals the extent of the buying and selling official positions when the cadre tenure system was introduced. Wang Xinkang was party secretary of the CCP's Hua County committee, Henan province. During his tenure, from 1994 to 1997, the whole county made 865 official appointments: 445 were promoted locally and 420 were appointed from elsewhere. Wang divided sales into three functions: promotion, transferring to a new post and retaining one's existing post. These three different arrangements were priced differently. To increase the scope for collecting bribes from those wishing to be promoted, appointed or retained, he even took advantage of an organisational reform to vacate more than 280 positions and then refill them. He was found to have taken bribes on more than seventy occasions, totalling almost a half a million of Chinese yuan, a huge amount by the standards of the time. As a result, he was nicknamed a 'wholesaler' of official positions (Fan et al. 1999). This reflects a core problem: if a county party secretary could control more than a thousand posts in this way, how many public servant positions are still within reach for other people in the open employment market?

New Social Dynamics and Responses

It was also in the late 1990s, on 12 October 1998, that China's official Xinhua News Agency re-posted an article under the rather provoking heading '20 Years of Reform and Opening Up: Who Gets Rich First'. Some left-wing commentators seized on the second half of the heading to criticise the concept of letting some people get rich first, proposed by Deng Xiaoping, who passed away in early 1997. This was the start of a debate over the 'original sin of the new rich' and the 'criminality and punishment of the first bucket of gold', even though many critics and researchers believe this debate to have started only recently (Fan 2007, n.p.). After the question of who became rich was raised in this high-profile manner – generally called *zhuanzai*, or *zhuanfa* (reposting) – by Xinhua, the attention of many concerned citizens was drawn to a number of new issues caused by the changes in social structure and dynamics. These issues and concerns had contributed jointly with other factors to a number of changes in general attitudes and thinking in the early years of the post-Deng era.

First, the attention of left-wing thinkers and activists was moving step by step away from the liberal-minded intellectuals and their arguments as a result of the extensive changes that had also occurred within the latter, which will be detailed next. Within years of Deng's passing, many left-wing ideologues turned their attention to whether, as many critics claimed, 'practitioners of other forms of commercial ventures, such as private and foreign-funded enterprises, those who use state monopoly to control both social and natural resources, the power-money brokers, and many illegal income receivers, such as tax evaders, have become rich first' (Fan 2007, n.p.). In the words of Wang Hui, a Tsinghua University professor and an alleged theorist of the Chinese New Left, the most striking feature of the 1990s was marketisation or the beginning of the market era. This key aspect is believed to have changed both state and society in China

(Wang 2009). Those exponents of Maoism and other similar isms, as well as those with vested interests from the Mao era, therefore, took aim at new groups of people who were found to have benefitted from the marketisation.

New entrepreneurs of both rural and urban origin were elevated during this round of debate to become the main target of left-wing criticism. They were regarded as a new breed of capitalists, responsible for class exploitation, income inequality and widespread injustices. It was partly true that these new entrepreneurs in both urban and rural areas were becoming more influential among ordinary citizens, young and old, than the ruling CCP, if not actually exceeding the number of CCP members as some alarmists claimed. As noted, these new economic realities had also attracted a huge number of CCP members and officials, who were joining the entrepreneurs either on a full-time basis or a part-time basis, or even indirectly such as through collusion with business people. However, in the eyes of reformers, these business people were the result of the strategy of supporting TVEs and reforming SOEs, and up to the late 1990s these people had proven to be front-runners in socio-economic expansion. More importantly, their role was considered to be irreplaceable. They were, therefore, also admired by young aspiring people, impacting the latter more significantly than other groups.

The new target of political attack by left-wing activists also helped generate a new concern among less radical left-leaning people and other citizens over the increasing inequality in China. Such concerns were well founded, but in the midst of the post-1992 reform and the social redistribution of economic resources, they did not detract from the persuasiveness of two dominant narratives. The first of these was that, despite the inequality, 'over the past 20 years of reform and opening up, with the development of the economy, people's living standards have generally improved' (Xu 1999b, 73). This stance has been accepted by a substantial majority of the Chinese population. The second narrative was put forward by Dengist reformers, insisting that the inequality problem could only be effectively tackled once the economy was well developed, and that the top priority for China was to deepen and accelerate economic structural reforms to expand its economy further. Despite the persuasiveness of these viewpoints, public concern about inequality has never been laid to rest. This is partly because of the increasing level of inequality since then, and partly because of the constant push from the discontented people and the dissidents of the time, who sought to alter the path of China's reform, especially its market liberalisation and deregulation. The latter meant that many people, including the above two groups, failed to properly reposition themselves at different stages of this social change process.

Second, the reformist ruling elites were also forced by the anti-reform rhetoric to reaffirm their commitment to reform and opening-up and their determination to implement Dengist governing principles and strategy to focus attention on economic development. This governing idea has since normally been expressed in the terms Deng used in his 1992 inspection tour – namely, that 'development is the only hard principle' (Nan 2014). Based on this governing principle, the reform of SOEs was pushed firmly forward. As noted in Chapters six and seven, SOE reform commenced years before the mid-1990s, but with the rapid development of TVEs and businesses under other forms of ownership, SOEs were failing badly in competing in the deregulated market by the mid-1990s. In 1997, the total loss of the loss-making SOEs had risen by more than ten times compared with that in 1987 (Xu and Hua 2015). Therefore, 1998 saw an intensified effort, with the central leadership issuing an order to solve this problem within three years (Yang 2019). From this year on, not only was the contract system of SOEs further strengthened, but other ways of handling enterprises – such as auction, contracting, insolvency, ownership transfer as well as the creation of job centres to manage laid-off workers – also began to be piloted and implemented. These actions dealt a blow to those remained in their positions rather than joining the *xiahai* cohort. What was more frustrating was that new enterprise owners or managers were often those who had actively repositioned themselves in time earlier than them.

The strong determination of the post-Deng leadership to deal with the inequality issue through economic expansion also led to some other reform schemes, including the urban housing reform in 1998. This urban housing reform added fuel to the flames ignited by the final effort to restructure SOEs. This combination helped the rapid expansion of a number of grassroots groups, including Falun Gong groups. On 25 April 1999, thousands of Falun Gong practitioners from neighbouring regions gathered in central Beijing to protest against the negative coverage of their practices in the Chinese official media. This large demonstration, and the organisational ability that it revealed, was considered by the post-Deng leadership to be a warning, reminding them of the other key part of Deng Xiaoping's political legacy – *Wending yadao yiqie* (stability overrides everything) (Fewsmith 2011). The Falun Gong was outlawed in July 1999 and a nationwide anti-Falun Gong campaign was launched. This was a turning point in the CCP's history. The ruling elites were less concerned by liberal-minded intellectuals than by the Falun Gong and other grassroots forces. Although claims that Falun Gong practitioners outnumbered the CCP were inaccurate, the Falun Gong was a strong social activist force, representing disappointed workers dismissed from SOEs and other disadvantaged urban groups. It would also be inaccurate to say that the Falun Gong posed a political threat to the CCP, but the events described earlier do suggest a change in social class relations in China. This point is much clearer taking into consideration the support the CCP had given new entrepreneurs and other business elites.

As a result of the focus on the reform of SOEs and the laid-off workers, a new class alliance formed between the ruling CCP reformers, new entrepreneurs and other economic elites. As this class alliance became the mainstay of China's economic expansion and its strategic internationalisation, it also, from the late 1990s, created changes in social power relations. From the left-wing viewpoint, this involved the emergence of what is now widely known as *guanshang goujie* (the collusion of government officials and commercial sectors or businesspeople). This has since gradually evolved into what is more recently and vividly portrayed as officials kneeling down at the feet of new rich entrepreneurs. As a special manifestation of the above problem, this depiction exemplifies a radical view of China's social change. Two components of this alliance have, in the minds of many ordinary citizens, however, illustrated two main career options and directions that were not preferred by many in the early years. While critics were condemning the alliance, the two economically and politically advantaged groups were quietly influencing many people in Chinese society, laying the foundation for more changes in the early 2000s.

Third, the liberal-minded intellectuals and wayward young students became a lesser concern not only for the CCP leadership and other ruling elites but also for various left-wing groups. These latter groups worked together to effectively reduce the influence of liberal-minded groups through several strategies. As noted, the termination of the job assignment, or allocation, system in 1996 for university undergraduates was a major change. It was followed by a significant increase in university enrolment intake several years later. This was seen as another major step to minimise the influence of free thinking and liberal ideas on young people, while many others viewed it as a deregulation effort to reform the higher education system. In practice, this was in reality a two-pronged approach: to enrol more students to dilute the university student composition, and to remove the power of assigning students to jobs from universities and redistribute that power to employers, or other institutions in the case of selecting loyal public servants or low-ranking cadres. Some other new social trends and pushes, such as studying abroad and *xiahai*, also diverted a relatively high proportion of liberal-minded intellectuals and young students away from the public sectors and other party-state-controlled organisations. All these measures radically changed the composition of both the student population and the intellectual community.

Apart from the loss of the social and political governance functions of universities in terms of student job allocation, the status of intellectuals also changed drastically during this period of time. Sun Liping, who taught sociology at Peking University and Tsinghua University, once pointed out that the concept of intellectuals almost disappeared from public discourse in the 1990s (Sun 2005). The intellectuals were highly divided, between those outside the party-state system and those within the system, with both groups further divided into various categories. Xiao Gongqin, a leading scholar of neo-authoritarianism in China, also observes that since the 1990s the ideological trend of radical liberalism has gradually disappeared from Chinese ideological discussion, and the tension between the liberal intellectuals and those in power in the 1980s also eased. The intellectuals as a whole became less hostile to the government, which even made the argument between liberalism and new authoritarianism less confrontational (Xiao 2007). One folklorist even described the change in the 1990s as the last fading ray of idealism, with a new era that was more open and diverse, recognising self-expression and individuality, arriving in China (Han 2009).

The above changes and trends were also reflected in the patterns of life of ordinary Chinese, including how they approached their career choices and decisions in this changing social context. The following changes are pertinent to this analysis.

The first clear change involved perceptions of wealth, social status, occupations and prosperity. The new concept of wealth had altered people's understanding of social status, resulting in changes in the reputation and attractiveness of many occupations. This was a rapid and widespread change, sweeping the country both vertically and horizontally. As Bian Yanjie and his colleagues reveal, significant erosion had already occurred in the privileges and superior social status of the cadre official class in comparison to businesspeople and intellectuals since the 1980s. Based on their survey, undertaken in

China in 1998, they notice that as a result of increasing levels of marketisation, China's class structure had changed dramatically, with the class structure of urban China becoming 'more fragmented and less clearly hierarchical than in the late 1970s and early 1980s' (Bian et al. 2005, 1445). Based on a large-scale nationwide survey undertaken in 2001, Li Chunling, a CASS-based sociologist, notes similar but slightly different changes. The results of this survey showed that Chinese society's deep-rooted bureaucracy-based hierarchical mentality (*guanbenwei* in Chinese) was still influential in the evaluation of social status in the late 1990s.[5] At the same time, the social prestige of intellectuals was found to have declined, corroborating Sun Liping's and Xiao Gongqin's observations about this period (Li 2005).

The second crucial shift was the actual occupational choices of young people, which were closely correlated with the changing perceptions outlined previously. Yang Xiong, former director of Shanghai Youth Research Institute, has documented these changes as early as 1997. At the time, university graduates alone were already attracted by two new opportunities. The first was the so-called *sanzi qiye* (three types of foreign-invested enterprises: foreign-owned, Sino-foreign joint and cooperative enterprises). The second was China's new economic zones in some coastal regions. The social status previously prioritised by educated Chinese began taking third place behind two new considerations: level of income, and the probability of making use of their expertise. The latter was believed to be an alternative expression for the opportunity of smooth promotion according to other observers (Yang 1997). Based on several surveys, Yang also concludes that the growth of the market economy fostered a very strong individual consciousness among young Chinese, including university graduates. On the other hand, the utilitarian tendency of these people also became more prominent than ever before, especially in the process of making their career choices and positioning themselves in society.

The third major change was the re-emergence of social class barriers, preventing many people from positioning themselves freely in different social class groups and at different levels of society. Obviously, this was a social structural change, more tangible and fundamental than others. More importantly, it not only modified the landscape of Chinese politics but also transformed its physical underpinnings or the social structural conditions in which people lived and worked. As mentioned, Bian and his colleagues identify this new issue as an increase in fragmentation (Bian et al. 2005). This finding has been supported by many other studies. However, the process of breaking society into fragments also indicates the formation and existence of some social class barriers. Li Lulu, my old classmate and colleague at Renmin University of China, and his collaborators have articulated the same issue in a different way, arguing that 'China has gradually formed a relatively stable societal structure formed by vested interest groups' (Li et al. 2018, 14). These vested interest groups have made every effort and used a wide range of resources and mechanisms to protect their vested interest. Li et al. consider three types of capital: cultural, political and economic. While cultural capital can be gained and inherited by ordinary people and families, they find that the other two types of capital, political and economic, were accumulated more and faster by particular class groups. As a result, 'strengthening intergenerational inheritance and hindering [other people's] intergenerational mobility has become a crucial means to maintain their vested interest' (Li et al. 2018, 14). In their analysis, political and economic capital were behind the social class solidification that started taking shape in the latter half of the 1990s.

Overall, people from different social groups were active and entrepreneurial in the second half of the 1990s. As a result, many achieved favourable positionings and reached new horizons in their careers. No matter whether these changes are defined as fragmentation, solidification or social class barriers, Chinese society has since then entered the twenty-first century with a growing sense of social inequality and a highly aspiring population.

Notes

1. *Wenhui Daily*, or *Wenhui Bao* in Chinese, or *Wen Hui Pao* as it was also called, is one of the oldest newspapers in China. Founded in Shanghai in the late 1930s, the newspaper became even more famous after 1 July 1957, when Mao Zedong wrote and published an editorial for *People's Daily* titled 'Wen Hui Pao's bourgeois orientation should be criticised'. This editorial is considered to be one of the most important articles marking the official beginning of the Anti-Rightist Campaign. The campaign 'lasted almost one year and designated 552,877 to 1.02 million people as Rightists' (Wang 2014c, 89). *Wenhui Daily* was seen as a newspaper for educated Chinese, promoting ideas of liberalisation, freedom of speech and press freedom. Since 1957 it has been under strict control by the party-state system and has become one of the political weathercocks in China. Apart from Wang (2014c), interested readers are also referred to (Yang 1995) and (Shirk 2011).
2. Rong Yiren (1916–2005) and Wang Guangying (1919–2018) were very different from the new entrepreneurs in terms of age. In fact, they were also different in other ways. These two old industrialists of the Republican period (1911–49) were from traditional industrialist families. After 1949, they became representatives of national capitalists, who were called the Red Capitalists. In the early reform years, Rong Yiren was appointed a national economic advisor, helping China establish China International Trust and Investment Corporation. He was the PRC's vice president from 1993 to 1998. Wang Guangying, who was from Tianjin, was a famous representative of Republican industrialists from northern China. Interestingly, he was also a brother-in-law of Liu Shaoqi, the PRC's second president. In the 1980s, he helped set up China Everbright Group before serving as vice chairperson of China's People's Congress and its Consultative Conference successively.
3. *Qigong* is a general term, also transliterated *chi kung*, *ch'i kung* and a few other forms. It refers to a set of traditional Chinese healing practices. While the term is widely known around the world, there are many types of such practices, which have emerged one after the other. The Falun Gong was redesigned by Li Hongzhi in 1992 based on the ideas of traditional *qigong*, but it formed a new sequence of body movements. Interested readers can read more about *Qigong* in Garripoli (1999), Liu (2010) and Mitchell (2011).
4. I attended Yan Xin's talk twice, one in a public forum and once in a closed-door workshop, in my capacity as a standing committee member of the association of social psychology. These face-to-face meetings helped me understand a number of his tactics. For example, he claimed that he could make *qi* energy flow, or even radiate, while giving a talk. Apart from using large seminars to collect more fees, his approach was also believed to be a smart use of collective psychology. To cope with our closed-door workshop, attended by people from several national scientific research institutions and universities, Yan Xin delayed his talk a few times during the day and turned up after 10 o'clock in the evening. All the attendees were joking about his making use of the attendees' tiredness to avoid his problems being detected by the attendees. Interested readers can read more about Yan Xin in Chen (2003), Lewis and Peterson (2005) and Ashiwa and Wank (2009).

5. The structure of the phrase *guanbenwei* is identical to that of *jinbenwei* or *huangjin benwei* (gold standard). These refer to the system by which the value of a currency is defined in terms of gold. In terms of *guanbenwei*, the level of a person's social status is matched to and assessed in accordance with an equivalent to an official position in the party-state system. It has been a very useful perspective for observing and analysing Chinese culture, the mentality of Chinese people and their behaviours. In addition to the definition provided in the text, which is that of the deep-rooted bureaucracy-based hierarchical mentality and standard, some scholars have defined it as 'the bureaucratic standard' (Wang 1998a, 142), an 'official-entered' culture (Kinkley 2007, 119) and a 'bureaucracy-oriented consciousness' (Ce and Rui 2016, 68). Interested readers are referred to the above-quoted books for details.

Chapter Nine

TOWARDS A THEORY OF COMPETITIVE SOCIAL REPOSITIONING

This short chapter concludes this book, with a focus on theoretical insights into how societal dynamics and changes in China's recent past can be better understood and what practical inferences may be drawn from this analysis. As noted in Chapter one, this analysis is conducted from the perspective of competitive social repositioning, some features of which need to be further considered. Special attention must also be paid to the political importance of the Three-Represents theory. This theory was initially put forward by Jiang Zemin in early 2000 as the ideological responses of his leadership generation to the new social class structure, societal dynamics and many other changes taking place in post-Mao China. Two decades after it was proposed, the Three-Represents theory is virtually abandoned by the post-Jiang leadership, despite the occasional, and largely ceremonial, mention in some official media reports. However, it remains not only a conclusion drawn by reformist Chinese leaders from the previous reforming decades, but also a set of ideological and political responses to the main hurdles in modernising the CCP from a revolutionary party to a ruling party.

The first section of this final chapter summarises the analysis in earlier discussion chapters and offers further explication of the competitive social repositioning perspective, especially its theoretical and analytical usefulness and importance in examining deep-rooted social dynamics and subsequent social changes. The second section considers the practical implications of this study, including a brief analysis of the fate of Jiang Zemin's Three-Represents ideas over the past two decades. Suggestions for future research are offered with the objective of promoting the use of a competitive social repositioning lens in future studies.

Perspective Matters

The three and a half decades from 1964 to 2000, which form the subject of this book, were a historical period when China's economy, people's living conditions and political culture deteriorated to a new crisis level and then started climbing upwards. Specifically, during this period, the Chinese people suffered from the famine of the early 1960s and were then dragged into a decade-long Cultural Revolution. The latter led to widespread support for leaders who had different ideas and governing strategies from Mao, driving China onto the reform track from the late 1970s. Throughout the above social process, a high proportion of Chinese people actively participated in continuous and competitive social repositionings, making the whole country both chaotic and dynamic. However, as examined in Chapter one, many observations and analyses of China's recent past have been influenced by binary thinking about contemporary China, focusing narrowly either on the decision-making elites or on those who suffered from and were angered by the new policies and procedures. Under the influence of these dichotomous approaches, and also despite the fact that these approaches have generated considerable insight into Chinese society and social change, past studies have in some way overlooked, if not excluded, some crucial social aspects, such as social actors, motivations, processes and dynamics, from their understanding of contemporary Chinese society.

This analysis is based on a comprehensive and critical examination of the research literature on contemporary China. As stated, the literature is characterised by two types of research interest and focus, either prioritising elitist views on Chinese society or devoting attention to the reactions of those angered by numerous changes. While there are a small number of studies analysing the role of everyday people side in social changes, the majority of the Chinese population and their behavioural responses to social changes are largely understudied, if not completely absent from the scholarly literature. Based on a review of the literature, this analysis identified not only the analytical gap, but also the suitability of the concept of competitive social repositioning to guide this analysis. Perspective matters in studying social changes and processes. The competitive social repositioning perspective not only places this study on the right course but also focuses attention on people's actual reactions and actions.

Guided by the competitive social repositioning viewpoint, this book has offered insights into how ordinary Chinese had reacted to social changes and how societal dynamics were generated and played out over the course of three and a half decades, from 1964 to 2000. The main findings may be summarised as follows:

The recovery from the famine of the early 1960s started with the appeal of the Red and Expert ideal, on which basis the successor narrative was developed and widely propagated in 1964. Despite being positive to breathe new hope into the post-famine years, the intensifying competition to be both Red and Expert made those from politically sound families feel threatened, because most of such families gained new privileges through participation in the Chinese armed revolution, not through the utilisation of their intellectual or cultural capital. Their anxieties helped Mao embark on the Cultural Revolution, the aim of which was to consolidate his position in power, different from what his followers expected. It was very soon that Mao's imprudent decision to send urban youth to remote rural areas tore the veil of his utopianism and Chinese revolutionary romanticism, putting an end to both the worship of Mao and his personal charisma. It was replaced by utilitarianism and individualism, the influence of which gave rise to the bottom-up push for change in the second half of the 1970s, with the 1976 Tiananmen Incident reflecting fundamental change in Chinese society.

To satisfy ambitious young people, the university entrance examination and selection system was restored in late 1977, adding another contentious issue into post-Mao China because it brought disadvantages to many people from communist revolutionary families with little intellectual capital. The 1980s was a busy decade for the Chinese people, who had not only to fit into new political and social class relations, but also to seize on chances to realise their potential or personal goal and ambitions. While some liberal-minded citizens devoted their attention and energies to various forms of ideo-logical activism, rural people and some workers started making efforts to achieve their own economic freedom in the increasingly deregulated market. However, the post-Mao generation of university students was fairly supercilious and soon found themselves on a collision course with other left-leaning groups, with their clear advantages in career progression slowly depleted by such tensions.

China's attention to economic development had, since the mid-1980s, created more favourable social conditions for business people from both rural and urban settings than for people interested in ideological and political debates. The student protests from late 1986 to mid-1989 changed China's political landscape, driving numerous liberal-minded people out of public sectors and politics. The vacuums left by educated lib-erals and those choosing to enter the commercial world were slowly but calculatedly filled by left-leaning loyalists, and single-minded and ambitious social climbers as well. Behind this replacement process, a number of new institutional measures were taken to minimise the reliance on universities to train future leaders. These changes to the rules, paths and patterns of upward social mobility did not, however, generate much serious attention and awareness at the time, as China was entering the most entrepreneurial period of its modern history after Deng's inspection tour in early 1992. While most people focused on accumulating wealth, a new alliance of political and economic elites began to take shape and new social class barriers emerged.

More theoretically, the social changes over these decades started with policies and measures that were rather unfavourable for many members of the ruling class and its allies. This was partly due to the absence of off-the-shelf models for the distri-bution of interests, social resources and powers of influence among Chinese citizens in early post-revolutionary years, except a range of revolutionary rules and orders. Both the post-famine recovery in the early- to mid-1960s and the post-1978 reform had, little by little, altered those transitional rules with the aim of rallying more people to participate in China's social and economic development. The involvement of more able citizens in the processes forced the new ruling classes to make society more inclusive and to open up some of the areas they had monopolised from the 1950s to much of the 1970s. Similar changes and compromises were also made in the post-1992 years.

As a result, from the early- to mid-1960s more Chinese people started making extra efforts to reposition themselves in this slowly opening social system and class structure. Since then, such efforts have been an almost constant phenomenon in this changing soci-ety as citizens reacted to their changing positions in the distribution of social resources, benefits and powers of influence. This reaction process has, therefore, become a vital and permanent feature of Chinese society. To a great degree, these efforts have also from time to time acted as a disruptive force on the pre-existing patterns in the distri-bution of benefits, resources and political influences. Such disruptions have gradually become routine and commonplace due to economic growth and increase in wealth, driving a big proportion of the population to keep repositioning themselves to either stay relevant or climb the social ladder. Their efforts have made their repositioning process not only constant but also competitive.

Because of the vital significance of individuals' positions, or precisely, people's feelings about their positions, in the social distribution of social resources, benefits and influences, people constantly make judgements and adjustments to their status throughout their lifetime. In fact, active social members have always calculated their gain or loss, or the progress or regress in their relations with the changing patterns of social resources and benefit distribution. Such calculation is especially necessary in the case of China, where the ruling elites have had a very strong sense of ruling. The typical clue running through the period covered by this study has to be the bloodline theory, or *xuetong lun* in Chinese. This was often represented by a rhyming couplet: *laozi yingxiong er haohan, laozi fandong er hundan* (the sons of heroes are real men; the sons of reactionaries are bastards), which typically concluded with a general statement: *jiben ruci* (no exception). This view was publicly and viciously promulgated by the children or the relatives of some revolutionary seniors in the earlier days of the Cultural Revolution, showing their determination to maintain dominance in the distribution of social resources and benefits. Such class interest-based societal rivalries have continued into the present, as typified by the recent 'red-genes' (*hongse jiyin*) theory, which has in recent years been publicly advocated in a top-down manner in China. This historical thread confirms that social positionings are based on class interests and dominance with hardly any ideological element present, although they are often articulated in or covered with ideological concepts and terms.

The reuse and existence of the bloodline theory seriously prevents or delays China's socio-political system from being changed and advanced further, making China's socio-economic realities of the twenty-first century – for example, the dominance of market economy – coexist with the political or institutional choices of the mid-twentieth century. Such contradiction sows the seeds for sudden and violent changes and other disruptive changes. Of course, the politicised perspectives, or abstract interpretations, that distort these normal social reactions, dynamics and processes are not only those of the elites, but also those of their rivals, who have rarely understood the intrinsic nature of social processes and explained them convincingly. As pointed out earlier, the attention of many analysts has also been drawn to various politicised interpretations offered by both the ruling elites and their rivals, leaving actual social dynamics and processes unexplored.

When citizens adjust or readjust their position in society to respond to changing conditions, they often reacted according to their own personal circumstances and are usually driven by their own needs and hopes. As a result, the distribution of benefits, social resources and influences has become ever more diverse and complex, making social repositionings increasingly competitive and tactical. What has also surfaced from these social reactions is the periodicity of the reaction and repositioning. On the one hand, there are some zigzag patterns throughout the course of China's reforming decades. The country, precisely its population, has also been frequently pushed by the political left and right so strongly that the pattern of the 'negation of the negation' has occurred even within the space of a few decades. Observers have noted China's public sentiment shifting from the appetite for reform under Deng Xiaoping to the revival of Mao fever, from the post-Mao liberal tendency to the fresh surge of nationalism and from the worship of everything Western to rising anti-Western sentiment. These social responses reveal that when some citizens are placed in an advantageous position by various forms of new change and policy, others often feel disadvantaged. Once such feelings, real or imagined, become widespread among the population, a fresh round of competitive social repositionings is imminent.

On the other hand, the persistence of competitive social repositioning has been so significant that various forms of grassroots understanding of them, or folk philosophical ideas and beliefs, have arisen. In recent years, the following humorous remarks or jokes about ten major life mistakes in the life of Chinese people over the past hundred or so years have been widely circulated on social media, reminding people of the importance and seriousness of social positionings while warning against miscalculations and missteps:

1. Became a eunuch in 1911 (i.e., as the Qing Dynasty collapsed in 1911).
2. Joined the puppet army in 1945 (just before the end of the Japanese occupation).
3. Purchased land in the countryside in 1948 (just before the CCP's land reforms).
4. Expressed criticism in 1957 (just before the Anti-Rightist campaign).
5. Urban sent-down youth marrying a rural person after 1966 (when it became almost impossible to return to cities).
6. Supported the Gang of Four in 1976 (just before the end of Cultural Revolution).
7. Veterans obeying their assignment and transferring to SOEs before 1999 (when most SOEs were shut down).
8. Spent big money on converting rural household registrations into urban ones in 2000 (before the rural land price rose).
9. Refused to buy an apartment before 2004 (since when the price has since risen significantly).
10. Underwent sterilisation done before 2015 (when the one-child policy was abandoned) (Zhihu 2021).

While ordinary people have condensed part of their understanding about social repositionings into various folk beliefs outlining the boundaries of the repositionings, the ruling elites have also demonstrated political or even philosophical responses to the challenges from the aspirational segment of the population. Of course, the folk philosophies or beliefs are far more powerful and persuasive in shaping how people respond to the changes in society than the efforts made by the ruling class. There are a huge number of idioms, proverbs, maxims, jingles and allegories in Chinese that have been used for centuries to carry and spread philosophical messages and beliefs. More Chinese people have in fact been influenced in their life by the folk philosophies or beliefs carried by those everyday sayings than the officially advocated ideologies and teachings. This is another understudied aspect of Chinese culture and society, and the knowledge vacuum in this area has been partially filled by those who are overtrained in concepts and theories and believing that a large proportion of the Chinese population are highly ideological and political, being easily influenced by various forms of political belief and ideology.

Among the responses of China's ruling elites to mounting pressures for further reform, Jiang Zemin's Three Represents theory is the last and most characteristic response to

China's changing social conditions. As noted, it suggests turning attention not only to the changes in social class structure and relation, as Deng Xiaoping did in the late 1970s and early 1980s, but also to the construction of the CCP's ruling ideology and the membership composition of the CCP. That is to say, all those social changes pressed the CCP leadership to reset its political agenda and ideological compass to maintain its relevance. Jiang Zemin gave a long speech in Guangdong in February 2000, stressing that 'to run China well, the key lies with our Party', especially the soundness of the party's ideology; its work style, organisation and discipline; its leading capacity; and its leadership level (Jiang 2002, 7). He put forward his Three Represents as follows:

> [The] Party *represents* the requirements of development of the advanced productive forces. [...] Our Party *represents* the orientation of the advanced Chinese culture. [...] Our Party *represents* the fundamental interests of the broadest masses of the people. (Jiang 2002, 8)

The above two forms of responses – the folk philosophical beliefs and the official Three Represents theory – while hailing from opposite directions both confirm what has occurred in Chinese society and the magnitude of social transformations. Behind these apparent manifestations stands a basic narrative, that is, the incessant societal positioning and repositioning of large numbers of people who wish to be better placed vis-à-vis social resources, benefits and power distribution, or at least to maintain their position in society. Such efforts have changed the composition of social classes and groups, which is also characterised by its cyclicity. If there is anything especially important in the conclusion, it must be the analytical perspective that combines social actors, motivations, behaviours and their dynamic processes in the analysis of social change processes. This useful analytical perspective is referred to as competitive social repositioning in this book.

Future Studies and Practical Implications

Guided by the concept of competitive social repositioning, this study has re-examined a topic that has yet to be systematically and satisfactorily studied, painting a dynamic picture of how large numbers of aspirational ordinary Chinese have lived through recent decades of turbulent social change. This analysis has revealed the various different shared preferences and choices that have effectively driven social changes during each specific period of transformation and at each historical turning point. Because the motivations of large parts of Chinese society and their overall inclinations are largely absent from many earlier studies, China has become a rather unpredictable place in the eyes of those who rely on published research. By adopting the perspective of competitive social repositionings, this analysis has not only dealt with the analytical gaps in the academic literature on China's social changes and dynamics, but also revealed the areas where competitive social repositionings occurred. Based on the above findings, the discussion of this section focuses on three issues.

First, as indicated by the above-quoted folk ideas about the importance of social repositionings, a range of major events or social processes taking place in the past decades need to be examined or further re-analysed so that the strong theoretical meanings expressed in numerous folk philosophical beliefs are equally reflected in academic discussions, and novel analytical perspectives could also be identified. To achieve these goals, three main research areas deserve special research attention.

The first possible future research topic is the *xiahai* people who left the party-state system for the business world. They have joined with hundreds of thousands of rural industrialists to become China's new generations of business leaders, if not economic elites, performing a significant role in revitalising the Chinese economy over the course of recent decades. This analysis has noted that *xiahai* has been seen as a heroic epic in the eyes of many ordinary Chinese people, because of the enterprising spirit, visionary thinking and courageous action of *xiahai* individuals. While their roles in China's economic restructuring and growth should never be undervalued, there are many aspects of their experiences that remain under-researched and deserve more research attention. There is an apparent need to further examine the long-term trajectory of their ventures and careers, while also exploring the many directions many *xiahai* people have since taken in their business ventures and life journeys. What is also needed, as mentioned in Chapter seven, is an examination of who has filled the gaps left by those *xiahai* people. The option of *xiahai* has been part of people's efforts to reposition themselves in changing social settings, and the new social classes that have emerged from them will need to be observed over the long term.

A second topic that requires more research attention is peasants-turned industrialists or entrepreneurs. These active participants in China's reform have emerged, as social actors, from China's rural reform trilogy of rural agricultural reform, rural industrialisation and rural urbanisation. Although this study does not address the most recent stage of rural urbanisation, as it occurred predominantly after the early 2000s, the first two stages of China's rural economic reform were so fundamental and extensive that hundreds of thousands of aspirational rural people turned themselves into entrepreneurs. These businessmen and women often started their ventures locally in small village and towns, and then expanded to larger markets. If the societal trend of *xiahai* is regarded as a heroic epic of the Chinese reform period, the rural reform in China and the changing socio-economic status of numerous rural residents must be defined as the main melody of this transitional period of Chinese history. The ups and downs of these peasants-turned entrepreneurs merit special attention and further research.

These enthusiastic rural reform participants are also among the several hundreds of millions of rural people who have relocated to urban centres. Because of their under-theorised influence in both rural and urban China, future studies are needed to further examine how their business activities, individual and family lives and perceptions of social status have evolved and progressed over the course of recent decades. Since many of those new rural entrepreneurs and other former rural residents have moved to urban centres since the 1990s and now form a substantial portion of China's new middle- and upper-middle-class population, there is a need for research into their influences on urban society and culture. Additional longitudinal and empirical studies of this type of reform participants over a long time span would help form better understanding of China's recent social changes.

The third possible future research area concerns the changes in and current situation of China's educated youth, especially university-educated young Chinese. One obvious reason this particular issue stands out from other understudied topics in the field is that the student protests have largely disappeared from China's socio-political landscape since the early 1990s, except the student protests taking place in late 2022 against China's 'zero-COVID-19' policy and lockdowns. However, in general, young students have become the main force behind China's fast-growing and spreading nationalistic sentiments. The latter was symbolised by the book entitled *China Can Say No*, published in 1996. At the same time, however, more young Chinese than ever before have also chosen to study in foreign, but predominantly Western, countries, becoming the largest segment of the international student population in recent decades. This occurred within a few years of the Tiananmen protest of 1989. While these rapid and radical changes in social attitudes and positions are recognised by many Chinese analysts, no thorough analysis has been undertaken.

One special issue related to China's educated youth is their responses to and attitudes towards changing practices and patterns of elite selection and promotion over the decades. As discussed in earlier chapters, the successor issue and the loyalty of future leaders have been a major source of political tensions in China since the post-famine years of the mid-1960s. The post-1989 political situation in China had significantly diminished the influence of educated and liberal-minded people, while permitting more citizens to establish themselves in non-government-controlled business sectors by engaging in commercial activities. Many people from the latter groups have become economically well off, but it is quite unclear how young Chinese – the educated youth in particular – have reacted to many aspects of China's socio-political reality. Many people have also felt that their opportunities to position or reposition themselves in post-industrial China have become very limited. Such a situation makes it critical to find out if, and for how long, young social ladder climbers in the country will tolerate the dominance of pre-existing elites, especially those with 'red genes' (*hongse jiyin*).

Second, as a special, but very important, case of the practical political implications of this study, the Three Represents theory quoted in the first section of this chapter is worth serious research attention. This is because the theory seems to be the only systematic theoretical attempt to reassess and modify the ruling party's ideology orientation, re-alignment of social class relations and membership composition since Deng Xiaoping's push for seeking truth from facts (*shishi qiushi*). The importance of the Three Represents theory also lies in the fact that the theory has some potential in modernising the CCP but has quietly been set aside by the two leadership generations after Jiang Zemin. This study has examined events in Chinese society over the past three and a half decades, from 1964 to 2000, ending right at the time Jiang proposed his Three Represents theory as the political response of the ruling CCP to changes in society. It is because of the latter that the potential of the theory for improving societal environments and clearing the way for more ordinary but aspiring individuals to position or reposition themselves in society needs to be further examined, to assess its theoretical and political relevance and strength.

Without any intent of praising Jiang himself, the ruling party's political responses represented by the Three Represents theory seem to be highly relevant to the many changes and challenges examined in this study. Jiang Zemin suggested a set of radical reformist ideas at the start of the twenty-first century, when Chinese society was undergoing a sequence of socio-economic and socio-political changes. Apart from the quote in the section above, Jiang also advocated that the ruling party should aim to liberate and expand the productive forces and to make an effort to absorb and develop the best cultural traditions, both Chinese and foreign. To be legitimate in representing the overwhelming majority of the population, the ruling CCP is also encouraged to include those people who represent the most active and dynamic productive social forces in Chinese society in the ruling party. This particular position has since been interpreted as a reactionary push to allow capitalists to become members of the CCP, switching the topic into the politicised issue many people were very familiar with under the Maoist regime. In fact, many detailed accounts included in the Three Represents theory seem to reflect the social transformations and needs discussed in this analysis.

As hinted earlier, the fate of this particular endeavour to create a new political identity for China's ruling elite has not been as promising as the social transformation taking place in China in the past two decades. Jiang Zemin's Three Represents idea has been regarded by many reformers as a promising proposal for the ruling CCP to reform and transform itself from a revolutionary political party to a ruling party in the twenty-first century. The neglect of this suggestion is considered by many to be a retrogressive movement away from the collective goal of comprehensive reform. In other words, without serious attention to the proposals contained in Jiang's Three Represents theory, the CCP's ruling ideology and its manner of responding to social transformations have reflected a backsliding towards Maoism in the more recent decade. More fundamentally, political conditions are a vital part of social relations and can determine the outcomes of any future reform programme. Recent ideological retrogression to Maoism has not only buried the promises of Jiang's idea, allowing the opportunity to reform the CCP to slip away, but also left the party mired in its identity crisis and ideological confusion. Regular efforts to renew the ruling party's ideological and political stance are a necessary condition for preventing socio-political instability. In this context, future studies are required to examine why the post-Jiang leadership has given up on this opportunity to renew their party.

The final practical implication of this analysis is the significance and practicality of the competitive social repositioning stance itself. Because this viewpoint has not been widely used in social science studies, nor in studies of contemporary Chinese society, work is needed to validate this new approach through more studies and to develop it to its full analytical potential. This is important considering that the main shortcomings in the scholarly literature have been the lack of a right approach to incorporate social actors, motivations, actions and their dynamic processes into the analysis of social transformation processes. As a result of this analytical gap, more studies in the field of China studies are needed to complement the present study. Further, this perspective needs to be tried and evaluated in different societal and demographic settings.

In short, it is critical that future research focus on aspiring social actors and the social dynamics and processes generated by social actors. Future researchers need to be urged and supported to look at the process of social transformation itself, especially the substantial number of active members of society. It may be of some benefit to focus on the dominant minority in the ruling elite, or on small groups of citizens who would express strong dissenting opinions, but such approaches in isolation may be detrimental to an accurate understanding of Chinese society. The former type of research has in fact put China in the hands of two types of people, who account for a small proportion of the total population. Those two types of people can be dominant, often having a lot to say, but they are only part of the whole societal system and landscape. What it needs now is to learn more about the majority of the Chinese population, especially those aspirational groups.

In addition to who and how many people are observed and studied, the perspective and analytical stance taken by researchers are always critical. One obvious problem in studying Chinese society arises from the use of 'long-distance' observations, including studies undertaken from different cultural perspectives. This approach is still popular among Chinese and foreign researchers, and in many macro-level studies. These studies often come to very different conclusions from those that take social actors, their motivations, behaviours, dynamics and processes into consideration. This analysis has sought to provide a new perspective on examining Chinese society and its population, which is expected to be of some help to future researchers.

REFERENCES

Aglietta, Michel, and Guo Bai. 2013. *China's Development: Capitalism and Empire*. Abingdon: Routledge.

Ah, Cheng. 2011. *The Best Selection of Ah Cheng*. Beijing: Yanshan Publishing House.

Andreas, Joel. 2009. *Rise of the Red Engineers: The Cultural Revolution and the Origins of China's New Class*. Stanford: Stanford University Press.

Anghel, Remus, Margit Fauser, and Paolo Boccagni, eds. 2019. *Transnational Return and Social Change: Hierarchies, Identities and Ideas*. London: Anthem Press.

Ashiwa, Yoshiko, and David Wank, eds. 2009. *Marking Religion, Make the State: The Politics of Religion in Modern China*. Stanford: Stanford University Press.

Åström, Thomas. 2006. 'Moral Positioning: A Formal Theory'. *Grounded Theory Review: An International Journal* 6(1): 29–60.

Bakken, Borge. 2000. *The Exemplary Society: Human Improvement, Social Control, and the Dangers of Modernity in China*. Oxford: Oxford University Press.

Barmé, Geremie. 2000. *In the Red: On Contemporary Chinese Culture*. New York: Columbia University Press.

Barmé, Geremie, and Linda Jaivin, eds. 1992. *New Ghosts, Old Dreams: Chinese Rebel Voices*. New York: Times Books.

Barnett, Doak. 1967. *China after Mao*. Princeton: Princeton University Press.

Baum, Richard. 1964. '"Red and Expert": The Politico-Ideological Foundations of China's Great Leap Forward'. *Asian Survey* 4(9): 1048–57.

Baum, Richard. 1994. *Burying Mao: Chinese Politics in the Age of Deng Xiaoping*. Princeton: Princeton University Press.

Baum, Richard, and Frederick Teiwes. 1968. *Ssu-Ch'ing: The Socialist Education Movement of 1962–1966*. Berkeley: University of California Press.

Bedeski, Robert. 1986. 'China's 1979 Election Law and its Implementation'. *Electoral Studies* 5(2): 153–65.

Beijing Local Gazetteers. 2000. *Municipal Volume 15: Real Estate*. Beijing: Beijing Press.

Beijing Review. 1966. 'Chinaman Mac Reviews a Total of 11 Million of Might Cultural Revolution Army'. *Beijing Review* 9: 49.

Bell, Daniel. 2010. *China's New Confucianism: Politics and Everyday Life in a Changing Society*. Princeton: Princeton University Press.

Bennett, Gordon, and Ronald Montaperto. 1972. *Red Guards: The Political Biography of Dai Hsiao-Ai*. New York: Doubleday.

Benney, Jonathan. 2013. *Defending Rights in Contemporary China*. Abingdon: Routledge.

Bernstein, Thomas. 1977. *Up to the Mountains and Down to the Villages: The Transfer of Youth from Urban to Rural China*. New Haven: Yale University Press.

Bian, Morris. 2015. 'Explaining the Dynamics of Change: Transformation and Evolution of China's Public Economy through War, Revolution, and Peace, 1928–2008'. In *Stat Capitalism, Institutional Adaptation and the Chinese Miracle*, edited by Barry Naughton, and Kelle Tsai, 201–22. Cambridge: Cambridge University Press.

Bian, Yanjie. 2002. 'Chinese Social Stratification and Social Mobility'. *Annual Review of Sociology* 28: 91–116.

Bian, Yanjie, Breiger Ronald, Deborah Davis, and Joseph Galaskiewicz. 2005. 'Occupation, Class, and Social Networks in Urban China'. *Social Forces* 83(4): 1443–68.

Bian, Yanjie, Xiaogang Wu, and Lulu, Li. 2008. *Social Stratification and Mobility: The Overseas Scholars' Advanced Research on China*. Beijing: Renmin University of China Press.

Blecher, Marc, and Vivienne Shue. 1996. *Tethered Deer: Government and Economy in a Chinese County*. Stanford: Stanford University Press.

Bo, Zhiyue. 2007. *China's Elite Politics: Political Transition and Power Balancing*. Singapore: World Scientific Publishing.

Bonnin, Michel, and Yves Chevrier. 1991. 'The Intellectual and the State: Social Dynamics of Intellectual Autonomy during the Post-Mao Era'. *China Quarterly* 127: 569–93.

Bonnin, Michel (Pan, Mingxiao). 2005. 'Shangshan Xiaxiang Yundong Zaipingjia' (A Historical Assessment of the 'Up to the Mountains, Down to the Villages' Movement). *Sociological Studies* 20(5): 154–81.

Bonnin, Michel. 2013. *The Lost Generation: The Rustication of China's Educated Youth (1968–1980)*. Hong Kong: The Chinese University Press.

Bonnin, Michel. 2016. 'Restricted, Distorted but Alive: The Memory of the "Lost Generation" of Chinese Educated Youth'. *China Quarterly* 227: 752–72.

Bramall, Chris. 2007. *The Industrialization of Rural China*, Oxford: Oxford University Press.

Breslin, Shaun. 1996. *China in the 1980s: Center-Province Relations in a Reforming Socialist State*. Basingstoke: Macmillan Press.

Bridgham, Philip. 1967. 'Mao's "Cultural Revolution": Origin and Development'. *China Quarterly* 29: 1–35.

Brown, Jeremy. 2021. *June Fourth: The Tiananmen Protests and Beijing Massacre of 1989*. Cambridge: Cambridge University Press.

Bu, Weihua. 2009a. 'Yan Yangsheng's "Tsinghua Fuzhong Hongweibing 100 Tian" Ruogan Shishi Bianzheng' (Corrections on Some Historical Facts in Yan Yangsheng's *100 Days of the Red Guards at Tsinghua High*). *China News Digest*, No. 518. www.cnd.org/cr/ZK09/cr518.gb .html. Accessed 10 June 2021.

Bu, Weihua. 2009b. 'Zhide Zhuyi de Shui Luzhou Xianxiang' (The Notable Phenomenon of Shui Luzhou). https://bbs.creaders.net/history/bbsviewer.php?trd_id=337502. Accessed 31 May 2022.

Buck, Daniel. 2012. *Constructing China's Capitalism: Shanghai and the Nexus of Urban-Rural Industries*. London: Palgrave Macmillan.

Burke, Sandra. 2011. 'Competitive Positioning Strength: Market Measurement'. *Journal of Strategic Marketing* 19(5): 421–28.

Burns, John. 1988. *Political Participation in Rural China*. Berkeley: University of California Press.

Byrd, William, and Qingsong Li, eds. 1990. *China's Rural Industry: Structure, Development and Reform*. Oxford: Oxford University Press.

Cai, Fang, Yang Du, and Meiyun Wang. 2009. 'Employment and Inequality Outcomes in China', Presented at the OECD Seminar on Employment and Inequality Outcomes: New Evidence, Links and Policy Responses in Brazil, China and India, April 2009. www.oecd.org /employment/emp/42546043.pdf. Accessed 31 May 2022.

Cai, Xiaopeng. 2017. 'Renda Xinsanjie Xiaoyuan Wangshi Gouchen' (Recollections of the Life of Renda's Three New Cohorts). https://freewechat.com/a/MzA3ODY0NDkwOA== /2651925100/1. Accessed 12 December 2021.

Cai, Yongshun. 2002. 'The Resistance of Chinese Laid-off Workers in the Reform Period'. *China Quarterly* 170: 327–44.

Cai, Yongshun. 2010. *Collective Resistance in China: Why Popular Protests Succeed or Fail*. Stanford: Stanford University Press.

Cao, Jinghui, Juan Liu, and Lingli Hu. 2018. 'The Implementation Dilemma and Governance of the Tenure System of Local Officials'. *Journal of South China University of Technology (Social Science Edition)* 20(3): 92–99.

Cao, Pu. 2008. 'Zhongguo Gaige Kaifang de Lishi Youlai' (The Historical Origin of China's Reform and Opening Up). *Study Times*, 29 September 2008.

Cao, Pu. 2019. *Zhongguo Gaige Kaifang Sishinian Jianshi (A Brief History of China's 40 Years of Reform and Opening-up)*. Beijing: Foreign Languages Press.

CCTV (China Central Television). 2021. 'Xi Jinping he Muqin: Liangdai Gongchandangren de "Yueding"' (Xi Jinping and his Mother: The 'Promise' of the Two Generations of Communists). news.cctv.com/2021/05/08/ARTIiQ9SRlcSvTNhXoOnERwL210429.shtml. Accessed 2 July 2021.

Ce, Liang, and Racheal Rui. 2016. '"Development" as a Means to an Unknown End: Chinese National Identity in 2013'. In *Making Identity Count: Building a National Identity Database*, edited by Ted Hopf, and Bentley Allan, 63–82. Oxford: Oxford University Press.

Central Committee, the CCP. 1995. *Zhongguo Gongchandang Dangxiao Gongzuo Zanxing Tiaoli (Interim Regulations on the Work of the Party School of the Communist Party of China)*. http://fgcx.bjcourt.gov.cn:4601/law?fn=chl065s207.txt&truetag=1813&ti. Accessed 31 May 2022.

Chan, Anita. 1982. 'Images of China's Social Structure: The Changing Perspective of Canton Students'. *World Politics* 34(3): 295–323.

Chan, Anita. 1985. *Children of Mao: Personality Development and Political Activism in the Red Guard Generation*. London: Palgrave Macmillan.

Chan, Anita. 1996. 'The Changing Ruling Elite and Political Opposition in China'. In *Political Oppositions in Industrialising Asia*, edited by Garry Rodan, 163–87. New York: Routledge.

Chan, Cheris. 2004. 'The Falun Gong in China: A Sociological Perspective'. *China Quarterly* 179: 665–83.

Chang, Jung. 2013. *Empress Dowager Cixi: The Concubine Who Launched Modern China*. London: Jonathan Cape.

Cheek, Timothy. 1997. *Deng Tuo and the Intelligentsia*. Oxford: Clarendon Press.

Chen, An. 1999a. *Restructuring Political Power in China: Alliances and Opposition, 1978–1998*. Boulder: Lynne Rienner.

Chen, Chih-Jou. 2009. 'Growing Social Unrest in China: Rising Social Discontents and Popular Protest'. In *Socialist China, Capitalist China*, edited by Guoguang Wu, and Helen Lansdowne, 10–28. Abingdon: Routledge.

Chen, Danqing. 2014. 'Womende Tongnian Gengxiang Tongnian' (Our Childhood was more like the Childhood). *Zhongxiaoxue Guanli (Primary and Secondary School Management)* 8: 7–9.

Chen, Fong-ching. 2001. 'The Popular Cultural Movement of the 1980s'. In *Voicing Concerns: Contemporary Chinese Critical Inquiry*, edited by Gloria Davies, 71–86. Lanham: Rowman & Littlefield.

Chen, Hongyi. 1997. 'The Transition in TVEs' Ownership Structure: A Valuable Reference for the Reform of SOEs'. In *The Reformability of China's State Sector*, edited by Guanzhong Wen, and Dianqing Du, 131–55. Singapore: World Scientific.

Chen, Hongyi. 2000. *The Institutional Transition of China's Township and Village Enterprises: Market Liberalization, Contractual from Innovation and Privatization*. Abingdon: Routledge.

Chen, Huai. 1999b. 'Zhongguo Jiuye Wenti de Fenxi yu Duice Jianyi' (Analysis and Countermeasures of Employment Problems in China). *Management World* 1: 97–112.

Chen, Jibing. 1992. 'Jiaoshou "Xiahai"' (Professors Jumping into the Sea of Business). *Wenhui Newspaper*, 26 December 1992.

Chen, Jian. 2018a. 'Gaige Kaifang 40nian Dangfeng Lianzheng Jianshe he Fanfubai Douzheng Lishi Huigu' (A Historical Review of the Construction of a Clean Government and the Fight against Corruption in the Past 40 Years of Reform and Opening Up). http://fanfu.people.com.cn/n1/2018/1123/c64371-30432123.html. Accessed 31 August 2022.

Chen, Jian. 2021. 'Fuzhong Qianxing ke Daren: Gongnongbing Xueyuan Pingshu' (Carrying a Heavy Load to Undertake a Big Task: A Commentary on the Worker-Peasant-Soldier University Trainees). http://chen-jian.blog.caixin.com/archives/242914. Accessed 31 May 2022.

Chen, Jianguang. 2019a. 'Zhongguo Xiangcun Chanye Fazhan 70nian: Cong Jiannan Yunyu dao Baige Zhengliu' (70 Years of Development of China's Rural Industry: From the Difficult Conception to the Intense Competition). www.farmer.com.cn/2019/09/23/843309.html. Accessed 12 December 2021.

Chen, Kanzhang. 2019b. '77ji, 78ji Daxuesheng de Lishi Luhen' (The Historical Traces of University Students in Grades 1977 and 1978). https://mp.weixin.qq.com/s/fVqqoAWuiA mxrsK6w5j-xQ. Accessed 12 December 2021.

Chen, King, ed. 2018b. *China and the Three Worlds: A Foreign Policy Reader*. Abingdon: Routledge.

Chen, Lixu. 2011. 'Mao Zedong Zuihou Yici Zhuchi Zhongyang Zhengzhiju Huihi' (Mao Zedong's Last Politburo Meeting). *Dangshi Zongheng* (*Over the Party History*) 1: 7–10.

Chen, Lu. 2015. 'Report: Persecution of Falun Gong Continues in China'. https://fofg.org/2015/01/13/report-persecution-of-falun-gong-continues-in-china/. Accessed 31 August 2022.

Chen, Minglu, and David Goodman, eds. 2013. *Middle Class China: Identity and Behaviour*. Cheltenham: Edward Elgar.

Chen, Nancy. 2003. *Breathing Spaces: Qigong, Psychiatry, and Healing in China*. New York: Columbia University Press.

Chen, Shih-hsiang. 1963. 'Metaphor and the Conscious in Chinese Poetry under Communism'. *China Quarterly* 13: 39–59.

Chen, Xi. 2012. *Social Protest and Contentious Authoritarianism in China*. Cambridge: Cambridge University Press.

Chen, Yixin. 1999c. 'Lost in Revolution and Reform: The Socioeconomic Pains of China's Red Guards Generation, 1966–1996'. *Journal of Contemporary China* 8(21): 219–39.

Chen, Yan. 2006a. '"Minzhuqiang Yundong" ji Lishi Diwei' ('The Democracy Wall' and its Historical Status). *Modern China Studies*. www.modernchinastudies.org/cn/issues/past-issues/92-mcs-2006-issue-2/956-2012-01-05-15-35-10.html. Accessed 12 December 2021.

Chen, Ziming. 2006b. 'Zhongguo Tizhiwai Zhengzhi Liliang de Dansheng' (The Birth of Political Forces Outside China's Party-State System). *Beijing Spring*. www.beijingspring.com/bj2/2006/120/200633100359.htm. Accessed 5 October 2021.

Chen, Ziming. 2006c. 'Lishi Da Shiye Zhong de Siwu Yundong' (The April 5th Movement in the View of History). *Huaxia Zhiqing*. www.hxzq.net/aspshow/showarticle.asp?id=9392. Accessed 5 October 2021.

Chen, Ziming. 2009. 'Guanyu Bashi Niandai Wenhua Sixiang Paibiede Tongxin' (Letters about the Different Schools of Culture and Thought in the 1980s). ww2.usc.cuhk.edu.hk/Paper Collection/Details.aspx?id=7227. Accessed 5 October 2021.

Cheng, Zhongyuan. 2015. 'Guanyu Deng Xiaoping Lingdao 1975nian Zhengdun Ruogan Wenti de Tantao' (Several Issues about the 1975 Rectification led by Deng Xiaoping). *Beijing Dangshi* 5: 24–8.

Cherrington, Ruth. 1997. *Deng's Generation: Young Intellectuals in 1980s China*. New York: St. Martin's Press.

Chin, Ko-lin. 1999. *Smuggled Chinese; Clandestine Immigration to the United States*. Philadelphia: Temple University Press.

Chun, Lin. 2013. *China and Global Capitalism: Reflections on Marxism, History, and Contemporary Politics*. New York: Palgrave Macmillan.

Cooke, Fang Lee. 2012. *Human Resource Management in China: New Trends and Practices*. Abingdon: Routledge.

CPCNews (News of the Communist Party of China [CCP]). 2005. 'Xinshiqi Zhishi Fenzi de Fazhan Bianhua Qushi' (The Development and Changing Trend of Intellectuals in the New Era). http://cpc.people.com.cn/GB/64107/65708/66072/66089/4471969.html. Accessed 31 May 2022.

Creaders Net. 2015. 'Nanxun Zhenxiang: Deng Xiaoping Tuxi "Paoda" Chen Yun' (The Truth of the Southern Inspection Tour: Deng Xiaoping's 'Booming' Raid on Chen Yun). https://news.creaders.net/china/2015/05/06/1526069.html. Accessed 31 May 2022.

Cui, Weiping. 2008. 'Sanshi Nianqian de Zhengzhi hejie' (Political Reconciliation 30 Years Ago). https://m.aisixiang.com/data/17813.html. Accessed 5 October 2021.

Cunningham, Philip. 2009 *Tiananmen Moon: Inside the Chinese Student Uprising of 1989*. New York: Rowman & Littlefield.

Davin, Delia. 2013. *Mao: A Very Short Introduction*. Oxford: Oxford University Press.

deLisle, Jacques, and Avery Goldstein. 2019. *To Get Rich is Glorious: Challenges facing China's Economic Reform and Opening at Forty*. Washington: Brookings Institution Press.

Deng, Peng. 2015. *Exiled Pilgrims: Memoirs of Pre-Cultural Revolution Zhiqing*. Leiden: Brill.

Deng, Rong. 2013. *Wode Fuqin Deng Xiaoping: 'Wenge' Suiyue (My Father Deng Xiaoping: The Cultural Revolution Years)*. Beijing: Sanlian Books.

Deng, Xiaoping. 1975. 'Jiaqiang Dangde Lingdao, Zhengdun Dangde Zuofeng' (Strengthen the Party Leadership and Rectify the Party's Style of Work). www.reformdata.org/1975/0704/5141.shtml. Accessed 5 October 2021.

Deng, Xiaoping. 1994. *Selected Works of Deng Xiaoping, Volume 3*. Beijing: Foreign Language Press.

Deng, Yanling. 2009. 'Lishu Zhongguo Xiahai Jingshang Guanyuan' (Counting Chinese Officials Jumping into the Sea of Business). *China Weekly*, 21 October 2009. http://news.sina.com.cn/c/2009-10-21/181718878437.shtml. Accessed 31 May 2022.

Dickson, Bruce. 1997. *The Adaptability of Leninist Parties: A Comparison of the Chinese Communist Party and the Kuomintang*. Oxford: Clarendon Press.

Dickson, Bruce. 2003. *Red Capitalists in China: The Party, Private Entrepreneurs, and Prospects for Political Change*. New York: Cambridge University Press.

Dikötter, Frank. 2010. *Mao's Great Famine*. London: Bloomsbury.

Dikötter, Frank. 2016. *The Cultural Revolution: A People's History, 1962–1976*. London: Bloomsbury.

Dillon, Michael. 2020. *Zhou Enlai: The Enigma Behind Chairman Mao*. London: Bloomsbury.

Ding, Changyan. 2020. 'Gaige Kaifang Yilai Zhongguo de Xiangzhen Qiye Weishenme Neng?' (Why did China's TVEs 'Can' since Reform and Opening?). www.sssa.org.cn/mtbd/681348.htm. Accessed 12 December 2021.

Ding, Xiaohe. 2006. *Niepan: Laosanjie Suixiang Qu (Nirvana: The Capriccio of the Old-Three-Year Grades)*. Beijing: CCP History Press.

Dittmer, Lowell. 1987. *China's Continuous Revolution: The Post-Liberation Epoch, 1949–1981*. Berkeley: University of California Press.

Dittmer, Lowell. 2015. *Liu Shaoqi and the Cultural Revolution*. Abingdon: Routledge.

Dong, Guoqiang, and Andrew Walder. 2021. *A Decade of Upheaval: The Cultural Revolution in Rural China*. Princeton: Princeton University Press.

Dongen, Els van. 2019. *Realistic Revolution: Contesting Chinese History, Culture and Politics after 1989*. Cambridge: Cambridge University Press.

Drulhe, Christile, and Michael Black. 2002. 'The Little Emperor in the City: The Child and the Family in Urban China'. *China Perspectives* 39: 17–26.

Du, Honglin, and Shengde Li. 2017. '130wan Fancheng Zhiqing Chuangzao Shishang Zuiqite Bingtui Fengchao' (1.3 Million *Zhiqing* Created the Most Peculiar *Bingtui* Wave of Returning to the Cities in the History). www.myoldtime.com/m/view.php?aid=11871. Accessed 2 August 2021.

Dwyer, Peter, and Monica Minnegal. 2010. 'Theorizing Social Change'. *Journal of the Royal Anthropological Institute* 16(3): 629–45.

Elejabarrieta, Fran. 1994. 'Social Positioning: A Way to Link Social Identity and Social Representations'. *Social Science Information* 33(2): 241–53.

Englesberg, Paul. 1992. *University Student Cultural in China, 1978–1990: Formal and Informal Organization*. PhD Thesis, University of Massachusetts Amherst.

Ezra, Vogel. 1989. *One Step Ahead in China: Guangdong Under Reform*. Cambridge: Harvard University Press.

Fan, Huawei, Yan Zhang, and Jun Wang. 1999. 'Anli Fenxi: Henan yi Xianweishuji Dasi Maiguan Liancai' (Case Study: A County Party Secretary in Henan Sells Officials to Make

Money). *Southern Metropolis Daily*, 8 December 1999. https://news.sina.com.cn/comment/1999-12-8/39522.html. Accessed 31 August 2022.

Fan, Jie, Thomas Heberer, and Wolfgang Taubmann. 2006. *Rural China: Economic and Social Change in the Late Twentieth Century*. Abingdon: Routledge.

Fan, Shenggen, Linxiu Zhang, and Xiaopo Zhang. 2002. *Jingji Zengzhang, Diqu Chaju yu Pinkun: Zhongguo Nongcun Gonggong Touzi yanjiu (Economic Growth, Regional Disparity and Poverty: A Study of Public Investment in Rural China)*. Beijing: China Agriculture Press.

Fan, Wen. 2016. 'Turning Point or Selection? The Effect of Rustication on Subsequent Health for the Chinese Cultural Revolution Cohort'. *Social Science and Medicine* 157: 68–77.

Fan, Xingwei. 2007. 'Dui "Yunxu Yibufen Ren Xian Fu Qilai" de Zhiyi' (Questions about "Allowing Some People to Get Rich First"). www.wyzxwk.com/e/DoPrint/?classid=27&id=24175. Accessed 31 August 2022.

Fang, Huijian, and Zhang Sijing. 2001. *Qinghua Daxue Zhi, Shangjuan (Chronicle of Tsinghua University Vol. I)*. Beijing: Tsinghua University Press.

Feng, Lun. 2020. 'Neixie Baitan Qijia de Fuhaomen' (Those Rich People Who Started With Setting up a Stall). www.cyzone.cn/article/589200.html. Accessed 12 December 2021.

Feng, Lun. 2022. 'Fengyu Renwu Zhi' (List of Famous People). WeChat ID: fengluntalk. Accessed 31 March 2022.

Feng, Xiang. 2004. *Zhengfa Biji (Political and Legal Notes)*. Nanjing: Jiangsu People's Publishing.

Feurtado, Gardel. 1986. *Mao Tse-tung and the Politics of Science in Communist China, 1949–1965*. Stanford: Stanford University Press.

Fewsmith, Joseph. 2001. *Elite Politics in Contemporary China*. New York: M. E. Sharpe.

Fewsmith, Joseph. 2010. 'Inner-Party Democracy: Development and Limitations'. *China Leadership Monitor* 31: 1–11.

Fewsmith, Joseph. 2011. 'Reaction, Resurgence, and Succession: Chinese Politics since Tiananmen'. In *The Politics of China: Sixty Years of the People's Republic of China*, edited by Roderick MacFarquhar, 468–526. Cambridge: Cambridge University Press.

Fewsmith, Joseph. 2013. *The Logic and Limits of Political Reform in China*. Cambridge: Cambridge University Press.

Fiskesjo, Magnus. 2018. 'Bury me with Comrades: Memorializing Mao's Sent-Down Youth'. *Asia-Pacific Journal* 16(14/4): 1–25.

Fu, Wei. 2021. 'Zhongguo Gongyehua Jinchengzhong de Jiating Jingying jiqi Jingshen Dongli: Yi Zhejiangshang H shi Chaozhen Kuaizhuang Chanyequn Weili' (Family Operation and Its Psychological Power in the Process of China's Industrialisation: Cases of the Massive Industrial Cluster of Chao Town, H City, Zhejiang). *Social Science in China* 4: 146–65.

Fu, Zhengyuan. 1993. *Autocratic Tradition and Chinese Politics*. New York: Cambridge University Press.

Fuming, E. 2015. 'Lao "Jintian" Zazhi de Chuban yu Faxing' (The Publication and Distribution of the Old *Today* Magazine). *Today*. www.jintian.net/today/?action-viewnews-itemid-52520. Accessed 12 December 2021.

Gan, Yang, and Meng Li. 2004. *Zhongguo Daxue Gaige zhi Dao (The Road of Reforming Chinese Universities)*. Shanghai: Shanghai People's Press.

Gao, Bai. 2009. 'The Rubik's Cube State: A Reconceptualization of Political Change in Contemporary China'. In *Work and Organisations in China after Thirty Years of Transition*, edited by Lisa Keister, 409–38. Bingley: Emerald.

Gao, Falin. 2012. 'Zhiqingde Beiju yu Guanyuande Beiju (*Zhiqing*'s Tragedy and the Tragedy of Officials). *Xin Shiji* 10: 196–203.

Gao, Jia. 2013a. *Chinese Activism of a Different Kind: The Chinese Students' Campaign to Stay in Australia*. Leiden: Brill.

Gao, Jia. 2013b. 'Feng Lun'. In *Biographical Dictionary of the People's Republic of China*, edited by Yuwu Song, 83–5. Jefferson: McFarland & Co.

Gao, Jia. 2015. *Chinese Migrant Entrepreneurship in Australia from the 1990s: Case Studies of Success in Sino-Australian Relations.* Waltham: Elsevier.

Gao, Jia. 2021. 'Sick Returnees among China's Sent-Down Youth and Contemporary Chinese Practices of Identity Performance'. *East Asia: An International Quarterly* 38(2): 139–56.

Gao, Jia, Hong He, and Weiling He, trans. 1986. *Wenhua yu Geren (Culture and Individual).* Hangzhou: Zhejiang People's Press.

Gao, Jia, and Peter Pugsley. 2008. 'Utilizing Satire in Post-Deng Chinese Politics: Zhao Benshan Xiaopin vs. the Falun Gong'. *China Information* 22: 451–76.

Gao, Jia, and Yuanyuan Su. 2019. *Social Mobilisation in Post-Industrial China: The Case of Rural Urbanisation.* Cheltenham: Edward Elgar.

Gao, Jing. 2017. 'Pohai Falun Gong Zao Eyun, Minghui Wang Jizai 7Sheng yue 7qianli' (Persecution of Falun Gong Suffers Bad Luck, Minghui Websites Records about 7,000 Cases in 7 Provinces). www.epochtimes.com/gb/17/3/24/n8963750.htm. Accessed 31 August 2022.

Gao, Mobo. 1999. *Gao Village: A Portrait of Rural Life in Modern China.* Honolulu: University of Hawai'i Press.

Gao, Wenqian. 2008. *Zhou Enlai: The Last Perfect Revolutionary.* New York: Public Affairs.

Gao, Yifei. 2005. 'Zhiyi "Dangxiao Xueli" Yingdang Lizhiqizhuang' (Questioning "Party School Education" Should be Justifiable). www.aisixiang.com/data/7060.html. Accessed 31 August 2022.

Gardner, John. 1982. *Chinese Politics and the Succession to Mao.* London: Macmillan.

Garnaut, Ross, Ligang Song, and Fang Cai, eds. 2018. *China's 40 Years of Reform and Development 1978–2018.* Canberra: ANU Press.

Garripoli, Garri. 1999. *Qigong: Essence of the Healing Dance.* New York: Simon & Schuster.

Gary, Jack. 2002. *Rebellions and Revolutions: China from 1880s to 2000.* Oxford: Oxford University Press.

Ge, Liangyan. 2001. *Out of the Margins: The Rise of Chinese Vernacular Fiction.* Honolulu: University of Hawai'i Press.

Gilley, Bruce. 1998. *Tiger on the Brink: Jiang Zemin and China's New Elite.* Berkeley: University of California Press.

Gilley, Bruce. 2001. *Model Rebels: The Rise and Fall of China's Richest Village.* Berkeley: University of California Press.

Girard, Bonnie. 2018. '40 Years of Social Change in China'. *The Diplomat*, 20 December 2018. https://thediplomat.com/2018/12/40-years-of-social-change-in-china/. Accessed 10 March 2021.

Gittings, John. 1964. 'The "Learn from the Army" Campaign'. *China Quarterly* 18: 153–59.

Gittings, John. 1990. *China Changes Face: The Road from Revolution, 1949–1989.* New York: Oxford University Press.

Gold, Thomas. 1980. 'Back to the City: The Return of Shanghai's Educated Youth'. *China Quarterly* 84: 755–70.

Goldman, Merle. 1981. *China's Intellectuals: Advise and Dissent.* Cambridge: Harvard University Press.

Goldman, Merle. 1994. *Sowing the Seeds of Democracy in China: Political Reform in the Deng Xiaoping Era.* Cambridge: Harvard University Press.

Gong, Ting. 1996. 'Jumping into the Sea: Cadre Entrepreneurs in China'. *Problems of Post-Communism* 43(4): 26–34.

Goodman, David. 1997. 'China in Reform: The View from the Provinces'. In *China's Provinces in Reform: Class, Community and Political Culture*, edited by David Goodman, 1–20. London: Routledge.

Goodman, David. 2014. *Class in Contemporary China.* Cambridge: Polity Press.

Gore, Lance. 1998. *Market Communist: The Institutional Foundation of China's Post-Mao Hyper Growth.* Hong Kong: Oxford University Press.

Grazianzi, Sofia. 2019. 'May Fourth Youth Day from Yan'an to the Early People's Republic: The Politics of Commemoration and the Discursive Construction of Youth'. *Twentieth-Century China* 44(2): 237–52.

Gries, Peter. 2004. 'Popular Nationalism and State Legitimation in China'. In *State and Society in 21st-Century China: Crisis, Contention, and Legitimation*, edited by Peter Gries, and Stanley Rosen, 180–94. New York: RoutledgeCurzon.

Gustafsson, Björn, and Ding Sai. 2013. 'Unemployment and the Rising Number of Nonworkers in Urban China: Causes and Distributional Consequences'. In *Rising Inequality in China: Challenges to a Harmonious Society*, edited by Shi Li et al., 289–331. Cambridge: Cambridge University Press.

Haggard, Stephan, and David Kang. 2020. *East Asia in the World: Twelve Events that Shaped the Modern International Order*. Cambridge: Cambridge University Press.

Hamrin, Carol. 2003. 'Social Dynamics and New Generation Politics'. In *China's Leadership in the 21st Century: The Rise of the Fourth Generation*, edited by David Finkelstein, and Maryanne Kivlehan, 204–22. Abingdon: Routledge.

Han, Aijing. 2006. 'Mao Zedong Zhuxi Zhaojian Wugeban Xiaoshi de Tanhua Jilu' (Notes on the Five-and-a-Half Hour Meeting Called by Chairman Mao Zedong). *Aisixiang*. www.aisixiang.com/data/10712-4.html. Accessed 2 July 2021.

Han, Qiang, and Guo Kaiyu. 2017. 'Fahui Jiceng Dangzhuzhi "Zhengzhi Hexin" Zuoyong de Tizhi Baozhang Yanjiu' (A Study on the Institutional Guarantee for the Full Play of the Role of 'Political Core' by Grass-Roots Party Organisations). *Journal of Zhejiang Party School of CPC* 4: 69–75.

Han, Xiaodong. 2009. '1989–1999 Dazhong Wenhua Quanqui Kuanghuan de Qianye' (1989–1999, The Eve of the Global Carnival of Popular Culture). www.chinesefolklore.org.cn/blog/?action-viewnews-itemid-10196. Accessed 31 August 2022.

Hansen, Mette. 2015. *Educating the Chinese Individual: Life in a Rural Boarding School*. Seattle: University of Washington Press.

Hardy, Grant, and Anne Kinney. 2005. *The Establishment of the Han Dynasty and Imperial China*. Westport: Greenwood Press.

Harmel, Robert, and Yao-Yuan Yeh. 2016. 'Attitudinal Differences within the Cultural Revolution Cohort: Effects of the Sent-Down Experience'. *China Quarterly* 225: 234–52.

Harré, Rom, and Luk van Langenhove. 1991. 'Varieties of Positioning'. *Journal for the Theory of Social Behaviour* 21(4): 393–407.

Harré, Rom, Fathali Moghaddam, Tracy Cairnie, Daniel Rothbart, and Steven Sabat. 2009. 'Recent Advances in Positioning Theory'. *Theory & Psychology* 19(1): 5–31.

Hawkins, John. 1974. *Mao Tse-tung and Education: His Thoughts and Teachings*. Hamden: Linnet Books.

He, Henry. 2001. *Dictionary of the Political Thought of the People's Republic of China*. New York: M. E. Sharpe.

He, Hui. 2009. 'Wuhan Daxue Qianxiaozhang Jianyi Dangxiao Yilu Buneng Zhaoshou Yanjiusheng' (The Former President of Wuhan University Suggests No Party Schools be Allowed to Run Graduate Courses). *Changjiang Times*, 3 March 2009. https://news.ifeng.com/mainland/200903/0303_17_1040456_3.shtml. Accessed 31 May 2022.

He, Ping, and Gao Xin. 1996. *Zhonggong Taizidang* (*Princelings of the CCP*). New York: Mirror Media Group.

He, Qinglian, and Xiaonong Cheng. 2017. *Zhongguo: Kui er bu Beng* (*China: Crumbling but not Collapsing*). Taipei: Book Republic.

He, Xin. 1998. *Gudu yu Tiaozhan: Yige Gongheguo Tonglingren de Fendou yu Sikao* (*Solitude and Challenge: The Struggle and Thinking as a Coeval of the PRC*). Jinan: Shandong Friendship Publishing.

He, Xin. 2012. *Hong yu Hei: 60niandai Zhongguo Qingnian Wenti de Shehuixue Fenxi* (*Red and Black: A Sociological Analysis of the Chinese Youth Issues of the 1960s*). *Aisixiang*. www.aisixiang.com/data/49161.html. Accessed 10 March 2021.

He, Xin. 2014. 'The Party's Leadership as a Living Constitution in China'. In *Constitutions in Authoritarian Regimes*, edited by Tom Ginsburg, and Alberto Simpser, 245–64. Cambridge: Cambridge University Press.

He, Yan-Ling. 1991. 'The Struggling against Poverty and Hunger in China'. In *Poverty, Progress and Development*, edited by Paul-Marc Henry, 228–52. London: Routledge.

He, Yunfeng. 2007. 'Mao Zedong tichu jiebanren wuxiang tiaojian zhenshi yitu tanxi' (A Probe into Mao Zedong's Real Intention for Putting Forward the Five Conditions for the Successors). *Jinyang Journal* 1: 95–100.

Herrmann-Pillath, Carsten. 2017. *China's Economic Culture: The Ritual Order of State and Markets*. Abingdon: Routledge.

Heurlin, Christopher. 2017. *Responsive Authoritarianism in China: Land, Protests, and Policy Making*. New York: Cambridge University Press.

History Museum. 2020. *The Nanjing University Chronicle: Part 4. A Fight Without Hesitation*. https://historymuseum.nju.edu.cn/jypx/ndxs/ndxs/njdx1949/dszwgsn19661976/sywfgddz/index.html. Accessed 5 October 2021.

Ho, Peter, and Richard Edmonds. 2008. *China's Embedded Activism: Opportunities and Constraints of a Social Movement*. London: Routledge.

Ho, Wing-Chung, and Fen-Ling Chen. 2016. 'Compromising Citizenry: The Perceived Irrelevance of Rightful Resistance among Peasant Coal Miners Suffering from Pneumoconiosis'. *China Review* 16(2): 85–103.

Hong, Zicheng, and Cheng Guangwei, eds. 2009. *Chongfan Bashi Niandai* (*Returning to the 80s*). Beijing: Peking University Press.

Honig, Emily, and Zhao Xiaojian. 2019. *Across the Great Divide: The Sent-Down Youth Movement in Mao's China, 1968–1980*. Cambridge: Cambridge University Press.

Hooley, Graham, and John Saunders. 1993. *Competitive Positioning: The Key to Market Success*. London: Prentice-Hall.

Hou, Li. 2018. *Building for Oil: Daqing and the Formation of the Chinese Socialist State*. Cambridge: Harvard University Press.

Hou, Xiaoshuo. 2013. *Community Capitalism in China: The State, the Market, and Collectivism*. New York: Cambridge University Press.

Hsing, You-Tien. 2010. *The Great Urban Transformation: Politics of Land and Property in China*. Oxford: Oxford University Press.

Hsu, Carolyn. 2007. *Creating Market Socialism: How Ordinary People are Shaping Class and Status in China*. Durham: Duke University Press.

Hsü, Immanuel. 1990. *China without Mao: The Search for a New Order*. Oxford: Oxford University Press.

Hu, Angang. 1998. 'Zhongguo Chengzhen Shiye Zhuangkuang Fenxi' (An Analysis of Unemployment in China's Urban Areas). *Management World* 4: 47–63.

Hu, Jiwei. 2004. 'Hu Yaobang yu Xidan Minzhuqiang' (Hu Yaobang and the Xidan Democracy Wall). *China News Digest*. http://my.cnd.org/modules/wfsection/article.php?articleid=6187. Accessed 12 December 2021.

Hu, Ping. 1988. 'Chuguo Chao' (The Tide of Going Abroad). *Guangming Daily*, 22 to 28 February 1988.

Hu, Sheng. 1991. *From the Opium War to the May Fourth Movement*. Beijing: Foreign Language Press.

Hu, Xianzhong. 2018. 'Zhishi Qingnian Shangshan Xiaxiang Dongyuan Jieguo Bianqian Kaocha' (A Study of the Structural Changes of Mobilisation of Sent-down Youth). *China Youth Studies* 9: 11–8. www.aisixiang.com/data/112418-2.html. Accessed 2 July 2021.

Hua, Sheng. 2005. 'The Beginning and the End of Dual-Track System'. *China's Reform* 1: 22–5.

Hua, Shiping, ed. 2001. *Chinese Political Culture, 1989–2000*. Abingdon: Routledge.

Huang, Jiangang. 2003. *Zhengzhi Minzhu yu Qunti Xintai* (*Political Democracy and Mass Intention*). Beijing: CITIC Publishing House.

Huang, Jing. 2000. *Factionalism in Chinese Communist Politics*. Cambridge: Cambridge University Press.

Huang, Shouhong. 1990. 'Xiangzhen Qiye shi Guomin Jingji Fazhan de Tuidong Liliang' (TVEs are the Driving Force of National Economic Development). *Economic Research Journal*, 5: 39–80.

Huang, Pengjin. 2010a. '"Yi Ziyou Kandai Fazhan": "Zhejiang Moshi" de Jiedu yu Fanxi' (Considering Development from a Freedom Perspective: Interpretations and Reflections of the Zhejiang Model). *Journal of Hangzhou Party School* 1: 81–86.

Huang, Xiaoming, ed. 2010b. *The Institutional Dynamics of China's Great Transformation*. Abingdon: Routledge.

Huang, Yao. 2004. 'Luo Ruiqing zai 1965nian Aipiaizhengde Neimu Zhenxiang (Secrets of Luo Ruiqing's Downfall in 1965)'. news.sohu.com/20040929/n222294245.shtml. Accessed 10 June 2021.

Huang, Yasheng. 2008. *Capitalism with Chinese Characteristics: Entrepreneurship and the State*. New York: Cambridge University Press.

Hughes, Neil. 2002. *China's Economic Challenge: Smashing the Iron Rice Bowl*. New York: M. E. Sharpe.

Hurst, William, ed. 2019. *Urban Chinese Governance, Contention, and Social Control in the New Millennium*. Leiden: Brill.

Hurun China Rich List. 1999. *1999 Hurun China Rich List*. www.hurun.net/en-US/Rank/ HsRankDetails?pagetype=rich&num=CUY998QL. Accessed 31 August 2022.

Hurun China Rich List. 2000. *2000 Hurun China Rich List*. www.hurun.net/en-US/Rank/ HsRankDetails?pagetype=rich&num=ZX2LRTYM. Accessed 31 August 2022.

Hurun China Rich List. 2001. *2001 Hurun China Rich List*. www.hurun.net/en-US/Rank/ HsRankDetails?pagetype=rich&num=CV5RRTYQ. Accessed 31 August 2022.

Irwin, Sarah. 2005. *Reshaping Social Life*. Abingdon: Routledge.

Jacobs, Bruce. 1991. 'Elections in China'. *Australian Journal of Chinese Affairs* 25: 171–99.

Jakobson, Linda. 1998. *A Million Truths: A Decade in China*. New York: M. Evans and Company.

Jeffreys, Elaine. 2016. 'Political Celebrities and Elite Politics in Contemporary China'. *China Information* 30(1): 58–80.

Jeffries, Ian. 1993. *Socialist Economies and the Transition to the Market*. London: Routledge.

Jian, Guo, Yongyi Song, and Yuan Zhou. 2009. *The A to Z of the Chinese Revolution*. Lanham: Scarecrow Press.

Jiang, Qisheng. 2009. *Zhongguo Liusi Shouhaizhe Zhuangkuang Minjian Baogao (A Civil Report on the Situations of June Fourth Victims in China)*. Independent Chinese PEN Center. www.chinesepen .org/blog/archives/130358. Accessed 31 May 2022.

Jiang, and Tang. 2014. '"Lishi Zhuanzhe zhong de Deng Xiaoping" Diqi, baji Juqing Jingyao: Huifu Gaokao' (The Summary of the Plot of Episodes 7 and 8 of *Deng Xiaoping at the Turning Point of History*: The Restoration of the University Entrance examination). www.thepaper.cn/ newsDetail_forward_1261609. Accessed 5 October 2021.

Jiang, Yarong, and David Ashley. 2000. *Mao's Children in the New China: Voices from the Red Guard Generation*. Abingdon: Routledge.

Jiang, Zemin. 1990. *Guanyu Jiaqiang Dangxiao Jianshe de Jige Wenti* (Several Issues on Strengthening the Construction of Party Schools). www.reformdata.org/1990/0612/4124.shtml. Accessed 31 May 2022.

Jiang, Zemin. 1997. 'Eulogy for Comrade Deng Xiaoping'. *People's Daily*, 15 February 1997.

Jiang, Zemin. 2002. *On the "Three Represents"*. Beijing: Foreign Language Press.

Jin, Dalu. 2014. 'Zhiqing Fancheng yu Xiaxiang: Tuxian Lishide Zhuanzhe' (The Returning and the Sending Down of *Zhiqing*: Highlights of Historical Transformations). *Exploration and Free Views* 11: 95–8.

Jin, Guangyao. 2015. 'Houzhiqing Shidaide Zhiqing Lishi Shuxie' (Writing of the *Zhiqing* History in the Post-*Zhiqing* Era). *Studies of Chinese Communist Party History* 4: 117–19.

Jing, Wen. 2021. 'Zhaogong zhi Nongmin yu Xuesheng de Duijue' (The Rivalry between the Peasants and the Students over Worker Recruitment). *Xinsanjie*. WeChat ID: df3p1113-2. Accessed 2 August 2021.

Karl, Rebecca. 2002. *Staging the World: Chinese Nationalism at the Turn of the Twentieth Century*. Durham: Duke University Press.

Karl, Rebecca, and Peter Zarrow, eds. 2002. *Rethinking the 1898 Reform Period: Political and Cultural Change in Late Qing China*. Leiden: Brill.

Keith, Michael, Scott Lash, Jakob Arnoldi, and Tyler Rooker. 2014. *China Constructing Capitalism: Economic Life and Urban Change*. Abingdon: Routledge.

Keith, Ronald, and Zhiqiu Lin. 2003. 'The "Falun Gong Problem": Politics and the Struggle for the Rule of Law in China'. *China Quarterly* 175: 623–42.

Kelliher, Daniel. 1992. *Peasant Power in China: The Era of Rural Reform, 1979–1989*. New Haven: Yale University Press.

Kelliher, Daniel. 1993. 'Keeping Democracy Safe from the Masses: Intellectuals and Elitism in the Chinese Protest Movement'. *Comparative Politics* 25(4): 379–96.

Kennedy, Scott, ed. 2011. *Beyond the Middle Kingdom: Comparative Perspectives on China's Capitalist Transformation*. Sandford: Stanford University Press.

Kim, Samuel. 2006. 'Chinese Foreign Policy Faces Globalization Challenges'. In *New Directions in the Study of China's Foreign Policy*, edited by Alastair Johnstone, and Robert Ross, 276–308. Stanford: Stanford University Press.

Kinkley, Jeffrey. 2007. *Corruption and Realism in Late Socialist China: The Return of the Political Novel*. Stanford: Stanford University Press.

Kleinberg, Robert. 2018. *China's 'Opening' to the Outside World: The Experiment with Foreign Capitalism*. Abingdon: Routledge.

Knight, John, and Lina Song. 1999. *The Rural-Urban Divide: Economic Disparities and Interactions in China*. Oxford: Oxford University Press.

Kor, Kian Beng. 2016. 'Cultural Revolution Ruined his Life, says Former Sent-Down Youth'. www.straitstimes.com/asia/east-asia/cultural-revolution-ruined-his-life-says-former-sent-down-youth. Accessed 2 July 2021.

Kou, Chien-wen, and Xiaowei Zang, eds. 2014. *Choosing China's Leaders*. Abingdon: Routledge.

Kraus, Richard. 1981. *Class Conflicts in Chinese Socialism*. New York: Columbia University Press.

Kuhn, Robert. 2011. *How China's Leaders Think: The Inside Story of China's Past, Current and Future Leaders*. Chichester: John Wiley & Sons.

Kwong, Luke. 1984. *A Mosaic of the Hundred Days: Personalities, Politics, and Ideas of 1898*. Leiden: Brill.

Lam, Catherine, and Xu Huang. 2012. 'Managing Social Comparison Processes among Chinese Employees'. In *Handbook of Chinese Organizational Behavior: Integrating Theory, Research and Practice*, edited by Xu Huang, and Michael Bons, 118–39. Cheltenham: Edward Elgar.

Lam, Willy. 1999. *The Era of Jiang Zemin*. Singapore: Prentice Hill.

Lampton, David. 1987. 'Chinese Politics: The Bargaining Treadmill'. *Issues and Studies* 23(3): 11–41.

Lardy, Nicholas. 2014. *Markets Over Mao: The Rise of Private Business in China*. Washington: Peterson Institute for International Economics.

Le, Hu. 2017. 'Bingtui de Beixiju' (Tragedy and Comedy of *bingtui*). www.jianzi103.com. Accessed 2 July 2021.

Lee, Ching Kwan, and Yonghong Zhang. 2013. 'The Power of Instability: Unraveling the Microfoundations of Bargained Authoritarianism in China'. *American Journal of Sociology* 118(6): 1475–508.

Lee, Ming-kwan. 2000. *Chinese Occupational Welfare I Market Transition*. London: Palgrave Macmillan.

Leese, Daniel. 2011. *Mao Cult: Rhetoric and Ritual in China's Cultural Revolution*. Cambridge: Cambridge University Press.

Leung, Laifong. 1994. *Morning Sun: Interviews with Chinese Writers of the Lost Generation*. New York: M. E. Sharpe.

Lewis, James, and Jesper Peterson, eds. 2005. *Controversial New Religions*. Oxford: Oxford University Press.

Lewis, Orion. 2012. 'The Evolution of Chinese Authoritarianism'. In *China in and Beyond the Headlines*, edited by Timothy Weston, and Lionel Jenson, 249–70. Lanham: Rowman & Littlefield.

Li, Botao. 2005a. 'Wuqian Yuming Dazhuan Yingjie Biyesheng Canjia Gongwuyuan Zige Kaoshi' (More than 5,000 Young Graduates Take the Civil Servant Qualification Examination). *Beijing Daily*, 21 March 2005.

Li, Cheng. 1997. *Rediscovering China: Dynamics and Dilemmas of Reform*. Lanham: Rowman & Littlefield.

Li, Cheng. 2001. *China's Leaders: The New Generation*. Lanham: Rowman & Littlefield.

Li, Cheng, ed. 2010. *China's Emerging Middle Class: Beyond Economic Transformation*. Washington: Brooking Institution Press.

Li, Cheng, and David Backman. 1989. 'Localism, Elitism, and Immobilism: Elite Formation and Social Change in Post-Mao China'. *World Politics* 42(1): 64–94.

Li, Chuncheng, Yalin Tang, and Xie Baofu. 2014. 'Ganbu Xiahai: Chaoqi Chaoluo yu Daode Kunjing' (Cadres' *Xiahai*: The Ebb and Flow and the Moral Dilemma). *Beijing Daily*, 21 May 2014. http://cpc.people.com.cn/n/2014/0519/c64387-25033254.html. Accessed 31 May 2022.

Li, Chunling. 2005. 'Prestige Stratification in Contemporary China: Occupational Prestige Measure and Socio-Economic Index'. *Sociological Studies* 20(2): 74–102.

Li, Chunling, ed. 2012. *The Rising Middle Classes in China*. Reading: Paths International.

Li, Danhui, and Yafeng Xia. 2018. *Mao and the Sino-Soviet Split, 1959–1973*. Lanham: Lexington Books.

Li, He. 2015. *Political Thought and China's Transformation: Ideas Shaping Reforms in Post-Mao China*. New York: Palgrave Macmillan.

Li, Jiangyuan. 2006a. *Wo shi yige Gongnongbing Xueyuan: Fanzhengzhihua Jiaoyu zhong de Shoujiayuzhe, Shang* (*I am a Worker-Peasant-Solider Trainee: A Trainee in Pan-Politicised Education, I*). Fuzhou: Fujian People's Press.

Li, Jiangyuan. 2006b. *Wo shi yige Gongnongbing Xueyuan: Fanzhengzhihua Jiaoyu zhong de Shoujiayuzhe, Xia* (*I am a Worker-Peasant-Solider Trainee: A Trainee in Pan-Politicised Education, II*). Fuzhou: Fujian People's Press.

Li, Jingpeng, and Song Dingguo, eds. 1992. *Dangdai Zhongguo Qingnian de Zhengzhi Yishi he Zhengzhi Xingwei* (*Political Consciousness and Political Behavior of Contemporary Chinese Youth*). Beijing: China Police University Publishing House.

Li, Junfu. 2017. *Beijing de Zhufang Bianqian yu Zhufang Zhengce* (*Beijing's Housing Changes and Policies*). Beijing: Central Compilation and Translation Press.

Li, Junpeng. 2014a. 'The Religion of the Nonreligious and the Politics of the Apolitical: The Transformation of Falun Gong from Healing Practice to Political Movement'. *Politics and Religion* 7(1): 177–208.

Li, Keji. 2014b. 'Guanyuan "Xueli Fubai" Dang E' (Officials' "Educational Corruption" Should be Curbed). http://cpc.people.com.cn/pinglun/n/2014/0404/c78779-24829535.html. Accessed 31 August 2022.

Li, Linda. 1998. *Centre and Provinces: China 1978–1993, Power as Non-Zero Sum*. Oxford: Clarendon Press.

Li, Linzi. 2018. '*Bingtui*, Wo Zui Jihui de Ci' (*Bingtui*, My Taboo Phrase). www.hnzqw.com. Accessed 2 July 2021.

Li, Lulu, Lei Shi, and Bin Zhu. 2018. 'Guhua haishi Liudong?: Dangdai Zhongguo Jieceng Jieguo Bianqian 40nian' (Solidification or Fluidity?: 40 Years of Class Structure Changes in Contemporary China). *Sociological Studies* 33(6): 1–34.

Li, Peilin. 2022. *Another Invisible Hand: The Transformation of Social Structure*. Abingdon: Routledge.

Li, Qiang. 2004. *Nongmingong yu Zhongguo Shehui Fenceng (Rural Migrant Workers and Chinese Social Stratification)*. Beijing: Social Sciences Academic Press.

Li, Qiang, Jianwei Deng, and Zheng Xiao. 1999. 'Social Change and Individual Development: The Paradigm and Method of Life Course'. *Sociological Studies* 14(6): 1–18.

Li, Qinggang. 2012. '20shiji wuliushi niandai "Hongzhuan" wenti de taolun' (The 'Red-Expert' Debates in the 1950s and 1960s). *Contemporary China History Studies* 1: 67–72.

Li, Ruihuan. 2005b. *Xue Zhexue Yong Zhexue (Study Philosophy and Use Philosophy)*. Beijing: Renmin University of China Press.

Li, Shi. 2002. 'Zhongguo Geren Shouru Fenpei Yanjiu Huigu yu Zhanwang' (Review and Outlook of Research on Personal Income Distribution in China). ww2.usc.cuhk.edu.hk/PaperCollection/Details.aspx?id=2324. Accessed 5 October 2021.

Li, Weijian. 1995. 'Xinjiang Gaoxiao Shizi Weishenme Wailiu' (Why Do Teaching Staff Members in Xinjiang Universities Leave). *China Higher Education* 4: 41–42.

Li, Xiaobing. 2007. *A History of the Modern Chinese Army*. Lexington: University Press of Kentucky.

Li, Xiaoyun, Yu Lerong, and Lixia Tang. 2019. 'Xin Zhongguo Chengli hou 70nian de Fanpinkun Licheng ji Jianpin Zhizhi' (The Process and Mechanism of China's Poverty-Reduction in the Past 70 Years). *China's Rural Economy* 10: 1–17.

Li, Zhenghua. 2013. 'Lun Deng Xiaoping de "Sannong" Sixiang dui Zhongguo Nongcun Gaige de Zhongda Yiyi' (On the Significance of Deng Xiaoping's 'Three Rural' Thoughts to China's Rural Reform). www.dswxyjy.org.cn/n1/2019/0228/c423719-30917177.html. Accessed 12 December 2021.

Li, Zhongjie. 2021. 'Zhongguo Gongchandang Chengwei Shijie Diyi da Zhizhengdang, "Shishang Zuiqiang Chuangye Tuandui"' (The Communist Party of China Has Become the World's Largest Ruling Party, "The Most Innovative Party in History"). *Beijing Daily*, 28 June 2021. www.bjd.com.cn/theory/2021/06/28/117407t118.html. Accessed 31 August 2022.

Liang, Heng, and Judith Shapiro. 1984. *Intellectual Freedom in China after Mao: With a Focus on 1983*. New York: Fund for Free Expression.

Liang, Xiao. 1976. 'Lun Dangqian Jiaoyu Zhanxian shang de Liangtiao Luxian Douzheng' (On the Two-line Struggle on the Education Front). *The Chinese Cultural Revolution Database*. ccradb.appspot.com/post/3804. Accessed 10 June 2021.

Liang, Xiaosheng. 2019. *Neixie Suiyue (In Those Years)*. Beijing: Beijing Shiyue Wenyi Press.

Lieberthal, Kenneth. 1995. *Governing China: From Revolution through Reform*. New York: W. W Norton.

Lin, Jing. 1991. *The Red Guards' Path to Violence: Political, Educational, and Psychological Factors*. New York: Praeger.

Lin, Jing, and Xiaoyan Sun. 2010. 'Higher Education Expansions and China's Middle Class'. In *China's Emerging Middles Class: Beyond Economic Transformation*, edited by Cheng Li, 217–44. Washington: Brooking Institution Press.

Lin, Justin. 1988. 'The Household Responsibility System in China's Agricultural Reform: A Theoretical and Empirical Study'. *Economic Development and Cultural Change* 36(3): 199–224.

Lin, Justin, Fang Cai, and Zhou Li. 2001. *State-Owned Enterprise Reform in China*. Hong Kong: Chinese University Press.

Lin, Zhe. 2010. 'It's Not Age That Really Matters'. *China Daily*, 15 January 2020. www.chinadaily.com.cn/thinktank/2010-01/15/content_9324612.htm. Accessed 31 August 2022.

LiPuma, Edward. 2001. *Encompassing Others: The Magic of Modernity in Melanesia*. Ann Arbor: University of Michigan Press.

Liu, Alan. 1988. 'How Can We Evaluate Communist China's Political System Performance?' In *Changes and Continuities in Chinese Communism, Volume 1: Ideology, Politics, and Foreign Policy*, edited by Yu-Ming Shaw, 1–32. Abingdon: Routledge.

Liu, Bing. 1998. *Fengyu Suiyue: Qinghua Daxue 'Wenhua Da Geming' Yishi (Stormy Year: Recollections of the 'Cultural Revolution' at Tsinghua University)*. Beijing: Tsinghua University Press.

Liu, Chuanzhi. 2012. 'Wo ruanruo dan bu yaobai, wo xiwang gaige dan fandui baoli geming' (I am Weak But Not Swaying, I Hope to Reform But Oppose Violent Revolution). http://finance.sina.com.cn/review/hgds/20121015/150213371057.shtml. Accessed 5 October 2021.

Liu, Fuzhi. 1990. *The Work Report of the Supreme People's Procuratorate: To the Third Session of the Seventh National People's Congress om.* 29 March 1990. www.people.com.cn/zgrdxw/zlk/rd/7jie/newfiles/c1160.html. Accessed 31 May 2022.

Liu, Haifeng. 2007. *Gaokao Gaige de Lilun Sikao (Theoretical Analyses of the Reform of University Entrance Examination).* Wuhan: Huazhong Normal University Press.

Liu, Jianzhou. 2014. *Nongmingong de Jieji Xingcheng yu Jiejiyishi Yanjiu (An Analysis on the Class Formation and Class Consciousness of Peasant Workers).* Beijing: China Social Sciences Press.

Liu, Qingfeng. 2001a. 'The Topography of Intellectual Culture in 1990s Mainland China: A Survey'. In *Voicing Concerns: Contemporary Chinese Critical Inquiry,* edited by Gloria Davies, 47–70. Lanham: Rowman & Littlefield.

Liu, Tianjun, ed. 2010. *Chinese Medical Qigong.* London: Singing Dragan.

Liu, Yuan. 2020. 'Liu Yuan 1980nian Jingxuan Renda Daibiao Shi de Shengming' (Statement by Liu Yuan When He Was Running for the District People's Congress in 1980). www.163.com/dy/article/FQASC39B05439UIT.html. Accessed 12 December 2021.

Liu, Wanzhen, and Qinggui Li, eds. 2003. *Mao Zedong Guoji Jiaowanglu (Records of Mao Zedong's International Exchanges).* Beijing: Zhonggong Dangshi Chubanshe (CCO History Press).

Liu, Xiaomeng. 2006 'Biandi Qingnian Xia Xiyan' (The Youth Everywhere Work Until the Evening Mist). *Economic Observer.* finance.sina.com.cn/xiaofei/consume/20060618/17432660434.shtml. Accessed 2 July 2021.

Liu, Xiaomeng. 2009. *History of China's Educated Youth: The Big Wave (1966–1980).* Beijing: Contemporary China Publishing House.

Liu, Xinkui. 2012. 'Beijing Urban Renewal: The Theory Evolvement and Practice Characteristics'. *Chengshi Fazhan Yanjiu (Urban Development Studies)* 21(10): 129–36.

Liu, Xiuwu. 2001b. *Jumping into the Sea: From Academics to Entrepreneurs in South China.* Lanham: Rowman & Littlefield.

Loewe, Michael. 2011. *Dong Zhongshu, a 'Confucian' Heritage and the Chunqiu Fanlu.* Leiden: Brill.

Long, Pingping, Huang Yazhou, Zhang Qiang, and Wen Ren. 2014. *Lishi Zhuanzhe Zhong de Deng Xiaoping (Deng Xiaoping at History's Crossroads).* Chengdu: Sichuan People's Press.

Long, Pingping, and Zhang Shu. 2016. 'Jiemi Deng Xiaoping Huifu Gaokao' (Demystifying Deng Xiaoping's Decision to restore the University Entrance Examination). www.dswxyjy.org.cn/n1/2016/0530/c222139-28393825.html. Accessed 5 October 2021.

Lü, Xiaobo. 2000. *Cadres and Corruption: The Organizational Involution of the Chinese Communist Party.* Stanford: Stanford University Press.

Lu, Di. 2010. *Mao Zedong he tade Chenpumen (Mao Zedong and his Servants).* New York: Mirror Media Group.

Lu, Xing. 2017. *The Rhetoric of Mao Zedong: Transforming China and its People.* Columbia: University of South Carolina.

Lu, Yunfeng. 2005. 'Entrepreneurial Logic and the Evolution of Falun Gong'. *Journal for the Scientific Study of Religion* 44(2): 173–85.

Luo, Chenxi. 1988. 'China's Economic Reforms Face Major Constraints'. *Far Eastern Economic Review* 139(January 28): 72–73.

Luo, Xiaohai. 2009. 'xinli lucheng' (The journey of mind). https://difangwenge.org/archiver/?tid-366.html. Accessed 5 October 2021.

Ma, Damien. 2012. 'After 20 Years of "Peaceful Evolution," China Faces Another Historic Moment'. *The Atlantic,* 24 January 2012.

Ma, Guochuan. 2010. 'Zhongguo Xuyao Shenmeyang de Xiandaixing' (What Kind of Modernity Does China Need). *Caijing Biweekly.* finance.sina.com.cn/review/20101123/18088997867.shtml. Accessed 31 March 2022.

Ma, Licheng. 2011. *Dangdai Zhongguo Bazhong Shehui Sichao (Eight Social Trends of Thought in Contemporary China)*. Beijing: Social Sciences Academic Press.

MacFarquhar, Roderick. 1974. *The Origin of the Cultural Revolution: 3. The Coming of the Cataclysm, 1961–1966*. New York: Columbia University Press.

MacFarquhar, Roderick, and John Fairbank, eds. 1991. *The Cambridge History of China, Vol. 15, The People's Republic, Part 2: Revolutions within the Chinese Revolution 1966–1982*. New York: Cambridge University Press.

MacFarquhar, Roderick, and Michael Schoenhals. 2006. *Mao's Last Revolution*. Cambridge: Harvard University Press.

MacMillan, Margaret. 2007. *Nixon and Mao: The Week That Changed the World*. New York: Random House.

Majid, Nomaan. 2015. *The Great Employment Transformation in China*. Geneva: ILO (International Labour Organization) Working Paper No. 5.

Mao, Huahe. 2019. *The Ebb and Flow of Chinese Petroleum: A Story told by a Witness*. Leiden: Brill.

Mao, Min. 2017. *Marshal Lin Biao: Topic 6 of the Selected Topics from the Revival of China*. California: CreateSpace.

MARA (Ministry of Agriculture and Rural Affairs). 2009. *Xin Zhongguo Chengli 60nian: Xiangzhen Qiye Fazhan Chengjiu (60th Anniversary of the Founding of New China: Achievements in the Development of Township and Village Enterprises)*. www.moa.gov.cn/ztzl/xzgnylsn/gd_1/200909/t20090918_1353912.htm. Accessed 12 December 2021.

Maslow, Abraham. 1954. *Motivation and Personality*. New York: Harper & Row.

Mason, David. 1994. 'Modernization and Its Discontents Revisited: The Political Economy of Urban Unrest in the People's Republic of China'. *Journal of Politics* 56(2): 400–24.

McDermott, Kevin, and Jeremy Agnew. 1996. *The Comintern: A History of International Communist from Lenin to Stalin*. Basingstoke: Macmillan Press.

McLaren, Anne. 1979. 'The Educated Youth Return: The Poster Campaign in Shanghai from November 1978 to March 1979'. *Australian Journal of Chinese Affairs* 2: 1–20.

McMahon, Keith. 1988. *Causality and Containment in Seventeenth-Century Chinese Fiction*. Leiden: Brill.

Mei, Zhimin, ed. 2006. 'Fang Zhongguo Zuihou de Gongnongbing Daxuesheng: Yong Madai Zhuang Zhishi' (Interviews with China's Final Group of Worker-Peasant-Soldier University Students: Packing Knowledge in Sacks). http://news.sohu.com/20060821/n244897404_8.shtml. Accessed 12 December 2021.

Mi, Hedu. 1993. 'Shangshan Xiaxiang Yundong de Yuanqi' (The Origin of the Sent-down Youth Movement). *Huaxia Zhiqing*. www.hxzq.net/aspshow/showarticle.asp?id=4984. Accessed 2 July 2021.

Mi, Hedu. 2011. *Xinlu: Toushi Gongheguo Tonglingren (Intentions: Examining my Peers in the Republic)*. Beijing: Central Party Literature Press.

Mi, Hedu. 2014. 'Jilu Hongweibing Yidai' (Documenting the Red Guard Generation). *Southern People Weekly*. www.bannedbook.org/bnews/zh-tw/ssgc/20131231/690946.html/amp. Accessed 2 August 2021.

Miao, Ying. 2017. *Being Middle Class in China: Identity, Attitudes and Behaviour*. Abingdon: Routledge.

Miles, James. 1997. *The Legacy of Tiananmen: China in Disarray*. Ann Arbor: University of Michigan Press.

Minghui.org. 1998. 'Falun Gong Jianshen Gongxiao Beijing Wanli Diaocha baogao' (A Report on the Fitness Effect of Falun Gong Based on More Than 10,000 Cases in Beijing). http://media.minghui.org/gb/0001/Feb/21/fujian23.html. Accessed 31 August 2022.

Ministry of Education (China). 2020. '2019nian Quanguo Jiaoyu Shiye Fazhan Tongji Gongbao' (Statistical Report on the Development of China's Education Sector in 2019). www.moe.gov.cn/jyb_sjzl/sjzl_fztjgb/202005/t20200520_456751.html. Accessed 10 March 2021.

Misra, Kalpana. 2016. 'Curing the Sickness and Saving the Party: Neo-Maoism and Neo-Conservativism in the 1990s'. In *Chinese Political Culture, 1989–2000*, edited by Shiping Hua, 133–60. Abingdon: Routledge.

Mitchell, Damo. 2011. *Daoist Nei Gong: The Philosophical Art of Change*. London: Singing Dragon.

Mitter, Rana. 2000. *The Manchurian Myth: Nationalism, Resistance, and Collaboration in Modern China*. Berkeley: University of California Press.

Mitter, Rana. 2004. *A Bitter Revolution: China's Struggle with the Modern World*. Oxford: Oxford University Press.

Mittler, Barbara. 2012. *A Continuous Revolution: Making Sense of Cultural Revolution Culture*. Boston: Harvard University Press.

Mo, Rong, and Wei Yue. 2001. 'Zengjia Xiagang Zhigong Jiuye Jihui Yanjiu' (A Study of Increasing Employment Opportunities of Laid-off Workers). *Management World* 2: 88–94.

Moody, Peter. 1994. 'Trends in the Study of Chinese Political Culture'. *China Quarterly* 139: 731–40.

Mosher, Steven. 1998. 'Are the Chinese Ready for Liberty and Self-Government?'. *American Enterprise* 9, no. 4: 50–3.

Myers, Ramon. 1987. 'How Can We Evaluate Communist China's Economic Development Performance?'. *Issues and Studies* 23(2): 122–55.

Nan, Chen. 2014. 'Deng Xiaoping Nanxun de Bada Neimu, "Jianghua" Zuichu Buzhun Baodao' (Eight Insider Stories of Deng Xiaoping's Southern Inspection Tour, 'Speeches' Were Initially Not Allowed to be Reported). http://history.sina.com.cn/bk/ggkfs/2014-08-25/154998639 .shtml. Accessed 31 May 2022.

Nathan, Andrew. 1985. *Chinese Democracy*. Berkeley: University of California Press.

Nathan, Andrew, and Tianjian Shi. 1993. 'Cultural Requisites for Democracy in China: Findings from a Survey'. *Daedalus* 122: 95–124.

Naughton, Barry. 1988. 'The Third Front: Defence Industrialization in the Chinese Interior'. *China Quarterly* 115: 351–86.

Naughton, Barry. 2007. *The Chinese Economy: Transitions and Growth*. Cambridge: The MIT Press.

Nolas, Sevasti-Melissa, Christos Varvantakis, and Vinnarasan Aruldoss. 2017. 'Political Activism across the Life Course'. *Contemporary Social Science* 12(1–2): 1–12.

NBSC (National Bureau of Statistics of China). 1999. 'Xin Zhongguo 50nian Xilie Fenxi Baogao' (Analytical Report Series Over 50 Years of New China). www.stats.gov.cn/ztjc/ztfx /xzg50nxlfxbg/. Accessed 5 October 2021.

NBSC. 2005. *China Labour Statistical Yearbook*. www.mohrss.gov.cn/ImportedImageFile/2711031 6153762520791.pdf. Accessed 12 December 2021.

NBSC. 2009. 'Xin Zhongguo 60nian Renkou Shidu Zengzhang' (A Moderate Population Growth Over 60 Years of the New China). www.gov.cn/gzdt/2009-09/11/content_1415054 .htm. Accessed 10 March 2021.

NBSC. 2011a. *Statistics of the Second Census*. www.stats.gov.cn/tjsj/tjgb/rkpcgb/qgrkpcgb/. Accessed 2 July 2021.

NBSC. 2011b. *Communique of the Third Census*. www.stats.gov.cn/tjsj/tjgb/rkpcgb/qgrkpcgb/. Accessed 2 July 2021.

NBSC. 2015. *Xin Zhongguo 65 Zhounian (New China 65 Years)*. www.stats.gov.cn/tjzs/tjbk/201502/ t20150213_683631.html. Accessed 2 July 2021.

NBSC. 2018. 'Jiuye Zongliang Chixu Zengzhang Jiuye Jieguo Tiaozheng Youhua' (The Total Number of Employment Continued to Grow, and the Employment Structure Was Further Optimised).   www.stats.gov.cn/ztjc/ztfx/ggkf40n/201809/t20180912_1622409.html. Accessed 31 March 2022.

NBSC. 2020. *China Statistical Yearbook 2020*. www.stats.gov.cn/tjsj/ndsj/2020/indexch.htm. Accessed 10 March 2021.

Nee, Victor, and David Stark, eds. 1989. *Remaking the Economic Institutions of Socialism: China and Eastern Europe*. Stanford: Stanford University Press.

Nee, Victor, and Frank Young. 1991. 'Peasant Entrepreneurs in China's "Second Economy": An Institutional Analysis'. *Economic Development and Cultural Change* 39(2): 293–310.

Neubert, Dieter. 2019. *Inequality, Socio-cultural Differentiation and Social Structures in Africa: Beyond Class*. London: Palgrave Macmillan.

Nolan, Peter. 1988. *The Political Economy of Collective Farms: An Analysis of China's Post-Mao Rural Reforms*. Boulder: Westview Press.

O'Brien, Kevin, ed. 2008. *Popular Protest in China*. Cambridge: Harvard University Press.

O'Brien, Kevin, and Lianjiang Li. 2006. *Rightful Resistance in Rural China*. New York: Cambridge University Press.

Oksenberg, Michel, Carl Riskin, Robert Scalapino, and Ezra Vogel. 1968. *The Cultural Revolution, 1967 in Review*. Ann Arbor: University of Michigan Press.

O'Leary, Greg, ed. 1998. *Adjusting to Capitalism: Chinese Workers and the State*. New York: M. E. Sharpe.

Osburg, John. 2013. *Anxious Wealth: Money and Morality among China's New Rich*. Stanford: Stanford University Press.

Palmer, David. 2007. *Qigong Fever: Body, Science, and Utopia in China*. New York: Columbia University Press.

Pan, Yihong. 2003. *Tempered in the Revolutionary Furnace: China's Youth in the Rustication Movement*. Lanham: Lexington books.

Pei, Minxin. 1994. *From Reform to Revolution: The Demise of Communism in China and the Soviet Union*. Cambridge: Harvard University Press.

Pei, Minxin. 2008. *China's Trapped Transition: The Limits of Development and Autocracy*. Cambridge: Harvard University Press.

People's Daily and Red Flag. 1964. *On Khrushchev's Phoney Communism and its Historical Lessons for the World: The Nineth Comment on the Open Letter of the Central Committee of the CPSU* [Communist Party of the Soviet Union]. Beijing: Foreign Languages Press.

Penny, Benjamin. 2012. *The Religion of Falun Gong*. Chicago: University of Chicago Press.

Perry, Elizabeth. 2001. 'Challenging the Mandate of Heaven: Popular Protest in Modern China'. *Critical Asian Studies* 33(2): 163–80.

Perry, Elizabeth. 2007. 'Studying Chinese Politics: Farewell to Revolution'. *China Journal* 57: 1–22.

Pieke, Frank. 2009. *The Good Communist: Elite Training and State Building in Today's China*. Cambridge: Cambridge University Press.

Powell, Ralph. 1965. 'Commissars in the Economy: "Learn from the PLA" Movement in China'. *Asian Survey* 5(3): 125–38.

Preston, Peter, and Aifen Xing. 2003. 'State-owned Enterprises: A Review of Development Dynamics, Contemporary Problems and the Shape of the Future'. In *Contemporary China: The Dynamics of Change at the Start of the New Millennium*, edited by Peter Preston, and Jürgen Haacke, 73–88. London: Routledge/Curzon.

Pugsley, Peter, and Gao Jia. 2009. 'Invisible Women: Chinese Media Responses to the "Japanese Orgy"'. In *Local Violence, Global Media: Feminist Analyses of Gendered Representations*, edited by Lisa Cuklanz, and Sujata Moorti, 109–31. New York: Peter Lang.

Pye, Lucian. 1981. *The Dynamics of Chinese Politics*. Cambridge: Oelgeschlager, Gunn & Hain.

Qian, Liqun. 2008. 'Buneng Yiwang de Sixiang: 1980nian Zhongguo Xiaoyuan Minzhu Yundong Shuping' (Unforgettable thoughts: A Review of China's Campus Democracy Movement in 1980). *Modern China Studies*, www.modernchinastudies.org/us/issues/past-issues/99-mcs-2008-issue-1/1034--1950.html. Accessed 12 December 2021.

Qian, Liqun. 2012. *Mao Zedong Shidai he Hou Mao Zedong Shidai (1949–2009): Ling Yizhong Lishi Shuxie (Shang)* (*The Mao Era and the Post-Mao Era (1949–2009): An Alternative Historical Narrative, Vol. 1*). Taipei: Linking Publishing.

Qiu, Jin. 1999. *The Culture of Power: The Lin Biao Incident in the Cultural Revolution*. Stanford: Stanford University Press.

Rankin, Mary. 1986. *Elite Activism and Political Transformation in China: Zhejiang Province, 1865–1911*. Stanford: Stanford University Press.

Reformdata. 2004. '1986 niandi dui "yiqie xiang qian kan" de pipan' (Criticism of 'Always Thinking of Money' at the End of 1986). www.reformdata.org/2004/0623/5944.shtml. Accessed 31 March 2022.

Ren, Hai. 2013. *The Middle Class in Neoliberal China: Governing Risk, Life-Building, and Themed spaces*. Abingdon: Routledge.

Rene, Helena. 2013. *China's Sent-Down Generation: Public Administration and the Legacies of Mao's Rustication Program*. Washington: Georgetown University Press.

Robinson, Thomas. 1971. 'The Wuhan Incident: Local Strife and Provincial Rebellion during the Cultural Revolution'. *China Quarterly* 47: 413–438.

Rosen, Stanley. 1981. *The Role of Sent-Down Youth in the Chinese Cultural Revolution: The Case of Guangzhou*. Berkeley: University of California Press.

Saich, Tony. 2001. *Governance and Politics of China*. New York: Palgrave Macmillan.

Sammut, Gordon, and George Gaskell. 2010. 'Points of View, Social Positioning and Intercultural Relations'. *Journal of the Theory of Social Behaviour* 40(1): 47–64.

Schrift, Melissa. 2001. *Biography of a Chairman Mao Badge: The Creation and Mass Consumption of a Personality Cult*. New Brunswick: Rutgers University Press.

Schubert, Gunter, and Anna Ahlers. 2012. *Participation and Empowerment at the Grassroots: Chinese Village Elections in Perspective*. Lanham: Lexington Books.

Schwarcz, Vera. 1986. *The Chinese Enlightenment: Intellectuals and the Legacy of the May Fourth Movement of 1919*. Berkeley: University of California Press.

Seybolt, Peter. 2018. *Revolutionary Education in China: Documents and Commentary*. Abingdon: Routledge.

Shambaugh, David. 2008. *China's Communist Party: Atrophy and Adaptation*. Berkeley: University of California Press.

Shan, Feng. 2018. 'Shangshan Xiaxiang 50nian: Fansi zhi Fansi' (50 Years of up to the Mountains and down to the Villages: Reflection of Reflection). Shanghai Zhiqing Forum. pjq.shzq.org/Print.asp?tid=17067. Accessed 2 July 2021.

Shan, He, and Li Lu. 2002. 'Cong Siheyuan dao Tongzilou' (From Siheyuan to Tongzilou). *Old Beijing Net*. http://cn.obj.cc/article-15548-1.html. Accessed 5 October 2021.

Shen, Qiaosheng. 2017. 'Zhiqing Fancheng Hou' (After *Zhiqing*'s Return). his.cn-n.net/d2.php?id=4083. Accessed 2 August 2021.

Shen, Zhihua, ed. 2020. *A History of Sino-Soviet Relations, 1917–1991*. Singapore: Palgrave Macmillan.

Shi, Shujun. 2004. 'Maiguan Maiguan: Wan'e Zhiyuan' (Buying and Selling Official Positions: The Root of All Evil). www.aisixiang.com/data/4217.html. Accessed 31 August 2022.

Shi, Tianjian. 1997. *Political Participation in Beijing*. Cambridge: Harvard University Press.

Shi, Weimin. 1995. 'Shangshan Xiaxiang Zhishi Qingnian de "Bingtui", "Kuntui" Wenti' (The *Bingtui* and *Kuntui* Issues of the Sent-Down Youth). *Youth Studies* 5: 46–9.

Shirk, Susan. 1993. *The Political Logic of Economic Reform in China*. Berkeley: University of California Press.

Shirk, Susan, ed. 2011. *Changing Media, Changing China*. Oxford: Oxford University Press.

Shui, Luzhou. 2004. *Deng Xiaoping de Wannian zhi Lu* (*Deng Xiaoping's Path in his Final Years*). www.2002n.com/book/biography/dengxiaopingwannian/7705.html. Accessed 31 May 2022.

Sigurdson, Jon. 1977. *Rural Industrialization in China*. Cambridge: Harvard University Press.

Simon, Amanda. 2018. *Supplementary Schools and Ethnic Minority Communities: A Social Positioning Perspective*. London: Palgrave Macmillan.

SinaNews. 2007. *Zhongguo Gongchandang Dashiji (1990)* (*Chronicle of the Chinese Communist Party, 1990*). http://news.sina.com.cn/s/2007-08-08/142913620295.shtml. Accessed 31 May 2022.

Singer, Martin. 1971. *Educated Youth and the Cultural Revolution in China*. Ann Arbor: University of Michigan Press.

Smith, Aminda. 2012. *Thought Reform and China's Dangerous Classes: Reeducation, Resistance and the People*. Lanham: Rowman & Littlefield.

Song, Chunhui. 2008. 'Mao Zedong Shidai Yipie' (A Glimpse of Mao Zedong's Era). *Wuyou Zhixiang Zhoukan* (*Utopia Weekly*). www.wyzxwk.com/Article/zatan/2009/09/58299.html. Accessed 10 March 2021.

Song, Qiang. 2008b. *Renmin Jiyi* (*People's Memory*). Nanchang: Jiangxi People's Press. https://news.ifeng.com/history/1/jishi/200810/1006_2663_817558.shtml. Accessed 12 December 2021.

Song, Yongyi, ed. 2006. *The Cultural Revolution: Historical Truth and Collective Memories*. Hong Kong: Dianji Press.

Song, Yongyi, ed. 2016. *Guangxi Wenge Jimi Dang'an Ziliao, 16* (*Secret Archives about the Cultural Revolution in Guangxi, Classified Documents, Vol. 16*). New York: Guoshi Books.

Starr, John. 1979. *Continuing the Revolution: The Political thought of Mao*. Princeton: Princeton University Press.

Stavis, Benedict. 1988. *China's Political Reforms: An Interim Report*. New York: Praeger.

Sun, Liping. 1993. '"Ziyou Liudong Ziyuan" yu "Ziyou Huodong Kongjian": Lun Gaige Guochengzhong Zhongguo Shehui Jiegou de Bianqian' ('Freely Flowing Resources' and 'Free Activity Spaces': On the Changes of China's Social Structure in the Process of Reform). *Tansuo* (Probe), 1: 64–8.

Sun, Liping. 2005. '90 Niandi Yilai Pinfu Chaju de Jige Xin Tezheng' (Several New Features of the Gap between the Rich and the Poor since the 1990s). www.aisixiang.com/data/7643-2.html. Accessed 31 August 2022.

Sun, Liping. 2007. 'Jizhi yu Luoji: Guanyu Zhongguo Shehui Wending de Yanjiu' (Mechanism and Logic: A Study of Chinese Social Stability). https://m.aisixiang.com/data/15264-3.html. Accessed 31 August 2022.

Sun, Liping. 2008. 'Societal Transition: New Issues in the Field of the Sociology of Development'. *Modern China* 34(1): 88–113.

Sun, Nutao. 2013. *Liangzhi de Kaower: Yige Qinghua Wenge Toutoude Xinlu Licheng* (*The Torment of the Conscience: The Mental Journey of a Red Guard Leader at Tsinghua University*). Hong Kong: China Cultural Propagation Press.

Sun, Wanning. 2020. 'Rural Migrant Workers in Chinese Cities'. In *Routledge Handbook of Chinese Culture and Society*, edited by Kevin Latham, 115–28. London: Routledge.

Sun, Xiaosheng. 2004. 'Beijing Chengzhen Junmin Renjun Zhufang Shiyong Mianji 18.7pingmi' (Beijing's Urban Residents' Housing Area Reaches 18.7sqm Per Capita). Xinhua News Agency. 11 March 2004. https://business.sohu.com/2004/03/11/54/article219385416.shtml. Accessed 5 October 2021.

Sun, Yan. 1995. *The Chinese Reassessment of Socialism, 1976–1992*. Princeton: Princeton University Press.

Sun, Yingshuai. 2009. 'Zhongguo Gongchandang Dangyuan Shuliang yu Jieguo Bianhua ji Fazhan Qushi' (Changes and Development Trends in the Number and Structure of the CCP). *Journal of Beijing Administration Institute* 5: 28–32.

Tang, Beibei. 2014. 'Development and Prospects of Deliberative Democracy in China: The Dimensions of Deliberative Capacity Building'. *Journal of Chinese Political Science* 19: 115–32.

Tang, Wenfang, and William Parish. 2000. *Chinese Urban Life under Reform: The Changing Social Contract*. New York: Cambridge University Press.

Tao, Jianqun. 2006. '59sui Renzuo Chaliang 39sui Jiyu Shangtaijie? Tanguan Shoukun Liangdaokan' (The Tea Cools Down as soon as Reaching 59 Years Old and 39 Years Old

Eager to Climb the Stairs? Corrupt Officials are Trapped in Two Hurdles). www.chinanews .com.cn/other/news/2006/08-17/775366.shtml. Accessed 31 August 2022.

Teiwes, Frederick. 1989. 'Book Reviews – *China's Continuous Revolution*'. *China Journal* 21: 177–79.

Teiwes, Frederick, and Warren Sun. 1996. *The Tragedy of Lin Biao: Riding the Tiger during the Cultural Revolution*. Honolulu: University of Hawaii Press.

Teiwes, Frederick, and Warren Sun. 1999. *China's Road to Disaster: Mao, Central Politicians, and Provincial Leaders in the Unfolding of the Great Leap Forward 1955–1959*. Armonk: M. E. Sharpe.

Teiwes, Frederick, and Warren Sun. 2016. *Paradoxes of Post-Mao Rural Reform: Initial Steps Toward a New Chinese Countryside, 1976–1981*. Abingdon: Routledge.

Tencent.com. (2021). 'Linian Gaokao Renshu he Luqulu Tongji' (Statistics on the Number of University Entrance Examination Participants and Admission Rate over the Years). https:// new.qq.com/omn/20210608/20210608A02MXL00.html. Accessed 12 December 2021.

Thøgersen, Stig, and Ane Bislev. 2012. 'Organizing Rural China: Rural China Organizing'. In *Organizing Rural China: Rural China Organizing*, edited by Ane Bislev, and Stig Thøgersen, 1–13. Lanham: Lexington Books.

Thurston, Anne. 1983. 'The Social Sciences and Fieldwork in China: An Overview'. In *The Social Sciences and Fieldwork in China: Views from the Field*, edited by Anne Thurston, and Burton Pasternak, 3–36. Boulder: Westview Press.

Thurston, Anne. 1984. 'Victims of China's Cultural Revolution: The Invisible Wounds: Part I'. *Pacific Affairs*, 57(4): 599–620.

Tirole, Jean. 2017. *Economics for the Common Good*. Princeton: Princeton University Press.

Tomba, Luigi. 2011. 'Remaking China's Working Class: Gongren and Nongmingong'. In *China's Changing Workplace: Dynamism, Diversity and Disparity*, edited by Peter Sheldon, Sunghoon Kim, Yiqiong Li, and Malcolm Warner, 144–60. London: Routledge.

Tong, Qinglin. 2008. *Huishou 1978: Lishi zai Zheli Zhuanzhe (Looking Back at 1978: History Turned Here)*. Beijing: People's Press.

Tsai, Kellee. 2007. *Capitalism without Democracy: The Private Sector in Contemporary China*. Ithaca: Cornell University Press.

Tsou, Tang. 1986. *The Cultural Revolution and Post-Mao Reforms: A Historical Perspective*. Chicago: University Chicago Press.

Unger, Jonathan. 1979. 'China's Troubled Down-to-the-Countryside Campaign'. *Contemporary China* 3(2): 79–92.

Unger, Jonathan. 1982. *Education Under Mao: Class and Competition in Canton Schools, 1960–1980*. New York: Columbia University Press.

Unger, Jonathan. 2007. 'The Cultural Revolution at the Grass Roots'. *China Journal* 57: 109–37.

Veg, Sebastian. 2019a. *Minjian: The Rise of China's Grassroots Intellectuals*. New York: Columbia University Press.

Veg, Sebastian, ed. 2019b. *Popular Memories of the Mao Era: From Critical Debate to Reassessing History*. Hong Kong: Hong Kong University Press.

Wagoner, Brady, ed. 2010. *Symbolic Transformation: The Mind in Movement through Culture and Society*. Abingdon: Routledge.

Walder, Andrew. 1989. 'Social Change in Post-Revolution China'. *Annual Review of Sociology* 15: 405–24.

Walder, Andrew, Bobai Li, and Donald Treiman. 2000. 'Politics and Life Chances in a State Socialist Regime: Dual Career Paths into the Urban Chinese Elite, 1949 to 1996'. *American Sociological Review* 65(2): 191–209.

Walker, Anne. 2012. *China Calls: Paving the Way for Nixon's Historic Journey to China*. Lanham: Madison Books.

Wan, Zhaoyuan. 2021. *Science and the Confucian Religion of Kang Youwei (1858–1927): China Before the Conflict Thesis*. Leiden: Brill.

Wang, Fei-ling. 1998a. *From Family to Market: Labor Allocation in Contemporary China*. Lanham: Rowman & Littlefield.

Wang, Heyan. 2008a. 'Zhongyang Dangxiao Xueli bu zai Xiangshou Tongdeng Jiaoyu Daiyu' (The Central Party School Degree No Longer Enjoys the Same Educational Treatment). https://news.boxun.com/news/gb/china/2008/10/200810072205.shtml. Accessed 31 May 2022.

Wang, Hui. 2009. '90 Niandai de Zhongjie' (The End of the 1990s). https://m.aisixiang.com/data/30102.html. Accessed 31 August 2022.

Wang, Huisheng. 2017a. 'Ganen Lin Hujia, Kuozhao Shang Daxue' (Thanks Lin Hujia, Enroled in University through the Expanded Enrolment Plan). *Xinsanjie*. WeChat ID: df3p1113-2. Accessed 5 October 2021.

Wang, James. 1980. *Contemporary Chinese Politics: An Introduction*. Englewood Cliffs: Prentice-Hall.

Wang, Juntao. 2014a. 'Caifang Wang Juntao' (An Interview with Wang Juntao). https://pekinger-fruehling.univie.ac.at/index.php?id=189357&L=27. Accessed 5 October 2021.

Wang, Mingjian, ed. 1998b. *Shangshan Xiaxiang: Yichang jueding 3000wan Zhongguoren Mingyun de Yundong Zhimi (Going Up the Mountains to the Countryside: The Mystery of a Movement that Determines the Fate of 30 Million Chinese)*. Beijing: Guangming Daily Press.

Wang, Ning. 2017b. *Banished to the Great Northern Wilderness: Political Exile and Re-education in Mao's China*. Vancouver: UBC Press.

Wang, Ruijie. 2018a. 'Beijing Jinru "Juzhe Youqiwu" Shidai' (Beijing Enters the Era of 'Living in Better Houses'). *BJ House*. https://bj.house.163.com/18/1112/07/E0D7JF0D000782A4.html. Accessed 5 October 2021.

Wang, Ruize. 2014b. *Zhidu Bianqian xiade Zhongguo Jingji Zengzhang Yanjiu (Studies on China's Economic Growth During Institutional Transformations)*. Beijing: China Social Sciences Press.

Wang, Ruowang. 1991. *Hunger Trilogy: Translated by Kyna Rubin with Ira Kasoff*. New York: M. E. Sharpe.

Wang, Shaoguang. 2017c. 'The Wuhan Incident Revisited'. *Chinese Historical Review* 13(2): 241–270.

Wang, Shaoguang, and Angang Hu. 1999. *The Political Economy of Uneven Development: The Case of China*. New York: M. E. Sharpe.

Wang, Weibo. 2008b. 'Dangxiao Xueli zhi Zheng: Shifou Xiangshou Guomin Jiaoyu Daiyu reng Xuaner Weijue' (Dispute Over Party School Education: Whether to Enjoy National Education Treatment Is Still Pending). www.chinanews.com.cn/gn/news/2008/10-31/1432827.shtml. Accessed 31 May 2022.

Wang, Xiaolu. 2018b. 'Gaige 40nian yu Zhongguo Jingji de Weilai' (40 Years of Reform and the Future of China's Economy). https://finance.sina.cn/china/cjpl/2018-08-22/zl-ihhzsnec0756193.d.html. Accessed 12 December 2021.

Wang, Xiaolu. 2018c. 'Gaige 40nian de Huigu yu Sikao' (Retrospect and Reflection on the 40 Years of Reform). www.aisixiang.com/data/113386.html. Accessed 12 December 2021.

Wang, Yanzhong. 2000. 'Xinshiqi Zhongguo de Jiuye Guanli Zhibiao yu Zhengce Xuanze' (China's Controlled Employment Indictor and Policy Selection in the New Stage). *Management World* 5: 49–60.

Wang, Yinfei. 2012. 'Xiangzhen Qiye de "1984": Zhejiangsheng Zhujishi Diankouzhen Xiaowujingye Yanjiu' (TVEs' '1984': Research on Small Hardware Industry in Diankou Town, Zhuji City, Zhejiang). *China Economic History*. http://economy.guoxue.com/?p=8935. Accessed 31 March 2022.

Wang, Youqin. 2004. *Victim of the Cultural Revolution: An Investigative Account of Persecution, Imprisonment and Murder*. Hong Kong: Kaifang Press.

Wang, Yonghong. 2019. 'Kuangren Yehua: Zhiqing Bingtui Ji' (Evening Chats of a Madman: A Journey of a *Zhiqing*'s *Bingtui*). www.myoldtime.com/plus/view.php?aid=19063. Accessed 2 August 2021.

Wang, Zhouyi. 2014c. *Revolutionary Cycles in Chinese Cinema, 1951–1979*. New York: Palgrave Macmillan.

Watson, Andrew, ed. 1992. *Economic Reform and Social Change in China*. London: Routledge.

Wemheuer, Felix. 2019. *A Social history of Maoist China: Conflicts and Change, 1949–1976*. Cambridge: Cambridge University Press.

Wen, Yuankai. 2007. 'Deng Xiaoping Caina wo Sifen Zhisan Yijian' (Deng Xiaoping Accepted Three-Quarters of My Recommendation). http://news.sina.com.cn/c/2007-05-28/110213093575.shtml. Accessed 5 October 2021.

Weng, Hansong. 2015. *Zhonggong shi Zenyang Lianchengde?: Mao Zedong Zhou Enlai 44nian Quanduoshi (How the CCP was Forged: Mao Zedong and Zhou Enlai's 44-Year History of Power Struggle)*. New York: Mirror Media Group.

Weng, Yanqing. 2016. *Zhongguo Minzhu Yundongshi: Cong Yan'an Wang Shiwei Zheng Minzhu dao Xidan Minzhuqiang (History of Chinese Democracy Movement: From Yan'an Wang Shiwei's Struggle for Democracy to the Xidan Democracy Wall)*. Taipei: Independent & Unique.

White, Gordon. 1981. *Party and Professionals: The Political Role of Teachers in Contemporary China*. New York: M. E. Sharpe.

White, Lynn. 1989. *Policies of Chaos: The Organizational Causes of Violence in China's Cultural Revolution*. Princeton: Princeton University Press.

White, Lynn. 1998. *Unstately Power, Volume I: Local Causes of China's Economic Reforms*. New York: M. E. Sharpe.

Whiting, Susan. 2000. *Power and Wealth in Rural China: The Political Economy of Institutional Change*. Cambridge: Cambridge University Press.

Womack, Brantly. 1982. *The Foundations of Mao Zedong's Political Thought, 1917–1935*. Honolulu: University Press of Hawaii.

Woodman, Sophia. 2011. 'Law, Translation, and Voice: Transformation of a Struggle for Social Justice in a Chinese Village'. *Critical Asian Studies* 43(2): 185–210.

Wong, Linda. 1998. *Marginalization and Social Welfare in China*. London: Routledge.

Wong, Yiu-chung. 2005. *From Deng Xiaoping to Jiang Zemin: Two Decades of Political Reform in the People's Republic of China*. Lanham: University Press of America.

The World Bank. 2020. *Inflation, Consumer Prices (Annual %) – China*. https://data.worldbank.org/indicator/FP.CPI.TOTL.ZG?locations=CN. Accessed 31 May 2022.

The World Bank. 2022. *Population, Total – China*. https://data.worldbank.org/indicator/SP.POP.TOTL?locations=CN. Accessed 31 August 2022.

Wright, Teresa. 2013. 'Protest as Participation: China's Local Protest Movements'. *World Politics Review*, 16 April 2013.

Wright, Teresa. 2018. *Popular Protest in China*. Hoboken: Wiley.

Wu, Jiaxiang. 2006. 'Rongjiexing Gongnengzhuyi: Zhongguo Gaige de Shijie Zhexue Yiyi' (Dissolving Functionalism: The World Philosophical Significance of China's Reform). https://m.aisixiang.com/data/9823.html. Accessed 31 May 2022.

Wu, Jing, and Bai Long. 2008. 'Gongwuyuan "Xiahai": Zhengfu ying Jiji Guli Haishi chi Zhongli Taidu' (Civil Servants 'Xiahai': The Government Should Actively Encourage or Maintain a Neutral Attitude). www.chinanews.com.cn/gn/news/2008/07-02/1299252.shtml. Accessed 31 August 2022.

Wu, Wei. 2014. '70 Niandaimo Zhongguo de Sixiang Qimeng Yundong' (China's Enlightenment Movement in the Late 1970s). *New York Times* (Chinese Edition). https://cn.nytimes.com/china/20140113/cc13reform/. Accessed 12 December 2021.

Wu, Weiyi, and Fan Hong. 2016. *The Identity of Zhiqing: The Last Generation*. Abingdon: Routledge.

Wu, Guoguang, Yuan Feng, and Helen Lansdowne, eds. 2019. *Gender Dynamics, Feminist Activism and Social Transformation in China*. Abingdon: Routledge.

Wu, Xinsheng. 2015. *Gongheguo Lingxiu Shouxi Baojian Zhuanjia (Chief Health Care Specialist of the Leaders of the PRC)*. Beijing: Chinese Literature and History Press.

Xiao, Donglian. 2019. *Tanlu Zhiyi: 1978–1992 de Zhongguo Jingji Gaige (Exploring the Paths: China's Economic Reform from 1978 to 1992)*. Beijing: Social Sciences Academic Press.

Xiao, Gongqin. 2007. 'Dangdai Zhongguo Zhishifenzi de Sixiang Fenhua jiqi Zhengzhi Yingxiang' (The Ideological Divergence of Contemporary Chinese Intellectuals and Their Political Influence). https://www.aisixiang.com/data/12642.html. Accessed 31 August 2022.

Xiao, Gongqin. 2009. 'Dangdai Zhongguo Liuda Shehui Sichao de Lishi Yanbian yu Weilai Zhanwang' (The Historical Evolution and Future Prospect of the Six Social Thought Trends in Contemporary China). www.aisixiang.com/data/30283.html. Accessed 31 March 2022.

Xie, Houzhi. 2008. *Yecao* (*Weeds*). www.jintian.net/sanwen/2008/xiehouzhi5.html. Accessed 2 August 2021.

Xie, Lizhong, ed. 2010. *Jieguo-zhidu fenxi, haishi guocheng-shijian fenxi?* (*Structural-Institutional Analysis or Process-Event Analysis?*) Beijing: Social Sciences Academic Press.

Xie, Qingqing. 2016. 'Wenge' koushushi diaocha (Oral History Survey of the Cultural Revolution). www.bannedbook.org/bnews/lishi/20161109/671912.html. Accessed 2 August 2021.

Xie, Xuanjun. 2021. *Complete Works of Xie Xuanjun, Vol. 119*. New York: Xie Xuanjun.

Xin, Yimei. 2021. 'Jingcheng Jiyi: 1953–1987' (Memory of Beijing: 1953 to 1987). *Siren Shi* (*PerHistory*). WeChat ID: PerHistory. Accessed 2 July 2021.

Xu, Bin. 1999a. *Disenchanted Democracy: Chinese Criticism after 1989*. Ann Arbor: University of Michigan Press.

Xu, Bin. 2016. 'Memory and Reconciliation in Post-Mao China, 1976–1982'. In *Routledge Handbook of Memory and Reconciliation in East Asia*, edited by Mikyoung Kim, 47–60. Abingdon: Routledge.

Xu, Hui. 2021. 'Cong Xiahaichao dao Jijin Tizhire' (From the Tide of Jumping into the Sea of Commerce to the Fever of Squeezing into the System). *careerengine.us*. WeChat ID: yigeshidaidejilu. https://posts.careerengine.us/p/6179ccb8e97e4432bf795d63. Accessed 31 May 2022.

Xu, Sheng, and Yedi Huan. 2015. 'Beijing Xinwen: Guoqi Gaige de "Neixie Nian, Neixie Shi"' (Background News: "Those Years, Those Things" in the Reform of State-Owned Enterprises). www.xinhuanet.com/politics/2015-09/13/c_1116547220.htm. Accessed 31 August 2022.

Xu, Xiaodi. 2012. *Diandao Suiyue* (*Upside-down Years*). Beijing: Sanlian Books.

Xu, Xinxin, 1999b. 'Zhongguo Chengzhen Jumin Pinfu Chaju Yanbian Qushi' (The Evolution Trend of the Gap between the Rich and the Poor among China's Urban Residents). *Sociological Studies* 14(5): 66–74.

Xu, Youyu. 2013. 'Shangshan Xiaxiang dui Zhiqing Yidai Sixiang Xingcheng de Yingxiang' (The Influence of the Sent-Down Drive on the Formation of Thoughts of the Sent-Down Youth Generation). *Twenty-First Century* 4: 15–22.

Yan, Yangsheng. 2009. 'Wengeqiande Qinghua Fuzhong' (Tsinghua High School before the Cultural Revolution). *Beijing Youth Daily*, 11 December 2009. www.chinanews.com/cul/news/2009/12-11/2012642.shtml. Accessed 10 March 2021.

Yan, Yangsheng. 2021. 'Beijing Sizhong "Xiao Siqing" he Qinghua Fuzhong "Da Yuke"' (The Small-Scale Four Clean-ups Campaign at Beijing Sizhong and the University Foundation [Programme] at Tsinghua High). *Xinsanjie*. WeChat ID: df3p1113-2. Accessed 2 July 2021.

Yan, Yunxiang. 2003. *Private Life under Socialism: Love, Intimacy, and Family Change in a Chinese Village, 1949–1999*. Stanford: Stanford University Press.

Yang, Chen. 2011. 'Spatial Practice of Socialist City: Worker's New Village in Shanghai (1949–1978)'. *Human Geography* 26(3): 35–64.

Yang, Dongping. 2006. *Zhongguo Jiaoyu Gongping de Lixiang yu Xianshi* (*The Ideal and Reality of China's Education Equity*). Beijing: Peking University Press.

Yang, Guobin. 2000. *China's Red Guard Generation: The Ritual Process of Identity Transformation, 1966–1999*. PhD Thesis, New York University.

Yang, Guobin. 2006. 'Hongweibing Yidai de Rentong Zhuanbian' (Identity Change of the Red Guard Generation). *China News Digest*, No. 545. www.cnd.org/cr/ZK06/cr379.gb.html. Accessed 5 October 2021.

Yang, Dali. 1996. *Calamity and Reform in China: State, Rural Society, and Institutional Chane since the Great Leap Famine*. Stanford: Stanford University Press.

Yang, Deguang, and Ma Kali. 1997. *Zhongguo Dangdai Daxuesheng Jiezhiguan Yanjiu (Research on the Values of Contemporary Chinese University Students)*. Shanghai: Shanghai Education Press.

Yang, Jisheng. 2016. 'Wenge Shiqide Guomin Jingji' (National economy during the Culture Revolution). *Twenty-First Century* 156: 42–60.

Yang, Jisheng. 2018. *Tianfan Difu: Zhongguo Wenhua Geminshi (The World Turning Upside Down: A History of the Chinese Cultural Revolution)*. Hong Kong: Cosmos Books.

Yang, Meirong. 1995. 'A Long Way toward a Free Press: The Case of the World Economic Herald'. In *Decision-Making in Deng's China: Perspectives from Insiders*, edited by Carol Hamrin, Suisheng Zhao, and Doak Barnett, 183–88. Abingdon: Routledge.

Yang, Ray. 2015. 'Political Process and Widespread Protests in China: The 2010 Labor Protest'. *Journal of Contemporary China* 24(91): 21–42.

Yang, Xiong. 1997. '90 Niandai Zhongguo Daxuesheng Zeyeguan Bianhua Tedian he Fazhan' (The Changing Characteristics and Development Trend of Chinese College Students' Career Choices in the 1990s). *Youth Studies* 11: 19–24.

Yang, Ye. 2019. 'Guoqi 70 Nian: Cong "Baishou Qijia" dao Maixiang "Shijie Yiliu"' (70 Years of SOEs: From "Starting from Scratch" to "World-Class"). www.jjckb.cn/2019-09/18/c _138399838.htm. Accessed 31 August 2022.

Yao, Cunshe. 2005. 'Yige Beijing Zhiqing de Shaanxi Rensheng' (The Shaanxi Life of an Educated Youth from Beijing). news.sina.com.cn/o/2005-12-27/10007828747s.shtml. Accessed 2 July 2021.

Yao, Xinzhong, ed. 2003. *The Encyclopedia of Confucianism, 2-Volume Set*. London: Routledge.

Yao, Yang. 2011. *Global Implications of the Chinese Experience*. Beijing: Peking University Press.

Yao, Zhikang. 2019. 'Tianshan "Penghuqu" Bianqian Jiekai Shanghai Renjun Zhufang Mianji Zhengzhang 8.5bei zhimi' (Changes in Tianshan 'Shanty Town' Reveals the Mystery of Shanghai's Growth of 8.5 Times in Housing Area Per Capita), *Xinmin Evening News*. 7 January 2019. https://wap.xinmin.cn/content/31474228.html. Accessed 5 October 2021

Ye, Weili, and Ma Xiaodong. 2019. '"Liangge Shijie" de Jiaocha' (The Intersection of 'Two Worlds'). *China News Digest*, No. 197. museums.cnd.org/CR/ZK19/cr1029.gb.html. Accessed 2 July 2021.

Ye, Yonglie. 2008. *Deng Xiaoping Gaibian Zhongguo, 1978: Zhongguo Minyun Dazhuanbian (Deng Xiaoping Changed China, 1978: China's Destiny is Turning)*. Nanchang: Jiangxi People's Press.

Yin, Hongbiao. 2009. *Footprints of the Missing: Thoughts of the Youth during the Cultural Revolution*. Hong Kong: The Chinese University Press.

You, Ji. 1998. *China's Enterprise Reform: Changing State/Society Relations after Mao*. Abingdon: Routledge.

Young, Louise. 1998. *Japan's Total Empire: Manchuria and the Culture of Wartime Imperialism*. Berkeley: University of California Press.

Young, Susan. 2015. *Private Business and Economic Reform in China*. Abington: Routledge.

Yu, Jianxing, and Jun Zhou. 2012. 'Chinese Civil Society Research in Recent Years: A Critical Review'. *China Review* 12(2): 111–40.

Yu, Xilai. 2011. 'Beijing Gaoxiao Jingxuan Yundong' (The University Election Campaigns in Beijing). https://lvhonglai.wordpress.com/2011/01/05. Accessed 12 December 2021.

Yue, Gang. 1999. *The Mouth That Begs: Hunger, Cannibalism, and the Politics of Eating in Modern China*. Durham: Duke University Press.

Yun, Hua. 2008. 'Gao Bingtui' (To Make a Case of *Bingtui*). blog.wenxuecity.com/myblog/2 1795. Accessed 2 August 2021.

Zang, Xiaowei. 2000. *Children of the Cultural Revolution: Family Life and Political Behavior in Mao's China*. Boulder: Westview Press.

Zang, Xiaowei. 2006. 'Technical Training, Sponsored Mobility, and Functional Differentiation: Elite Formation in China in the Reform Era'. *Communist and Post-Communist Studies* 39: 39–57.

Zang, Xiaowei. 2008. 'Market Transition, Wealth, and Status Claims'. In *The New Rich in China: Future Rulers, Present Lives*, edited by David Goodman, 53–70. Abingdon: Routledge.

Zeng, Peiyan. 1999. *Xin Zhongguo Jingji 50nian (50 Years of New China's Economy)*. Beijing: China Planning Press.

Zeng, Qinghong. 2005. *Zai Quanguo Shishi Gongwuyuanfa Gongzuo Huiyi Shang de Jianghua (Speech at the National Work Conference on Implementing the Civil Servant Law)*. www.reformdata.org/2005/0920/4843.shtml. Accessed 31 May 2022.

Zhang, Boshu. 2016. *Gaibian Zhongguo: Zhongguo Sixiangjie Gege Liupai (Changing China: Various Schools of Thought in China)*. New York: China Independent Writers Publishing.

Zhang, Chengsi. 2017. 'Soft Landing'. In *Major Issues and Policies in China's Financial Reform, Volume 3*, edited by Chen Yulu, and Guo Qingwang, 109–32. Honolulu: Enrich Professional Publishing.

Zhang, Chunsheng. 2018a. 'Taoli' (Escape). www.chinazhiqing.com/portal.php?mod=view&aid=19636. Accessed 2 August 2021.

Zhang, Dong, and Freestone Owen. 2013. *China's Unfinished State-Owned Enterprise Reforms*. https://treasury.gov.au/publication/economic-roundup-issue-2-2013-2/economic-roundup-issue-2-2013/chinas-unfinished-state-owned-enterprise-reforms. Accessed 31 August 2022.

Zhang, Fei'an. 2012. 'Pingxi Dangdai Zhongguo Wuda Shehui Sichao' (An Analysis on the Five Trends of Social Thought in Contemporary China). *Social Sciences Weekly*, 18 June 2012.

Zhang, Jinfeng. 2008a. 'Yiduan Zhongshen Nanwang de Jingli' (An Unforgettable Experience). *RUC News*, 21 October 2008. https://news.ruc.edu.cn/archives/30271. Accessed 12 October 2021.

Zhang, Jun. 2018b. 'China's Price Liberalisation and Market Reform: A Historical Perspective'. In *China's 40 Years of Reform and Development 1978–2018*, edited by Ross Garnaut, Ligang Song, and Cai Fang, 215–34. Canberra: ANU Press.

Zhang, Lei. 2007. 'Tanguan "59 Xianxiang": Zhengzhi Jingying Lunluo yu Guanchang Shiyi Miqie Xiangguan' (The "59 Phenomenon" of Corrupt Officials: The Decline of Political Elites is Closely Related to Official Disappointment). www.chinanews.com.cn/gn/news/2007/05-11/932749.shtml. Accessed 31 August 2022.

Zhang, Li. 2019. 'Shiwu Qianli de "Daxue Fenxiao Shiqi"' (An Unprecedented Period of 'University Branch Campuses'. *Xinsanjie*. WeChat ID: df3p1113-2. Accessed 5 October 2021.

Zhang, Liqun, and Zhang Zhenxing. 2011. '"Chongfan 80niandai"de "Wenxue Xintai" jiqi Lishi Wenti' (The 'Literary Mindset' of 'Returning to the 1980s' and its Historical Issues). *Art Panorama* 9: 4–10.

Zhang, Sheldon. 2008b. *Chinese Human Smuggling Organizations: Families, Social Networks, and Cultural Imperatives*. Stanford: Stanford University Press.

Zhang, Shu. 2015. 'Chen Yun Lizhu Qingli "Sanzhong Ren"' (Chen Yun Urged to Clean up the 'Three Types of People'). www.dswxyjy.org.cn/n/2015/0713/c222139-27294988.html. Accessed 12 December 2021.

Zhang, Shujun. 1998. *Da Zhuanzhe: Zhonggong Shiyijie Sanzhong Quanhui Shilu (The Great Turning Point: True Records of the 3rd Plenary Session of the CCP's 11th Central Committee)*. Hangzhou: Zhejiang People's Press.

Zhang, Xin. 2000. *Social Transformation in Modern China: The State and Local Elites in Henan, 1900–1937*. Cambridge: Cambridge University Press.

Zhang, Xudong, and Xu Yong. 2012. 'Chongfan 80niandai de Xiandu jiqi Kenong: Zhang Xudong Jiaoshou Fangtanlu' (Limitations and Possibilities of Returning to the 1980s: An

Interview with Professor Zhang Xudong). *Wenyi Zhengming* (*Literary and Artistic Contention*) 1: 97–102.

Zhang, Zhongfa. 2008c. '1949 dao 2007: Zhongguo Nongcun Gaige yu Fazhan 58nian' (1949 to 2007: 58 Years of Rural Reform and Development in China). https://business.sohu.com /20080219/n255239489.shtml. Accessed 12 December 2021.

Zhao, Chenggen. 2003a. 'Rational Authoritarianism and Chinese Economic Reform'. In *Contemporary China: The Dynamics of Change at the State of New Millennium*, edited by Peter Preston, and Jürgen Haacke, 175–89. London: Routledge.

Zhao, Deyu. 2016a. '1966–1976 nianjian Woguo Liangshi Tongguo Tongxiao Zhengce de Zhiding jiqi Xiaoyi' (The Formulation of Our Country's Grain Monopoly Purchase and Marketing Policy and Its Benefits from 1966 to 1976). *South China Agricultural University Journal* 2:1–11.

Zhao, Sheng. 2015. 'Shanghai Chengshi Sifang de Shehuizhuyi Gaizao' (The Socialist Transformation of Private Houses in Shanghai). http://61.129.65.112/Newsite/node2/ n88773/n88792/u1ai137898.html. Accessed 5 October 2021.

Zhao, Suisheng. 1994. 'China's Central-Local Relations: A Historical Perspective'. In *Changing Central-Local Relations in China: Reform and State Capacity*, edited by Jia Hao, and Zhimin Lin, 19–34. Boulder: Westview Press.

Zhao, Suisheng, ed. 2000. *China and Democracy: Reconsidering the Prospects for a Democratic China*. New York: Routledge.

Zhao, Suisheng, ed. 2006. *Debating Political Reform in China: Rule of Law vs. Democratization*. New York: M. E. Sharpe.

Zhao, Yong. 2016b. *Zhongguo Gaodeng Jiaoyu Xuqiu de Renkou Shehuixue Kaocha* (*A Demographic-Sociological Study of China's Demand for Higher Education*). Beijing: China Social Sciences Press.

Zhao, Yuezhi. 2003. 'Falun Gong, Identity, and the Struggle over Meaning inside and outside China'. In *Contesting Media Power: Alternative Media in a Networked World*, edited by Nick Couldry, and James Curran, 209–26. Lanham: Rowman & Littlefield.

Zhao, Yunqi. 2014. *Gonggong Caizheng yu Zhongguo Jingji Zenzhang Fangshi Zhuangbian* (*Public Finance and Transformation of Growth Model of China's Economy*). Beijing: China Financial & Economic Publishing House.

Zhao, Yunxian. 2021. 'Chongfan 90niandai zhi Xiagangchao' (A Revisit to the Laid-off Wave of the 1990s). https://m.jiemian.com/article/6485827.html. Accessed 31 May 2022.

Zheng, Hui, and Yunhui Lin. 2009. *60 Nian Guoshi Jiyao: Jingji Juan* (*Summary of 60 Years of National Affairs: Economy Edition*). Changsha: Hunan People's Press.

Zheng, Qian. 2013. '"Wenhua Da Geming" Zhong Zhishi Qingnian Shangshan Xiaxiang Yundong Wuti' (Five Topics about the Sent-down Youth Movement During the "Cultural Revolution"). *CPC [CCP] History Studies* 9: 43–58.

Zheng, Ruoling. 2007. *Keju, Gaokao yu Shehui zhi Guanxi Yanjiu* (*Research on Relationships between the Imperial Examination, University Entrance Examination and Society*). Wuhan: Huazhong Normal University Press.

Zheng, Yefu. 2018. 'Dalao Lishide Xijie: Xu Li Weidong's *Qinghua Fuzhong Gao631ban*) (Salvaging historical details: A Preface for Li Weidong's *The Class of 1963 at Tsinghua High School*). *China News Digest*, Special 952. www.cnd.org/cr/ZK18/cr952.gb.html. Accessed 10 June 2021.

Zheng, Yongnian. 2010. *The Chinese Communist Party as Organizational Emperor: Culture, Reproduction and Transformation*. Abingdon: Routledge.

Zhihu.com. 2021 '100Nianlai Zhongguo Laobaixing de Zhongda Rensheng Shiwu' (Major Life Mistakes of Chinese People in the Past 100 Years). www.zhihu.com/pin /1354780309276332032. Accessed 31 August 2022.

Zhong, Ninghua. 2011. 'Can Rural Industrialization Keep Working in China?: Am Empirical Study on TVEs' Effects in Reducing Urban-Rural Income Inequality'. *Economic Research Journal* 26(1): 18–28.

Zhou, Beilong, ed. 1999. *Mianxiang 21Shiji de Zhongguo Jiaoyu: Guoqing, Xuqiu, Guihua, Duice (Chinese Education Facing the 21st Century: National Conditions, Demands, Planning and Measures)*. Beijing: Higher Education Press.

Zhou, Qiren. 1997. 'Jihui yu Nengli: Zhongguo Nongcun Laodingli de Jiuye he Liudong' (Opportunity and Ability: Employment and Mobility of Rural Labor in China). *Management World* 5: 81–101.

Zhou, Ruijin. 2008. '"Huangfu ping Shijian" de Qianqian Houhou: Ceng Yinfa Yichang Sixiang Jiaofeng' (Before and After 'Huangfu ping' Incident: A Clash of Ideas Once Sparked). *China News*, 29 December 2008. www.chinanews.com.cn/cul/news/2008/12-29/1506687.shtml. Accessed 31 May 2022.

Zhou, Xiaohong. 2011. 'Zhongguo jingyan yu Zhongguo tiyan: Lijie shehui bianqiande shuangchong shijiao' (Chinese Experiences and Feelings: A Dual-Perspective on Understanding Social Changes). *Tianjin Social Sciences* 6: 12–9.

Zhou, Xueguang. 2004. *The State and Life Chances in Urban China: Redistribution and Stratification, 1949–1994*. New York: Cambridge University Press.

Zhou, Xueguang. 2009. *The State and Life Chances in Urban China: Redistribution and Stratification, 1949–1994*. Cambridge: Cambridge University Press.

Zhou, Xueguang, and Liren Hou. 1999. 'Children of the Cultural Revolution: The State and the Life Course in the People's Republic of China'. *American Sociological Review* 64(1): 12–36.

Zhu, Hanguo. 2012. *Dangdai Zhongguo Shehui Sichao (Research on Contemporary Chinese Social Thought Trends)*. Beijing: Beijing Normal University Press.

Zhu, Jianguo. 2006. 'Yige 14sui de "Xiaoyao Hongweibing"' (A 14-Year-Old 'Leisured Red Guard'). chinesepen.org/old/zyxz/11/011zjg.htm#first. Accessed 2 July 2021.

Zhu, Julie. 2017. 'China's "Glass King" to Complete U.S. Expansion despite Trump Tensions'. Reuters, 28 February 2017. www.reuters.com/article/us-fuyao-investment-idUSKBN1670KF. Accessed 12 December 2021.

Zweig, David. 1992. 'Urbanizing Rural China: Bureaucratic Authority and Local Autonomy'. In *Bureaucracy, Politics and Decision Making in Post-Mao China*, edited by Kenneth Lieberthal, and David Lampton, 334–59. Berkeley: University of California Press.

INDEX

9/13 Incident, the: *see* Lin Biao
1962 Seven-Thousand Cadres Conference, the 2–3, 25–29, 43, 71
1976 Tiananmen Incident, the 3, 23. 24, 72, 79–85, 91, 93, 96–97, 108, 119, 135–37, 192
1989 Tiananmen Incident, the 3, 12. 14–15, 24, 118–19, 128, 133–39, 141–46, 148, 152, 157–61, 165, 167, 169, 193, 198
571 Outline, the: *see* Outline of Project 571, the

alien class elements 64, 78, 143, 145
anti-intellectualism 88–89, 115
April 5th Movement, the: *see* 1976 Tiananmen Incident, the

bingtui of sent-down youth: *see* sick returnees of sent-down youth
bloodline theory, the 33, 63, 88, 194

cadre children 43–46, 63, 66, 68, 75, 87, 98, 112–13, 138–39, 146, 169, 194
cadre corruption 60, 134–35, 138–39, 146, 177–78, 180, 182–83
cadre families 30, 42–43, 45, 50, 51, 59–61, 63–66, 68, 75, 87, 89, 99, 110, 112, 136–37, 179, 192
cadre four modernisations 113, 180
cadre promotion 10–11, 54, 61, 67, 79, 88, 106, 114, 131, 134, 138, 142, 158, 150, 182–83, 198
cadre selection 1–11, 25, 30, 40, 113, 166, 178–79, 181–82, 198
cadre tenure system, the 180–83
cadre training 24, 142, 166, 178, 181
cadre *xiahai* 155
CCP: *see* Chinese Communist Party (CCP), the
CCYL: *see* Chinese Communist Youth League (CCYL), the
Chen Yun 111–12, 138, 159
Chen Ziming 80–84, 97, 108
chi daguofan: *see* eating from one big pot
chi Huangliang: *see* eat imperial food

Chinese Communist Party (CCP), the 2–4, 7, 23, 27–31, 35, 37, 40, 42, 45, 48, 54, 59, 62–63, 70, 73–74, 79–80, 83–86, 89–90, 94, 99, 106–8, 111–13, 116, 122, 134–35, 138, 141–43, 145–46, 149, 156–59, 161–62, 167, 169–70, 177, 179, 181–81, 184–86, 191, 196, 198–99
Chinese Communist Youth League (CCYL), the 4, 30–34, 36, 54, 89, 128
Chinese Young Pioneers, the 33, 36
communist heir narrative, the: *see* communist successor narrative, the
Communist Party of China (CPC): *see* Chinese Communist Party (CCP), the
communist successor narrative, the 3–4, 7, 11, 22, 28–34, 40, 48, 50–52, 54–55, 57, 59, 71, 73, 97, 104, 110, 117, 130, 138, 192, 196
Confucianism 12, 27, 48, 115, 120

dapo tiefanwan: *see* smashing the iron rice bowl
Deng Xiaoping 3, 14, 23–24, 42, 50, 73, 79–80, 82–88, 97, 99, 101, 103, 111, 113–14, 118, 121–22, 126, 142–43, 148–50, 152, 154–56, 159–60, 162–63, 165, 167, 183–85, 193–94, 196, 198
Dengist 10, 12, 18, 36, 44, 80, 83, 85, 86, 93, 97, 108, 113, 114, 122, 126, 132, 149–50, 152, 156, 159–61, 163, 165, 167, 173, 184
de-utopianisation 22, 50, 55
disan tidui: *see* third echelon (of leadership team), the
diyitong jin: *see* first bucket of gold, the

eat imperial food 154, 156
eating from one big pot 105, 131
eryue niliu, The 47, 51, 69

Falun Gong, the 3, 15, 24, 165–66, 172, 175–77, 185, 188
February counter-current, the: *see eryue niliu*, the
Feng Lun 101, 116, 126–28, 131, 132, 155, 170
first bucket of gold, the 24, 166–67, 169, 171, 177, 183
five black categories 47
five great rebel leaders 69, 71, 112

www.ingramcontent.com/pod-product-compliance
Lightning Source LLC
Chambersburg PA
CBHW030647270326
41929CB00007B/239